THE TIES THAT BIND

The Ties that Bind

Siblings, Family, and Society in Early Modern England

BERNARD CAPP

OXFORD

UNIVERSITY PRESS

OXFORD

UNIVERSITY PRESS

Great Clarendon Street, Oxford, OX2 6DP,
United Kingdom

Oxford University Press is a department of the University of Oxford.
It furthers the University's objective of excellence in research, scholarship,
and education by publishing worldwide. Oxford is a registered trade mark of
Oxford University Press in the UK and in certain other countries

First Edition published in 2018

Impression: 3

Published in the United States of America by Oxford University Press
198 Madison Avenue, New York, NY 10016, United States of America

British Library Cataloguing in Publication Data
Data available

Library of Congress Control Number: 2018933091

ISBN 978–0–19–882338–4

Printed and bound by
CPI Group (UK) Ltd, Croydon, CR0 4YY

In memory of my only sibling,
David Walter Capp
1939–2016

Preface

The subject of this book is at once narrow and immensely broad. It covers only one dimension of family relationships in early modern England. Yet this dimension played a significant role in the lives of almost the entire population, and it has been unduly neglected. In Part I, the book explores how contemporaries understood this relationship, and how both adults and children behaved in practice. Part II focuses on several individual families where unusually rich source materials allow us to explore these issues in depth. The book ranges from the mid-sixteenth century to the early eighteenth, and excludes only royalty and the aristocracy (except for the children of Lord North, in the final chapter). I would like to thank OUP's readers for their very helpful comments and suggestions, and also the audiences at seminars and conferences where I have presented early versions, at the Institute of Historical Research, London, Birkbeck, Reading, The Shakespeare Institute, Stratford, the University of East Anglia, and Warwick. For fifty years, Warwick's History Department has provided a congenial and stimulating academic home, with early modern English history continuing to flourish in the hands of Peter Marshall, Mark Knights, and their colleagues. I am also very grateful for the warm encouragement of my friends Angela McShane, Jasmine Kilburn-Toppin, Naomi Pullin, and latterly, Iman Sheeha, and Edith Roberts. The death of my brother, David, when the book was almost complete, has given it a poignant dimension I had not anticipated.

I have modernized the spelling of quotations. In references, the place of publication is London unless otherwise stated. In pre-decimal currency, twelve pence (12d) made a shilling, and twenty shillings (20s) a pound. A groat was 4d, a mark 13s 4d. And when contemporaries spoke of mothers- or fathers-in-law, they usually meant what we now call step-parents.

December 2017

Contents

Abbreviations

BI, CP	Borthwick Institute, York, Cause Papers
BL	British Library
brs	broadside
D'Ewes, *Autobiography*	*The Autobiography and Correspondence of Sir Simonds D'Ewes,* ed. J. O. Halliwell (1845)
Flemings in Oxford	*The Flemings in Oxford*, ed. J. R. Magrath, Oxford Historical Society, 44, 62, 79 (1904–24)
Heywood, *Autobiography*	*The Rev. Oliver Heywood BA, 1630–1702. His Autobiography, Diaries, Anecdote and Event Books*, ed. J. H. Turner (Brighouse and Bingley, 1881–5)
HMC	Royal Commission on Historical Manuscripts
Isham, 'Diary'	'The Diary of Elizabeth Isham' (http://www.warwick.ac.uk/fac/arts/ren/projects/isham/)
Isham, 'Rememberance'	Elizabeth Isham, 'Book of Rememberance' (http://www.warwick.ac.uk/fac/arts/ren/projects/isham/)
Josselin, *Diary*	*The Diary of Ralph Josselin, 1606–1683*, ed. Alan Macfarlane (1976)
LRRO	Leicestershire and Rutland Record Office
Newcome, Autobiography	*The Autobiography of Henry Newcome*, ed. R. Parkinson (Chetham Society, 26–7, 1852)
OBOA	*Old Bailey, Ordinary's Accounts*
OBSP	*Old Bailey Sessions Papers*
ODNB	*The Oxford Dictionary of National Biography* (Oxford, 2004, and http://www.oxforddnb.com/)
Oxinden Letters 1607–1642	*The Oxinden Letters 1607–1642*, ed. Dorothy Gardner (1933)
Oxinden Letters 1642–1670	*The Oxinden Letters 1642–1670*, ed. Dorothy Gardner (1937)
Pepys, *Diary*	*The Diary of Samuel Pepys*, ed. R. C. Latham and W. Matthews (1971–83)
SQSR	E. H. Bates Harbin, ed., *Quarter Sessions Records for the County of Somerset*, Somerset Record Society, 23–4, 28, 34 (1908–19)
TNA, SP	The National Archives, Kew, State Papers
Verney, *Memoirs*	*The Memoirs of the Verney Family*, ed. Frances Parthenope Verney and Margaret M. Verney, 4 vols, 1892, repr. 1970
Wood, *Life and Times*	*The Life and Times of Anthony Wood*, ed. Andrew Clark (Oxford Historical Society, 1891–1900)
WSRO	West Sussex Record Office

1

Introduction

Lucy Apsley, born in 1620, did not like the company of other little girls. When they came to play, she would snatch their dolls and pull them to pieces. She preferred her brothers, and longed to share in their activities and academic studies. For Lucy was a serious, bookish child, already a fluent reader at 4. Her mother, puzzled and increasingly concerned, thought too much reading would damage Lucy's health, and wanted her to focus instead on needlework, music, and dancing. Her father, by contrast, was impressed by his daughter's ambition, and encouraged her desire to learn Latin. And when she quickly outstripped her brothers, he was pleased to see envy prompting them to greater efforts. After three boys, Lucy's mother had been 'very desirous of a daughter', and the child quickly became the favourite of both parents. But Lucy's lack of interest in conventional feminine accomplishments eventually became a problem. She would not practise her lute or harpsichord, and 'for my needle', she recalled years later, 'I absolutely hated it.' When Lucy was 5, her mother gave birth to another girl, Barbara, who proved more conventionally feminine in personality and tastes. Her mother grew to be 'infinitely fond of [this child] above all the rest', Lucy wrote in her fragmentary autobiography, 'and I being of too serious a temper was not so pleasing to my . . .'.[1]

There the fragmentary autobiography breaks off in mid-sentence, never to be resumed. We can only guess at the painful emotions these memories had revived, over forty years later. At the age of 10 Lucy had lost her father, and losing her mother's special favour had hurt. She remained bookish, and Barbara thought her too 'reserved and studious' to attract men. Barbara was perhaps surprised to find her sister wooed and wed by an accomplished young gentleman, John Hutchinson. The young couple, both ardent puritans, proved well matched, and John went on to become an MP and Governor of Nottingham during the civil war. Barbara, perhaps surprisingly, married Hutchinson's younger brother, and this younger couple followed a similar political course. Lucy's brother Allen, by contrast, became a staunch cavalier. The sibling bonds they had forged in childhood remained nonetheless intact; Allen found refuge with his sister and brother-in-law after the civil war, while after the Restoration, his intervention helped save the regicide Hutchinson from the scaffold.[2]

---

[1] Lucy Hutchinson, *Memoirs of the Life of Colonel John Hutchinson*, ed. John Sutherland (Oxford, 1973), 287–9.
[2] Hutchinson, *Memoirs*, 29–33, 170; *ODNB*, John and Lucy Hutchinson.

Lucy's narrative touches on many of the issues explored in this book. Love between siblings was seen as rooted in nature itself, yet parental favouritism and sibling rivalry are timeless. They lie at the heart of the Old Testament stories of Esau and Jacob, Joseph and his brethren, and many others. The tensions between the world's very first brothers (in the Genesis story) culminate in fratricide, Cain's murder of Abel. God felt it necessary to issue a stern command to the people of Israel through Moses, 'Thou shalt not hate thy brother,' and a New Testament commandment that 'he who loveth God love his brother also'. He who hates his brother 'is in darkness'.[3] Sibling relationships in the past, as today, were heavily shaped by the interplay of individual personality. Close ties and fierce rivalries in childhood sometimes persisted for a lifetime, while other siblings drifted out of one another's lives. All these are patterns familiar across the generations. Moreover, high rates of mortality and remarriage meant that, as today, many families contained half-siblings or step-siblings. Yet sibling roles and relationships, like marriage and the family more broadly, also possess a significant historical dimension. Our ancestors' very different beliefs on gender roles shaped the ways in which they treated their sons and daughters, and how siblings viewed each other. Contemporary attitudes and practices on issues such as inheritance, especially among the propertied, had equally profound ramifications. In landed families, birth order and gender were the crucial factors, and as Hans Medick and David Sabean have argued, material interests and emotion were tightly entwined.[4] In England, unlike much of continental Europe, land was most often passed on to the next generation by primogeniture, inheritance by the eldest son. That had a huge impact on sibling relationships. Contemporaries expected the heir's brothers and sisters to respect his status and authority as head of the family, and follow his guidance. At the same time, they believed he had a moral obligation to promote his siblings' welfare. The disparity in their fortunes, and the heir's readiness to honour these obligations, created a set of potentially fraught relationships. Though primogeniture was less dominant among ordinary families, here too sibling relationships and responsibilities played a significant role throughout the lives of both men and women.[5]

Contemporaries had a clear sense of the sibling ideal, spelled out by the merchant James Houblon in a memoir he composed for his numerous progeny. 'I have loved you all,' he wrote, 'wherefore so live together that when I am gone men may say, these are the children of such a father, see how they love one another.' Gratifying his wish, they became famous for their affection and solidarity.[6] Yet, predictably, many families fell far short of the ideal, and parents often worried about their children's ability to live together harmoniously. In 1635, Sir John Coke urged his eldest son to be kind to a younger brother, insisting plaintively that 'No small part

---

[3] *Leviticus*, xix.17; *1 John*, ii.11, iii.15, iv.20–1.

[4] Hans Medick and David Sabean, eds, *Interest and Emotion. Essays in the Study of Family and Kinship* (Cambridge, 1984), 9–27.

[5] Amy Louise Erickson, *Women and Property in Early Modern England* (1993).

[6] Alice Archer Houblon, *The Houblon Family. Its Story and Times* (2 vols, 1907), i.347; Pepys, *Diary*, vii.36, 39, 370, ix.68.

of the comfort of both your lives will proceed from that which you give one another.'[7] Wills occasionally contained similar exhortations, and many included clauses cancelling bequests if the heir failed to convey specified money, goods, or lands to his siblings. John Davenant, Jacobean mayor of Oxford, even stipulated that within three months of his death his younger son William (the future playwright) was to be removed from the family home. Otherwise, he anticipated, discord would almost certainly erupt.[8] This book explores the expectations surrounding siblings in early modern England, and the complex relationship between expectations and behaviour. Rivalries and resentments form one prominent theme, but sibling bonds and responsibilities were far from empty ideals. They emerge as significant social forces at every level of society.

The family is a long-established subject of historical, literary, sociological, and anthropological research. It played a central role in every sphere—social, political, cultural, economic, and religious. Historical research has focused on demographic issues, inheritance, and relationships between husbands and wives, parents and children.[9] The roles and relationships of siblings in early modern England remain far less explored. Most households were 'nuclear', comprising only a husband, wife, children, and perhaps one or more servants. Property generally passed vertically from parents to children, not horizontally to other kin. The Poor Laws of 1598/1601 laid down that the young were to be supported, wherever possible, by parents or grandparents, and the destitute elderly by their adult children or grandchildren. No legal obligations were laid upon brothers or sisters, uncles or aunts. The destitute often turned to their neighbours for help, and increasingly across the seventeenth century to poor relief funded by the parish. This context helps to explain why the significance of sibling relationships has remained relatively neglected. Miranda Chaytor and Naomi Tadmor have shown how the contribution of close kin (including brothers-in-law and sisters-in-law) might be crucial in sustaining the nuclear family of parents and children, but siblings feature barely, if at all, in chapters on the family in most social histories. Patricia Crawford included a valuable chapter in her survey of the early modern family and we have fine studies of particular families, such as the Verneys of Claydon and the families of Ralph Josselin and Katharine and Philip Henry.[10] The most substantial works on England, Amy

[7] HMC, 23, *Cowper*, ii.102.

[8] Ralph Houlbrooke, *Death, Religion and the Family in England 1480–1750* (Oxford, 1998), 144; Mary Prior, 'Women and the urban economy: Oxford 1500–1800', in Mary Prior, ed., *Women in Early Modern Society 1500–1800* (1985), 97.

[9] The literature is vast. On demography, see E. A. Wrigley and R. S. Schofield, *The Population History of England 1541–1871. A Reconstruction* (1981). On family relationships, see e.g. Ralph A. Houlbrooke, *The English Family* (1984); Keith Wrightson, *English Society 1580–1680* (1982), chaps 3–4; Anthony Fletcher, *Gender, Sex and Subordination in England 1500–1800* (1985); Lawrence Stone, *The Family, Sex and Marriage in England 1500–1800* (New York, 1977).

[10] Miranda Chaytor, 'Household and Kinship: Ryton in the late 16th and early 17th Centuries', *History Workshop*, 10 (1980), 25–60; Naomi Tadmor, *Family and Friends in Eighteenth-Century England* (Cambridge, 2001); Miriam Slater, *Family Life in the Seventeenth Century. The Verneys of Claydon House* (1984); Susan E. Whyman, *Sociability and Power in Late-Stuart England. The Cultural Worlds of the Verneys 1660–1720* (Oxford, 1999); Alan Macfarlane, *The Family Life of Ralph Josselin. A Seventeenth-Century Clergyman* (Cambridge, 1970), chaps 7–10.

Harris's *Siblinghood* and Leonore Davidoff's *Thicker than Water*, both focus on later periods, and on the upper levels of society.[11] More has been published on contin-ental Europe and North America, where the context was often very different. In much of Europe, especially the south and east, families were extended rather than nuclear, with land and often houses shared by several generations. Brides were usually far younger than in England, and they married men considerably older, with a new couple living for years with the bridegroom's parents. Primogeniture held less sway, and in many areas sons and daughters inherited equal shares. All this made for a very different set of family relationships.[12] Primogeniture also had much less sway in colonial America.[13]

A stream of domestic conduct books sought to guide family relationships in early modern England, reinforcing the message of countless sermons.[14] They spelled out appropriate codes of behaviour for husbands, wives, parents, children, and domes-tic servants. They had remarkably little to say about sibling relationships, and almost nothing about in-laws. Families would generally refer to and address a brother- or sister-in-law as 'Brother' or 'Sister' (using the surname), and such kin often played a significant role in family life. The broader concept of fraternity pervaded the culture of the period. Members of corporations, guilds, and profes-sions viewed one another as members of an imagined family. Puritans and Non-conformists habitually spoke of 'Brother Smith' and 'Sister Green', and Anglican clergy occasionally referred to each other as brothers.[15] Fraternity as a universal ideal extended further still in the language and literature of the age. Shakespeare's *Henry V* rallies his desperate forces before Agincourt as 'we band of brothers', and similar images were ubiquitous in everyday language. Radicals could imagine all Englishmen as brothers, and every Londoner as a 'brother citizen'.[16] Twinship suggested an even closer bond. Robert Symcotts, who died in 1639, left his twin brother a ring inscribed 'Death cannot separate us', while the Independent minister Charles Nichols addressed a long-standing friend as 'Dear Twin'.[17] Preachers

---

[11] Amy Harris, *Siblinghood and Social Relations in Georgian England* (Manchester, 2012); Leonore Davidoff, *Thicker than Water. Siblings and their Relations 1780–1920* (Oxford, 2012).

[12] David Sabean and Christopher H. Johnson, *Sibling Relations and the Transformation of European Kinship* (2011); Naomi J. Miller and Naomi Yavneh, eds, *Sibling Relations and Gender in the Early Modern World* (Aldershot, 2006).

[13] C. Dallett Hemphill, *Siblings. Brothers and Sisters in American History* (Oxford, 2011), 16–17, 24–5.

[14] Fletcher, *Gender*, chap. 11; Bernard Capp, *When Gossips Meet. Women, Family and Neighbourhood in Early Modern England* (Oxford, 2003), 7–11 and works there cited.

[15] *The Diary and Letter Book of the Rev. Thomas Brockbank 1671–1709*, ed. Richard Trappes-Lomax, Chetham Society, N.S., 89 (1930), 118–19.

[16] Shakespeare, *Henry V*, IV.iii.60; Gerrard Winstanley, *The Law of Freedom in a Platform* (1652), title page; Abiezer Coppe, *A Fiery Flying Roll* (1650), 6; A. L., *To all the honest, wise, and grave citizens of London* (1648), brs.

[17] F. N. L. Poynter and W. J. Bishop, eds, *A Seventeenth-Century Doctor and his Patients. John Symcotts 1592?–1662*, Bedfordshire Historical Record Society, 31 (1951), xii; *Oxinden Letters 1642–1670*, 256; *The Diary of Roger Lowe of Ashton-in-Makerfield, Lancashire, 1663–74*, ed. William L. Sachse (1938), 21.

bracketed faith and obedience, or prayer and thanksgiving, as 'God's twins'.[18] The image of sisterhood, though less common, carried similar associations. Two close friends in Somerset were described as being 'like sworn sisters'.[19] Jane Sharp, author of a pioneering work on midwifery, addressed midwives across the nation as her 'Sisters', and contemporaries spoke of 'sister-churches' and 'sister counties'.[20]

Yet contemporary images also reflected the darker qualities and conflicts found in sibling relationships. A fanciful depiction of the underworld of criminals and rogues was entitled *The Fraternity of Vagabonds*, while a Jacobean diarist denounced the brotherhood of drunken, violent 'roaring boys' that plagued the capital.[21] Satirists ridiculed puritan and sectarian women as 'the holy sisters', accusing them of hypocrisy, lechery, and sinister designs to subvert male supremacy. Puritans countered by identifying 'popery and profaneness' as 'two sisters in evil'.[22] The imagery of twins could be similarly ambiguous. Preachers twinned ignorance and wickedness, and popery and prelacy, while a Whig polemicist smeared James II and Louis XIV as popish and tyrannical twins.[23] A balladeer explained that Rome and Geneva were also 'a sort of twins,/ Sworn sisters and sworn enemies to kings'.[24] Twins and siblings could also be imagined as bitter rivals. The poet Anne Bradstreet, inventing a dialogue between Flesh and Spirit, made Spirit declare defiantly, 'Sisters we are, yea, twins we be,/ Yet deadly feud 'twixt thee and me'.[25] Her image echoed the biblical story of Jacob and Esau fighting in the womb, reinforced by pagan myths such as the rivalry of Romulus and Remus. Charles I's hawkish minister Strafford and Archbishop Laud were vilified as twins vying to outdo one another in evil.[26]

Sibling relationships also provided a striking metaphor for the tensions between the rich and the poor. In his biting analysis of the social order, the Digger Gerrard Winstanley frequently used 'elder brother' to stand for the rich and powerful, 'younger brother' for the poor and oppressed.[27] The image even surfaced, bizarrely, at an Old Bailey trial in 1693, when a burglar claimed he had received only a small share of the booty, 'because he was but a younger brother' in the gang.[28] Yet the same image could also convey admiration and emulation. A rake in Restoration

[18] Henry Adis, *A Fanaticks Mite Cast into the Kings Treasury* (1660), 9; Vincent Alsop, *Duty and Interest United* (1695), 11.

[19] *The Chronicles of John Cannon, Excise Officer and Writing Master, 1684–1743*, ed. John Money (Oxford, 2010), i.139.

[20] Jane Sharp, *The Midwives Book* (1671), sig. A; *Certain Quaeres Humbly Presented* (1649), 6; *Flemings in Oxford*, i.217.

[21] John Awdeley, *The Fraternity of Vagabonds* [1561], Camden Society, Old Series, 41 (1848), 70–1.

[22] e.g. *The Holy Sisters Conspiracy against their Husbands* (1661); William Hinde, *A Faithfull Remonstrance of the Holy Life and Happy Death of Iohn Bruen* (1641), 89.

[23] Richard Ames, *The Character of a Bigotted Prince* (1693), 14; Lancelot Andrewes, *Aposasmatia Sacra* (1617), 420; *Good Newes from all Quarters* (1643), 6.

[24] *A Parallel betwixt Popery and Phanaticism* [1681], brs.

[25] *The Works of Anne Bradstreet*, ed. Jeannine Hensley (1967), 216.

[26] *Genesis*, xxv.22–3; *The Discontented Conference betwixt the two Great Associates* (1641), brs.

[27] Gerrard Winstanley, *A New-yeers Gift for the Parliament and Armie* (1650), 20; idem, *The Law of Freedom in a Platform* (1652), 61–2.

[28] *OBSP*, t16930713-24.

Yorkshire was so impressed to learn that two illegitimate babies, fathered by the same man, had been christened on the same day that he felt moved to 'acknowledge him for his elder brother'. His witticism disgusted the pious.[29]

The ubiquity of these powerful yet contradictory images underlines the importance and complexity of sibling relationships in early modern England. Perhaps we should not be surprised, then, to find that two pioneering studies arrived at diametrically opposite conclusions. Joan Thirsk identified a pattern of bitter conflict and resentment between older and younger brothers, while Linda Pollock argued for a widespread sense of family solidarity.[30] We can find plentiful evidence of both patterns. Many siblings expressed deep affection for one another. Philip Gawdy assured his brother in 1589 that 'the faithful love I bear you may be compared to the love that was between David and Jonathan, which was exceeding the love of women'. Tom Oxinden, writing home a few weeks after marrying his teenage bride in 1653, closed by sending 'my best respects to my wife and love to my sisters', a formulation that sounds very strange to modern ears.[31] But there is also abundant evidence of fierce sibling rivalries, rooted in the social, cultural, and legal structures of the period as well as in personal antipathies.

So how far can we recover the character and significance of sibling relationships in the past? Could children hope or expect to be loved equally by their parents? How far did elder and younger brothers honour their reciprocal obligations? And how far would a sense of responsibility guide their behaviour if personal affection was absent? How did sisters relate to each other, and to their brothers? How successfully did families handle the challenge of accommodating half-siblings and stepchildren? Were cruel step-parents a threat to orphaned children, or merely figures of cultural myth? On all these issues, the evidence is predictably far more abundant for the upper levels of society. Letters, diaries, and memoirs often reveal in vivid detail the social dynamics of their families. For ordinary people, by contrast, the evidence is almost always fragmentary, prompting one scholar to conclude that this world 'may well remain closed to us for ever'.[32] But by piecing together the fragments we can discern at least the broad shape of popular attitudes and behaviour.

Sibling tensions in landed families were closely related to the issue of primogeniture. The practice of passing on landed property to the eldest son had a solid economic rationale. Even a large estate, divided between several children and divided again in subsequent generations, would quickly become too fragmented to support any family at an acceptable level. Primogeniture was deeply entrenched in the social and cultural values of the propertied, as the best way to preserve the status and wealth of their families. The puritan minister William Gouge insisted this was both right and just. 'God hath so appointed it', he declared, claiming

[29] Heywood, *Autobiography*, ii.274.

[30] Joan Thirsk, 'Younger Sons in the Seventeenth Century', *History*, 54 (1961), 358–77; Linda Pollock, 'Younger Sons in Tudor and Stuart England', *History Today*, 39 (June 1989), 23–9.

[31] *Letters of Philip Gawdy of West Harling, Norfolk*, ed. Isaac Herbert Jeayes (1906), 44; *Oxinden Letters 1642–1670*, 183.

[32] Peter Laslett, *Family Life and Illicit Love in Earlier Generations* (Cambridge, 1977), 167.

mistakenly that 'the laws in all nations do order as much'. His domestic conduct book condemned the disinheritance of any 'rightful' heir, unless 'notoriously wicked'. Thomas Fuller explained that while a good father would love all his sons, 'his main land he settles on the eldest: for where man takes away the birth right, God commonly takes the blessing from a family'. Another guide pronounced it 'unnatural, injurious, and ungodly' for a father to disinherit his eldest son other than in the most exceptional circumstances.[33]

Younger siblings grew up fully aware of the rationale behind primogeniture, and its implications. Understanding, of course, did not equate with satisfaction. Joan Thirsk identified the discontent of younger brothers as a major social fault line in early modern England. In landed families, fathers were expected to make provision for their younger sons, whether through annuities or by entering them into a profession (law, medicine, the Church, or the military), or apprenticing them to a wholesale trade. In practice, negligent or indebted fathers often failed to make any such provision, leaving younger brothers at the mercy of the heir's favour. Moreover, most annuities were too small to provide a satisfactory livelihood, and payments were often irregular and delayed. And, as Thirsk points out, young men who not been brought up to accept the idea of working for a living found it hard to buckle down to the demands of a profession or trade. Many 'hung around at home, idle, bored, and increasingly resentful'.[34]

These frustrations prompted a huge tide of complaint. Thomas Wilson, a younger brother analysing England's social structure in 1600, commented bitterly that 'my elder brother forsooth must be my master. He must have all', while younger siblings must be content with 'that which the cat left on the malt heap'. All too often, another writer complained, heirs 'grow like infidels or Turks, neither providing for their own families, nor regarding their brothers nor sisters'. Francis Osborn, another younger brother, railed that 'first-born' was a term 'pernicious to the major part of mankind'. Most elder brothers, he raged, were thieves who cheated their brethren and laid 'cruelties and unnatural burdens' upon them.[35]

Primogeniture thus left younger brothers facing steep downward mobility and perhaps penury. Many found life in trade tedious and demeaning, and dropped out without completing their apprenticeships. Many others abandoned their legal studies. Soldiering, far more congenial, was hazardous and ill-paid, and few made their fortunes. Lucy Hutchinson's uncles had taken this route, and were all dead by the time she was born. Between them, she observed, they had left only three daughters, 'who bestowed themselves meanly, and their generations are worn out except two or three unregarded children'. The descent from gentility to oblivion had taken only two generations. Lucy's own father was the youngest of seven

[33] William Gouge, *Of Domesticall Duties* (1622), 576–7, 579–80; Thomas Fuller, *The Holy State* (1642), 12; John Dod and Robert Cleaver, *A Godly Forme of Household Government* (1612), 336–40; *The Office of Christian Parents* (Cambridge, 1616), 128–9.

[34] Thirsk, 'Younger Sons', 368.

[35] Thomas Wilson, *The State of England Anno Dom. 1600*, ed. F. J. Fisher, in *Camden Miscellany*, 16 (Camden Society, 3rd series, 52, 1936), 23–4; Hinde, *Faithfull Remonstrance of Bruen*, 48; *The Works of Francis Osborn, Esquire* (8th edn, 1682), 141.

brothers, and only luck and their early deaths had brought him the means to live as his father had done.[36]

Sibling discontents feature prominently in the literature of the period. They shape Shakespeare's *As You Like It*, with Orlando chafing at his ill-treatment by Oliver, eldest son and heir of Sir Roland de Boys. Sir Roland had left a thousand crowns for Orlando, charging Oliver to see him well educated. Instead, Orlando complains, his brother detains the money, keeps him 'rustically at home', bars him from his table, and 'undermines my gentility'. Orlando acknowledges the social and cultural conventions of the age: 'The courtesy of nations allows you my better, in that you are the first-born; but the same tradition takes not away my blood.' Oliver has abused his rights and neglected his responsibilities, driving Orlando to the point of mutiny.[37] Similar resentments surfaced in many other literary forms. The essayist John Earle characterized the 'younger brother' as a pitiful figure brought up to behave as a gentleman, but denied the means to do so. 'His birth and bringing up will not suffer him to descend to the means to get wealth . . . He is commonly discontented, and desperate, and the form of his exclamation is, that churl my brother.'[38] In 1618, a Welsh gentleman named Ap Robert published a treatise entitled *The Younger Brother*, prompted, he explained, by conversations among his friends. A younger brother himself, he accepted the economic rationale of primogeniture but criticized its rigidity. As it rested merely on social convention, he urged fathers to redirect the inheritance whenever the eldest son was patently unfit to succeed.[39] The treatise passed through six editions, confirming that this was a hot issue. Most readers, we may suppose, were younger brothers too.

Ap Robert's theme also surfaced in popular comedies, such as John Fletcher's *The Elder Brother*, penned in the early 1620s. Its plot revolves around a wealthy father who does resolve to disinherit his elder son. This particular heir is no wastrel but an obsessive bookworm, indifferent to worldly concerns and women. His father considers him unfit to manage an estate, and fears he will never marry and so condemn the family line to extinction. Two generations later Aphra Behn addressed the same issue in *The Younger Brother*, also performed on the London stage. Its hero, a spirited young man, has abandoned his apprenticeship and scrapes a living by his wits. His elder brother is an idle, dim-witted drunkard and gamester. The younger brother wants his father to disinherit this useless heir, and his father repeatedly vows to do so. Yet in neither play does the threat of disinheritance materialize. In Fletcher's comedy, the bookworm suddenly develops all the conventional qualities and appetites of a fine gentleman. In Behn's play, where the heir remains a drunken sot, she supplies a happy ending by having the younger brother marry a beautiful young woman with an independent fortune. Both plays thus underline the strength of primogeniture's hold over the social and cultural values

---

[36] Hutchinson, *Memoirs*, 283.
[37] *As You Like It*, I.i. For an excellent discussion see Louis Montrose, '"The Place of a Brother" in *As You Like It*: Social Process and Comic Form', *Shakespeare Quarterly*, 32 (1981), 28–54.
[38] John Earle, *Micro-Cosmographie* (1628), *sig.* C5v–7.
[39] I. Ap Robert, *The Younger Brother His Apology* ([St. Omer,] 1618).

of the age.[40] Shakespeare's *As You Like It* does the same. Orlando is fully justified in his sense of grievance, but the play ends with his elder brother still in possession of his estate and transformed into a paragon of fraternal love. Orlando, for his part, has secured an implausibly happy future by marrying the Duke's daughter and becoming heir to the Dukedom. As Louis Montrose has argued, these plays were escapist fantasies, not serious social critiques.[41]

Ap Robert had pointed out that inheritance patterns rested on custom rather than law, and that custom did not bind. Moreover, customs varied. In Kent, under the system of gavelkind, property was partible among sons, to the frustration of many landowners. In areas that followed 'borough English', it passed to the youngest son. Land could also be devised by will, if there was no 'strict settlement' to tie the owner's hands.[42] A few fathers chose to divide their property equally, while Thomas Wood of Oxford left most of his estate to the longest-lived of his three surviving sons.[43] Men did occasionally disinherit the natural heir. Sir George Croke, for example, left his estate to his brother, spurning his son as a dissolute drunkard. The baronet Sir George Stonehouse, outraged that his eldest son had become 'debauched and married his kitchen maid', arranged for both title and estate to pass to his second son.[44] But most landowners viewed such disruptions of the social order with deep unease. When Sir John Holles heard in 1616 that an old friend had disinherited his eldest son, he penned a long and passionate letter begging him to reconsider. How could his friend have 'strayed out of the way of nature, of charity, of justice'? Arguing that fathers had a duty to sons, as well as sons to fathers, he hoped God would 'show you the foulness of your error'.[45] Disinheritance, moreover, might well breed new troubles and strife. In 1632, the Court of High Commission tried a case of multiple adulteries against Dr Francis Gibbons of Shrewsbury, on a charge brought by Gibbons's elder brother. The defence counsel told the court that this was a malicious prosecution, brought because their father had disinherited the elder brother, and that the doctor was lawfully married to the woman in question.[46]

The public debate was dominated by resentful younger brothers (and wholly ignored their sisters). In private debate, conducted in person or by letter, elder brothers spelled out their own grievances. Many inherited heavy debts along with the estate, and saw the portions and annuities they were required to pay as an unfair or impossible burden. Sometimes they came as a shock. Sir Thomas Peyton, orphaned as a child, was not told how much he would have to provide one day

---

[40] *The Elder Brother*, ed. Fredson Bowers, in *The Dramatic Works in the Beaumont and Fletcher Canon*, ix (Cambridge, 1994); *The Younger Brother*, in *The Works of Aphra Behn*, ed. Janet Todd, 7 vols, (1992–6), vii.

[41] *As You Like It*, IV.iii–V.iv; Montrose, 'Place of a Brother', 53.

[42] Erickson, *Women and Property*.   [43] Wood, *Life and Times*, i.284.

[44] Wood, *Life and Times*, ii.137–8, 311.

[45] *Letters of John Holles 1587–1637*, ed. P. R. Seddon, Thoroton Society, 31, 35 (1975, 1983), i.111–12.

[46] Samuel Rawson Gardiner, ed., *Reports of Cases in the Courts of Star Chamber and High Commission*, Camden Society, New Series, 39 (1886), 277, 282–3.

for his sisters, and refused to believe it when his mother finally informed him.[47] Many an heir saw his siblings as idle, spendthrift, and ungrateful, and tried to evade his obligations. The more he gave away, he would reason, the less he would have to maintain the estate, pay off inherited debts, and provide for his own family. Many elder brothers thus reciprocated the resentment their younger siblings harboured, with both parties convinced they occupied the moral high ground.

Ordinary families with some land generally also bequeathed it to the eldest son, but most also tried to provide generously for his siblings. The eldest son of a yeoman, husbandman, or tradesman always knew, moreover, that he would have to work for his living, just like his brothers. Many humbler folk owned only movable goods such as furniture, clothes, and the tools of their trade. Here, as we will see, the spirit of equity usually prevailed. In this sphere, sibling relationships often involved different issues and challenges. How far could siblings even remain in contact, when many were barely literate and perhaps lived far apart? And how far would those of modest means be able or willing to help kin in need? Historians face a different set of challenges, too, for the poor did not keep diaries or write autobiographies, and any letters were unlikely to survive. Like the poor themselves, we have to resort to an 'economy of makeshifts', piecing together the fragments that survive from a range of disparate sources.

This book has two parts. The first is thematic, with Chapter 2 exploring childhood issues: parental attitudes and favouritism, sibling friendships and competition. Chapter 3 looks beyond inheritance to focus on the heir's responsibilities throughout adult life, and patterns of support, deference, affection, and resentment between brothers. Starting with the gentry and upper middling classes, it moves on to explore fraternal relationships among ordinary people and the poor. Chapter 4 turns to ties, responsibilities, and conflicts across the gender divide, including the ways in which sisters might be able to support their brothers, despite the gendered structures of a male-dominated society. Chapter 5 focuses on the emotional and material dimensions of adult relationships between sisters, while Chapter 6 addresses the issues raised by families rebuilt after bereavement and remarriage: the world of half-siblings, step-siblings. Chapter 7 shifts focus again. This was an age of religious as well as social upheaval, with the Reformation creating deep tensions between Catholics and Protestants, and between different Protestant denominations. The chapter looks at how religious divisions and different levels of commitment affected family relationships. Part II of the book adopts a different approach, exploring issues through a series of in-depth case studies. The evidence that survives to enable such studies comes largely from families in the middle and higher levels of society in the second half of the period, and the case studies in Part II reflect this. Whenever the evidence does enable us to explore sibling relationships in depth, they emerge as powerful, complex, and contradictory. And while some aspects appear familiar, others were very clearly the product of an age with its own distinctive values and culture.

---

[47] *Oxinden Letters 1607–1642*, 87.

PART I

SIBLING ISSUES

2

The Experience of Childhood

Sibling relationships in childhood have always been characterized by close bonds and fierce rivalries, reflecting individual temperament, age difference, competition, and parental favouritism. But equally important is the context of time and place: gendered assumptions and conventions on the upbringing and value of boys and girls, and the behaviour deemed appropriate for each. Significant too are the parents' social and economic circumstances. Family dynamics in the early modern period can appear both startlingly familiar and very alien to our own.

THE CONTEXT OF CHILDHOOD

A woman in early modern England might bear six or seven children over the course of a lifetime. The wives of gentlemen and wealthy merchants and professionals often bore more, because they were less likely to breastfeed their infants, which reduced the intervals between births. Very rarely did all children survive to reach adulthood, and roughly a quarter died before the age of 10. Infant mortality was higher in the children put out to nurse, and infant and child mortality rates were higher in the period after 1650, sometimes as high as a quarter. Older children would usually leave home at around puberty to enter service or an apprenticeship. A typical ordinary household might therefore include only three children at any particular time. Young children lived, played, and slept in close proximity. But when a large age gap existed between the surviving siblings, their relationships were inevitably very different, in some cases quasi-parental, in others almost non-existent. Older siblings who had left home might barely know their younger brothers or sisters. Elizabeth Osborne, for example, who was seventeen years older than her sister Dorothy, married and moved away when Dorothy was only 9, and died six years later. They had had little opportunity to build a close relationship. Between half-siblings the gap might be still wider. The lawyer Bulstrode Whitelocke fathered seventeen children by three wives, with twenty-eight years between the oldest and youngest.[1]

Among the elite, the former practice of sending boys to be raised and trained in the household of a magnate was in decline. Instead, it became increasingly

---

[1] Peter Laslett, *The World We Have Lost Further Explored* (1983), 96, 112; *The Letters of Dorothy Osborne to William Temple*, ed. G. C. Moore Smith (Oxford, 1928), 90, 235, 320; *The Diary of Bulstrode Whitelocke 1605–1675*, ed. Ruth Spalding (Oxford, 1990), viii.

common for them to be sent away to school, where they received a classical education, often accompanied by a deliberately harsh disciplinary regime. Their education was designed to equip them for public life and leadership, and to set them apart from both women and 'ordinary' men. The harsh regime was intended to foster physical and mental toughness, to balance the civility and polish.[2] Their sisters were generally tutored at home, with a focus on appropriate housewifely skills. In Tudor families that valued humanist learning, some girls reached very high standards, but academic learning became less acceptable as the seventeenth century advanced. Lucy Apsley, at the age of 7, had eight tutors and additional tuition in Latin from her father's chaplain, but her mother feared her addiction to books would damage her health, and locked them away. The girls' boarding schools that flourished from the mid-seventeenth century were essentially finishing schools, focusing on music, dancing, and other social accomplishments.[3] When boys came home from their boarding schools, their sisters would have been very conscious of their wider horizons and superior learning.

Boys in ordinary families were similarly far more likely than their sisters to receive an elementary education. Literacy levels were always much higher among men than women, though many girls learned to read without acquiring the skill of writing.[4] The ability to write brought them little material advantage, and parents often decided they were more useful at home, helping with housework and caring for younger siblings. The Lancashire yeoman William Stout sent all his children to school, but his only daughter was soon withdrawn to help at home. Thereafter she looked after her young brothers, freeing her mother to devote herself to farm work.[5]

These gendered contrasts were equally visible in patterns of play.[6] In poorer families, parents set their children to work from an early age, running errands, fetching water, minding animals, and assisting with other tasks.[7] Even so, many boys at all levels of society found opportunities to roam abroad and engage in adventurous and sometimes antisocial activities. Isaac Barrow, later a Cambridge professor, had been an idle schoolboy, 'his chief delight being in fighting' with schoolmates and butchers' boys in the Shambles.[8] William Coe, as a schoolboy, had deliberately led 'a poor blind man out of his way' into a river, while a diarist noting

---

[2] Anthony Fletcher, *Growing Up in England: the Experience of Childhood 1600–1914* (New Haven, 2008), chaps 11–13; idem, *Gender, Sex and Subordination in England 1500–1800* (New Haven, 1991), chap. 16; Kenneth Charlton, *Women, Religion and Education in Early Modern England* (1999).

[3] Lucy Hutchinson, *Memoirs of the Life of Colonel John Hutchinson*, ed. John Sutherland (Oxford, 1973), 288; Fletcher, *Growing Up*, chaps 15–17; idem, *Gender*, chap. 19.

[4] David Cressy, *Literacy and the Social Order. Reading and Writing in Tudor and Stuart England* (Cambridge, 1980); Margaret Spufford, 'First steps in Literacy: the Reading and Writing Experiences of the humblest seventeenth-century Spiritual Autobiographers', *Social History*, 4 (1979): 407–35.

[5] *The Autobiography of William Stout of Lancaster 1665–1752*, ed. J. D. Marshall (Manchester, 1967), 68.

[6] Keith Thomas, 'Children in Early Modern England', in Gillian Avery and Julia Briggs, eds, *Children and their Books* (Oxford, 1989), 45–77.

[7] Ilana Krausman Ben-Amos, *Adolescence and Youth in Early Modern England* (New Haven 1994), 40–7.

[8] Walter Pope, *The Life of Seth [Ward], Lord Bishop of Salisbury* (1697), 131; Kate Bennett, ed., *John Aubrey: Brief Lives* (Oxford, 2016), i.703; Pepys, *Diary*, iv.12–13.

the death of a vagrant observed that 'the night before some bad boys set dogs upon him, which bit him very much, which it is thought occasioned his death'.[9] Young vandals in Somerset found their fun in breaking down gates and bridges, killing geese and ducks, and stealing chickens. They were far from unique.[10]

Gentry and professional families had no need, of course, to call on their children's labour, and outside school boys might enjoy remarkable freedom. William Blundell, a Catholic squire in Restoration Lancashire, described how his 14-year-old grandson was often to be found at 'the head of a whole regiment of pitiful tatterdemalions', beating through the brambles to start a hare.[11] It would have been unthinkable for a girl of that age and class to mix with girls of such lowly origins. Boys too young for school were often left largely unsupervised. William Coe's diary records the repeated misadventures of his young sons: one, aged 6, almost drowned after falling into a creek, 'none with him'; another, 4, almost hanged while squeezing out of a window, 'being left alone in the house'; a third, aged 2, kicked by a horse after wandering into a stable to play.[12] Even puritan ministers allowed their young sons to roam abroad. Henry Newcome, for example, recorded one child playing on a bridge and left hanging when the railings broke, and another, aged 5, falling into the river while fishing. In a similar mishap, two years later, his only companion had been his 2-year-old brother.[13] If such an anxious parent allowed his young sons this degree of freedom, boys in less caring families can have faced few constraints.

The young daughters of elite or professional men enjoyed no such licence. Any mishaps generally occurred in or near the home, from swallowing pins, falling into the fire, or in the kitchen. Girls were expected to play at home, and with more decorum. In 1663, William Blundell penned a revealing 'Exercise' for his three young daughters to perform, to foster their self-confidence. It focuses on the behaviour of Mall (Mary), aged 7, who, we learn, had frequently been whipped for such grave offences as 'unreverend' praying, an 'untidy gait', and 'wild, unhandsome laughing'. Even at this age, she was expected to behave in a decorous manner. In the Exercise, her sisters Frances and Bridget (9 and 4 respectively) are playing, with the little one pretending to be a horse. But when little Bridget suggests more boisterous games, such as kneading cockle bread or performing somersaults, Mall objects. Endeavouring now to be a 'grave gentlewoman', after her father's scolding, she declares that such things were wholly unfitting, and 'plays for boys'.[14]

---

[9] 'The Diary of William Coe 1693–1729', in Matthew Storey, ed., *Two East Anglian Diaries, 1641–1729*, Suffolk Records Society, 36 (1994), 204; 'The Journal of Mr John Hobson', ed. Charles Jackson, in *Yorkshire Diaries and Autobiographies of the Seventeenth and Eighteenth Centuries*, Surtees Society, 65 (1877), 323.

[10] *The Chronicles of John Cannon, Excise Officer and Writing Master, 1684–1743*, ed. John Money (Oxford, 2010), i.42.

[11] Margaret Blundell, ed., *Cavalier. Letters of William Blundell to his Friends 1620–1698* (1933), 177.

[12] Coe, 'Diary', 210, 225, 230–1, 239; cf. 223, 235, 241.

[13] Newcome, *Autobiography*, 74, 104–5, 108; cf. 'The Diary of Isaac Archer 1641–1700', in Storey, ed., *Two East Anglian Diaries*, 45.

[14] Blundell, *Cavalier*, 45–6, 304–12.

Many parents shared Blundell's views. Thomas Meautys, a professional soldier, wrote admiringly in 1636 that his eldest daughter, aged about 8, serious and studious, 'hath already sowed her wild oats, so much a woman is she grown, God bless her'.[15]

Mall was clearly something of a tomboy, a term already familiar in this period. Her father's efforts eventually prevailed, and Mall later became a nun, but in every age we can find spirited girls reluctant to conform to the manners deemed appropriate. Even Jane Austen's demure heroine Catherine Morland had been, at the age of 10, a 'noisy and wild' child, 'fond of all boys' plays' and preferring cricket and baseball to dolls.[16] We learn that Kate Thornton, aged 5, had been a boisterous girl, 'very full of sport and play'. Her mother preferred her sister, a quieter and more conventional child.[17] Ann Harrison, the daughter of a London merchant, recalled that she too had been a 'wild' child. Though taught French, needlework, and dancing, she preferred riding, 'running, and all active pastimes; and in fine I was that which we graver people call a hoiting girl'. The death of her mother, when Ann was 15, brought all that to an abrupt end. Her father placed her in charge of his house and family, and Ann had to metamorphose overnight into a responsible matron, a life-changing experience that was shared by many other adolescent girls.[18]

There were similarly boisterous girls, of course, at every level of society. Ralph Josselin, a yeoman's son, recalled that one of his sisters, another 'wild child', had once 'stabbed him in the forehead'.[19] But in ordinary families, girls from the age of 7 or 8 were generally kept busy with household chores and caring for younger siblings, with games and sports confined mainly to Sunday afternoons and holidays. Coroners' inquests on child fatalities show that accidents to girls usually occurred while engaged in domestic chores, such as fetching water from a well. Most at risk were the very young, too small to help with such chores and left almost unsupervised. The Old Bailey records present a melancholy succession of little girls, some as young as 3 or 4, run over by carts and wagons while playing in the street.[20]

GENDER PREFERENCES

In many parts of today's world, as in the past, parents display a strong preference for boys rather than girls. Many parents in early modern England displayed a similar

---

[15] *The Private Correspondence of Jane Lady Cornwallis 1613–1644* (1842), 277.

[16] Jane Austen, *Northanger Abbey* (1818), chap. 1.

[17] *The Autobiography of Alice Thornton*, ed. Charles Jackson, Surtees Society, 62 (1873), 129–30, 133–4, 170.

[18] *The Memoirs of Anne, Lady Halkett and Ann, Lady Fanshawe*, ed. John Loftis, (Oxford, 1979), 110.

[19] Josselin, *Diary*, 1.

[20] R. F. Hunnisett, ed., *Sussex Coroners' Inquests 1558–1603* (Kew, 1996), 29, 39, 47, 49, 51, 54, 108, 135; Barbara A. Hanawalt 'Childrearing among the Lower Classes of Late Medieval England', *Journal of Interdisciplinary History*, 8 (1977), 15–18; *OBSP*, t16811017-1; t16840903-19; t16860414-3; t16900903-16; cf. Paul Seaver, *Wallington's World. A Puritan Artisan in Seventeenth-Century London* (1985), 90.

preference, and for broadly similar reasons. A boy might be raised to take over his father's farm or trade. He would keep alive the family's name and, in elite families, preserve its estate and title. A girl's destiny, by contrast, was generally marriage. For the 'middling sorts' and above, that required a substantial portion in cash or land, transferring resources from her family to that of her husband. While younger sons might find a livelihood in a craft, trade, or profession, daughters had far fewer opportunities. In families where money was tight, another daughter might be viewed as an unwelcome burden. Single women from humble backgrounds faced a life in service, or earned a hard living by knitting, charring, laundering, and the like.

Men's preference for sons thus rested on both emotional and pragmatic foundations. The story of the Blundell family, Lancashire Catholics, provides a telling example. The Blundells were blessed or cursed with extraordinary fertility, with wives across three generations each bearing thirteen children. Ten of the middle couple's children were girls, and William, their father, greeted their arrival with bleakly humorous dismay. Writing to a friend after the birth of his sixth daughter he reported that the infant had already died; 'finding herself not so welcome in this world as a son, [she] hath made already a discreet choice of a better'. On the birth of his tenth daughter, he wrote wearily that 'the thing is called Bridget'. Having fathered three daughters born within the space of thirty-two months, he added wryly, 'You may well think that this is not the way to get rich.' Despite these jaundiced comments, Blundell was in fact a caring and affectionate father, and he was desolate many years later when 'the thing called Bridget' married and left home. But Blundell had suffered heavy financial penalties during and after the civil wars, as a Catholic and a cavalier, and his brood of daughters was a financial burden.[21]

If Blundell's circumstances were extreme, his sentiments were commonplace in elite circles. When Sir William Cecil's wife bore her first child, a daughter, in 1556, he tried to overcome his disappointment by hoping a boy would soon follow. After fathering several girls, William Thornton was overjoyed at the birth of his son, 'whom he had begged of God, to continue his family'.[22] Isaac Archer had similarly prayed for a boy, and when his wife gave birth to a 'lusty girl' he feared God was punishing him. To console himself, he reflected that she was less likely to grow into a disobedient and difficult child (as he had been), 'for I considered girls are not so dangerous'.[23]

Many women expressed the same gender preference. When the gentlewoman Ann Brograve gave birth in 1629, after many barren years, we learn that 'the child, *though a daughter*, was very welcome both to her and her husband, because it gave them hope of further issue'. That was a common response.[24] After bearing three daughters, Katherine, Lady Berkeley, shared her husband's desperation for a son to perpetuate the Berkeley line and name. She was delighted to hear of a man who

---

[21] Blundell, *Cavalier, passim* (quotations at 44, 79).
[22] HMC, 9, *Salisbury*, i.138; Thornton, *Autobiography*, 143; cf. A. Hassell Smith et al., eds, *The Papers of Nathaniel Bacon of Stiffkey*, 5 vols, Norfolk Record Society (1979–2010), i.254.
[23] Archer, 'Diary', 118.
[24] D'Ewes, *Autobiography*, i.416 (emphasis added); cf. Isham, 'Rememberance', f.29v.

guaranteed that she would conceive again and bear a son, provided she and her husband followed his elaborate instructions. Taking the charlatan into her household, she diligently observed his directions and was overjoyed when she did indeed bear a son and heir in 1575.[25] Many others shared her longing for a son. The poet Anne Bradstreet called her son Samuel,

> The son of prayers, of vows, of tears,
> The child I stayed for many years.

Ralph Josselin tells us that his own birth in 1617 had been 'to the great joy of father and mother', because though their third child he was the first and only son.[26]

Women were naturally aware of their husbands' hopes, and many may have simply wanted to please them. But many had also come to identify with their new family and its name and aspirations. Some pious women, like Katherine Henry, reflected that sons might one day establish godly households of their own, whereas daughters might have to adapt to their husbands' values. Her daughters recognized that she preferred Matthew, her only son, and appear to have accepted this as natural. They had all been raised to imbibe their parents' conviction that women occupied a lesser place in God's order.[27] Alice Thornton similarly felt a special love for her only son, the 'child of my vows and tears'. Ill and close to death in 1665, she feared for her children's futures. 'For my son, the hope of my house,' she wrote, 'I humbly committed him into the protection of Almighty God, as also his two sisters.' The construction of that sentence is revealing. With her son's birth she had come to identify her husband's family as her own, and the welfare of her son clearly took priority. Similarly, Ann Fanshawe loved all her children, but when her only son Richard (aged 11) contracted smallpox in 1659 at the same time as two of his sisters, she admitted having 'neglected them, and day and night tended my dear son'. Richard died while the girls recovered despite her neglect, leaving Ann devastated. Another woman recalled similar despair at the sudden death of her son, 'the chief comfort that my heart was fixed upon in this world'. She explained that her other child, 'which was a girl, I did not so much value'.[28]

Yet it is clear that many parents were devoted to their little daughters as well as sons, and charted their early progress with equal pride.[29] The preference for boys, strongest among the elite, was also less evident in ordinary families.[30] A woman might long for the special relationship she could expect with a daughter, with shared female tastes and values. One woman recalled how her mother, a pious

---

[25] John Smyth, *The Berkeley Manuscripts, The Lives of the Berkeleys*, 3 vols (Glasgow, 1883–5), ii.385–6.
[26] *The Works of Anne Bradstreet*, ed. Jeanne Hensley (Cambridge, Mass.,1967), 258; cf. 237; Josselin, *Diary*, 1.
[27] Patricia Crawford, *Blood, Bodies and Families in Early Modern England* (Harlow, 2004), 181, 186–8, 191.
[28] Thornton, *Autobiography*, 139–40, 145, 309; Fanshawe, *Memoirs*, 139; [Henry Walker,] *Spirituall Experiences of Sundry Beleevers* (1653), 69–70.
[29] Fletcher, *Growing Up*, chaps 5–6; Linda Pollock, *A Lasting Relationship. Parents and Children over Three Centuries* (Hanover, New Hampshire, and London, 1987).
[30] Sara Mendelson and Patricia Crawford, *Women in Early Modern England* (Oxford, 1998), 80–2.

gentlewoman, 'from amongst her twelve children, chose me to set her love and affection upon', and developed a special bond with her from the age of 7.[31] Fathers too might yearn for the different rewards a young daughter could bring. Lucy Hutchinson records that 'After my mother had had three sons she was very desirous of a daughter', and was overjoyed at Lucy's birth. Both parents thought their little girl beautiful and clever, lavished care on her education, and heaped praise on her early accomplishments. Similarly, the minister Henry Newcome recalled that his parents had produced a daughter in 1641, after seven sons, 'which was great joy to them, they desiring much (as is usual in that case) a daughter, if it were the will of God'. The bracketed aside suggests that while a son was the initial priority, couples often hoped for children of both sexes. One gentlewoman expressed the wish that her niece, having borne two sons, would now have a daughter.[32]

Moreover, whatever initial disappointment parents might feel at the birth of a daughter was often forgotten as the child grew older. Fathers could certainly become powerfully attached to their girls. In a sentimentally quixotic gesture, William Coe even had a wig made from the hair of his three eldest daughters, after a visit from their hairdresser.[33] Parents were often stricken with grief at the loss of a child of either sex. Ralph Josselin and his wife were both devastated when their daughter Mary, 'a bundle of sweetness', died at the age of eight years and forty-five days, as he calculated precisely. She was 'a child of ten thousand', he wrote in his diary, and he described her funeral in loving and emotional detail, adding that 'I kissed her lips last.' Weeks later, he was still 'ready to be overwhelmed in remembrance of dear Mary'.[34] Ann Fanshawe recorded in similarly painful detail the death of 'our most dearly beloved daughter Ann', 'the dear companion of our travails and sorrows', and its precise moment: 3 p.m. on 20 July 1654. Her 'beauty and wit exceeded all that ever I saw of her age', she recalled, and she marvelled at the dying child's precocious wisdom and piety. Even more striking, Fanshawe recalled that she and her husband had both 'wished to have gone into the ground with her'. They could not bear to remain in the house where she had died, 'that fatal place to us', and had moved out within a week.[35]

The economic factors that could make girls a burden for the elite weighed far less heavily on ordinary families, which must have mitigated the preference for sons. In many parts of Europe and Asia, girls were married off in their early teens, to men considerably older, a pattern that reinforced gender inequality. In England, by contrast, and other parts of north-western Europe, women married relatively late, in their mid-twenties. The English pattern of nuclear households, with husbands and wives roughly similar in age, encouraged a marital relationship based more on partnership and interdependence, if still far from equal. Late female marriage also meant that a young woman's labour was an asset that remained available to her

---

[31] [Walker,] *Spirituall Experiences*, 161–3.

[32] Hutchinson, *Memoirs*, 287–8; Newcome, *Autobiography*, i.4; Hassell Smith et al., *Papers of Nathaniel Bacon*, iv.53.

[33] Coe, 'Diary', 35–6.   [34] Josselin, *Diary*, 200–4, 207; cf. Fletcher, *Growing Up*, chap. 7.

[35] Fanshawe, *Memoirs*, 136.

family for a number of years. Daughters could engage in seasonal farm work, help with domestic chores, and look after younger siblings. That in turn might save the expense of hiring a maidservant and free their mother to work on the farm, run the shop, or supplement the family's income with waged labour. Girls were usually more able than boys to make their own small contribution to that income, and were often kept longer at home. And those who had gone into service could be summoned home should family circumstances change.[36] There is no evidence of the deliberate neglect of female infants, as found in many societies. A combination of boys and girls may well have appeared the ideal family composition.[37]

PARENTAL FAVOURITISM AND SIBLING RIVALRY

The issues become more complex when we turn from gender preferences to favouritism. Francis Bacon deplored the overt preference that many parents displayed towards particular offspring. In families with numerous children, he observed, we often find 'one or two of the eldest respected, and the youngest made wantons', spoiled by parental indulgence. Middle children tended to be forgotten and neglected.[38] The puritan William Gouge denounced favouritism in forthright terms. 'Many parents have their darling children', he complained, and while these 'are hugged in the bosom, others are neglected as if they were not of their own, but basely born'. Such partiality bred 'envy, malice and much contention', and would provoke God's wrath. Jacob's favouritism towards Joseph, he cautioned, had made his brethren hate him.[39] A father and mother did not necessarily have the same favourite, of course; a father might favour whichever son seemed most apt to take over his farm or trade one day. Preferences might also change over time. Josselin's ninth child, Elizabeth, features little in his diary until he married her off cheaply at the age of 16 to a modest London tradesman. Yet over the next few years she seems to have become a favourite, perhaps because her sisters proved far more difficult to satisfy over matches and dowries. When Elizabeth came back to visit, he referred to her as 'my good daughter', 'my good child', 'my dear child'. And when she and her baby son stayed for two months in the summer of 1682, it was 'with sweetness and content, that made her company pleasant to me, I parted with her in all love'.[40]

The firstborn were seen as natural favourites. Sir John Oglander and his wife were devastated when their eldest son, George, died of smallpox in France in July

---

[36] Mary S. Hartman, *The Household and the Making of History* (Cambridge, 2004), chaps 1–3; Patricia Crawford, *Parents of Poor Children in England, 1580–1800* (Oxford, 2010), 159, 169–70; Ben-Amos, *Adolescence*, 42, 76–8.

[37] Hanawalt, 'Childrearing', 9–10; E. A. Wrigley and R. S. Schofield, *The Population History of England 1541–1871* (Cambridge, 1981), 249.

[38] Francis Bacon, *The Essays*, ed. John Pitcher (1985), 79–80; *The Office of Christian Parents* (Cambridge, 1616), 143–4.

[39] William Gouge, *Of Domesticall Duties* (1622), 578; Gen, xxxvii.4; John Dod and Robert Cleaver, *A Godlie Forme of Household Government* (1612), 322–4; John Oliver, *A Present to be Given to Teeming Women* (1688), 16.

[40] Josselin, *Diary*, 632, 633, 639.

1632, only a few weeks after leaving home. 'O George, my beloved George, is dead and with him most of my terrestrial comforts', he lamented. Oglander reminded himself that 'I have good and dutiful sons left', but none could fill George's place in his parents' hearts. The Suffolk squire Edmund Bohun felt similarly. Recalling the suicide of his eldest son, a Cambridge undergraduate, he added that it had 'almost broke my heart; and I have not, nor perhaps never shall overgrow that intolerable grief'. Bohun also had other sons, but again none meant as much to him.[41] The eldest were not always so favoured, however. While parents accepted that the estate should pass to the eldest son, they were often fondest of the child who most resembled them in personality. Sir Edmund Verney was very close to his third son and namesake, which made it all the more painful when he went off the rails at Oxford, drinking heavily and running up debts. 'Son,' his father wrote sadly, 'you were a son in whom I took delight, that I had a particular affection for . . . above most of my children. But God has in you punished me for that partiality . . . you are now grown so lewd and false that I blush to think you mine.' Edmund was disgraced, though before long he was restored to favour once more. Verney's little daughter Mary was also a favourite, so much so that he had to hide his 'overfond-ness', to prevent the other children becoming jealous.[42]

Contemporaries recognized that the youngest might also command a special place in parents' hearts. Thomas Shepard, ninth child of a Towcester grocer, was born in 1604 only a few weeks before his father's death. He recalled that, 'I being the youngest', his widowed mother 'did bear exceeding great love to me'. The clergyman John Shaw dedicated his memoirs to his last-born child, who was only a few weeks old. 'You are the son of my old age,' he wrote, 'and therefore none may wonder if you have a Benjamin's portion of my affection.' The child was Shaw's only surviving son, and his longing for a male heir was clearly the decisive factor. Gervase Disney recalled how his little brother Samuel had been their father's 'great favourite and darling', and how they would take little walks together, hand in hand. Samuel had died at 4, so we cannot know whether that special relationship would have lasted.[43] Some fathers felt a similar affection for their youngest daughter. Ralph Thoresby treasured the memory of his daughter Betty, who also died young, partly because she had 'a peculiar loveliness in her countenance' but primarily, he insisted, because she 'was pious above her years'. By contrast, it was the bright personality of little Betty Paston, aged about 9, that endeared her to her father, Sir Robert. She 'entertains me with pretty discourses,' he wrote to his wife, 'we are wondrous great'. Moreover, Betty loved her books, unlike her idle brothers.

---

[41] Francis Bamford, ed., *A Royalist's Notebook. The Commonplace Book of Sir John Oglander Kt. of Nunwell* (1936), 80–2; *The Diary and Autobiography of Edmund Bohun, Esq.*, ed. S. Wilton Rix (Beccles, 1853), 98–9.

[42] Verney, *Memoirs*, i.162–3; Miriam Slater, *Family Life in the Seventeenth Century. The Verneys of Claydon House* (1984), 120–1.

[43] 'Thomas Shepard's Memoir of his Own Life', in Alexander Young, ed., *Chronicles of the First Planters of the Colony of Massachusetts Bay* (Boston, 1846), 500; 'The Life of Master John Shaw', ed. Charles Jackson, in *Yorkshire Diaries*, 122; *Some Remarkable Passages in the Holy Life and Death of Gervase Disney, Esq.* (1692), 13–15.

In the case of Hester Pinney, youngest daughter of a lace merchant and Noncon-formist minister, her favoured status continued into adulthood. Her father was deeply hurt when he sensed some unkindness on her part, and reminded her of her position as 'My youngest and for that usually ye dearest to parents'.[44]

Contemporaries warned, however, that indulging a favourite child, especially the youngest, was misguided and potentially ruinous. Thomas Meautys wrote proudly of his little daughter in 1632 that 'she is beloved where she comes, and I love her very well, and so doth she me; and yet sometimes I can whip her and love her too'.[45] Joseph Pike, raised in a Quaker family, had a more indulgent parent. His mother had deplored his childish misdeeds, he recalled, 'yet she loved me exceedingly, even beyond any of her children, which I well knew, and therefore in some measure presumed upon it'. Oliver Heywood recalled how his attractive, sweet-natured brother Josiah had similarly been his 'mother's darling, being her youngest child', and how his parents were devastated when he was led astray by bad company.[46] Richard Gough told the dark story of another spoiled younger son, one Thomas Elks. His widowed mother had 'loved him best of any of her children; and by supplying him with money to feed his extravagances, she undid him'. When her money ran out, he was unwilling to live on his small wages as a journeyman shoemaker, and looked greedily at the estate his infant nephew had inherited. Hatching an evil plan to secure it for himself, he lured the child into a cornfield and murdered him. The crime was soon exposed, and he died on the gallows. The mother of another felon, hanged at Tyburn, lamented that 'she had been partly guilty of his untimely end, by her fond indulgence of him, above any of her children'.[47]

Favouritism carried with it, of course, the corollary of discrimination and neglect, and generated sibling tensions that might last a lifetime.[48] It also stoked predictable resentment towards the parents. Thomas Ellwood, a bright younger son, deeply resented the fact that his father had taken him out of grammar school to save on the fees, so that he could afford to maintain his elder son as a privileged Fellow-Commoner at Oxford.[49] In Restoration Halifax, the undisguised favouritism of William and Susanna Appleyard backfired badly. They 'doted' on their elder son John at the expense of his younger brother, who was eventually disowned, and his sisters. But when his father died, John turned his mother out of the house, leaving her broken-hearted and dazed, while his sisters shunned both parents, and did not attend their funerals. William was described as an 'exacting' father, and his harsh parenting and overt favouritism had proved a toxic combination.[50]

---

[44] *The Diary of Ralph Thoresby FRS*, ed. Joseph Hunter, 2 vols (1830), i.333; Jean Agnew, ed., *The Whirlpool of Misadventures. Letters of Robert Paston, First Earl of Yarmouth 1663–1679*, Norfolk Record Society, 76 (2011), 214; *Letters of John Pinney 1679–1699*, ed. Geoffrey F. Nuttall (1939), 32–4, 37.

[45] *Private Correspondence of Jane Cornwallis*, 253.

[46] John Barclay, ed., *Some Account of the Life of Joseph Pike* (1837), 23; Heywood, *Autobiography*, i.35.

[47] Richard Gough, *The History of Myddle*, ed. David Hey (Harmondsworth, 1981), 122; OBOA, 16850904.

[48] See Chapter 11.

[49] *The History of the Life of Thomas Ellwood*, ed. C. G. Crump (1900), 3–4.

[50] Heywood, *Autobiography*, iii.190–1.

In this instance, both parents had favoured the same child, which, inevitably, was not always the case. The Elizabethan astrologer Simon Forman recalled that as a small boy 'his father loved him above all the rest, but his mother nor brethren loved him not'. His father had a little bed placed for him at the foot of the parents' own, but his sudden death when Simon was 11 left the boy with no protection against his siblings' resentment. Henceforth, 'what fault soever was committed by any of the rest he was beaten for it'. His mother took him out of school and set him to keep sheep, plough, and gather firewood, all of which he hated. Simon's bookish tastes and lively mind, which had won his father's favour, stoked the resentment of the rest of the family. 'Seeing the hatred of his mother and of the rest of his brethren and sisters towards him', he escaped by having himself bound apprentice at the age of 14.[51] Arise Evans, born around 1607, had a similar experience. He was his father's favourite, but his father died before Arise was 7 and inexplicably left him out of his will. Thereafter, Arise recalled, 'my brethren who afore envied me begin to glory over me, saying, what was I but a beggar?' His mother was never fond of him, and when she married again he was 'put away from all, and tossed from place to place to do any drudgery'.[52]

While few writers were so blunt, we can find resentful sons at every level of society. John Rastrick, the only son of a Lincolnshire husbandman, found himself the unhappy object of a prolonged tussle between his warring parents. His father encouraged his bookish aspirations, while his more forceful mother considered education pointless and wanted him to be set to work on the farm.[53] His contemporary Thomas Raymond, the second of his father's four children, always thought himself the 'least beloved' and 'on all occasions (though I was not above 12 years old at his death) felt the effects of his choler, which was of great mischief unto me, being of a soft and timorous complexion'. Sent to a boarding school with a younger brother, he experienced harsher treatment and the humiliation of being placed in a lower form than his clever sibling. Cruelty both at home and school, he was convinced, had scarred him for life.[54] The diary of Isaac Archer records another fraught relationship between father and son, and rivalry with his sister added a further dimension to the family dynamics. 'My father loved her entirely', he recalled, and was stricken by her death. Isaac, by contrast, felt little sense of loss and thought she had deliberately turned his father against him. After her burial, he adds guiltily, his father 'wrote to me bitterly that my eye-sore was taken away'. Only after his father's own death did Isaac discover the full depth of his hostility. Though he was the only surviving child, his father had remained determined to punish him for his behaviour and for what he saw as his religious betrayal. For Isaac had conformed to the Church re-established at the Restoration, after much heart-searching, whereas his father had remained a steadfast Nonconformist. He therefore

[51] A. L. Rowse, *The Case Books of Simon Forman* (1976), 273, 276.
[52] Arise Evans, *An Eccho to the Voice from Heaven* (1653), 4–6, 38–9.
[53] *The Life of John Rastrick 1650–1727*, ed. Andrew Cambers, Camden Society, 5th series, 36 (2010), 35–42; cf. D'Ewes, *Autobiography*, i.29–33, 118, 148; Fiona McCall, *Baal's Priests. The Loyalist Clergy and the English Revolution* (Farnham, 2013), 220; Chapter 10.
[54] *Autobiography of Thomas Raymond*, ed. G. Davies, Camden Society, 3rd series, 28 (1917), 19.

bequeathed his estate not to Isaac but to Isaac's children—despite the fact that at the time of his father's death there were none. The will inevitably raised a host of legal complications.[55]

Most diaries and memoirs were written by men, and we know far less of daughters who felt neglected or ill-used. Elizabeth Isham was aware that her mother thought her reserved, melancholy, and slow, and preferred her younger daughter, who shared her own 'lightsome' temperament. Elizabeth insisted that she bore no resentment towards her more favoured sister, but many passages in her autobiography suggest otherwise.[56] Letters and wills allow us to glimpse other resentments. Elizabeth Phelips, for example, daughter of a Somerset landowner, was grateful when her father promised a generous portion to attract a good husband. But he was heavily in debt, and in 1632 he made over almost his whole estate to his only son, to facilitate a lucrative match. That left Elizabeth without any portion, and her brother, when he inherited, showed little inclination to help. It took her ten years, with 'great fear and trouble', to find a suitable husband.[57] At every level of society, daughters faced parental wrath if they showed too independent a spirit. Nicholas Blundell reminded his elder daughter of his ability to disinherit her when she resisted his plans for her.[58] Henry Oxinden, a Kentish gentleman, went much further, and disowned his daughter Margaret, aged 12, after her foolish flirtation with a young man lodging in the house. She 'hath undone herself,' he raged, 'let her like Cain wander as a vagabond.' Though he later relented in part, he married her off (to the same young man) at 14, without any fixed portion, and never fully forgave her. When the marriage soured, he vowed never to allow her back home. She was 'too too headstrong', he told his wife, and her wilful spirit had to be broken.[59] His younger daughter Betty, equally refractory, was told to obey his directions or leave home and go into service. In one extraordinary outburst, Oxinden raged that 'Should a heathen, Turk, or infidel use a parent as some of my children have used me,...I would ride twenty miles to see such a wretch hanged as high as Haman.'[60] Oxinden's children felt equally ill-used by their stern and capricious father.

Responsible parents tried to conceal any partiality they felt towards a particular child. But in an age of high child mortality, they may often have nurtured a secret wish that an infant or less favoured child would be taken, and some privately admitted as much. Isaac Archer did not hide his relief in 1675 that God had taken his newborn baby and spared little Will, aged 3, who had fallen dangerously ill at the same time. Will's own death, only two months later, left Archer devastated.

[55] Archer, 'Diary', 11, 96, 123–4, 186–8.

[56] Katharine Hodgkin, 'Elizabeth Isham's Everlasting Library: Memory and Self in Early Modern Autobiography', in Sally Alexander and Barbara Taylor, eds, *History and Psyche: Culture, Psychoanalysis, and the Past* (Basingstoke, 2012), 251–5.

[57] J. H. Bettey, ed., *Calendar of the Correspondence of the Smyth Family of Ashton Court 1548–1642*, Bristol Record Society, 35 (1982), 113–15, 140, 146, 157.

[58] Margaret Blundell, *Blundell's Diary and Letter Book 1702–1728* (Liverpool, 1952), 206–7.

[59] *Oxinden Letters 1642–1670*, 113, 167–8, 171–2; BL, Add. MS 28002, fos. 317–18, 326-v, 328, 342.

[60] *Oxinden Letters 1642–1670*, 173; BL, Add. MS 28001, f.120; Add. MS 28002, f.308.

'The Lord knew how to strike to the heart,' he confided to his diary, 'by taking away my joy, strength, builder of my house, and by casting my crown to the ground.' His poor wife was equally distraught, he added, for she 'had too much set her heart on this lovely, manly boy'.[61] Elizabeth Avery did not hide her own partiality when she publicly recalled the pain of losing three children, and 'one child above all, a most sweet child'. Neither did a grief-stricken Cheshire woman, who shocked mourners at the funeral of her teenage daughter in 1705 by screaming hysterically that she would rather have buried her husband or two or three of her other children.[62] In 1635 a plague epidemic prompted the London turner Nehemiah Wallington to muse despondently which of his family he could least spare should it invade his house. He would surrender the maidservant first, an easy choice, then, in order, his little son John, his daughter Elizabeth, and himself. It is surprising to see him sacrificing his son before his daughter. But John was little more than a baby and subject to severe fits, so Wallington probably thought him unlikely to survive long, as indeed proved the case.[63] Henry Newcome also found himself pondering which child he could least bear to lose, when two of his young sons fell dangerously ill within a matter of days. He was emotionally torn. When little Daniel appeared close to death, he grieved for 'my finest boy'; when Daniel recovered and Henry sickened, he now feared 'I should lose my best child. This one then seemed to have better parts some way, the other a better disposition. It may be', he mused, 'that which is to go is usually, with us, the best, which we can worst part with'.[64] These were, of course, very private reflections. The puritan minister John Angier, by contrast, unforgivably asked his dangerously ill little daughter whether she felt more love for him or for her mother, who had died only a few weeks earlier. The wise child replied that she loved them both equally.[65]

Far less evidence survives on favouritism and discrimination in ordinary families. Martha Bairstow, a humble Yorkshire girl, had been 'sent abroad into service and hardship when but ten years of age', her master recalled, adding that 'her relations much disowned her' and 'often sent her home weeping' when she visited them. When her father died, many years later, she was left far less than other members of the family, and her relations proved 'churlish'. We have no explanation for Martha's harsh treatment, but she had at least found a caring employer. She remained with him for sixteen years, keeping house after his wife died, and he came to 'love her as a child'.[66] Wills provide some further evidence, though only a small minority of people left a will and we rarely know all the circumstances that lay behind them. A testator would often already have helped his older children, and the will would take that into account. Wills tell us more about gender and birth order

[61] Archer, 'Diary', 150–2; cf. Slater, *Family Life*, 119–21.

[62] John Rogers, *Ohel or Beth-shemesh. A Tabernacle for the Sun* (1653), 403; J. B. Williams, ed., *Memoirs of the Life and Character of Mrs Sarah Savage*, 4th edition (1829), 189–90; cf. [Walker,] *Spirituall Experiences*, 69–70.

[63] *The Notebooks of Nehemiah Wallington, 1618–1654*, ed. David Booy (Aldershot, 2007), 90. He could not bear to imagine losing his wife, father, or brother.

[64] Newcome, *Autobiography*, 97.   [65] Heywood, *Autobiography*, i.75.

[66] Heywood, *Autobiography*, iii.137–8, 159–60.

than favouritism towards individuals. Will-makers generally left land and other real estate to the eldest son, with reversion to other sons in order of age should he die without issue. Daughters more often inherited money, household furniture and goods, clothes, and livestock.[67] When the Essex mariner John Love died in 1561, leaving three young daughters and a pregnant wife, he bequeathed his house to his wife for life and then to their unborn child—provided it was a boy. If it was another girl, however, the house was to be sold and the proceeds shared equally between all four daughters. By contrast, John Grave, another mariner, left his whole estate, which included several houses, to be divided equally between his young son and daughter.[68] Where an estate comprised only movables, testators often treated their children more or less equally. When a widow left clothes or furnishings to be divided equally between her daughters, she would sometimes specify that the eldest should receive the best, or have first choice.[69] A cluster of mid-Tudor Essex wills illustrates some typical arrangements. John Hatche, a husbandman and widower, left 20s each to his six young children, four boys and two girls. John Hockman, another poor man, left each of his daughters 20s, two pewter platters, and one pewter dish. John Champney, a tenant farmer, bequeathed his land to his wife and then their eldest son, but stipulated that two younger sons and a daughter were each to inherit £4, one cow, and ten sheep. Edmund Radley appears to have prioritized age over gender; his three sons and daughter Agnes were each to inherit £5 at age 20; three other daughters, probably younger, would inherit £3 6s 8d at the same age.[70] In such arrangements a sense of equity appears to have outweighed favouritism, and would have been reinforced by the manorial customs governing inheritance when the deceased had made no will.

When testators explicitly favoured a particular child, they often provided an explanation. If a daughter had remained at home, for example, acting as house-keeper and nurse for ageing parents, she might well have earned their special gratitude. In 1695, the minister Henry Newcome left his entire estate to his wife, to maintain her and their unmarried daughter Rose, 'who I know will not leave her in her old age'. After his wife's death, the largest share of the estate was to go to Rose 'in consideration that she hath denied herself, and spent her time and strength in a painful, tender attendance upon us both in our old age and great infirmities'.[71] Other testamentary arrangements, by contrast, reflected powerful negative emotions. Giles Storie of Newcastle, dying in 1586, told those gathered around his bedside that he was leaving everything to his wife and thereafter to their son George. When asked about their other son, Ralph, he exclaimed 'hang him'. 'God's malison light upon him,' he raged, 'for he hath beggared me, and would

---

[67] Amy Louise Erickson, *Women and Property in Early Modern England* (1993); Jack Goody, Joan Thirsk, and E. P. Thompson, eds, *Family and Inheritance. Rural Society in Western Europe 1200–1800* (Cambridge, 1976), esp. the essays of Cicely Howell and Margaret Spufford.

[68] F. G. Emmison, ed., *Wills of the County of Essex (England), vol. 1, 1558–1565* (Washington, D.C., 1982), 42, 59. For parallels to Love's will see Nesta Evans, ed., *Wills of the Archdeaconry of Sudbury 1630–1635*, Suffolk Records Society, 29 (1987), 144, 276, but cf. Erickson, *Women and Property*, 73.

[69] Emmison, *Wills of Essex*, 2, 5, 38, 145.   [70] Emmison, *Wills of Essex*, 5, 6–7, 13, 59.

[71] Newcome, *Autobiography*, ii.284–6.

not follow my counsel; I shall rive him out of the earth that ever giveth him one groat of my gear.' In 1629, a Suffolk husbandman passed over both his daughters and bequeathed his house to a granddaughter, on the strict condition that she must never allow her parents to live there. Elizabeth Bumsted left only 5s 'and no more' to her son Thomas, with almost everything else passing to her 'loving daughter Elizabeth'. The widow Vinca Ellis was still blunter, complaining that her sons had failed to pay the annuities bequeathed by her husband, leaving her almost destitute. She left almost everything to her 'well-beloved' son-in-law and his children.[72] John Cannon, the Somerset diarist, recorded an equally striking case. Summoned to take down a will for one John Lamport, he found four of Lamport's children and their spouses squabbling around his bed, 'like as the fowls of the air on a dying sheep'. Ordering them from the room, he listened while the old man explained that he wanted his will to reflect his children's 'untoward' behaviour. Two were to receive only one or two shillings apiece, and another daughter was awarded £4. Everything else he bequeathed to his better-behaved son, John.[73]

Parental discrimination was, of course, only one of many factors that might provoke sibling rivalries and resentment. Gervase Disney, crippled by rickets as a child and forced to shuffle around on a cushion, must have envied his able-bodied siblings. Years later, he confessed that he had pilfered money from both his brothers and sisters.[74] Friction more often reflected clashing personalities or differences in age, status, and authority. All these factors appear in Anthony Wood's account of his childhood during the civil war. His father had died soon after Wood's tenth birthday, he had little respect for his mother, and his eldest brother had become 'a rude and boisterous soldier'. The next oldest, Edward, became Wood's tutor for a time but was 'so far from being a governor or tutor to others, that he could scarce govern himself'. For his part, Edward considered Anthony slow-witted, and often beat him. Wood enjoyed better relations with two other brothers, much closer in age, and they remained on friendly terms throughout their lives.[75] Oliver Heywood left similarly mixed verdicts on his brothers and sisters. He criticized his sister Alice's 'rugged and knotty' character, and reflected that God had sent her a correspondingly bad husband, and six disobedient children. By contrast, Heywood loved his 'dear, very dear brother' Nathaniel, and deeply admired an older sister whose early death had proved she was too good for this world.[76]

CHILDHOOD BONDS: FRIENDSHIP AND CARING

Rivalry was the dark side of the sibling coin. Many other children, by contrast, developed close and lasting bonds that reflected their early companionship and

[72] James Raine, ed., *Depositions and other Ecclesiastical Proceedings from the Courts of Durham*, Surtees Society, 21 (1845), 318–19; Evans, *Wills of Sudbury*, 71, 146, 193.
[73] Cannon, *Chronicles*, ii.351–2, 355.   [74] Disney, *Some Remarkable Passages*, 27, 34–5.
[75] Wood, *Life and Times*, i.93, 129–30, 162.   [76] Heywood, *Autobiography*, i.100–2.

temperamental affinity. Thomas Paston greatly missed the company of his older brother William, who left home for Cambridge at 14 in 1624. Their mother told William that 'there is no meal since you went but he [doth] drink to thee'. She told him later that Thomas was delighted with a present William had sent; he returned his 'lovingest love' and thanks for the 'fine knife . . . which he will wear on high days'.[77] George Coke, who attended a family reunion in Derbyshire in 1602, especially enjoyed the company of his 'kindest' sister, 'with whom I was ever merry'. Sir Thomas Barrington was similarly recalling childhood days when he sent greetings in 1631 to his sister Joan, 'my honest and beloved playfellow'.[78]

Siblings were not only playfellows, of course. Older and younger children also forged close bonds through the care they had given or received from one another. Adam Martindale tells us that he had learned to read at the age of 6 or 7 'by the help of my brethren and sisters that could read'. Richard Norwood similarly remembered how, as a small child at a dame school in the late 1590s, his mistress would 'praise me for learning so well, and teaching my sisters'.[79] Siblings often attended school together, which helped them adjust and further strengthened their bonds. Four of Recorder Fleetwood's sons, aged between 6 and 16, were boarding together at a school in Ealing in 1599, and most of the other pupils also had siblings there. The five sons of Thomas Offley, Esquire, aged between 11 and 17, boarded together at Lichfield in 1695.[80] The same pattern applied for girls. Henry Oxinden sent his two daughters, aged 11 and 12, to a private school in Kent, and two of Josselin's daughters boarded together.[81] Very occasionally, we catch a glimpse of the close bonds that might develop in these circumstances. Thus, John Bramston was so outraged by the savage flogging his younger brother endured at the hands of a sadistic master that he wrote home to report the abuse, which led their father to remove them both. John and George Hutchinson also attended school together, in the 1620s, and John's stronger personality meant that he 'was as a father over his brother, and having some advantage of years, took upon him to be the guide of his youth'. They were 'happy in mutual affection', and when George developed epilepsy, John became his carer too. Their childhood bond matured into a close, lifelong relationship, cemented years later when they married two sisters.[82] Such

[77] Ruth Hughey, ed., *The Correspondence of Lady Katherine Paston 1603–1627*, Norfolk Record Society, 14 (1941), 87, 90.

[78] HMC, 23, *Cowper*, iii.132; Arthur Searle, ed., *Barrington Family Letters 1628–1632*, Camden Society, 3rd series, 28 (1983), 191.

[79] *The Life of Adam Martindale*, ed. Richard Parkinson, Chetham Society, 4 (1845), 5; *The Journal of Richard Norwood, Surveyor of Bermuda*, ed. Wesley Craven and Walter Haywood (New York, 1945), 6–7.

[80] K. J. Allison, ed., 'An Elizabethan Village "Census"', *Bulletin of the Institute of Historical Research*, 36 (1963), 97; Birmingham & Midland Society for Genealogy, 'Census of Lichfield carried out for Gregory King in 1695', transcript, 5.

[81] *Oxinden Letters 1642–1670*, 128–9; Josselin, *Diary*, 574, 585; cf. *The Autobiography of Sir John Bramston*, ed. Lord Braybrooke, Camden Society, OS, 32 (1845), 107–8; Charlton, *Women, Religion and Education*, 136–8.

[82] Bramston, *Autobiography*, 100–1; Hutchinson, *Memoirs*, 22, 170.

double marriages were not uncommon, and they offer another suggestive glimpse of the strength of sibling bonds.[83]

Hutchinson was far from alone in this protective, quasi-parental role. Thomas Shepard had lost both parents by the age of 10, and was left in the care of a stepmother who disliked and neglected him. He was rescued by his elder brother John, 'who showed much love unto me, and unto whom I owe much; for him God made to be both father and mother unto me'. Sir Francis Willoughby, also orphaned as a child, escaped from a hated stepfather to find refuge with an aunt, and at the age of only 12 dared to remove his younger brother too, taking it upon himself to arrange his brother's education. As his sister Cassandra recalled years later, 'he chiefly governed both my brother and self, who were both very willing to follow his directions and be guided by him'. At the age of 19, Willoughby took possession of the family's main estate at Wollaton, and invited Cassandra (aged 17) to manage the household. It was a daunting prospect, and she was grateful that he 'behaved himself like a father to me', supporting and supervising her activities.[84] Care and protection could also take very different forms. Nehemiah Wallington, a depressed young artisan, was closely monitored by his older brother and sister, who thwarted several suicide attempts. Edward and John Coxere, sailors from Dover, provide another striking example of support. At the age of about 15 Edward enlisted in a warship where his older brother was already serving and could look out for him. When a devastating fire broke out, John refused to leave the blazing vessel until he was certain his brother was safe, and risked his life by going back below deck to search for him. Both survived to serve together again, and continued to care for one another.[85]

Childhood bonds and care took on special significance when one or both parents died prematurely. We have a poignant example in the family of the bereaved minister John Angier, who overheard his young son and daughter, aged 11 and 8, praying anxiously together in the parlour. They thought it was their disobedience that had led God to take away their mother, and prayed their father would not be taken too. Religion generally provided comfort in times of loss, but it could also aggravate the pain.[86] A fifth of all children had lost their father by the age of 11, and an elder brother was sometimes called on to assume a quasi-parental role to fill the gap. Alice Thornton recalled how her brother George had been 'a father to us all', while a clergyman, writing to console his widowed sister, observed that her eldest son was now '*in loco parentis*', and must 'show all manner of kindness and tenderness' to his younger siblings. The Derbyshire tailor Leonard Wheatcroft was 19 when his father died in 1648, and as the eldest of nine children took on the task of teaching his

---

[83] See e.g. Nicholas Guy, *Pieties Pillar* (1626), 38–9 (William Gouge and his brother); Barclay, ed., *Some Account of Joseph Pike*, 7; Pepys, *Diary*, x.211–12; Cannon, *Chronicles*, i.51; Bennett, *John Aubrey*, i.260.

[84] 'Thomas Shepard's Memoir', 502; Cassandra, Duchess of Chandos, *The Continuation of the History of the Willoughby Family*, ed. A. C. Wood (Eton, Windsor, 1958), 123–4, 126, 129.

[85] Seaver, *Wallington's World*, 23, 25, 78–9; *Adventures by Sea of Edward Coxere*, ed. E. H. W. Meyerstein (Oxford, 1945), 5–7, 24–5, 31, 107.

[86] Heywood, *Autobiography*, i.74.

craft to four younger brothers.[87] The children of the minister Stephen Newcome faced a still greater challenge when both parents died within a few days in 1642, only a few weeks after the birth of their baby daughter. The seven sons displayed a remarkable solidarity and sense of responsibility. The eldest son, Robert, a young graduate, returned home to assume responsibility for his siblings, taking on a lowly position as curate. The older brothers all pledged to remain single until the younger were old enough to be apprenticed or sent to university. Robert opened a private school to boost his small income, enrolling two younger siblings among his pupils. The brothers hired a maidservant to keep house, and presumably put out the baby to nurse. The fourth son, Henry, 14 at his parents' death, always remembered the brothers' solidarity with deep respect. There was 'great love and concord amongst the children,' he recalled in his autobiography, 'the elder brothers being careful and tender of all the younger, and the younger bowing to be ruled by them'. Henry was schooled by his brother Robert, and went on to teach his own younger brother Richard. Close bonds endured throughout their lives.[88]

Girls were expected, almost from infancy, to look after their younger siblings as a matter of course. Ralph Josselin recorded with pride how his daughter Mary, aged two and a half, had saved her baby brother from disaster; just learning to walk, he 'was held out of the fire by his little sister, who held and cried until I came to him'.[89] Many older girls, as we have seen, had weighty responsibilities thrust upon them at an early age. One woman recalled how at her mother's death, and at the age of only 12, she 'was suddenly made my father's housekeeper, so as it were a mother to ten children, a mistress over six servants, none to do anything without my command or consent'. Her life was utterly transformed overnight.[90] Many women remembered how much they had owed, as orphans, to an older sister who had cared for them. Bridget Sherd, a young Suffolk spinster who died in 1628, left all her goods to her sister, 'because she is most worthy of them for she hath taken great pains about me'. Ann-Mary Freeman, a Quaker, remembered her older sister with similar gratitude: 'when I was but a child she took me unto her care, and tenderly educated and helped me many years . . . I can truly say I honoured her as a mother.'[91]

We also find some girls playing a caring and protective role they had fashioned for themselves. Some would attempt, for example, to save a delinquent brother from parental wrath, as in the case of the orphaned Elizabeth Angier and her slightly older, wayward brother. Years later her husband recalled that the boy's 'extravagances broke her heart, as if she had been his mother, she loved him so dearly whiles they were both young, that she could have wished to have borne his corrections for him'. That relationship survived into adult life. Elizabeth would send him letters of

---

[87] Thornton, *Autobiography*, 57; Letter Book of Charles Allestree, BL. Add. MS 27440, f.49v; *The Autobiography of Leonard Wheatcroft of Ashover 1627–1705*, ed. Dorothy Riden, *Derbyshire Record Society*, 20 (1993), 83; 'Family History begun by James Fretwell', ed. C. Jackson, *Yorkshire Diaries*, 201.

[88] Newcome, *Autobiography*, i.5–7.   [89] Josselin, *Diary*, 29–30.

[90] [Walker,] *Spirituall Experiences*, 163–4.

[91] Evans, *Wills of Sudbury*, 16; George Whitehead et al., *Piety Promoted by Faithfulness* (1686), 16–17; cf. John Whiting, *Early Piety Exemplified* (1711), 8.

exhortation, even after he had migrated to New England, and was gratified whenever she received a suitably penitential reply.[92] We can find a similar pattern in families at every social level. Mary Isham, a baronet's daughter, took it upon herself to reprimand her younger brother Justinian, aged 17, when he went off the rails after their father's death in 1681. Unless he stopped mixing with 'such debauched people', she warned, he would be 'accounted a lewd foolish person'. She hoped her intervention would prevent their widowed mother from hearing of his escapades, and suffering further distress. At the other end of the social spectrum, young William Inchbald of Knaresborough had similarly gone off the rails after his father's death, and now lived by begging and stealing. In 1638, he was whipped for theft, a disgrace that prompted his sister Ellen to petition magistrates to have him bound apprentice, to save him from ruin. And 'out of her love and affection' she offered to lend £5 to cover the cost of having him indentured and provided with appropriate clothes. She explained that he had been left a parcel of land that he could enter at 21, which could then be sold to reimburse her. Magistrates sensibly accepted her offer.[93] Samuel Pepys's diary provides another example of sisterly care, the better-known story of Jane and Wayneman Birch. Jane had entered Pepys's household as a servant, aged 14, and two years later she persuaded him to take on her younger brother, who turned out, alas, to be lazy, dishonest, and undisciplined. When Pepys took him down to the cellar one day and beat him, Jane followed and pleaded with him to cease. Even after leaving the family, she and her older brother William, a groom, continued to feel responsible for Wayneman's welfare. Pepys summoned them both in December 1662 to tell them he had decided to turn Wayneman away, but they begged him to keep him for another week while they found him a new position, a week that in the event stretched to six months. The end came after Wayneman absconded, and was dismissed. A few weeks later Jane and William came to beg for him to be taken back. Pepys's diary records that Jane pleaded for two hours, distressed and desperate, and that the 'poor girl cried all the time she was with me'. Wayneman did find a new master, probably through his siblings' efforts, though he was soon packed off to Barbados as an indentured servant. Whatever his ultimate fate, Jane and William had demonstrated a powerful sense of responsibility to help and protect an incorrigible younger brother.[94]

* * *

It comes as little surprise that many parents favoured sons over daughters, and especially the firstborn, though we have seen that such preferences were neither as general nor as strong as is often assumed. The most distinctive feature of English family relationships, the practice of primogeniture, did much to shape both parental behaviour and relationships between siblings themselves. We turn next to the rights and responsibilities associated with the elder brother, the most contentious dimension of family life.

---

[92] Heywood, *Autobiography*, i.62–3.
[93] Isham, *Diary of Thomas Isham*, 37; John Lister, ed., *West Riding Session Records, ii, 1611–1642*, Yorkshire Archaeological Society, 54 (1915), 62, 68.
[94] Pepys, *Diary*, i.25, iii.66, 295, iv.7–8, 67, 113, 194, 202, 252, 382.

3

Fraternal Bonds

'Am I my brother's keeper?'
(Genesis, iv.9)

GENTLEMEN AND THEIR SIBLINGS

In landed families, the eldest son enjoyed from birth a highly privileged status. He could expect to inherit the estate, while his brothers could hope at best for small, outlying parcels of land, or more often cash payments or annuities. The significance of birth order, moreover, extended far beyond such material facts. Both heir and siblings were raised in a culture of order, deference, and reciprocity, principles intended to guide their adult relationships. Younger brothers should serve, respect, and defer to the heir, and seek his advice and approval for their actions. He, in turn, should direct, support, and protect them, as well as paying the annuities stipulated by their father. Sibling relationships in practice varied hugely according to individual personality and circumstance, but they were always shaped by these conventions and the tensions inherent within them.

Primogeniture locked many younger brothers into a pattern of lifelong dependency and subordination. Reliant on the heir for their annuities, they had little leverage if they failed to arrive. Annuities were rarely sufficient for them to marry, and they had nothing to offer by way of jointure to attract a bride. Many remained bachelors. Those who did marry usually found wives from humbler social origins, and their children were likely to sink further. Wealthy fathers sometimes mitigated the effects of primogeniture by leaving some outlying estates to their younger sons. Sir Henry Slingsby, a thoughtful father, denounced negligent parents who left their younger sons in a 'servile condition' of dependence on the heir. Assuring his own younger son of his love, he bequeathed him a modest estate 'competent for a younger brother: sure I am, it is all I can do for you'.[1] It was his response to the challenge of squaring the interests of the estate with the needs of each child. More often, gentlemen educated younger sons for a profession, or apprenticed them to a respectable wholesale trade. Young men blessed with ability, drive, and luck sometimes flourished, but many proved unable to adjust to a life so far removed from the one in which they had been raised. It was a recipe for resentment.

---

[1] Sir Henry Slingsby, *A Father's Legacy* (1658), 12, 52–3.

Sir William Wentworth, a Yorkshire landowner, gave his heir detailed instructions on the appropriate education, allowances, and careers of his younger brothers, and his lifelong responsibilities towards them. He explained that 'you must love and assist [them] in their honest causes with countenance and good counsel', and keep a watchful eye on the company they kept and their marriage plans. His heir, Sir Thomas, was conscientious in discharging his responsibilities.[2] Many others, throughout the period, were accused of ignoring both their moral and legal obligations. Sir Richard Whalley, old and ailing, feared that his eldest son would 'devour' his other children, and other fathers harboured similar fears.[3] But heirs frequently inherited estates already encumbered with large debts, and failure to pay annuities might reflect circumstance as much as selfishness. Sir Percival Willoughby, for example, must have felt fortunate in 1596 when he married an heiress who brought a large estate, but it came burdened with debts and encumbrances of £35,000. Inheriting further debts from his own father, he struggled under this double burden throughout his life. In consequence, his younger brothers inevitably struggled too, and their begging letters fell on deaf ears. Several were imprisoned for debt, but so too was Sir Percival.[4] The Verney family's story is somewhat similar. Sir Edmund Verney, slain at Edgehill, left his son Ralph an estate burdened with debts and other charges amounting to four times its annual value, along with responsibility for nine younger brothers and sisters. Ralph took his responsibilities seriously, but the combination of civil war and inherited debt left him unable to satisfy his brothers' expectations or provide the portions his sisters had been promised.[5]

Heirs thus faced competing pressures and competing moral obligations. They were expected to support their siblings, and praised when they did so. At the same time, they needed to pay off inherited debts, preserve the estate intact, maintain the household in appropriate style, and raise their children to continue the family line. Most also had to deal with a throng of other kin clamouring for support. So as heirs and siblings tussled over rights and obligations, both claimed the moral high ground. Many elder brothers dismissed their siblings as feckless and inferior, while their siblings resented them as tyrannical and mean. Sir Ralph Verney's heir, Edmund, idle and irresponsible, felt entitled to lecture his hard-working brother John in terms both offensive and patronizing: 'remember you are a gentleman,' he wrote loftily, 'otherwise I shall never own you, for I hate a poltroon.'[6]

Many heirs discharged their responsibilities with scrupulous care, especially in the first half of our period. John Bruen, a Cheshire gentleman, offers one striking

---

[2] J. P. Cooper, ed., *Wentworth Papers 1597–1628*, Camden Society, 4th series (1973), 13, 54–5.

[3] Arthur Searle, ed., *Barrington Family Letters 1628–1632*, Camden Society, 4th series, 28 (1983), 30–1; cf. *Flemings in Oxford*, iii.39–40.

[4] Lawrence Stone, *The Crisis of the Aristocracy 1558–1641* (Oxford, 1965), 540; Felicity Heal and Clive Holmes, *The Gentry in England and Wales, 1500–1700* (Oxford, 1994), 88; Cassandra, Duchess of Chandos, *The Continuation of the Willoughby Family* (Eton, Windsor, 1958), 38–52.

[5] Miriam Slater, *Family Life in the Seventeenth Century. The Verneys of Claydon House* (1984), chaps 2–4; Susan E. Whyman, *Sociability and Power in Late Stuart England* (Oxford, 1999), chap. 1.

[6] Whyman, *Sociability and Power*, 52.

example. As a young man, Bruen had lived a life of idle pleasure, hunting, and hawking. But when his father died in 1587, leaving him the estate and responsibility for twelve younger siblings, Bruen transformed his life to meet the challenge. Selling his hounds, he turned the deer park into arable farmland, and adopted an austere manner of life. He took pride in arranging good marriages for his sisters, and careers for his brothers. This was model rather than typical behaviour, and Bruen's early biographer (an admiring brother-in-law) pointedly contrasted it with the selfishness of most heirs.[7] Yet many other traditionalists also honoured the code, and some went far beyond their legal obligations. When Edward Herbert's father died intestate in 1596, he voluntarily settled annuities on his brothers and portions of £1,000 apiece on his sisters. A generation later Sir George Sondes, a Kent royalist, paid an annuity of £100 to his brother, despite his father having made no such provision. John Bramston even persuaded his father to increase the annuity he was planning for an indebted younger brother, brushing aside concern over the additional burden on his own finances.[8] Sir John Reresby, a Yorkshire knight, felt a similarly powerful obligation. The annuities stipulated in his father's will proved legally void, but Reresby was scrupulous in paying them, prompted by affection and a desire to honour his father's intentions. He apprenticed two brothers in London, and sent a third to Cambridge. And when one brother rebelled against the tedium of an apprentice's life, Reresby helped him switch to a military career.[9]

An heir's responsibilities extended far beyond annuities and portions. There were a multitude of other calls, large and small, on his purse. In 1669, for example, Daniel Fleming paid for his brother Roger, then in his thirties, to travel from Westmorland to London, to be touched by the king for scrofula, 'the king's evil'.[10] Many heirs found themselves expected to support younger brothers at school and university, and find them a profession or apprenticeship. Some had assumed such responsibilities even during the father's lifetime. Thus, Simonds D'Ewes arranged schooling for his brother Richard, thirteen years his junior, found him a tutor at Cambridge, and entered him at the Middle Temple to smooth his path should he opt for a legal career. D'Ewes also felt responsible for his brother's moral welfare. Having urged him to live a sober life at university, he removed him when he suspected his brother was being corrupted.[11] Similarly, Sir Edmund Verney, preoccupied with his career at court, left Ralph to run his estate and arrange a university place for his younger son Edmund. And when Edmund proved an idle student, it was to Ralph his tutor wrote, not their father. Throughout his late teens and twenties Ralph guided his brothers and sisters, acted as petitioner, mediator, and peacemaker on their behalf, covered their debts, and chided their

[7] William Hinde, *A Faithfull Remonstrance of the Holy Life and Happy Death of Iohn Bruen* (1641), 47–8.

[8] Sidney Lee, ed., *The Autobiography of Edward, Lord Herbert of Cherbury* (n.d., *c*.1906), 43; *Sir George Sondes his plaine Narrative to the World* (1655), 18; *The Autobiography of Sir John Bramston*, ed. Lord Braybrooke, Camden Society, OS, 32 (1845), 26–7, 97.

[9] *Memoirs of Sir John Reresby*, ed. Andrew Browning (2nd edition, ed. Mary Geiter and W. A. Speck, 1991), 53–4.

[10] *Flemings in Oxford*, i.453.   [11] D'Ewes, *Autobiography*, ii.69–70, 78.

failings.[12] Elder brothers might thus play a quasi-parental role long before inheriting their estate. Thereafter, many exercised a sternly parental authority, even towards those close in age. Henry Oxinden was only 20 when he inherited a modest estate in Kent and with it responsibility for five siblings, and immediately behaved like a strict parent. He kept his brother James, just entered at Cambridge, on a very tight allowance and demanded detailed accounts of his expenditure.[13]

After launching his brothers into the world, a responsible family head also felt it his duty to advance their careers. In most spheres, success depended heavily on patronage, and well-placed gentlemen exploited their connections to advance siblings, as well as sons and other close kin, at court and in the army, navy, and professions. Contemporaries would have seen nothing unusual or reprehensible when Humphrey May, groom of the privy chamber to James I, secured a higher position at court and contrived to install his younger brother in the post he was vacating.[14] Elder brothers could help in the business sphere too, at many levels. Nicholas Blundell, a Lancashire gentleman, assisted his younger brother Richard, a merchant's factor in Virginia, by dispatching goods to America for him to trade privately.[15]

Elder brothers might also be able to provide protection, sometimes of still greater value. Sir John Reresby had often tried to advance his brother Edmund's military career, but his most significant intervention came shortly after the Glorious Revolution, when Edmund was accused of encouraging his Guards battalion to desert. With powerful figures at court demanding retribution, Reresby lobbied hard on his brother's behalf. He assured ministers that Edmund was ill, had merely wished to lay down his commission, and had done nothing to subvert his men. When all this proved insufficient, he composed an apologia in his brother's name, and contrived to have it placed before the king. Edmund possessed no such connections or political skills, and without his brother's help might well have been destroyed.[16] Other family heads intervened to protect and defend a sibling's honour. When a duel in 1628 left one of the combatants branded a coward, his elder brother, Sir William Wittipoll, resolved to avenge the slur. The outcome was a bloody clash between two armed companies, after which Sir William paraded in triumph through Ipswich before surrendering to the authorities. Prosecution for murder, he considered, was a price worth paying to uphold his brother's honour. Like Reresby, he would have seen his younger brother's disgrace as tarnishing the honour of the whole family. Each individual's reputation affected the standing and credit of them all.[17]

Such incidents reflected the concept of siblings as partners in a collective enterprise, with each promoting the welfare and protecting the honour of the

---

[12] Slater, *Family Life*, 34–7; Verney, *Memoirs*, i, chaps 5–7.

[13] *Oxinden Letters, 1607–1642*, 114–15, 118–19, 158–9; BL, Add. MS 27999, fos. 84, 135, 138.

[14] John Bruce, ed., *Liber Famelicus of Sir James Whitelocke*, Camden Society, OS, 70 (1858), 26; Natalie Mears, *Queenship and Political Discourse in the Elizabethan Realm* (Cambridge, 2005), chap. 2; Linda Levy Peck, *Court Patronage and Corruption in Early Stuart England* (1993), esp. Chap. 2.

[15] Margaret Blundell, ed., *Blundell's Diary and Letter Book 1702–1728* (Liverpool, 1952), 39–48.

[16] Reresby, *Memoirs*, 563–4, 566.

[17] *Diary of John Rous, 1625–1642*, ed. M. A. E. Green, Camden Society, OS, 66 (1856), 22–4, 41. He was convicted only of manslaughter, and pardoned.

whole family. For some, like the Wittipolls, that ideal outweighed the rule of law, and they clung to the right of kin to exact private satisfaction. In one mid-Tudor Lancashire case, which involved the grandfather of the eminent Jacobean puritan John Preston, a court had judged an act of homicide to be self-defence, but the dead man's kin were determined on revenge, 'as the manner in those northern counties then was', as Preston's early biographer put it. His grandfather was confronted by the dead man's brother and forced to fight again—killing this assailant too. Recognizing that he would never be left in peace, he decided to uproot his family to the south.[18] Manners were different there, but not necessarily better. When Charles Walker provoked a quarrel in a Westminster coffee house in 1709, by flirting with the owner's niece, his behaviour led to insults, scuffles, and worse. His brother William declared that he 'would take his brother's part', and within hours he had arranged and fought a duel in the nearby churchyard, killing his opponent.[19]

Contemporaries saw the sibling relationship as founded on the principle of reciprocity. In return for support, patronage, and protection, elder brothers expected deference, obedience, and service. A younger sibling might remain living in his brother's household, assisting in his affairs. A sibling in London could provide useful contacts and information, and supply goods and services unavailable in the provinces. Philip Gawdy, who spent a lifetime on the fringes of the Elizabethan and Jacobean courts, discharged a multitude of commissions for his elder brother Bassingbourne, a Norfolk landowner. Gawdy bought fine clothes and fabrics for his brother and sister-in-law, reported on current fashions, sent them fine wines, books, and rare delicacies, and showed their son the London sights. Younger brothers performed similar services for countless other families.[20] A brother in the law could provide valuable help in the lawsuits that featured regularly in almost every landowner's life. As a contemporary remarked, that was why so many fathers steered a younger son into the profession.[21] A sibling living in a large provincial town could be useful too. John Thomlinson, in rural Cumberland, directed his younger brother at Newcastle to procure books and on one occasion virginals for him, and to settle his shop debts.[22] Equally, if the family head spent most of his time in London, a brother in the country might play a valuable role overseeing his estate business.[23]

This pattern, with the elder brother as patron and guide, was not set in stone, however. Fraternal support sometimes came from a different sibling, more affectionate or closer in age. George Fleming, a student at Oxford, was very grateful for

---

[18] Samuel Clarke, *The Lives of Two and Twenty English Divines* (1660), 95.

[19] *OBSP*, t17090302-13.

[20] Isaac Herbert Jeayes, ed., *Letters of Philip Gawdy of Harling, Norfolk* (1906), 20–1, 25, 27, 33, 92, 97, 107, 160; Heal and Holmes, *Gentry*, chap. 2.

[21] Thomas Adams, *The Devills Banket* (1614), 207; cf. J. H. Bettey, ed., *Calendar of the Correspondence of the Smyth Family of Ashton Court 1548–1642*, Bristol Record Society, 35 (1982), 15, 18, 20, 22, 25–6; John Smyth, *The Lives of the Berkeleys*, 3 vols (Gloucester, 1883–5), ii.348–9.

[22] 'The Diary of the Rev. John Thomlinson', ed. J. C. Hodgson, in *Six North Country Diaries*, Surtees Society, 118 (1910), 121, 140, 157.

[23] Louise Brown Osborn, ed., *The Life, Letters, and Writings of John Hoskyns 1566–1638* (New Haven, 1937), 75, 77–9, 248.

the 'loving care' of his brother Henry, who 'hath been a brother, a counsellor, and a tutor, yea even a second father unto me', as he told their father in 1689. George was the sixth of the Fleming brothers, Henry the second, eight years his senior. The eldest brother and heir, William, had a poor relationship with both his siblings and his father. Henry indeed had to take on a very different counselling role when William left home in high dudgeon and uttering alarming threats. Wanting financial independence, he declared that unless most of the estate was made over to him, he would take out expensive loans in London, using his future inheritance as security. Henry was appalled. Attempting to mediate, he warned his father that such an action would cripple the estate, and leave all the other siblings 'to the mercy of an offended brother'. His efforts prevailed.[24]

Anthony and Francis Bacon were the sons of their father's second marriage, and neither inherited his estate. In their case, the close sibling bond rested on mutual affection. On one occasion, in 1593, Anthony wrote to their widowed mother, urging her to make over a manor to Francis to help clear his debts, adding that he had said nothing of this approach to his brother. He was acting merely out of 'a brotherly care and affection'. Lady Anne commended his 'brotherly care', though she grumbled that Francis should live less extravagantly. Even so, she eventually did as Anthony asked.[25]

There were other exceptions to the conventional sibling relationship. If an heir was ruined by misfortune or folly, for example, he might have to seek help from more successful younger brothers. Henry Oxinden had adopted a lofty attitude towards his siblings, but after being ruined by lawsuits he found that he needed their help in launching a new career in the Church. They responded generously.[26] Ambitious and able younger brothers, moreover, sometimes carved out careers that raised them far above an easy-going or extravagant heir both in status and wealth.[27] The Cokes of Derbyshire provide a striking example. The family's head, Sir Francis, always struggled to live within his means, while his younger brother John forged a successful career in government service. In 1604, we find Sir Francis desperately begging for a loan, appealing to fraternal love and offering to pay interest at 10 per cent, a rate he acknowledged was illegal. John Coke eventually rose to become Secretary of State and *de facto* head of the family, taking over the responsibilities that normally belonged to the eldest brother. Siblings and other kin bombarded him with requests to use his influence on their behalf. Sir Francis, who was among them, accepted the reversal of roles with some grace.[28]

---

[24] *Flemings in Oxford*, ii.233, 261, 263–4, 266–71. Cf. a brother pressed by siblings to mollify their mother, the formidable matriarch Lady Joan Barrington: Searle, *Barrington Letters*, 47–8, 81. Sir John Bramston, less in awe, dismissed Lady Joan as 'that impertinent everlasting talker': Bramston, *Autobiography*, 94.

[25] Gemma Allen, ed., *The Letters of Lady Anne Bacon*, Camden Society, 5th series, 44 (2014), 121–3; cf.157.

[26] *Oxinden Letters 1642–1670*, 266–8, 273–4, 279–80.

[27] Thomas Fuller, *The Holy State* (1642), 47–50.

[28] HMC, 23, *Cowper*, i.54–5, 94, 110, 116, 143–4, 269, 282–3, 392, 427, 442, 454, 485; *ODNB*, Sir John Coke.

RIVALRIES AND RESENTMENTS

Stories of solidarity and support give us, of course, only half the picture. As noted earlier, many elder brothers resented the burdens and responsibilities they were expected to shoulder. Even the Cokes were exasperated by their brother Robert, an idle drifter. Sir Francis eventually packed him off to London with £5 in his purse, commenting that 'I look now that he live of his own'. When Robert found an honourable death, fighting in the Netherlands, his brothers did not hide their relief. One thanked God for having spared them any further trouble.[29] Similarly, Sir Thomas Wentworth warned his idle and extravagant brother, Michael, that he saw no reason to help him if he would not bother to help himself.[30] A mountain of contrasting evidence records the resentments of younger brothers, many without any livelihood or the skills to acquire one. Some allegedly wished they had been born into a yeoman family.[31] Tensions were often exacerbated by a sense of grievance on both sides. Denzel Holles, a Nottinghamshire squire, left a will in 1590 that directed his heir, John, to pay two younger siblings £300 each and an annuity. John inherited heavy debts along with the estate, and had to fund his brothers' education and see them launched into professional careers (soldiering and the law). All that, he decided, fully satisfied the spirit of his father's will. So when many years later, in 1617, his brother George demanded payment of the moneys specified in the will, John angrily refused and challenged him to sue. George appealed to the Privy Council, and Lord Keeper Bacon eventually ruled in favour of the younger brothers, leaving John deeply aggrieved. Their very public dispute had become the talk of the town.[32] Similar disputes often led to litigation, and some reached as far as parliament.[33] Other disgruntled siblings preferred direct action, assaulting rivals or seizing contested houses or lands. One Cheshire dispute in 1665–6, between three siblings, generated eleven indictments for dispossession or assault, and nine recognizances binding them to keep the peace or be of good behaviour.[34]

On rare occasions, such resentments could escalate still further, to murderous rage. In one such case Henry Welby, a Lincolnshire gentleman, was shot at close range by his embittered younger brother. The pistol misfired, but the trauma turned Welby into a nervous recluse, and for the remaining forty-four years of his life he never left his house or allowed visitors to enter.[35] Still more traumatic was

---

[29] HMC, 23, *Cowper*, i.22, 26.   [30] Cooper, *Wentworth Papers*, 171–2.

[31] Champianus Northtonus, *The Younger Brothers Advocate* (1655), 4; *The Office of Christian Parents* (Cambridge, 1616), 128.

[32] P. R. Seddon, ed., *Letters of John Holles 1587–1637*, Thoroton Society, 31, 35 (1975, 1983), i, pp. xxvi–vii, 160, 163–5.

[33] See e.g. A. Hassell Smith et al., eds, *The Papers of Nathaniel Bacon of Stiffkey*, 5 vols, Norfolk Record Society (1979–2010), ii.77–9, 81–2, 93–5, 101–5, 106–7; HMC, 53, *Montagu of Beaulieu*, 104; *The Case of Roger Price, Esq.* (n.d., ?1688); *An Answer to the Case of Roger Price, Esq*, (n.d., ?1688); Heal and Holmes, *Gentry*, 42–5.

[34] Garthine Walker, 'Keeping it in the Family: Crime and the early modern Household', in Helen Berry and Elizabeth Foyster, eds, *The Family in Early Modern England* (Cambridge, 2007), 85–7, 90–1.

[35] Thomas Heywood, *The Phoenix of these late Times. Or the Life of Henry Welby* (1637).

the murder of George Sondes, heir to a rich Kent estate, by his brother Freeman in 1655. Freeman deeply resented his father's alleged favouritism, refused to pursue any career, and hated the prospect of becoming eventually dependent on his brother. One night his anger erupted. Freeman stabbed his brother to death as he lay asleep, and smashed his head with a cleaver. The murder, and Freeman's trial and execution, attracted huge public interest.[36] A few fathers sought to avert such hatreds by devising very generous arrangements for their younger sons. But these inevitably dashed the heir's expectations and could also backfire and generate litigation.[37] Roger Carter, who divided his estate equally between his two sons, triggered a still greater calamity. His elder son, cursed with 'an extravagant wild temper', hired a gang of ruffians to waylay and murder his brother.[38]

Such horrific crimes, though of course exceptional, reflected tensions that were common and involved not only material grievances. Shakespeare's Henry V, succeeding to the throne, promises his younger brothers that 'I'll be your father and your brother too'. Such pledges, however well intentioned, perpetuated Oedipal tensions within the family.[39] How could younger brothers ever achieve full emotional adulthood, with their elder sibling simply taking over the father's role and authority? Primogeniture locked many men into psychological as well as material dependency and immaturity. James Oxinden, surviving on a pittance at Cambridge, thought his elder brother Henry parsimonious and controlling. His desperate pleas and bitter complaints turned to extravagant avowals of gratitude, devotion, and obedience whenever money did arrive. Henry, like other heirs, gave little credence to such effusions. 'I know you think some love you more than I do', he told James, insisting reproachfully that he was devoted to his brother's welfare—provided his directions were always obeyed. He knew that the other brothers harboured similar resentments.[40] Such feelings, sometimes concealed, festered in many families. As a young man Philip Gawdy had assured his elder brother that 'my worldly joys consisteth in yourself only', that he rejoiced in his brother's superior fortune, and that he would always 'rest content with that portion God hath provided for me'. But these extravagant declarations also told only part of the story. By the early 1600s, Philip felt more secure, while his elder brother was now heavily in debt, and owed money to Philip himself. The younger Philip had addressed letters to 'My only sweetest and best beloved brother'. By 1600, his letters begin with a curt 'Sir', and continue in a distinctly cool tone.[41] As contemporaries were well aware, deference rooted in dependence could quickly evaporate if circumstances changed. In one such case, the unexpected death of a wealthy

---

[36] *Sir George Sondes his plaine Narrative*; anon., *The Devils Reign upon Earth* (1655); William Ammond, *A Funeral Elegie upon the Death of George Sondes* (1655); R. Boreman, *A Mirrour of Mercy and Judgement* (1655).

[37] Heal and Holmes, *Gentry*, 143–4.

[38] *Strange and Wonderful News from Linconshire [sic]* (1679). For other fratricidal quarrels see e.g. Pepys, *Diary*, viii.208–9, 321; OBSP, t17080414-18; OBOA 17080428.

[39] *2 Henry IV*, V.ii.57; Louis Adrian Montrose, '"The Place of a Brother" in *As You Like It*: Social Process and Comic Form', *Shakespeare Quarterly*, 32 (1981), 35–7.

[40] *Oxinden Letters 1607–1642*, 81–3, 158–9.

[41] Jeayes, ed., *Letters of Gawdy*, 36–7, 56, 69, 103, 118, 137.

London alderman brought his younger sons far greater portions than he had intended, and instantly transformed the family dynamics. Thereafter, a kinsman observed, 'they (in truth) despised their eldest brother, and they never after lived in cordial affection'.[42]

Younger brothers without a profession remained dependent on the heir's good-will. Those in the Church were unlikely to become rich, while success in the law and trade demanded talent, hard work, and luck. Soldiering was dangerous and ill-paid, and an essayist warned that soldiers were quite likely to die in poverty, 'without a shirt'.[43] The majority of younger siblings experienced a steep and permanent decline in status. One of them, Henry Willoughby, proved wholly unable to live on his earnings as a lawyer, and by 1632 had amassed debts of £1,300. His youngest brother, Robert, failed even more spectacularly and was gaoled after stealing jewels and other valuables from their father.[44] Sir Ralph Verney's younger brothers struggled too. All three followed military careers, but only Edmund achieved any success, and this was cut brutally short by his murder at Drogheda in 1649. His brother Thomas, who survived to the age of 91, remained poor and shiftless to the end, an unscrupulous and sponging adventurer. A kinsman remarked that 'having flown over many knavish professions, he settled only in rogue'.[45]

A younger brother's best prospects lay, paradoxically, in the high mortality rates of the period. The death of a childless elder brother could instantly transform his life. It was through such common accidents that many gentlemen, knights, and peers had acquired their lands and status. Such transformations had a powerful impact on their sense of identity as well as their material prospects. No longer expected to defer, work hard, and obey, they found themselves suddenly the heirs or even owners of a landed estate. Gervase Disney remembered his euphoria at his elevation, feelings that would have been shared by many others. His elder brother had enjoyed an Oxford education while Gervase had been packed off to an apprenticeship in London, a life he hated. On his brother's death, he was promptly summoned home and installed as heir. Resolving that 'I must now carry it out, and live at the rate of my father's eldest son, and not as Mr Oglethorpe's apprentice and servant', he launched himself into a brave new world of fine clothes, heavy drinking, and gaming.[46]

MIDDLING SORT AND ORDINARY FAMILIES

The first part of this chapter has focused on the landed gentry, who comprised only a small proportion of the population. Below them, a social pyramid descended from prosperous merchants, professionals, and substantial yeomen, through modest

---

[42] Bramston, *Autobiography*, 106–7.   [43] John Earle, *Micro-cosmographie* (1628), sig. C6v.
[44] Chandos, *Continuation*, 49–52.
[45] Slater, *Family Life*, 20–4, 34–45, 73–6; Verney, *Memoirs*, iii.138–78 (quote at 139).
[46] *Some Remarkable Passages in the Holy Life and Death of Gervase Disney, Esq.* (1692), 46–7.

tenant farmers and craftsmen, to the labouring poor. What did sibling rights and responsibilities mean for these very varied groups? And how did their behavioural patterns compare with those of the elite?

Professional and mercantile families often retained close ties to the gentry, from which many had sprung, and shared many values and patterns of behaviour. Those at the upper levels held a similar view of the appropriate relationship between elder and younger brothers. Thus John Janeway, a minister's younger son, was deeply troubled at securing the top scholarship to King's College, Cambridge, in 1650, while his elder brother William was awarded only the sixth. Dismayed by such a reversal of due order, he insisted on transferring his top award to his brother, in exchange for the inferior sixth. And though his superior intellect was obvious to them both, John would always 'humbly and heartily respect and honour' his older sibling.[47] Elder brothers, for their part, often shared the gentleman's sense of a right to govern his siblings and a responsibility to promote their welfare. Samuel Pepys offers a particularly well-documented example, explored in a later chapter.[48] The Bristol physician Thomas Ducket, a near-contemporary, felt a similar responsibility and supplied his brother with medical books, recipes, materials, surgical instruments, and money, enabling him to set up his own practice. As in many elite families, both Pepys and Ducket supplied their help in a grudging spirit, resenting their siblings' fecklessness while honouring their responsibilities.[49] The Leeds merchant Ralph Thoresby did likewise, and in far more difficult circumstances. His extravagant younger brother Jeremiah and their brother-in-law, a clergyman aptly named Idle, had both run up heavy debts and fled to escape their creditors. Thoresby was left caring for their abandoned wives and numerous children, along with his own, a total of twelve. Moreover, he had acted as surety for their loans, so he was left also facing liabilities of over £1,600. The stress took a heavy toll, and as he confided to his diary, 'I was in a most piteous condition.'[50]

For their part, younger brothers living in London undertook commissions similar to those common among the gentry. In 1596, Christopher Honeywell arranged for an elaborate watch to be made for his brother William, a prosperous Devon yeoman; William collected it and reimbursed him on his next visit to the capital. Such patterns survived for generations. In 1731, for example, John Hobson, living near Barnsley, received two globes and an edition of Raphael's cartoons sent by his brother, a distiller in Holborn. Treasures like these were hardly to be found in the South Yorkshire countryside.[51]

[47] James Janeway, *Invisibles, Realities, Demonstrated in the Holy Life and Triumphant Death of Mr John Janeway* (1673), 4, 36.

[48] See Chapter 9.

[49] H. E. Nott, ed., *The Deposition Books of Bristol 1643–1647*, Bristol Record Society, 6 (1935), 84–5.

[50] Joseph Hunter, ed., *The Diary of Ralph Thoresby FRS*, 2 vols (1830), i.185, 322–4.

[51] F. J. Snell, ed., 'A Devonshire Yeoman's Diary: William Honeywell of Ashton 1596–1614', in G. L. Apperson, ed., *Gleanings after Time* (1907) 162; 'The Journal of Mr John Hobson', ed. Charles Jackson, in *Yorkshire Diaries and Autobiographies of the Seventeenth and Eighteenth Centuries*, Surtees Society, 65 (1875), 302–3.

The most distinctive feature of relationships in the business community was the widespread practice of choosing partners from among close kin, especially brothers, brothers-in-law, and sons. The partnership between the brothers John and Otwell Johnson, which flourished throughout the 1540s, just before our period, is particularly well documented. The brothers specialized in wool and hides, exporting the best through Calais, and selling the rest to English dealers. John, based mainly in Northamptonshire, sourced most of the goods, while Otwell, the brains of the operation, dealt with sales and accounts, and the import of grain, cloth, herring, and wine. Their close partnership was based on warm affection and mutual trust. In 1547, they made their younger brother Richard a junior partner, based in Calais, and they had an agent in Antwerp too.[52] Richard Grassby, tracing the origins of business partnerships between 1580 and 1740, found that 51 per cent of partners were kin, with 41 per cent close kin. With trust essential, men often placed more confidence in close kin than outsiders in the transfer of money and the repayment of loans and debts.[53] Merchants and prosperous tradesmen also created many other openings for their kin. Grassby found many employing brothers and other kin as apprentices, agents, and factors throughout Europe, across the Atlantic, and in India, and such arrangements generally appear to have worked well. At a much humbler level, we find John Harrys, an Elizabethan grocer in Warwick, taking on his brother as apprentice, and sibling partnerships occur among pewterers, drapers, and apothecaries in mid-seventeenth-century Bristol.[54] Joseph Pike opened a linen-draper's shop with his younger brother, and traded in partnership with his brother-in-law.[55] Kinship was a significant factor in the military and naval sphere too, with senior officers often securing places and promotion for close kin, including siblings.[56]

Many of the comfortably off were also ready to provide their siblings with gifts or loans, and cancel or defer debts. The key factor here was resources, not birth order. Oswald Hoskyns, a wealthy draper in Jacobean London, lent his elder brother John, head of the family, the money to buy new lands in Herefordshire. While John was usually in debt, Oswald died leaving a business worth £4,000. John later took care to provide well for his brother's widow and small children.[57] George Symcotts, a London mercer, wrote to his brother in 1629 that as 'for that little money which you do owe me, let it not trouble your mind a jot . . . If you cannot pay me this year,

[52] Barbara Winchester, *Tudor Family Portrait* (1955), esp, chap. 8.

[53] Richard Grassby, *Kinship and Capitalism. Marriage, Family, and Business in the English-Speaking World, 1580–1740* (Cambridge, 2001), 288–92; Craig Muldrew, *The Economy of Obligation: the Culture of Credit and Social Relations in Early Modern England* (Basingstoke, 1998), 123–30; Ilana Krausman Ben-Amos, *The Culture of Giving: Informal Support and Gift-Exchange in Early Modern England* (Cambridge, 2008), 53–4.

[54] Grassby, *Kinship and Capitalism*, 210–14, 292–6; 'Diary of John Thomlinson', pedigree facing p. 166; Thomas Kemp, ed., *The Book of John Fisher, Town Clerk and Deputy-Recorder of Warwick 1580–1588* (Warwick [,1945]), 159; Nott, *Deposition Books 1643–1647*, 54–5; H. E. Nott and Elizabeth Ralph, eds, *The Deposition Books of Bristol 1650–1654*, Bristol Record Society, 13 (1948), 35, 52–4; Ilana Krausman Ben-Amos, *Adolescence and Youth in Early Modern England* (1994), 124–5.

[55] John Barclay, ed., *Some Account of the Life of Joseph Pike* (1837), 121–3.

[56] On the navy, see e.g. Bernard Capp, *Cromwell's Navy. The Fleet and the English Revolution 1648–1660* (Oxford, 1989), 179–89.

[57] Osborn, *Life of John Hoskyns*, 82, 85–6.

why then, if you have it to spare, pay it me the next.' Similarly, George Davenport, a Yorkshire clergyman, lent £50 to his brother, a farmer, and assured him that he was in no hurry to have it repaid. In his will, ten years later, he wrote off the debt altogether.[58] In an uncertain world, flexibility made sense, for at some point the lender might also need help and forbearance. Adam Martindale always remembered his brother Henry as 'a most kind brother to me'. Adam was a prisoner at Liverpool for over two months after its capture by Prince Rupert, and on his release, 'bare in clothes and money', Henry 'furnished me handsomely at his own charge, though his own circumstances were then but hard'. Adam made a point of adding that years later he had 'requited this his kindness to himself and the son he left behind him'.[59]

Moving further down the social pyramid, we find sibling support and solidarity in a wide variety of forms. Here too, men lent money to one another, and frequently cancelled such debts in their wills.[60] They might occasionally negotiate to rent land as joint tenants, or even devise a form of job-sharing.[61] Migrants to London often provided openings for close kin to follow. Leonard Wheatcroft's eldest son, who had migrated to London and flourished, arranged for two younger brothers to follow him.[62] And though it was uncommon for married brothers to live together, householders might provide a temporary or occasional home for a younger sibling. One Essex villager stipulated in his will that his widow was to keep a chamber and bed in the house for his brother John to use, without charge, 'whensoever he cometh'. John was presumably a younger man, perhaps a farm servant, and not yet a householder.[63] We also find farmers, artisans, and craftsmen providing training and employment. Several Essex and Lancashire Quakers employed siblings as farm servants, and in 1662 we find two Gloucestershire brothers working in partnership as blacksmiths. A Norfolk shoemaker also worked with his brother, and when they fell into debt they both fled to London, setting up together again in the city. They passed off the apprentice they had brought with them as another brother.[64] We find a Sussex thatcher employing his brother in

---

[58] F. N. L. Poynter and W. J. Bishop, eds, *A Seventeenth Century Doctor and his Patients. John Symcotts 1592?–1662*, Bedfordshire Historical Record Society, 31 (1951), 1; Brenda M. Pask with Margaret Harvey, eds, *The Letters of George Davenport 1651–1677*, Surtees Society, 215 (2011), 198, 263–4; Grassby, *Kinship and Capitalism*, 214; Fiona McCall, *Baal's Priests. The Loyalist Clergy and the English Revolution* (Farnham, 2013), 217.

[59] *The Life of Adam Martindale*, ed. Richard Parkinson, Chetham Society, 4 (1845), 41, 109–10.

[60] See e.g. F. G. Emmison, ed., *Wills of the County of Essex (England). Volume 1, 1558–1565* (Washington, D.C., 1982), 278; Nesta Evans, ed., *Wills of the Archdeaconry of Sudbury 1630–1635*, Suffolk Records Society, 29 (1987), 233.

[61] *The Diary of Bulstrode Whitelocke 1605–1675*, ed. Ruth Spalding (Oxford, 1990), 658; J. Bagley, ed., *The Great Diurnall of Nicholas Blundell of Little Crosby, Lancashire, 1702–1728*, 3 vols, Record Society of Lancashire and Cheshire (1968–72), ii.81; Hassell Smith, *Papers of Bacon*, v.286n, 290–1.

[62] *The Autobiography of Leonard Wheatcroft of Ashover 1627–1706*, ed. Dorothy Riden, Derbyshire Record Society, 20 (1993), 93, 95; *OBOA*, 17090803; R. C. Anderson, ed., *The Book of Examinations and Depositions 1622–1644*, 4 vols, Southampton Record Society (1929–36), i.7–8.

[63] Emmison, *Wills of Essex*, 14–15; Birmingham & Midland Genealogy Society, 'Lichfield Census', 54; *OBOA*, 16910918; *OBOA*, 17090803.

[64] *Memoirs of Benjamin Lay* (New York, 1842), 7; Joseph Besse, *The Sufferings of the Quakers*, 2 vols (1753), i.216, 319; Joseph Hobson, ed., *Memoirs of the Life and Convincement of Benjamin Bangs* (1757), 11–13.

1669, and other craftsmen doing likewise.[65] More casual arrangements were no doubt still more common, if rarely recorded. We learn that George Mayne's brother had paid him a shilling to drive some pigs to market only because the animals were stolen and the brothers ended up on trial at the Old Bailey.[66]

Siblings also played an important role in marriage formation, at almost every level of society. Most young couples hoped for the support of their close kin, and both brothers and parents would often identify suitable partners or facilitate a courtship.[67] And, as with the gentry, family involvement did not end with the marriage ceremony. A brother might intervene, for example, to patch up a troubled relationship. A feckless Essex miller, who abandoned his family after being scolded for his drinking and gaming, was promptly pursued by his brother and brought back home.[68] Wills confirm that fraternal bonds often survived throughout life. Testators bequeathed most of their property to their wives and children, and these were also by far the most popular choices as executors. But siblings would usually receive small bequests, and brothers and brothers-in-law were the next most favoured choice as executors. In a sample of about 650 wills from Suffolk in the early 1630s, forty-one male testators named a brother or brother-in-law as an executor. Only sixteen named other kin, while twenty-five chose apparently unrelated friends, or local worthies such as a minister or gentleman. Another sixteen testators named a brother as a supervisor, to support and monitor the executor (usually a son or wife), more than chose other kin or friends. Brothers were also often asked to raise underage children, and sometimes entrusted to approve a daughter's marriage plans.[69]

Many siblings played an equally important role as a safety net for the destitute, sick, or mentally ill. The poor laws assigned responsibility to vertical kin, the parents or adult children of those in need, but if no such help was available, communities and officials were relieved when siblings or other close kin stepped in.[70] Thus in Somerset John Maltravers took in his brother Peter in 1622, 'a weak mazed man not able to govern himself', when Peter's wife proved unable or unwilling to care for him. Other men came to the aid of kin maimed in the wars. In 1625, Valentine Gill took in his brother Richard, whose yearly pension of £4 would not have covered his keep. Robert Collier, a Wiltshire soldier seriously wounded in the civil war, was nursed back to health by his brother.[71] Other destitute men turned to kin for shelter and employment. Henry Carre, a wounded veteran now scraping a living as a pedlar, told officials at Warwick in 1581 that he had come to visit his brother, confident he

[65] *The Journal of Giles Moore 1656–1679*, ed. Ruth Bird, Sussex Record Society (1971), 63; cf. 46, 50, 53; Bagley, ed., *Great Diurnall of Nicholas Blundell*, i.245, 291; *OBSP*, t17201012-19.

[66] *OBSP*, t16931206-21.

[67] Diana O'Hara, *Courtship and Constraint: Rethinking the Making of Marriage in Tudor England* (Manchester, 2000); David Cressy, *Birth, Marriage and Death* (Oxford, 1997), 233–60.

[68] Josselin, *Diary*, 393–4.   [69] Evans, *Wills of Sudbury*, 182, 206, 263, 307, and *passim*.

[70] Steve Hindle, *On the Parish? The Micro-Politics of Poor Relief in Rural England c.1550–1750* (Oxford, 2004), 48–52; Jonathan Healey, *The First Century of Welfare. Poverty and Poor Relief in Lancashire 1620–1730* (Woodbridge, 2014), 146–52.

[71] *SQSR*, i.313, ii.8–9; B. Howard Cunnington, ed., *Records of the County of Wilts.* (Devizes, 1932), 233.

could find him work.[72] Magistrates were sceptical about such claims, but the stories were clearly plausible and sometimes genuine. Richard Greneway, a former servant in London, had indeed found help in Warwick from his brother, who had given him 10s for his immediate needs.[73] Such informal assistance rarely found its way into the record, so we will never know its scale, but we should not underestimate its significance. The authorities in Elizabethan Norwich gave most paupers only two or three pence a week, and clearly saw these tiny sums as merely supplementing help from family or friends. The story of a Somerset villager named William Hayle is also suggestive. Old, blind, and crippled, Hayle had been maintained for years by his brother Thomas, with the help of a pittance from the local overseers. By 1620, however, Thomas had also sunk into destitution under his burden, and begged magistrates to order an increase in the overseers' allowance. But for his petition, we would never have known of his years of generosity and self-sacrifice. Informal help came to light only when it failed.[74]

Support for the sick and poor was welcomed. Help for those entangled in the law was more problematic. It was common and wholly acceptable for kin to act as sureties for loans, or to secure the release of someone under arrest. Many contemporaries would also have sympathized with men sheltering a brother hiding from his creditors, though the authorities would not have approved.[75] In many other contexts, however, kin solidarity clashed directly with the law's demands. A Yorkshire constable who ignored a warrant to arrest his own brother soon found himself in trouble.[76] Solidarity and duty clashed more seriously when families spirited away a member accused of fathering an illegitimate child, to save him from punishment and shame. The authorities took a stern view of this practice.[77] When John Edgell fled in 1623 to escape such an accusation, his brother tried to thwart an order for his arrest, and tried to bribe the mother to drop her claims. His efforts backfired.[78] Resorting to violence to help a sibling enmeshed in legal proceedings was certain to provoke a stern response. When Somerset magistrates issued a warrant in 1616 against one Thomas Hippisley, his brother vowed to track down the complainant 'and run him through with his sword'. He too landed in trouble when his threat reached magistrates' ears.[79]

---

[72] Kemp, ed., *Book of John Fisher*, 75–8; cf. A. L. Beier, *Masterless Men. The Vagrancy Problem in England, 1560–1640* (1985); Paul Slack, 'Vagrants and Vagrancy in England, 1598–1664', in Peter Clark and David Souden, eds, *Migration and Society in Early Modern England* (1987), 49–76.

[73] Kemp, ed., *Book of John Fisher*, 48, 184–5.

[74] SQSR, i.268; cf. iii.184, 211–12; J. F. Pound, ed., *The Norwich Census of the Poor, 1570*, Norfolk Record Society, 40 (1971); Hindle, *On the Parish?*, 49.

[75] Heywood, *Autobiography*, ii.193; *Letters of John Pinney, 1679–1699*, ed. Geoffrey F. Nuttall (1939), 35; Pepys, *Diary*, ix.480.

[76] John Lister, ed., *West Riding Sessions Rolls, 1611–1642*, Yorkshire Archaeological Society, 54 (1915), 121; cf. SQSR, iii.350.

[77] SQSR, ii.128; William Le Hardy, ed., *County of Middlesex. Calendar to the Sessions Rolls, 1612–16*, 3 vols (1935–7), ii.45; S. C. Ratcliff and H. C. Johnson, eds, *Warwickshire County Records*, 9 vols (Warwick, 1935–64), i.7.

[78] SQSR, i.341–2.

[79] SQSR, i.173; cf. *The Notebook of Robert Doughty 1662–1665*, ed. J. M. Rosenheim, Norfolk Record Society, 54 (1989), 53.

Sibling violence was most common in the context of disputes between neighbours. Disputants often called on close kin for physical support, and the warring parties were frequently bound over to keep the peace or indicted for assault.[80] Men might also rush to the aid of a brother in immediate danger. Such incidents generally resulted in no more than cuts or bruises, but occasionally ended in tragedy. In 1570, for example, a sailor named Thomas Wright learned that his brother was being assaulted by a man armed with a dagger, and hastened to defend him. Only after giving the assailant a fatal blow to the head did he discover that the 'assailant' was in fact a constable trying to separate the combatants.[81] Any assault that resulted in death was, of course, a matter for the courts. In such circumstances, the victim's kin saw it as their responsibility to secure justice, and would supply information to a constable or magistrate. Some went much further. Thus, when John Thorley was assaulted and murdered in Staffordshire in 1586, his brother pursued the killer for several miles to carry out the arrest. When John Blanche was killed in a Somerset poaching affray, his brother resisted attempts to smother the crime, and scraped together the funds to travel to London to pursue justice.[82] And if kin failed to secure justice through the courts, they too, like the elite, might resort to violence. A Staffordshire man, who had secured a pardon after killing his opponent in a brawl, complained in 1606 that the dead man's father, brother, and stepbrother were nonetheless vowing to kill him in revenge.[83]

In other contexts, by contrast, we find siblings combining to break the law rather than secure justice. Alongside the numerous thieving partnerships, we find brothers as murderers, highwaymen, and coiners. Three London brothers even drew up a formal set of articles to govern their coining operation. It was not uncommon for the Tyburn crowds to see brothers hanged together.[84] Other siblings contrived to thwart the authorities by exploiting the law itself. Thus, four Staffordshire gamesters smothered attempts to curb their activities by launching vexatious suits against the constable. In the case of one Essex alehouse, suppressed as disorderly, its keeper recruited his brothers to launch a flood of suits against those who had informed against him.[85]

Despite these multiple forms of solidarity, sibling rivalry was also common at every level of society. Disputes frequently erupted over inheritance. Testators occasionally urged their heirs to behave with 'brotherly love', and many inserted penalty clauses if the main beneficiaries failed to honour the terms of the will.[86]

---

[80] Walker, 'Keeping it in the Family', 79, 84–6.

[81] J. S. Cockburn, ed., *Calendar of Assize Records: Kent Indictments, Elizabeth I* (1979), 101; cf. 227.

[82] S. A. H. Burns, ed., *The Staffordshire Quarter Sessions Rolls, 1581–1606*, 5 vols, William Salt Archaeological Society (1931–40), i.149–50; Bettey, ed., *Calendar of the Correspondence of the Smyth Family*, 19, 21, 25–6.

[83] D. H. G. Salt, ed., *Staffordshire Quarter Sessions Rolls, Easter 1608-Trinity 1609*, Staffordshire Record Society, 70 (1950), 109.

[84] *OBSP*, t16861013-8 (coiners); *Fair Warning from Tyburn* (1680); *OBOA*, 1680715; Cannon, *Chronicles*, ii.250 (highwaymen); J. S. Cockburn, ed., *Calendar of Assize Records: Essex Indictments, Elizabeth I* (1978), 338 (murderers).

[85] Burns, ed., *Staffordshire Quarter Sessions Rolls*, i.265–6; Searle, ed., *Barrington Letters*, 109.

[86] See e.g. Emmison, *Wills of Essex*, 152 and *passim*.

When the yeoman John Finch died in 1593, his widow hoped to perform his will concerning the younger children, but anticipated trouble. Her landlady promised to help, 'in case the eldest should be enticed by some advantage of law to forget the duty both of a son and a brother'.[87] Executors too sometimes discharged their responsibilities in a spirit of resentment or opportunistic greed. William Edmundson, who had lost both parents by the age of 8 recalled that he and his older siblings were treated harshly by the uncle who had raised them. The older ones left home as soon as they could, and later went to law 'about our portions, and other injuries and wrongs'.[88] Other tensions were rooted in resentment at a more successful sibling. Pepys found it amusing to hear how his cousin William Joyce, a well-to-do tradesman, was behaving 'like a prince' towards his struggling younger brother and sister-in-law. They found William's arrogance less entertaining.[89] Resentment was sometimes carried over from childhood, while fraternal solidarity might turn to rancour if a surety was forfeited or a loan was not repaid.[90] Other forms of misbehaviour could also create discord. Thomas Burbage was so disgusted by his brother William, a Leicestershire villager given to beating his wife with a rope, that when she sued for separation in 1589, he gave evidence in her support.[91] Hatreds could also suddenly burst into the open, sparked by some apparently trivial difference. In Kent, a husbandman turned on his brother as they were working together in the fields, and killed him with his spade. Two Londoners, who had spent a friendly afternoon drinking together, quarrelled over the bill and were soon locked in a fatal brawl. We will never know whether such tragedies reflected a sudden rush of blood, or had deeper roots now hidden from us.[92]

THE TIES OF BLOOD AND LOVE

This chapter has surveyed sibling relationships in a culture of reciprocal rights and responsibilities, a culture that was accepted almost universally in principle. In practice, as we have seen, relationships were frequently embittered by rivalries and resentments. But we should recognize too that in many families, at all social levels, close ties went far beyond the exchange of practical support, protection, and service. Many brothers valued their friendship for its own sake, for the emotional pleasure, satisfaction, and comfort it brought. One man, facing the gallows in

---

[87] Allen, *Letters of Lady Anne Bacon*, 160.

[88] *A Journal of the Life of William Edmundson* (1837), 5–6; cf. *SQSR*, i.283–4; W. J. Hardy and W. Le Hardy, ed., *Hertfordshire County Records* (Hertford, 1905–57), v.236; Cannon, *Chronicles*, ii.322–3; *OBOA*, t17080303a.

[89] Heywood, *Autobiography*, ii.248; Ratcliff and Johnson, eds, *Warwickshire County Records*, i.121, 126–7: Pepys, *Diary*, vii.398; x.211–12.

[90] *OBSP*, t16980504-11.

[91] LRRO, 1D 41/4/442; cf. Lawrence Stone, *Uncertain Unions. Marriage in England 1660–1753* (Oxford, 1992), 232–4.

[92] Cockburn, *Calendar, Kent, Elizabeth*, 257; *OBSP*, t16880711-9, *OBSP*, t17030426-40; J. A. Sharpe and J. R. Dickinson, 'Revisiting the "Violence We Have Lost": Homicide in Seventeenth-Century Cheshire', *English Historical Review*, 131 (2016), 305.

1693, spurned the comforting ministrations of a priest and asked instead for his brother to ride with him in the cart to Tyburn. Brothers shared a multitude of leisure activities, from drinking to sport, fishing, music, taking strolls, even performing in interludes.[93] Rings and other symbolic bequests hint at long-standing ties of affection, while many diaries and letters reveal close bonds among the middling sorts and above. In 1695, we find the Nonconformist minister Charles Nichols wailing to a friend, 'He is gone, he is gone, my dearest Joseph is gone, my darling brother, and so gone that I could not speak one word with him at parting.'[94] It was natural, of course, that siblings with similar views, interests, and personalities might well forge lasting ties. In the case of William Lawrence, a Berkshire gentleman, the bond is all the more striking given his crabbed personality. Financially hard-pressed into middle age, he was in no position to support his younger brother Isaac, who forged a mercantile career abroad. Yet the pair maintained a lifelong and intimate relationship through letters, each taking several months to arrive. When news came in 1679 that Isaac had died in Persia, William was devastated; 'my soul seemed deprived of all its organs,' he confided to his diary, 'for in him I saw the utmost limits of human goodness.' Isaac had been 'ten thousand times my dearest brother' and 'dearest friend'. Isaac had closed his last letter with a moving farewell from 'the very soul of your affectionate brother Isaac Lawrence, adieu, adieu my dearest friend'.[95]

Letters played an important role in sustaining elite and professional ties, and later those of the middling sort too.[96] Edward Bacon, learning French in Strasbourg in 1576–7, sent a stream of letters to his brother Nathaniel (and wrote to his sisters too). Richard Oxinden assured his brother in 1607 that he prized the 'mutual interchange of our letters, as the increase of our never changeable loves, the only means that absence affords to well affected minds to show their loving disposition'. A generation later, his nephew and namesake wrote in equally effusive terms to his own brother. But how much better, the younger Richard went on, if they could be together in person: 'Had I the Arabian gold or the Indian pearl it would not do me so much good as to enjoy your long desired and happy company.'[97] In the 1690s James Fleming sent his brother gossipy letters from Oxford about mutual friends, loose women, and gaming exploits, letters that were very different in tone from those addressed to his stern father.[98] These were all young, single men of very limited means. Gentlemen with substantial landed estates, by contrast, had the leisure and resources to sustain family ties through extended visits. Hospitality lay at the very heart of the elite lifestyle.[99]

---

[93] *OBOA,*161930616; James Stokes, ed., *Records of Early English Drama. Somerset* (Toronto, 1996), i.125, 144; Cannon, *Chronicles*, i.23; *OBSP*, t16911209-21.

[94] *Oxinden Letters 1642–1670*, 304.

[95] *The Diary of William Lawrence*, ed. G. E. Aylmer (Beaminster, 1961), 52–7, 59–61; Grassby, *Kinship and Capitalism*. 211–12.

[96] Susan E. Whyman, *The Pen and the People. English Letter Writers 1660–1800* (Oxford, 2009).

[97] Hassell Smith, *Papers of Nathaniel Bacon*, i.27–80; *Oxinden Letters, 1607–1642*, 5, 43–4.

[98] *Flemings in Oxford*, iii.217–21, 229–34.

[99] Heal and Holmes, *Gentry*, 282–9; Lawrence Stone, *The Crisis of the Aristocracy 1558–1641* (Oxford, 1965), 42–9.

Family visiting among the middling sort is less well documented. Though space, resources, and leisure were more limited, they were usually sufficient for occasional visits. The Newcomes provide one illuminating case from this milieu. As we have seen, a close bond existed between the brothers, who had grown up together following the early death of both parents. Three became ministers, with the others pursuing trades in London. As adults, the brothers initially appeared to be losing touch, and when Henry Newcome visited the old family home at Caldecote, Huntingdonshire, in 1649, he was surprised to find two of his older brothers now married. But the sibling ties revived after he returned to Cambridge in June 1651 to take his MA. He met his younger brother Richard, a student, and another brother, Thomas, came from London to celebrate the occasion. The trio then travelled to see their elder brother Robert at Caldecote, a reunion so enjoyable that Robert and Richard followed it in September with an unheralded visit to New-come in Cheshire. Delighted to see them, he rejoiced at the 'great love that was raised at our being together this summer'.[100] Many further reunions followed, and Newcome counted them among the high points of his life, ignoring criticism from his congregation about his lengthy absences. In 1660, he also took along his wife and two elder children, while Thomas and Stephen brought their wives from London. Newcome was away from home for six weeks in all. More visits were to follow over the next twenty years.[101] This was a close and enduring network, sustained by powerful bonds of affection. If middling-sort visiting was rarely so well documented, the Newcomes were far from unique. The ties between the Johnsons, mid-Tudor merchants, went far beyond their business arrangements, and they and their families enjoyed frequent social visits. The account book of the Sussex minister Giles Moore provides a later example of reunions for both business and pleasure, in this case including both brothers and sisters. Moore had a wealthy brother (Robert) on the Isle of Wight, and another brother (Francis, a husbandman) and two married sisters living in modest circumstances in Suffolk. Giles and Robert met on at least ten occasions between 1656 and 1670, in Sussex, the Isle of Wight, or London, usually spending several days together. Giles visited his three Suffolk siblings in 1664, and also met Francis both in Sussex and London.[102]

Some men in quite humble occupations also found the means to travel quite widely, to see brothers and other close kin. John Taylor the water poet, a Thames waterman, found the means to visit his brother in Germany in 1616, and the following year a Sussex musician was similarly able to visit a sibling in Middelburg. William Edmundson, a young soldier who left the parliamentary army in 1652, travelled from Derbyshire to visit his family in Westmorland before crossing to

---

[100] Newcome, *Autobiography*, i.16, 29–30, 33–4.

[101] Ibid., i.44, 59, 89–90, 121–5, 163–5, 178; ii.196–7. Ties with the London siblings weakened in later years, and after Robert's death in 1679, which deeply affected Newcome, reunions were more subdued: ii.226, 229, 239, 263, 268.

[102] Winchester, *Tudor Family Portrait*, 93–4, 109–10; *The Journal of Giles Moore 1656–1679*, ed. Ruth Bird, Sussex Record Society (1971), 279–83, 285, 292, 323, 343.

settle in Ireland. He visited them again the following year.[103] Leonard Wheatcroft, a Derbyshire tailor, gardener, and carpenter, provides us with an elaborate picture of family ties and visits extending over half a century. Wheatcroft visited London in the mid-1650s and tells us that a younger brother 'was no little glad to see me. Then did he leave all work and went along with me up and down London', to show him the sights.[104] Many years later, with his siblings and children now grown and scattered, Wheatcroft found numerous opportunities for more visits, and in his mid-sixties he embarked on an ambitious round of visits to all his surviving siblings. His children sometimes came home at Christmas to see him and one another, and again when he fell ill. His brothers, children, and other close kin took similar pleasure in family visits, and the pattern continued in the next generation. Some lived close enough for more frequent overnight visits, often timed to coincide with a local wake, or to celebrate a christening. Most of these gatherings, Wheatcroft makes clear, were simply for 'mirth and melody'.[105] Fairs, wakes, and markets provided many people with further opportunities for informal reunions, often imposing no burden beyond a drink in the alehouse.

Sibling relationships pervade the historical record, as well as the literature and drama of the period. The material surveyed in this chapter has revealed a patchwork of close bonds, bitter tensions, and contradictions. As John Taylor reminded his readers in 1642, 'brothers in one house do often jar and disagree, yet if one of them be injured by a stranger, the other will take his part'.[106] Fraternal solidarity, responsibility, and friendship were far more than empty ideals. It was the power of those ideals, the moral obligations they created, and the huge diversity of behaviour that honoured or betrayed them that made this a subject of such intense concern to contemporaries.

---

[103] John Taylor, *All the Workes* (1630), iii.86–7; HMC, 31, *Rye*, 151; *Journal of William Edmundson*, 9–11; cf. Basil Lubbock, ed., *Barlow's Journal of his Life at Sea* (1936), i.175–8.

[104] *The Courtship Narrative of Leonard Wheatcroft, Derbyshire Yeoman*, ed. Ralph Houlbrooke (Reading, 1986), 39.

[105] Wheatcroft, *Autobiography*, 83, 93–103; cf. *Oliver Heywood's Life of John Angier of Denton*, ed. Ernest Axon, Chetham Society, NS, 97 (1937), 58–9; Cannon, *Chronicles*, i.51, 90; Nott, *Deposition Books*, i.51.

[106] John Taylor, *An Humble Desired Union between Prerogative and Priviledge* (1642), 6.

4

Across the Gender Divide

BROTHERS AND THEIR SISTERS

The Gentry: Protection, Guidance, and Control

Parents educated daughters to equip them for marriage. A brother's influence would generally come to the fore, especially in the upper levels of society, when his father died. As heir, he would now be expected to arrange the education of his younger sisters, pay their annuities, and arrange suitable matches for those still single. Identifying potential husbands, negotiating terms, and raising portions could be a lengthy and complex process. And heirs sometimes had to take on such responsibilities even before inheriting, if the father was unable or unwilling to discharge them. Simonds D'Ewes was 19 when he helped negotiate an older sister's marriage settlement in 1621, smoothing over the objections their prickly father had raised. John Thomlinson, son of a Cumberland squire, stepped in because his father had done nothing to secure his sister's future.[1]

Sir Ralph Verney, who inherited his estate in 1642, was fairly typical in his interpretation of an heir's rights and responsibilities. He had already long supervised his sisters' lives, asserting his authority whenever they fell short of his expectations. He delivered a stern lecture to his teenaged sister Margaret in 1639 after hearing of her disrespectful behaviour towards her aunt. If the reports proved true, he warned, 'I know nothing bad enough for you'. When his 15-year-old sister Elizabeth jeopardized her reputation by flirting with a servant, he packed her off to boarding school, ignoring her threat to kill herself rather than endure such a dismal fate.[2] Like most landowners, Verney wanted to see his sisters well married, but the combination of civil war and inherited debts left him unable to raise the portions stipulated in his father's will. Throughout the 1640s, he struggled to protect his estate and clear it from debt while discharging his family responsibilities. The result was a series of negotiations, protracted and sometimes abortive, as Verney tried to marry off three unmarried sisters at minimum cost to his estate. All three did eventually marry, though less well than they had hoped or expected. One marriage failed, another proved unhappy, and Verney bore

---

[1] D'Ewes, *Autobiography*, i.175; 'The Diary of the Rev. John Thomlinson', ed. J. C. Hodgson, *Six North Country Diaries*, Surtees Society, 118 (1910), 109; cf. HMC, 23, *Cowper*, ii.283.

[2] Verney, *Memoirs*, i.290–1; Miriam Slater, *Family Life in the Seventeenth Century. The Verneys of Claydon House* (1984), 20, 79.

at least part of the blame. He took his responsibilities seriously, but always prioritized the interests of his estate.[3]

The problems facing the Verneys were common enough. If an heir had inherited debts along with the estate, as was often the case, he would have to borrow to pay a portion, or negotiate payment by instalments. William Heveningham needed £1,000 for his sister's marriage portion in 1629, and turned to his cousin for a loan.[4] An heir expected to arrange his sister's marriage, and would take offence if she married without his consent. Women who took such a step generally hoped to be allowed back into the fold, not least because they would otherwise find it hard to secure their portion or annuities. And if those moneys never materialized, the marriage would almost certainly suffer.[5] Frances Gifford was only a stepsister of Sir Hugh Smyth, and considerably older, but she was desperate to assuage his fury after matching one of her daughters in 1612 without seeking his approval. Pleading there had been no opportunity, she begged to be judged a 'careful mother', not a 'froward sister'. She needed his help to provide her daughter's portion, which made obsequious deference her only option.[6]

Over the period, women gradually gained more freedom to reject suitors they disliked. That was very different, of course, from freedom to choose. Moreover, brothers (like fathers) still insisted on their right to block any match they considered unsuitable. Sir John Reresby was determined to break a liaison between his sister Elizabeth, still single at 40, and an Irish soldier of fortune. He threatened to cut off her allowance, and challenged the Irishman to a duel. When Elizabeth contrived to marry her Irishman nonetheless, Reresby was outraged by her defiance, which had damaged the family's honour and dignity. Reresby felt a genuine sense of responsibility towards his siblings, but insisted on his right to supervise their lives. He was the family's head, and of its interests he alone was judge.[7]

Most women in this sphere accepted that it was proper and desirable for the head of the family to identify prospective suitors and negotiate a good marriage settlement. They knew that to secure his help, and the payment of annuities and portions, they would need to maintain his goodwill. If he chose to ignore his responsibilities, they could only plead, cajole, and complain. In desperation, they might perhaps broadcast his failings, to shame him in public. Penelope Verney was furious in 1645 when Sir Ralph's niggardliness wrecked a promising marriage negotiation, and warned him bluntly that 'you must look to be censured by the world to be the most unkind and unnatural brother'.[8] But such tactics carried obvious dangers. Few women would risk destroying the relationship on which they depended.

---

[3] Slater, *Family Life*, chaps 2 and 4.

[4] HMC, 11, *Gawdy*, 174. Seth Ward, as a young Oxford academic, borrowed £200 at interest to provide a dowry for his sister: Walter Pope, *The Life of Seth, Lord Bishop of Salisbury* (1697), 5.

[5] See e.g. HMC, 13, *Capt. Stewart*, 109.

[6] J. H. Bettey, ed., *Calendar of the Correspondence of the Smyth Family of Ashton Court 1548–1642*, Bristol Record Society, 35 (1982), 52.

[7] *Memoirs of Sir John Reresby*, ed. Andrew Browning (2nd edition, ed. Mary Geiter and W. A. Speck, 1991), 151, 195–7.

[8] Slater, *Family Life*, 39.

Responsible gentlemen accepted that a duty of care and support continued beyond a sister's marriage. As head of the lineage, an heir would still keep a protective eye on her welfare, just as he looked out for his brothers' interests.[9] Such care found expression in a multitude of ways. Lettice Kynnersley, struggling to cope with a feckless husband and domineering parents-in-law, depended heavily on the support of her brothers as well as kind neighbours. Lady Rebecca Paston, lonely in Norfolk in 1681 with her husband away in London, was hugely grateful for her brother's thoughtful attentions, 'his company and his coach everywhere'.[10] Brothers also felt bound to defend a sister's honour, both before and after marriage. A frustrated gentleman in one of Aphra Behn's comedies complains that a woman will forever be 'raving on her honour; then if she have a kinsman, or a brother, I must be challenged'. Edmund Verney challenged his brother-in-law to a duel, for deserting his sister. Sir Calisthenes Brook also faced a challenge after repudiating a woman he had got with child and promised to marry. He was seriously wounded by her brother, prompting a contemporary to observe that her injury had been 'justly revenged'.[11] Fraternal support might often continue beyond the grave, with brothers taking in a sister's orphaned children or intervening to protect their interests. After his sister Anne died in 1640, Sir Thomas Peyton repeatedly pressed her husband, Henry Oxinden, to settle an annuity on her son and a lump sum on each daughter, which would swell to a decent portion by the time they were of age to marry. 'I must not doubt of a denial,' he thundered. Peyton knew that his brother-in-law would probably remarry, and feared the estate might be diverted away from his sister's children. He maintained a watching brief on their behalf for the rest of his life. When Peyton himself was widowed and decided to remarry, he promised his father-in-law that he would always treasure the memory of his late wife and protect the interests of their children.[12]

Many men faced another responsibility: providing for those sisters unable or unwilling to marry. With the inflation of dowries, many families found themselves unable to arrange marriages for all their daughters, leaving many dependent on the hospitality of friends and relations. Others had to seek menial employment as a gentlewoman-companion, though one declared that she would 'rather serve hogs'.[13] Daughters who had remained at home might find shelter with a brother, or other close kin. The Jacobean diplomat Dudley Carleton took both his wife and his 'wisest and best esteemed sister' Alice with him when he was sent as ambassador

---

[9] Rosemary O'Day, *The Family and Family Relationships, 1500–1900* (Basingstoke, 1994), 71–4.

[10] Keith Wrightson, 'Mutualities and Obligations: Changing Social Relationships in Early Modern England', *Proceedings of the British Academy*, 139 (2006), 172; Jean Agnew, ed., *The Whirlpool of Misadventures. Letters of Robert Paston, First Earl of Yarmouth 1663–1679*, Norfolk Record Society, 76 (2013), 78–9.

[11] *The Younger Brother*, III.i, in *The Works of Aphra Behn*, ed. Janet Todd, 7 vols (1992–6), vii.391; Slater, *Family Life*, 98–9; I. H. Jeayes, ed., *Letters of Philip Gawdy of Harling, Norfolk* (1906), 103. But one Yorkshire gentlewoman, crossed in love, demanded personal satisfaction from her female rival, and fought a fatal duel: Wood, *Life and Times*, ii.32.

[12] *Oxinden Letters 1607–1642*, 179–80; *Oxinden Letters 1642–1670*, 186–7; BL, Add. MS 28003, f. 163; Add. MS 44846, fos. 43, 55. His father-in-law was Sir Peter Osborne, Dorothy's father.

[13] Susan E. Whyman, *Sociability and Power in Late-Stuart England. The Cultural Worlds of the Verneys 1660–1720* (Oxford, 1999), 128; Slater, *Family Life*, 84–90.

to Venice in 1612.[14] The Blundells, a Catholic family financially stretched, could find husbands for few of their girls, and while most became nuns, others remained at home with their brother William.[15] For many years Sir John Reresby's household included both his sister and his wife's sister, Honora Brown, also unmarried. Honora left in 1678 after a disagreement, and her fate underlined the vulnerability of such women. After drifting between other relations, she moved to London where she fell in with a fortune hunter, who promised marriage and then abandoned her after stripping her of her money. She died alone, miserable and desperately poor.[16]

Marriage offered security but could never guarantee it. A distressed wife would often turn to her birth family for support, and an embattled widow might seek protection against her husband's hostile or indifferent kin.[17] A widow might similarly turn to her brother for advice and assistance on remarriage. Nathaniel Bacon provided his sister with such help in 1577, 'wherein', their elderly father remarked approvingly, 'you do like a good brother'.[18] Widows often reverted to the fold of their birth family, and those in straitened circumstances might indeed become dependent on them once more. Sir Ralph Verney accepted some responsibility for several of his widowed sisters, as well as for his brother's abandoned wife. They all begged repeatedly for his support, and Cary, twice widowed, addressed him gratefully as a 'father as well as a brother'. He felt himself entitled to judge each request on its merits, and impose whatever conditions he saw fit. So when Cary ran up debts at the gaming table, he agreed to help only if she would renounce gaming and reduce her household expenses, demands she bitterly resented. But she and her sisters knew they depended on him, to pay their bills and maintain their genteel status.[19]

Middling Sorts, Ordinary Families, and the Poor

As we saw earlier, the gentry's sense of rights and responsibilities was often shared by the professional and mercantile classes. An elder brother would generally take the lead in seeking to support, guide, and govern his sisters. In ordinary families, any male sibling might feel it his right and duty to act, if he had the means to do so.

At almost every level of society, brothers helped to identify suitable marriage partners for their sisters, and facilitate courtships. When Hannah Newton, a yeoman's widow, was approached about a possible match with a local clergyman, she replied that 'she would be advised by her brother'. He then handled the

[14] *The Letters of John Chamberlain*, ed. N. E. McClure (Philadelphia, 1939), i.141, 417–19; *The Autobiography of Sir John Bramston*, ed. Lord Braybrooke, Camden Society, OS, 18 (1845), 380–2; *Flemings in Oxford*, iii.52, 156, 331, 335.

[15] Margaret Blundell, ed., *Cavalier. Letters between William Blundell and his Friends 1620–1698* (1933), *passim*.

[16] Reresby, *Memoirs*, 54, 151, 195–7.

[17] See e.g. O'Day, *Family*, 71–4; Slater, *Family Life*, 96–100; James Daybell, *Women Letter-Writers in Tudor England* (Oxford, 2006), 182–3.

[18] A. Hassell Smith et al., eds, *The Papers of Nathaniel Bacon of Stiffkey*, 5 vols, Norfolk Record Society (1979–2010), i.270; cf. HMC, 23, *Cowper*, i.202.

[19] O'Day, *Family*, 75; Whyman, *Sociability and Power*, 24–5; Verney, *Memoirs*, iv.273–8.

negotiations, though it was Hannah who dictated some of the terms.[20] Should a courtship fail, a brother might intervene to limit the damage. In 1579–80 Anne Tuttofte, orphaned daughter of a decayed family in Norfolk, was living in service in the household of a local yeoman, and a marriage was mooted with his son. But when the young man appeared grasping and his mother sneered at Anne's 'beggarly' family, she backed away and appealed to her brother for help and advice. He rose to the occasion. If she wanted to leave or was driven out, he wrote, he would willingly fetch her home; she was welcome to live with him, and if she was short of money, 'so long as I have you shall not want it'.[21] As among the gentry, brothers also felt entitled to block matches they considered unsuitable. Hester Pinney's two younger brothers combined with their father, a silk merchant, in heaping pressure on her to abandon matches they judged inappropriate. She resented their interference, but it proved effective. Ralph Josselin, a yeoman's son, felt similarly entitled, and was proud of preventing a marriage between his older sister Anne and a widower. His father had already cast her off but Ralph, only 16 at the time, succeeded in thwarting the marriage and then reconciling father and daughter. Throughout his life, Josselin felt it his right to supervise his sisters' affairs. He was furious, many years later, when Anne remarried after ten years as a widow, apparently without consulting him. She 'hath utterly undone herself and her children', he fumed.[22]

Protecting or avenging a sister's honour was another responsibility recognized throughout society. Extramarital sexual relations were sometimes tolerated when marriage appeared likely to follow, but kin would often intervene if it failed to materialize. If gossip had already compromised a woman's reputation, the best way to restore her good name and secure her future was to pressure the man into marrying her. Thus at Berwick in the 1560s, Agnes Neid's brother stepped in over rumours that she was living in sin with her lodger, a soldier in the garrison. He pressed the man to marry her, and threatened to have him court-martialled if he refused. Buckling under this pressure, the soldier complied—even though, as it transpired later, he already had a wife.[23] Richard Wolfe, a Cheshire villager, similarly intervened to protect his half-sister Margaret, whose lover was planning to marry another woman. When the banns were published in church, Wolfe

[20] Richard S. Westfall, *The Life of Isaac Newton* (Cambridge, 1993), 6–7; David Cressy, *Birth, Marriage and Death* (Oxford, 1997), chaps 10–11; Diana O'Hara, *Courtship and Constraint. Rethinking the Making of Marriage in Tudor England* (Manchester, 2000), chap. 3. For examples, see Amy Froide, *Never Married. Singlewomen in Early Modern England* (Oxford, 2005), 61; *The Courtship Narrative of Leonard Wheatcroft, Derbyshire Yeoman*, ed. Ralph Houlbrooke (Reading, 1986), 72–3; *The Diary of Adam Martindale*, ed. Richard Parkinson, Chetham Society, 4 (1845), 16–17; *The Diary of Roger Lowe*, ed. W. L. Sachse (1938), 72; J. J. Bagley, ed., *The Great Diurnall of Nicholas Blundell of Little Crosby, Lancashire, 1702–1728*, 3 vols, Record Society of Lancashire and Cheshire (1968–72), ii.71, 73.

[21] Hassell Smith, *Papers of Nathaniel Bacon*, ii.120–1, 124–5.

[22] Geoffrey F. Nuttall, ed., *Letters of John Pinney 1679–1693* (1939), 41–2, 104–8; Pamela Sharpe, *Population and Society in an East Devon Parish. Reproducing Colyton 1540–1840* (Exeter, 2002), 275–6; Josselin, *Diary*, 4, 425; cf. Lawrence Stone, *Uncertain Unions. Marriage in England 1660–1753* (Oxford, 1992), 80–2.

[23] James Raine, ed., *Depositions and other Ecclesiastical Proceedings from the Courts of Durham*, Surtees Society, 21 (1845), 254–7.

interrupted to object that Margaret was with child by the intended bridegroom, and that he had already pledged to marry her.[24]

Informal pressure often succeeded in making the faithless partner offer either marriage or a financial settlement. When Elizabeth Haddon of Banbury became pregnant by Robert Toms in 1634, her brother met with two of Toms's brothers on market day to negotiate a complex deal. Toms agreed to pay £4 10s to another man, who had been persuaded by Elizabeth's mistress (and cousin) to marry her and take on the child. Such intervention would relieve the woman in distress, and limit the damage to her family's good name. The latter concern was very evident in a Somerset case, where the woman had died during the course of her pregnancy, so that marriage and maintenance were no longer at issue. The local minister and several parishioners told magistrates there was no longer any need for the father to appear before them, adding that he had already 'satisfied her brothers and friends', that is, had paid compensation for the injury to the family's honour. They clearly accepted the brothers' right to demand satisfaction, and their responsibility to uphold the family's good name.[25]

Kin were also ready to use the law to apply pressure. In one case, where the father had been destitute when the mother gave birth, her brother learned that he had now found employment and urged magistrates to make him contribute henceforth to the child's keep. The family of Martha Beevor, a servant in North Yorkshire, proved still more determined. In 1690, Martha revealed that she was pregnant by her master, and her brother Joseph promptly launched a suit against him. Her parents and sisters testified against the alleged father, John Kay, stressing his shady sexual reputation, and Joseph secured the support of many other kin, friends, and neighbours. They insisted that Kay had promised to marry Martha or maintain her child. Martha bolstered her position by consulting a physician, who confirmed the pregnancy, and notifying two local justices. Kay denied some of the allegations, though far from all, and retaliated with a flood of counter-suits for defamation. Martha eventually turned out not to be pregnant after all, which makes this a very murky episode. The suit may have been a genuine attempt to salvage her lost honour or, as Kay claimed, a cynical plot to capitalize on his bad reputation. Whatever the truth, her brother had waged a determined campaign on her behalf.[26] Other men resorted to violence to defend family honour. When Elizabeth Dent was spurned by the man to whom she had long been betrothed, her brother vowed to stab him at the first opportunity. In Somerset, even a Quaker proved ready to beat a man for calling his sister a whore. She joined in the fray.[27]

Marriage was not always an option, of course. The father might already be married, or a penniless servant. When pregnant servants were turned away by their

[24] J. E. H. Bennett and J. C. Dewhurst, eds, *Quarter Sessions Records for the County Palatine of Chester 1559–1760*, Record Society of Lancashire and Cheshire, 94 (1940), 163–4.

[25] R. K. Gilkes, ed., *The 'Bawdy Court' of Banbury. The Act Book of the Peculiar Court of Banbury 1625–1638*, Banbury Historical Society, 26 (1997), 169–71; SQSR, i.5.

[26] J. W. Willis Bund, ed., *Worcestershire County Records: Calendar of the Quarter Sessions Records, 1591–1643* (Worcester, 1900), 309; BI, CP, H4315.

[27] Stone, *Uncertain Unions*, 210; Cannon, *Chronicles*, i.153.

employers, or fled, their most urgent need was to find a refuge. In some cases, the father or his male kin arranged temporary accommodation some distance away, where she could give birth privately and, with luck, escape punishment and avoid damaging their own good name. In other cases, women found refuge with compassionate parents or siblings. In 1628, one Leicestershire villager took in his sister Ann Heyford, arranged a midwife and nurse, stood godfather at the child's christening, and then spirited her away to spare her the shame of public penance. His sister escaped trouble; he did not.[28]

In ordinary families, as among the gentry, brothers often proved ready to assist and support their married sisters as well as those still single. In 1649, Jane Huett, a young Southampton bride, gave her brother £10 for safekeeping, a financial cushion should she ever be in want.[29] Brothers might provide protection if a marriage ran into difficulties, remonstrating with an abusive husband, or sheltering a sister who had fled or been abandoned. They could help and protect widows too.[30] Very often, the most immediate need was for financial assistance, if bad luck or a husband's incompetence had reduced the family to destitution. Ralph Thoresby, a Leeds merchant, came to his sister's rescue when her second husband ran up heavy debts and fled to escape arrest. Despite feeling little sympathy for the couple, who had always lived above their means, he took charge of his pregnant sister and her children, and borrowed money to pay off the debts.[31] Other men, some of very modest status, provided similar help. Elizabeth Collyns, labelled 'impotent' and 'foolish', had been abandoned by her husband, probably because of some mental incapacity, but had found shelter with her brother. In 1626, Anne Acton of Coleshill, similarly deserted and destitute, found refuge with her brother Thomas Slatford in Oxfordshire. Though of modest means, Slatford made her his housekeeper, promised to maintain one of her children, and made provision for the other. It was a striking example of sibling bonds operating over both distance and time. Suspicious overseers viewed Anne as a vagrant, but after examining the case magistrates gave the arrangement their full approval.[32]

Hard times and illness pushed many other families to the edge, placing demands on their close kin. Two of Ralph Josselin's sisters found themselves in dire circumstances in 1647, a period of harvest failure and chronic hardship, and both turned to him for relief. Josselin always tried to assist. When his sister Dorothy

[28] LRRO, ID 41/4, Box 7/131–2; cf. BI, CP H4587; LMA, MS 9064/16, fos. 109, 149v; Dave Postles, 'Surviving Lone Motherhood in Early-Modern England', *The Seventeenth Century*, 21 (2017); Patricia Crawford, *Blood, Bodies and Families in Early Modern England* (Harlow, 2004), 220; Froide, *Never Married*, 61.

[29] Sheila D. Thomson, ed., *The Book of Examinations and Depositions before the Mayor and Justices of Southampton 1648–1663*, Southampton Record Society, 37 (1994), 11.

[30] Joanne Bailey, *Marriage and Marriage Breakdown in England, 1660–1800* (Cambridge, 2003), 33 and n., 41; Amy Harris, *Siblinghood and Social Relations in Georgian England* (Manchester, 2012), 63.

[31] Joseph Hunter, ed., *The Diary of Ralph Thoresby FRS*, 2 vols (1830), i.185, 322–4.

[32] Thomas Kemp, ed., *The Book of John Fisher, Town Clerk and Deputy-Recorder of Warwick 1580–1588* (Warwick [,1945]), 171; S. C. Ratcliff and H. C. Johnson, eds, *Warwickshire County Records*, 9 vols (Warwick, 1935–64), i.25, 32; cf. 16; Steve Hindle, *On the Parish? The Micro-Politics of Poor Relief in Rural England c.1550–1750* (Oxford, 2004), 320.

visited with her husband, his diary records, 'we gave them such old things as we could anyways spare, I paid her 20s for her legacy, and I lent her 20s more'. Dorothy often returned and usually left with gifts in cash or kind, including some of his wife's spare clothes.[33] Josselin also took in her young son Tom, and kept him until he was old enough to be bound apprentice.[34] His sister Anne received similar support, especially after her husband's death in 1649. Josselin promised an annuity of 20s to help cover her rent, canvassed friends for further help, and rode over to deliver the additional largesse: £3 to trade with, 20s to buy wood for winter fuel, and 4s for her children.[35] And Josselin's sense of responsibility was by no means exceptional.[36] Female wills, generally made only by widows and single women, suggest the importance of brothers in women's lives. Widows generally named their adult children as executors, but childless women often turned to their siblings. A sample of wills by childless women in Suffolk in the early 1630s reveals twenty-seven naming brothers (or occasionally brothers-in-law), almost as many as the thirty-three women who chose executors from all other categories of kin and non-kin combined. One woman named one brother as executor and another as supervisor.[37]

Perhaps the greatest service kin could provide was to take in an orphaned child, a practice found throughout society. In Somerset, one Quaker came to the aid of his widowed sister, who was struggling to support five children on a smallholding, by taking in two of them. If both parents had died, such support became even more crucial. The merchant Samuel Jeake of Rye responded heroically when his widowed sister Anne died in 1666, by taking in her five youngest children to raise himself.[38] Quite often, we find arrangements of this kind anticipated in wills. Thus Alice Pressen, an Essex widow, asked her brother (and executor) to take in her daughter Grace, along with her stock, keep her to the age of 18, and 'use her well and well apparelled'.[39]

Marriage, as we have seen, was not the destiny of all women. In the later seventeenth century roughly 20 per cent never married, whether through circumstance or occasionally choice. Here too, brothers might accept a responsibility to help. Mary Braye, a crippled young woman in Elizabethan Sussex, was living with her elder brother when she died in 1568 after an accidental fall.[40] But even the

---

[33] Josselin, *Diary*, 106, 287, 382–3, 471, 593–4. On the late 1640s, see Steve Hindle, 'Dearth and the English Revolution: the Harvest Crisis of 1647-50', *Economic History Review*, 61 (2008), 64–98.

[34] Josselin, *Diary*, 217, 286, 349.

[35] Josselin, *Diary*, 105, 171, 173, 176, 181–2, 201, 269, 344, 370.

[36] See e.g. Nuttall, *Letters of John Pinney*, 67.

[37] Nesta Evans, ed., *Wills of the Archdeaconry of Sudbury 1630–1635*, Suffolk Records Society, 29 (1987), 362–3 and *passim*. A few women also named sisters, sometimes to act alongside brothers. Three women who had remarried named their husbands.

[38] Joseph Besse, *Sufferings of the Quakers* (1753), i.593–4; Michael Hunter and Annabel Gregory, eds, *An Astrological Diary of the Seventeenth Century. Samuel Jeake of Rye 1652–1699* (Oxford, 1988), 90 and n. Cf. *The Autobiography of William Stout of Lancaster 1665–1752*, ed. J. D. Marshall (Manchester, 1967), 73; D. E. Howell James, ed., *Norfolk Quarter Sessions Order Book 1650–1657*, Norfolk Record Society, 26 (1955) 74; Crawford, *Blood, Bodies*, 221–2.

[39] F. G. Emmison, ed., *Wills of the County of Essex (England). Volume 1, 1558–1565* (Washington, D.C., 1982), 180; cf. 32, 190.

[40] R. F. Hunnisett, ed., *Sussex Coroners' Inquests 1558–1603* (Kew, 1996), 11.

middling sort could rarely afford to maintain unmarried sisters on a permanent basis, and few women enjoyed annuities sufficient to cover their board. The poor generally had to choose between an ill-paid life in service and earning their own keep. A few occupations provided a reasonable livelihood, such as West Country lacemaking in the seventeenth century.[41] Most others, such as knitting, millinery, charring, nursing, spinning, and laundering, offered only a precarious living.

One option for middling-sort families, especially in London, was to set up an unmarried daughter with a shop. The Batelier family, wine merchants, set up their daughter Mary with a draper's shop in the Exchange, and similar arrangements can be found in the provinces.[42] A more common option was to take in a sister as a lodger or servant. One household in Stoke-on-Trent in 1701 contained both the husband's older sister and the wife's younger sister.[43] Samuel Pepys, who took in his sister as a servant, resolved to treat her like any other servant, but others adopted a kinder approach. When Josselin's sister Mary arrived in August 1644 to be his servant, he vowed that 'my respect is and shall be towards her as a sister'. Before long he had found her a better position with a local gentleman, his neighbour and patron, where he knew she would be well treated.[44] As the two cases suggest, sibling relationships in such circumstances varied widely. A young woman living with an easy-going brother might indeed enjoy a degree of freedom that few employers would have tolerated. Joan Bridges, who lived in Rochester with her brother, a baker, and sold his bread at market, stayed out late, drinking with her friends and ignoring all attempts to restrain her.[45]

Another option, in households headed by a bachelor or widower, was to install a sister as housekeeper. Such arrangements occur throughout the period, and often worked well. Alison Chambers managed her brother's house in County Durham in the 1580s 'as the housewife, till he was married', buying and selling goods at market for him. They clearly enjoyed a close bond, for she stayed on after he married, and when she died, she left him all her belongings.[46] William Stout of Lancaster and his sister enjoyed a similarly harmonious arrangement, and so did his neighbour Robert Mayor, a joiner and cooper. Only when his sister eventually left to marry did Mayor decide to marry too, at the age of 50.[47] And at the very end of our period, James Fretwell, a Yorkshire joiner and lifelong bachelor, took in his younger sister Mary as housekeeper in 1726, an arrangement that lasted for seven years. He was dismayed when she eventually left to marry, bringing their

[41] Sharpe, *Population and Society*, 92–117.

[42] Pepys, *Diary*, vi.73 and n., 170–1, 174, 334; Sharpe, *Population and Society*, 98–101; Norman Penney, *Record of the Sufferings of the Quakers in Cornwall 1655–1686* (1928), 33, 78–9, 139; Froide, *Never Married*, 48.

[43] D. A. Gatley et al., eds, 'The Stoke-upon-Trent Parish Listing, 1701', *Collections for a History of Staffordshire*, Staffordshire Record Society, 4th series, 16 (1994), 206; cf. K. J Allison, ed., 'An Elizabethan Village Census', *Bulletin of the Institute of Historical Research*, 36 (1963), 99, 100; Crawford, *Blood, Bodies*, 219; Eleanor Hubbard, *City Women. Money, Sex and the Social Order in Early Modern London* (Oxford, 2012), 71; cf. 46.

[44] Pepys, *Diary*, i.288, 290–1; Josselin, *Diary*,15, 39.

[45] *A Strange and Wonderfull Relation of the Burying Alive of Joan Bridges of Rochester* (1646), 2–3.

[46] Raine, *Depositions*, 328–30. [47] Stout, *Autobiography*, 153; and Chapter 8.

partnership to an end. Similar arrangements with other close kin generally worked less well, for the blood tie was weaker and the age gap usually wider. Fretwell later took in a young niece, not yet 18 commenting that her mother was 'weary of her at home, for she is of a very disagreeable temper'. Her mother had begged him 'to see what I could do with her', and the experiment predictably failed.[48] Even when these arrangements worked well, of course, a sister lacked the legal protection of a wife and always remained dependent on her brother's goodwill. Joan Whittle kept house for her brother at Eldersfield (Worcestershire) for over forty years, but in 1618, he turned her out to beg. Now that she had grown old and weak, he was unwilling or perhaps unable to support her. The parish officers, equally cold-hearted, labelled her a vagrant and attempted to drive her away.[49]

Poorer families who took in an unmarried sister would expect her to pay her way, for example by spinning and knitting. A survey of the poor in Norwich in 1570 revealed several such women doing whatever they could to earn their keep. Agnes Ysborne, living with her older brother, his wife, and their four children, 'doth work in the house', probably spinning and helping with housework and childcare. Another young woman, whose brother was out of work, had found casual employment but also worked as 'a harlot'.[50] A poor woman lodging with her brother in Elizabethan Warwick had been reduced to begging.[51] Even children taken in, usually as orphans, were expected to make some contribution. The Norwich surveyors recorded the case of Thomas Aleyne and his wife, who had taken in a sister's child aged 9 'that knit and is diseased'. Though sick, she still had to help pay her way.[52] An alternative solution was to have a destitute child bound as a pauper apprentice, a form of semi-servitude that would at least provide food, clothes, and shelter. But such arrangements often proved highly problematic. The Yorkshire yeoman Adam Eyre chronicled the miserable story of his apprentice Jane Goodyer, a truculent, dirty, and desperately unhappy girl, and the fruitless efforts of her brother to retrieve the situation.[53] At Lydd (Sussex), the overseers paid John Skiptone to keep his sister Joan as a servant, an arrangement that also broke down. Skiptone drove her out, penniless, to become a vagrant.[54]

---

[48] 'Family History begun by James Fretwell', ed. Charles Jackson, *Yorkshire Diaries of the Seventeenth and Eighteenth Centuries*, Surtees Society, 65 (1875), 204, 212–13, 242–3; cf. ibid. 237–8; Fiona McCall, *Baal's Priests. The Loyalist Clergy and the English Revolution* (Farnham, 2013), 211; Hunter, *Diary of Ralph Thoresby*, i.45–6. John Fell, Restoration bishop of Oxford, invited his widowed sister to manage his household: Wood, *Life and Times*, iii.81.

[49] Willis Bund, ed., *Worcestershire County Records*, 267–8.

[50] J. F. Pound, ed., *The Norwich Census of the Poor, 1570*, Norfolk Record Society, 40 (1971), 63; cf. 41.

[51] Kemp, *Book of John Fisher*, 166.   [52] Pound, *Norwich Census*, 60.

[53] 'A Dyurnall, or Catalogue . . . by Adam Eyre', ed. H. J. Morehouse, *Yorkshire Diaries*, 55, 58, 60, 64–8, 71; cf. Pepys, *Diary*, iv.282–4. On pauper apprenticeship see Hindle, *On the Parish?*, 191–226.

[54] HMC, 31, *Rye*, 151.

SISTERS AND THEIR BROTHERS

Dependency, Affection, and Agency

Girls were brought up to accept the gender hierarchy as natural, and to subordinate their own interests to those of their elder brothers and the lineal family. Even so, many chafed at their situation, especially when brothers failed to provide annuities or portions, quarrelled over inheritance, or pushed them into an unwanted marriage. Gertrude Savile's diary records enduring bitterness at her total dependence on a brother she saw as a cold tyrant. Their father, a clergyman, had died in 1701 when she was still a small child, and about the same time the accidents of inheritance had elevated her brother George to a baronetcy and a fortune. He was eighteen years older, which made their relationship more like that of parent and child. As she grew older, Gertrude came to loathe her dependency. 'I am the most abject slave', she confided to her diary, 'and must not speak or think.' She was 'treated like a hanger on upon the family', and openly scorned by the servants. Her brother eventually agreed to give her a modest annual allowance, which enabled her to live elsewhere, but the diary continued to reflect deep unhappiness at 'the damping mortifications' of her situation.[55]

By contrast, many other young women repeatedly professed their loving devotion to an elder brother. We should remember, of course, their need to retain his goodwill, something they would never have forgotten. In 1704, we find Elizabeth Coke thanking her brother Thomas for his kindness to her and her sister, 'especially these last few happy years we have lived together', and pledging their readiness to 'dispose of ourselves as formerly whenever you please'.[56] Their gratitude may well have been genuine, but they knew that their welfare depended on his continuing favour. As with younger brothers, sisters' self-effacement was the product of their situation, and could easily evaporate if circumstances changed. In the case of Anne and Vere Cook, a correspondent observed tartly in 1625 that they 'are become so much the prouder since they were the heirs; for their brother is very lately dead of a burning fever, and the land falls between them'.[57] Sisterly professions of love might also contain a competitive element. Sir Ralph Verney's sisters pledged their love and devotion while attempting to undermine one another by reporting their siblings' bad behaviour and disrespectful remarks. (His younger brothers did much the same.)[58] In the case of Elizabeth and Judith Isham, the sisters undoubtedly loved their brother Justinian. They fashioned gifts, talked about him endlessly when he was travelling abroad, and prayed for his speedy and safe return. They never married, and their father offered to set up a trust fund to save them having to depend on Justinian's goodwill in later life. Elizabeth declared that she saw no need,

---

[55] Alan Savile, ed., *Secret Comment. The Diaries of Gertrude Savile 1721–1757*, Thoroton Society, 41 (1997), 1–2, 4–5, 14–16, 150.

[56] HMC, 23, *Cowper*, iii.164.

[57] Lord Braybrooke, ed., *The Private Correspondence of Jane Lady Cornwallis 1613–1644* (1842), 131–2.

[58] Slater, *Family Life*, 40–5.

having total confidence in her brother's kindness. Her casual aside, that Judith felt differently, hints at an unacknowledged rivalry for his affection.[59]

It would be quite wrong, of course, to dismiss sisterly affection as merely instrumental. Some scholars have argued that affectionate ties between brothers and sisters developed only in a much later period, from the later eighteenth century.[60] But there is plentiful evidence to suggest otherwise. Though power and property structures certainly influenced emotional relationships, material dependency was by no means the only factor. We can find strong emotional ties between brothers and sisters, and in many situations dependency was not an issue. Ralph Thoresby's visit to his sister in Durham in May 1680, six months after their father's death, was a highly charged reunion for them both. She wept when they parted, and Ralph confided to his diary that 'my too violent affections were so strong, that I think I slept not an hour all night'.[61] Moreover, as material considerations played a significant role in most elite matches, it was natural for a woman's sense of identity to remain closely linked to the family of her birth. She might well feel stronger ties to her siblings than to her new spouse, at least during the early years. Many women were certainly eager to maintain contact with the brothers and sisters who had long been at the centre of their lives.[62] Francis Bussy told his brother-in-law, John Coke, in 1614 that his wife was pining for family news. If Coke came up to Derbyshire without paying them a visit, he added, 'she saith it will half kill her'.[63] Blood ties retained an even more powerful hold over Constance Fowler, a young Staffordshire gentlewoman, who maintained a passionate correspondence with her brother Herbert Aston when he was living in Madrid in the 1630s. Her letters reveal her emotional dependency, notwithstanding her recent marriage. Yet Herbert was only a younger son, with nothing material to offer. She asked, indeed, only for his verses and letters, and reassurances that he returned her love. 'Do you love me dearly,' she asked, 'pray let me know. I can never hear it too often.' 'I can go nowhere, but I miss you,' she told him, 'and to miss you so often, and never to find you, is worse than a continual death to me.' In one letter she signed herself, 'Your ever most affectionate sister, and oh I am your most true lover'. Constance never mentioned her new husband and did not use his surname, signing merely as Constance F, or C. F. She declared that Herbert was 'the comfort of my life', and 'my heart is ever with you'.[64] Her passionate nature was a quality that ran in the family, and few other writers displayed quite such intensity. But intimate letters between brothers and sisters were far from rare. Thomas Meautys, a professional soldier serving abroad in the early 1600s, exchanged numerous loving letters with his

---

[59] Isham, 'Rememberance', f.28.

[60] Christopher H. Johnson and David Warren Sabean, eds, *Sibling Relations and the Transformations of European Kinship 1300–1900* (New York, 2011), 2–6, 9–15.

[61] Hunter, *Diary of Thoresby*, i.44.

[62] J. H. Bettey, ed., *Calendar of the Correspondence of the Smyth Family of Ashton Court 1548–1642*, Bristol Record Society, 35 (1982), 80–1, 86, 88, 104, 115; O'Day, *Family*, 77.

[63] HMC, 23, *Cowper*, i.84.

[64] *Tixall Letters; or the Correspondence of the Aston Family and their Friends during the Seventeenth Century*, ed. Arthur Clifford (1815), i.85–126; cf. Laura Gowing, 'The Politics of Women's Friendship in Early Modern England', in *Love, Friendship and Faith in Early Modern Europe, 1300–1800*, ed. Laura Gowing, Michael Hunter, and Miri Rubin (Basingstoke, 2005), 140–2.

sister Jane over many years. When her letters eventually dwindled in the early 1620s, he told her reproachfully that he had spent a day rereading a hundred she had formerly written, as maid, wife, and widow. She had been 'a sister whose love and affection in those days was not to be equalised'.[65]

Sibling bonds were about practical as well as emotional support, and in a male-dominated society brothers were generally far better placed to provide it. Even so, help often flowed in both directions. We need, initially, to distinguish between the potential *value* of a sister to her brothers and kin, and the *agency* she might employ on their behalf. Through marriage, sisters were the means by which families built new alliances at many levels of society, with the dowry cementing that new alliance. The 'sister-wife' played an important role in early modern kinship throughout Europe.[66] Moreover, with office and advancement heavily dependent on patronage, elite women played an active part in what has been called 'the politics of intimacy'. Women at court, whether single or married, sought to advance their family's interests, some operating with skill and assurance. Bridget Carre, a gentlewoman at the Elizabethan court, felt sufficiently confident to send a brisk note to the Earl of Rutland in 1587, reminding him of his promise to appoint her brother to a local office.[67] A 'sister-wife' might persuade an influential brother to help her husband, or persuade an influential husband to help her brother. Mary Fulwood was behaving quite conventionally in 1601 when she begged her brother John Coke, a rising figure in the king's service, to assist her husband with a difficult lawsuit.[68] Other women provided support in different forms, such as sheltering brothers in the aftermath of the civil war. One royalist officer, who eventually escaped abroad, wrote from Brussels in 1649 to thank his sister Susan 'for her care and pains with me in my extremity'.[69] Major Thomas Hunt, a royalist condemned for treason after Penruddock's rising in 1655, owed his life to his sisters Elizabeth and Margery. One evening they visited him in prison, bringing some women's clothes. Hunt then walked out of the gaol dressed as a woman, with Margery, while Elizabeth lay that night in his prison bed and was not discovered till morning. Both women were arrested; their brother escaped. Lucy Hutchinson was able to help both her brother and her husband. After the war, her royalist brother, Sir Allen Apsley, found a refuge with Lucy and her parliamentarian husband. After the Restoration, with the situation reversed, her husband was facing execution as a regicide. Apsley now intervened on his behalf, 'with all the kindest zeal of friendship that can be imagined', Lucy recalled, 'as if it had been his own life'. Her husband escaped

[65] Braybrooke, *Correspondence of Cornwallis*, 79–80; cf. HMC, 23, *Cowper*, ii.361–3, 365–71; BL, Add MS 70231 (letters of Abigail Harley, unbound).

[66] This is a major theme in Johnson and Sabean, *Sibling Relations*.

[67] Natalie Mears, *Queenship and Political Discourse in the Elizabethan Realm* (Cambridge, 2005), chap. 2. HMC, 24, *Rutland*, i.226.

[68] HMC, 23, *Cowper*, i.29–30.

[69] HMC, 39, *Eliot Hodgkin*, 115; Thomas Birch, ed., *A Collection of the State Papers of John Thurloe* (1742), iii.453; cf. John Loftis, ed., *The Memoirs of Anne, Lady Halkett and Ann, Lady Fanshawe* (Oxford, 1979), 30.

the scaffold. Lucy's determination to protect both brother and husband was pivotal in shaping the behaviour of these political enemies.[70]

Within the family itself, sisters' agency more often took the form of conciliation, smoothing over rifts between brothers, or between a brother and father. In one such case Thomas Denne, a Kent gentleman and lawyer, had disowned his son (another Thomas) in 1643, and went to law vowing to ruin him. Fleeing abroad, the younger Thomas wrote despairingly to his twin sister, Thomasine, begging her to assuage the malice of their father and another brother.[71] Similarly, when Thomas Ellwood converted to Quakerism, his sisters did their best to soften their father's fury.[72]

Sisters might thus play a significant role in their brothers' lives. Some families also recognized that a sister close to her brother could be an effective instrument in promoting a courtship, by influencing him or the woman he was pursuing. Constance Fowler, cited above, proved a valuable ally in this regard. At her brother's request, she cultivated a close friendship with the woman he hoped one day to marry, and did all she could to foster a romance between them. Elizabeth Coke, also cited above, earned her brother's gratitude in a different way. Thomas, Vice-Chamberlain at court, was a widower and when attending on the monarch needed Elizabeth to care for his children and supervise his house in Derbyshire.[73] Abigail Harley provided similar help for her brother Robert, an MP also often away in London, sometimes with his wife. Abigail cared for their children at his Herefordshire home, and dealt with excise officials, tenants, and a host of other estate matters, even the construction of a new pigsty. On one occasion, she had to deliver his wife's baby, which arrived unexpectedly with no midwife on hand. Abigail had to cope with the children's emotional needs too, allaying their disappointment when their parents' return home yet again failed to materialize. In one letter, she added poignantly that the children sent their regards to their mother, 'whom they take great delight to talk of'. In many respects, Abigail was both proxy wife and mother.[74]

Help was especially valuable in very large families or where the wife was sickly, categories that often overlapped. Whether as resident or visitor, a sister could care for the children and if necessary take over household management. Gervase Disney, one of nine siblings and crippled in childhood by rickets, remembered how much he had owed to his widowed aunt. She had been 'both nurse and instructor', he recalled, for 'my mother having children thickly, and nursing us all herself, was rendered less capable'.[75] William Blundell's sisters played a similar role in raising his children and then grandchildren. In his later years, one of his daughters, financially

---

[70] Hutchinson, *Memoirs*, 170, 200–1, 230–3, 256.

[71] *Oxinden Letters 1642–1670*, 61–3. Cf. Isham, 'Rememberance', f.34v; see Chapter 10 (Thornton).

[72] *The History of the Life of Thomas Ellwood*, ed. G. C. Crump (1900), 40–1, 50.

[73] *Tixall Letters*, ed. Clifford, i.97–101, 107–26; HMC, 23, *Cowper*, iii.164–9; *Barrington Family Letters 1628–1632*, ed., Arthur Searle, Camden Society, 4th series, 26 (1983), 92.

[74] BL, Add. MS 70231, *passim*.

[75] *Some Remarkable Passages in the Holy Life and Death of Gervase Disney, Esq* (1692), 28–9; Froide, *Never Married*, 76–7.

stretched, sent her own sons to board with him, and it was his sister Frances who looked after them. She had been 'more than a mother' to one grandson, he recalled, and had 'made herself his nurse, his servant, his mistress, *his mother indeed.* Her money and pains and patience have been freely extended to him and in his behalf.' Frances lived with Blundell for most of their lives. Though he once grumbled at her readiness to list his faults, he added that she had 'been one of the best spokes in the wheel on which our fortunes have turned'. Far from being a burden or passive dependant, Frances was an integral and valued member of the family.[76]

Less predictably, perhaps, we also find some sisters able to provide financial support. A spinster might employ her assigned portion as security to raise a loan for a sibling in need. Edmund Bramston, younger son of a younger son, borrowed and spent his sisters' portions, money that may never have been repaid.[77] The younger sons of Sir Daniel Fleming, a Westmorland squire, were grateful for small contributions from older sisters (both single and married) when they left for Oxford.[78] Ralph Tyrer, vicar of Kendal (d.1627) had a different reason to be grateful, and his epitaph carried the striking refrain,

> London bred me, Westmorland fed me,
> Cambridge sped me, my sister wed me.

Rather than confessing to an incestuous marriage, Tyrer was acknowledging her key role in facilitating his marriage. William Blundell, heavily fined and sequestered as a Catholic and cavalier, had still more reason for gratitude. In 1654, his debts amounted to over £1,100, and he acknowledged that £520 of that sum was owed to his sisters. The huge debt, moral as well as financial, greatly strengthened their position within the household.[79]

For some elite women, a good marriage brought new opportunities to assist their kin. In the case of Susan Verney, it promised to transform the sibling relationship. While single, she had been wholly dependent on her brother Ralph. When she married, her husband gave her an impressively large sum to cover all her household and personal expenses for his entire lifetime, and she told Ralph that she would have £600 at her disposal to put out on loan. In the event, he was unwilling to borrow from a sister who had hitherto depended on him.[80] Others were less proud. Thomas Meautys was genuinely very fond of his sister Jane, but conscious too that as a wealthy widow she enjoyed a far superior financial position. Meautys never rose above the rank of captain, and his pay was often in arrears. So in 1625, wishing now to marry, he turned to Jane and another wealthy sister for financial support, to enable him to promise a jointure for his prospective bride. Several years later, we find him begging for a loan until his pay arrived, and Jane generously supporting two of his young children.[81] At the end of the century, Charles Allestree, vicar of

---

[76] Blundell, *Cavalier Letters*, 151–2, 283–7.   [77] Bramston, *Autobiography*, 21.

[78] *Flemings in Oxford*, iii.53, 114, 126, 156, 250; cf. *Oxinden Letters, 1607–1642*, 48.

[79] Joseph Nicholson and Richard Burn, *The History and Antiquities of the Counties of Westmorland and Cumberland* (1777), i.76; Blundell, *Cavalier Letters*, 40.

[80] Slater, *Family Life*, 104.

[81] *The Private Correspondence of Jane Lady Cornwallis, 1613–1644* (1842), 114–17, 180–2, 214–15.

Daventry, similarly benefited from the generosity of his sister Mary, who had married well. She sent him a stream of gifts in cash and kind, sometimes sent anonymously to spare his blushes. He found it embarrassing to be 'always receiving, and never repaying', but accepted the gifts with grace and gratitude. The siblings enjoyed a long and affectionate bond.[82]

Support for brothers took many other forms. Some women proved adept marriage brokers.[83] Alice Carleton sent her brother a medical recipe, while in 1608 her sister Elizabeth busied herself finding suitable lodgings for him in Westminster. Other women could offer hospitality themselves. In the early 1570s, for example, Nathaniel Bacon and his teenage wife were short of funds, and lived initially with his younger sister Elizabeth, who was married to a successful lawyer. When Bacon's wife was expecting their first child, it was accepted that she would lie in at the house of one of his sisters. The only issue was whose invitation to accept, and how to avoid offending the other.[84] A generation later, we find Lady Elizabeth Masham taking in an impoverished brother recovering from a broken leg.[85] In Westmorland John Kirkby, a lifelong bachelor, found a home for over thirty years with his widowed sister Alice. They were famously devoted to one another, and Alice did not long survive his death in 1680. She was buried next to her brother, not her husband.[86] In the case of families plunged into turmoil by the wife's premature death, a sister might also come to the rescue of her bereft brother. John Bramston broke up his household after his wife died in 1648, and found a refuge for himself, his son, and his youngest daughters with a married sister. The arrangement lasted several years. Elizabeth Isham, a spinster who managed her father's household, raised two small daughters of her brother Justinian, after his wife died in childbed.[87]

When gentry families took in a nephew or niece, such initiatives were as likely to come from a sister as a brother. A benevolent aunt might wish to relieve hard-pressed parents, or simply improve the accomplishments and opportunities of a favoured niece. Elizabeth Mostyn found a good match for her young niece Elizabeth Whitelocke, and the women remained friends for many years.[88] Childless wives and wealthy widows were particularly willing to provide such help. In the 1630s, we find Henry Cromwell begging his sister, the matriarch Lady Joan Barrington, to take in an orphaned niece. 'She is your brother's daughter,' he pleaded, 'it will be a deed of extraordinary charity, and I doubt not but God will repay you double.' Lady Joan's household already included another niece, as well as

---

[82] 'Letterbook of Charles Allestree', BL Add. MS 27440, fos. 34v–35v, 58-v.

[83] *The Diary of Bulstrode Whitelocke 1605–1675*, ed. Ruth Spalding (Oxford, 1990), 289; cf. HMC, 11, *Gawdy*, 147.

[84] *The Letters of John Chamberlain*, ed. N. E. McClure (Philadelphia, 1939), i.157, 275; Hassell Smith, *Papers of Nathaniel Bacon*, i.18–20, 23–4, 61, 64–5.

[85] *Barrington Letters*, 19–20, 117, 143.   [86] *Flemings in Oxford*, i.538–9.

[87] *The Autobiography of Alice Thornton*, ed. Charles Jackson, Surtees Society, 62 (1873), 39; Bramston, *Autobiography*, 107–8; Isham, 'Diary', 30–6; Ilana Ben-Amos, *The Culture of Giving. Informal Support and Gift Exchange in Early Modern England* (Cambridge, 2008), 50–1.

[88] Whitelocke, *Diary*, 247, 289; Bramston, *Autobiography*, 112; Isham, 'Rememberance', fos. 20v–21; Slater, *Family Life*, 46, 86, 88; Verney, *Memoirs*, i.167, 288–91.

two grandchildren.[89] Other women provided short-term help, for example when parents had to be away in London. In 1643 Thomas Knyvett, an imprisoned royalist, needed a home for his younger daughter so that his wife could devote all her time to lobbying for his release. He hoped his sister would oblige but was not sure she would agree, and asked his brother to take soundings. 'If she refuses,' he added, 'farewell all relation.'[90] It was a revealing choice of words. Though Knyvett felt she had a moral obligation to help, he accepted that the decision was hers alone. It was a not uncommon situation, and the effusive gratitude of some powerful men when such requests were granted shows that they recognized their dependence.[91] The plot of Shakespeare's *Measure for Measure* turns, of course, on a related issue of dependence, in very different circumstances: will the pure Isabella be prepared to sacrifice her virginity to save the life of her condemned brother, Claudio, as he begs? His desperate request is 'in probation of a sisterhood', but the decision is hers alone—and she refuses.[92]

Elite women were sometimes able to provide help in the political sphere too, and not only through patronage. Lady Grace Pierrepoint could promise in 1701 that all her tenants and family would be voting for her brother in a forthcoming election.[93] Sir Ralph Verney's sister Cary fed him political news and gossip, and when his son John returned from overseas and inherited the estate, she was able to guide him on the protocols of genteel behaviour. When John decided to enter politics, she played a significant role in his election campaigns, having better connections and some-times better information. Though the Verney women struggled financially, they could provide valuable services.[94] A well-connected sister could prove a still greater asset for public figures obliged to live far away from London's wheeling and dealing. General Cutts, as commander-in-chief of the English forces in Ireland, found himself in such an exposed situation in 1705, and asked his sister Joanna to keep him supplied with regular information on all the 'state intrigues, party designs, and . . . secret or cabinet news' in the capital. He trusted her to couch the informa-tion in suitably discreet language, and was confident that being single she would have no rival loyalties.[95]

Female Agency in Ordinary Families

These examples of sisterly support, drawn from the gentry, found numerous parallels in ordinary families. Perhaps the most striking is the story of Hester Pinney, a single woman in her twenties, who in 1685 contrived to save her young brother Azariah from the gallows after his involvement in Monmouth's rebellion. A pardon was out of the question but Hester, acting alone, was able to

---

[89] *Barrington Letters*, 126.
[90] Thornton, *Autobiography*, 5; *The Knyvett Letters (1620–1644)*, ed. Bertram Schofield, Norfolk Record Society, 20 (1949), 114.
[91] See Chapter 12.   [92] Shakespeare, *Measure for Measure*, quotation at V.i.72.
[93] HMC, 23, *Cowper*, iii.439–40; cf. BL, MS Egerton 2717, f.191.
[94] Whyman, *Sociability and Power*, 24, 96–9, 108, 162–5, 170–3.
[95] HMC, 52, *Frankland-Russell-Astley*, 93–4, 187, 194–5, 198.

raise the money and identify the right officials to bribe to have her brother transported instead, and as a free man, to Nevis. He 'owes his life to you, my dear daughter', their father John wrote in stunned relief. As a Nonconformist minister, he knew that any appeal he made for mercy would have been doomed to failure. Not only did Hester succeed: probably only she could have succeeded.[96]

Generally, of course, help took far less dramatic forms. As among the gentry, some women took in a nephew or niece. Edward Terrill, later a prominent Baptist, was taken in by his aunt at the age of 4 after losing his father. In rural Somerset, Oliver Sansom's father sent him at the age of 7 to board with his sister for three years, so he could attend a school close by.[97] Other women were able to steer work towards a brother, or join him in business or professional arrangements. The Lancashire widow Ann Greinsworth ran a business in association with a brother in London, hiring a scribe to pen business letters and prepare her accounts. In the 1690s, Humphrey and Rebecca Morris ran two linked schools in a Somerset village, his for older boys, hers for girls and younger boys.[98] Moreover, women keeping house for a bachelor or widowed brother were not necessarily the subordinate partners in such arrangements. When Lucy Shephard's brother summoned her to join his household, his need appears to have been far greater than hers; she was her mistress's favourite maid, and he had to make several requests, and resort to threats, before she consented.[99] A census at Stoke-on-Trent in 1701 identified Elizabeth Boulton, 24, as head of the household, with her brother Joseph, 22, listed as merely resident. Joseph was possibly physically or mentally incapacitated in some way, but whatever the circumstances Elizabeth was clearly in charge. Similarly, when John Hardy, a Leicestershire maltster aged 45, deposed that he lived with his sister and helped manage her public house, he was evidently a lodger, not heading the household.[100]

Even in very ordinary families, we can sometimes also find women providing brothers with financial help at critical points in their lives. We have seen Ralph Josselin supporting his sisters, but earlier, as a new graduate, he had lacked the resources to take up his first appointment. An older sister came to his rescue: by purchasing most of his scanty possessions, she was able to furnish him with sufficient money to cover the journey. A generation later, Ellen Stout lent her younger brother £10 at the end of his apprenticeship to help him set up in trade. It was many years before he repaid it.[101] Wills reveal loans that single women and widows had made to their brothers, as well as to other kin and outsiders. Such debts were often cancelled by the will, though one Suffolk widow preferred to reassign

[96] Nuttall, *Letters of John Pinney*, 27, 28–30; Sharpe, *Population and Society*, 99–100.
[97] Edward Bean Underhill, ed., *The Records of the Church of Christ meeting at Broadmead, Bristol, 1640–1687* (1847), 58–9; *An Account of Many Remarkable Passages in the Life of Oliver Sansom* (1710), 2.
[98] *The Diary and Letter Book of the Rev. Thomas Brockbank 1671–1709*, ed. Richard Trappes-Lomas, Chetham Society, NS, 89 (1930), 308, 315, 319; Lowe, *Diary*, 46, 62, 76, 86–7; Cannon, *Chronicles*, i.23, 27; cf. Sharpe, *Population and Society*, 100.
[99] Slater, *Family Life*, 112–13, 115–16.
[100] Gatley, 'Stoke-upon-Trent Parish Listing', 198; LRRO, 1D 41/4, Box 53/155.
[101] Josselin, *Diary*, 5–6; Stout, *Autobiography*, 89.

them to her brothers' children.[102] Other women played more traditional female roles as petitioners and mediators, sometimes trying to rescue brothers from troubles they had brought upon themselves. They might, for example, plead on behalf of a brother behind with his rent, or try to prevent a youngster going off the rails.[103] It is striking that employers sometimes recognized, indeed, that a sister might be the only person able to reform a delinquent male servant. Thus Gertrude Savile, exasperated by her young footman Abraham, sent for his sister, who pleaded on his behalf and had stern words with him in private. Abraham then apologized for his behaviour and Gertrude decided to forgive him, though she admitted that he had 'said little more than she [his sister] put into his mouth'. 'It was wholly upon her account I keep him,' she added. A similar scenario unfolded the following year over another feckless and drunken servant. Again, Gertrude thought that only his sister, also a London servant, might be able to reclaim him, and sent to her 'to put a stop to the course of ruin he was got into'.[104] Older women might intervene more forcefully to save a delinquent brother from himself. One striking instance emerges from what seems initially a typical defamation suit. It was triggered in 1692 when Martha Hardcastle, a Halifax wife, railed at a neighbour as 'the greatest whore in town', but takes on a different complexion when we discover that Martha's outburst was triggered by concern over a younger sibling. She complained bitterly that 'her brother Jonny could not be kept at home night nor day for going to whore with her'. She had been trying to save a wayward younger brother from his own folly.[105]

In rare cases, we can find women ready to elevate the sibling bond above every other consideration and loyalty. In 1602, for example, a Norfolk woman chose to help her brother at the expense of her own husband. Learning that her brother had got her maidservant with child, she pressed the maid to father it instead on her husband, to shield her brother from prosecution and shame. It was presumably a less than loving marriage.[106] A few women took solidarity still further, to literally murderous extremes. In one horrendous case, in 1671, Margaret Dine joined with her brothers in a barbarous assault on a maidservant in Enfield, who had rejected the advances of Robert Dine, a fellow servant. Robert resolved to kill the maid in revenge, and the three siblings devised a gruesome plot disguised as a burglary. One night, with his employers asleep, he let the other two into the house. His brother pinned down the victim while Margaret stabbed her in the face, gouged out an eye, slashed her nose, slit her tongue, and left her for dead. Robert was then tied up and left with some bruises to make his burglary story more plausible. But the maid recovered sufficiently to reveal what had happened, and the three siblings were hanged together at Tyburn for what was declared 'a crime unprecedented'. In another murder case, the sister's criminal solidarity appears, by contrast, to have

---

[102] Evans, *Wills of Sudbury*, 103, 160–1, 255; cf. Emmison, *Wills of Essex*, 221.
[103] *Great Diurnall of Nicholas Blundell*, ed. Bagley, i.166, 170; Cannon, *Chronicles*, ii.348; cf. Chapter 2, nn. 93–4.
[104] Savile, *Secret Comment*, 56–8, 116.   [105] BI, CP H4299.
[106] Hassell Smith, *Papers of Nathaniel Bacon*, iv.294–5.

been merely instinctive. Henry Jones of Monmouth had stabbed his mother for her money, and his young sister Mary then helped cover up the crime by washing his blood-stained clothes by night. She had apparently known nothing of his design, but was burned at the stake as an accessory after the crime. Her fate aroused some pity even in the pamphleteer reporting the case.[107]

In each of those extraordinary cases, the women had played an active role as their brothers' instruments or accessories. Very occasionally, however, we find that relationship reversed, with sisters recruiting brothers as instruments to advance their own sometimes nefarious agendas. One such case involved the Cheshire widow Isabel Hall, deeply implicated in a murder plot. One of her close friends, unhappily married, had a lover who was eager to be rid of the unwanted husband, and Hall suggested helpfully that her brother George would be willing to murder him for £5. George agreed and took the money, though he then failed to deliver. Isabel thereupon supplied some poisoned oatcakes, which proved more effective. The pamphlet account focused on her depravity, but equally striking is her confidence that she could recruit her brother as her agent.[108] Perhaps more suggestive is a case in the 1620s, from within the landed elites. Lettice Willoughby, the daughter of a Nottinghamshire baronet, felt pestered by an unwelcome suitor and decided that only drastic action would drive him away. So she asked her brother Henry to arrange for this 'base Jack' (actually a knight's son) to be beaten up. 'I would not have you foul your fingers with so dishonourable a man as he is', she added, explaining that in London he would find plenty of ruffians readily available for hire. She promised to reimburse his expenses, and stipulated that the victim was to be made aware who was behind the assault, to ensure her message was understood.[109] Brothers were, of course, expected to protect their sisters' honour and welfare. But as this incident reminds us, it might sometimes be the sister who decided when action was required, who was to provide it, and what form it should take.

[107] *OBOA*, 16770504; *The Bloody Murtherer, or the Unnatural Son his Just Condemnation* (1672), 11–12, 57–9.
[108] Gilbert Dugdale, *A True Relation of the Practices of Elizabeth Dugdale* (1604), sig. A4v-B.
[109] Cassandra, Duchess of Chandos, *The Continuation of the Willoughby Family*, ed. A. C. Wood (Eton, Windsor, 1958), 62.

5

The Sisters' World

Relationships between sisters differed in several important ways from those between their brothers. Common law stipulated an equal partition of land among daughters if there was no son to inherit, unless a will or settlement provided otherwise. Many women at all levels of society, both single or married, enjoyed close emotional ties with their sisters, ties more equal than those with or between their brothers. But we inevitably also find tensions and jealousies, triggered by clashing personalities, parental favouritism, or material grievances. Any woman given a smaller marriage portion than her sister was almost certain to harbour resentment.

AGE AND SENIORITY

While primogeniture was not an issue, the eldest daughter enjoyed a superior status that reflected her seniority and might sometimes find expression in material terms. Sir William Paston (d.1610) stipulated that, if he had daughters, the eldest at 18 was to receive £1,500 and her sisters £1,000 each. It was also considered appropriate for the eldest to marry first. Three of Sir Daniel Fleming's four daughters married, in order of age, and their traditionalist father provided them with descending portions of £1,000, £600, and £500 respectively.[1] The convention that the eldest should marry first helps drive the plot of Shakespeare's *The Taming of the Shrew*: Bianca's marriage cannot proceed until her father has found a husband for her truculent elder sister, Katherina.[2] A century later Sir John Verney's Aunt Gardiner voiced strong disapproval when one of his younger daughters married first, writing testily that 'It must not be so done in our country'. Elizabeth Freke felt the same way. The eldest daughter of a Wiltshire gentleman, Elizabeth found a partner before her three younger sisters, but her wedding was delayed for several years. She was mortified to find herself eventually the last, not first, to be married.[3]

Seniority also brought responsibility towards younger siblings, especially sisters. When Sir Edmund Verney and his wife stayed at their London home in the 1630s, for example, some of their children had to be left behind on his estate in

[1] Ruth Hughey, ed., *The Correspondence of Lady Katherine Paston 1603–1627*, Norfolk Record Society, 14 (1941), 137–8; *Flemings in Oxford*, ii.387–8.

[2] *The Taming of the Shrew*, I.i.

[3] Susan E. Whyman, *Sociability and Power in Late-Stuart England* (Oxford, 1999), 130; *The Remembrances of Elizabeth Freke, 1671–1714*, ed. Raymond A. Anselment, Camden Society, 5th series, 18 (2001), 37–8.

Buckinghamshire. Susan, the eldest daughter, was placed in charge of both house and children.[4] John Turner, a York lawyer, entrusted his daughter Theophila to take her younger sister and brothers to London in 1667, and settle them in school at Putney.[5] Sir Thomas Wentworth thought that when the elder of his two sisters married, it would be more appropriate for the younger to live with her rather than remain with him and his wife, or their widowed mother.[6] If a mother died, the eldest daughter might have to take on total responsibility for supervising her younger siblings and managing the household.[7] Older sisters would help raise younger siblings as a matter of course, and such relationships might easily take on a quasi-maternal flavour. Thomas Gwin and his wife left their daughter Anne in charge of her sick younger sister when they left on a journey in 1713, and testified later that she had tended her 'as if she had been her own child'. The flavour of such relationships sometimes survived into adulthood. Elizabeth Isham, devastated by the death of her younger sister, recalled 'that care and pity which I had of her as if she had been my child'. Her sister had always suffered chronic ill health, and years of tending her had no doubt reinforced Elizabeth's quasi-maternal feelings. More surprisingly, Elizabeth harboured rather similar feelings towards her brother, despite acknowledging his privileged status as heir and his intellectual superiority. 'I had in myself being eldest a motherly affection towards him', she wrote, even though the age gap was small.[8]

Occasionally we can trace the course of the relationship between sisters as they evolved over a lifetime. The autobiography of Anne Murray (later Lady Halkett) provides one such opportunity. In 1644, aged 21, Anne formed an inappropriate romantic liaison that her widowed mother ordered her to abandon. Anne begged her older sister Elizabeth to intercede, and when that failed, persuaded her to connive at a secret farewell tryst between the young lovers.[9] Anne was spirited and headstrong, and a few years later she became involved in a dangerous design to free Prince James (the future James II) from the Tower, a plot hatched by the adventurer Colonel Joseph Bampfield. Her sister and brother were deeply concerned for her safety, and equally alarmed by the liaison she struck up with the colonel. When Bampfield promised her marriage, they sent letters, 'his very severe, hers more compassionate', warning that he was a scoundrel already married. Anne preferred to believe his claim that his wife was dead.[10] That proved false, and she was left for several years in a fraught situation; she ran up substantial debts, unable to secure her inheritance after her mother's death, and her siblings remained vexed. When a more respectable suitor eventually appeared, Anne had to reveal her financial predicament. Her brother still refused to settle her debts, and it was her sister Elizabeth who came to the rescue. She and her husband, Sir Henry Newton,

---

[4] Verney, *Memoirs*, i.167; see also Chapter 3.   [5] Pepys, *Diary*, viii.210.
[6] J. P. Cooper, ed., *Wentworth Papers 1597–1628*, Camden Society, 4th series, 12 (1973), 55.
[7] See Chapter 2.
[8] Thomas Gwin, *A Memorial of Anne Gwin* (1715), 5–6; Isham, 'Diary', fos. 27v, 31.
[9] *The Memoirs of Anne, Lady Halkett and Ann, Lady Fanshawe*, ed. John Loftis (Oxford, 1979), 13–15.
[10] Ibid., 23–5, 32–4, 67.

took Anne to live with them at Charlton. She also accompanied Anne to plead with their brother, and together they managed to repair the family breach, at least in part. Though the debts remained, Newton generously lent his sister-in-law £300, no doubt prompted by his wife. Anne's very private wedding, in 1656, took place at her sister's home.[11] Anne's adventures naturally dominate her narrative, but it is clear how much she owed to the friendship and support of her elder sister.

The autobiography of Elizabeth Freke, which survives in two versions and extends over forty years, provides a far more comprehensive picture of relationships between older and younger sisters. It is remarkably frank on both the material and emotional dimensions. Freke married her cousin Percy in 1672, with their only son born a year later. The marriage proved deeply unhappy. Percy neglected his wife, abandoning her for months at a time, and left her desperately short of money. She was to have an equally unhappy relationship with her son, and dubbed him 'the undutifullest of sons to me'.[12] Freke often emerges from her narratives as bitter, self-pitying, and sour—qualities that were perhaps both cause and consequence of her unhappy situation. After the death of her father, whom she had loved dearly, her deepest relationships were with her sisters and their daughters. The early death of her sister Cecilia, and of Cecilia's daughter shortly afterwards, came as grievous blows. When her husband moved to Ireland in 1684, leaving her almost penniless, Freke became almost wholly dependent on the practical and emotional support of her two surviving sisters, Frances ('dear Sister Norton') and Judith ('dear Sister Austen'), and their husbands. Both sisters rose to the occasion. Over the next decade and more, Freke would often stay with one or other for weeks at a time, in London or the country, and they made their coaches available for her visits. Freke acknowledged that Frances had looked after her and her young son for several months in 1685 'with all the kindness and friendship imaginable'. Judith travelled to Freke's cottage at West Bilney, Norfolk, in 1687 to bring her back to London for another lengthy visit, and said that her husband would happily allow Freke to take up credit in his name while her own husband was absent.[13] In 1697, Freke finally gained possession of the manor house at Bilney, which she had claimed for twenty years, though with little money to furnish it. Again, both sisters came to her aid. Judith kept her company for several months in the half-empty house, and both sisters donated furniture and furnishings—a tea table, stools, cushions, china and delftware, a tortoiseshell cabinet, and family portraits. Some of these items they had crafted themselves, which imbued the gifts with still more emotional value.[14] Over the following years both sisters paid lengthy visits to Bilney, as Freke's deteriorating health repeatedly confined her to her chamber or bed. Judith, she recalled, had stayed for several months in the winter of 1698–9, 'for which I am ever thankful'. And when Frances arrived for another visit in May 1703, 'the very sight of my dear

[11] Ibid., 77–8, 80–5.
[12] Freke, *Remembrances*, 157. For overviews of Freke's unhappy life see Anselment's Introduction and Margaret George, *Women in the First Capitalist Society* (Brighton, 1988), chap. 10.
[13] Freke, *Remembrances*, 224, 226.   [14] Ibid., 70–2, 165, 169, 171–3, 179, 181–3, 188, 236.

sister revived and restored me again'. Frances took her back to London and then on to Bath, to revive her health and spirits.[15]

Given Freke's difficult personality, however, relations between the sisters were predictably often less harmonious. She found it mortifying to live without the comfort and security that her younger sisters both enjoyed. She felt ashamed in 1687 even to let them see her 'poor thatched house' at Bilney. And when Judith explained her husband's offer on credit, Freke brushed it aside. 'I thank God I had learned the way of shifting better than borrowing', she commented frostily, 'and ever esteemed it more honourable to unhappy me.'[16] The hurt pride and pain are palpable. The relationship between the two sisters was to change dramatically, however, after Robert Austen's sudden death in 1696. While his widow had a reasonable jointure, their elder son inherited debts of £3,000 to burden the estate, and Austen had left nothing at all to his younger son or two daughters.[17] Judith was now financially strained, while paradoxically Freke was finally coming to enjoy prosperity. She had at last secured properties that had long been rightfully hers, supplemented later by her jointure after her own husband's death in 1706. To her credit, now that she was a woman of substance, Freke displayed the same generosity her sisters had shown. She gave Austen's two bereft daughters 'all I were mistress of in the world, viz. 100*l* apiece', and the following year provided another £100 to have the younger son bound apprentice in Cork. Judith had generously placed all her jointure in her elder son's hands, to provide marriage portions for his sisters, renting for herself a little house in London. Freke furnished its best room, and gave her £200 for subsistence. Further substantial gifts followed over the years, including a coach ('second hand', but hardly used), and a New Year's gift of £100 in 1708. And when her brother-in-law, Sir George Norton, also found himself in financial straits, she lent him £1,300.[18]

These were generous gifts, but Freke made it clear that she expected favours in return. Always lonely at Bilney, her desire for company became a pressing need as failing health made it essential to have a sister or niece to manage the house. She was often unable to leave her room for long periods, and was distressed to find that several of her servants had conspired to prey on her weakness. Freke felt neglected whenever she was left alone.[19] Though Judith stayed for over six months in 1710, Freke was still bitterly resentful when she chose to return to London and take lodgings for the winter, and accused her sister of base ingratitude. She calculated that over the course of thirty years she had given or lent the Austens £1,732, and yet 'my sister would not bear my melancholy one winter. May God forgive her'.[20] Freke spent some time in London in 1711, and brought Judith's daughter Betty home with her early in December for company and assistance. It was Betty who entertained the tenants to dinner on New Year's Day ('my unhappy birthday'), with Freke again confined to her bed. Judith missed her daughter, however, and asked for her to be sent back home by Candlemas (2 February). Freke was furious at the request. 'And this is the sister that has had all the industry of my life',

[15] Ibid., 77, 237, 242.   [16] Ibid., 56, 226.   [17] Ibid., 66, 233.
[18] Ibid., 95, 267–8, 276.   [19] Ibid., 239, 271–2.   [20] Ibid., 266–8; cf. 239.

she fumed. It took three requests before Betty was finally allowed to leave. Freke thought her sister unreasonable, for 'she had another daughter with her, and I alone'. Surely she could 'have spared this [one] awhile to me, Elizabeth Freke; for I had deserved it and more of her that have been to her more like a mother from her childhood'.[21] In the later years of the narrative, it is Freke's other sibling, Frances Norton, who is her 'dearest sister'.[22]

Even in her affluent final years, Freke thus remained dependent on her sisters for both emotional and practical support. It was a situation she detested. Though gratified when Frances came to visit in May 1703, leaving her husband in London, she wrote with bleak, self-deprecating humour that she had come merely 'out of her pity and charity to do penance with me'.[23] Alone, frail, and acutely aware of her vulnerability in a household she could no longer oversee, Freke became increasingly bitter. And that bitterness triggered cruelty in actions as well as words. When she discovered that two maidservants had been thieving from her, in 1712, she persuaded magistrates to have them flogged, and to have the sentence carried out on her own premises. With grim satisfaction, she watched from her window as the two maids were whipped 'at the cart's tail . . . till the blood spun, for example sake'.[24]

Elizabeth Freke does not make an attractive subject, and she must have been a very difficult sibling. Nonetheless, despite her sharp tongue, her sisters gave her the practical and emotional support without which she could hardly have survived. She in turn gave generous help to her sister Judith, and nieces and nephew, when they were similarly in need. Freke never found the affection she longed for from her husband or child. She loved her young grandchildren but saw little of them. Her favourite, John, died at the age of only 4 in a shooting accident she blamed on her daughter-in-law's neglect. She vowed never to see her again.[25] Freke's emotional life came to focus on her sisters and their daughters, to whom she transferred the maternal feelings her son had repeatedly spurned. Towards her niece Betty Austen she said she had always felt 'like a mother', and her niece Grace Norton 'I loved as my own life and would have spared mine to have saved hers'. She was distraught when Grace made a secret marriage, and devastated when she succumbed to a fever only a few months later.[26]

Despite their difficult relationships, Freke and her sisters shared an enduring bond, and a powerful sense of mutual responsibility. Freke speaks kindly of her brothers-in-law, but they remain shadowy and marginal figures. The sisters' own ties were never relationships of equals. As the eldest, Freke always felt a sense of seniority, even if circumstances long conspired to mock that claim. She was the last to marry, had the worst husband and the most unsatisfactory child, and often had no money and no home. It is understandable that she frequently gave way to bursts of self-pity. Judith, by contrast, enjoyed a far more comfortable life. But when she too encountered adversity and relative penury, she displayed something of the same pride and prickliness. When she insisted on returning to London in September 1710, she chose to make her own travel arrangements, even though Freke had

---

[21] Ibid., 190–1, 278–9.   [22] Ibid., 157–8.   [23] Ibid., 77, 242.
[24] Ibid., 194, 284.   [25] Ibid., 81–3, 247–8.   [26] Ibid., 67, 69, 234–5.

offered the use of her coach. Like her elder sister, in adversity Judith needed to show that she too could retain some measure of independence and self-respect.[27]

FRIENDS AND ALLIES

The sibling ideal, for both sexes, was of mutual love, comfort, and support. Many women came much closer than Elizabeth Freke. Anne Dormer, for example, who almost sank under the burden of an abusive husband, eleven children, and chronic ill health, depended entirely on the love and support of her sister, Elizabeth Trumbull. Even when Elizabeth was far away in Constantinople, with her diplomat husband, her loving letters kept Anne afloat. Anne's replies, kept hidden from her husband's eyes, provided a crucial self-administered therapy. Anne's determination to survive, and one day see her sister again, helped keep her alive, and her dream was eventually realized.[28] Many other sisters provided emotional and practical support for women trapped in an unhappy marriage. In John Fletcher's sequel to Shakespeare's *The Taming of the Shrew*, Petruchio finds his attempt to crush his second wife thwarted by her fiery sister Livia, who launches a fierce and successful campaign to turn the tables.[29] Elizabeth Everard faced a different problem when her husband died intestate in 1605, fearing that she and her children would be left destitute by a harsh executor, Francis Gawdy. She turned to her sister, who was Gawdy's wife, and begged her to persuade him to show pity.[30]

Many sisters retained affectionate ties into old age. Sir John Bramston recalled how his widowed sister Dorothy, over 80, had grown anxious when she became too frail to travel to her daughter's house. Her sister Katherine, another elderly widow, offered a solution; 'bring your bed and come to me,' she urged, 'you shall set it up in my dining room, and we will be together.'[31] The twins Elizabeth and Judith Isham (nieces of their namesakes cited earlier) decided to set up home together in Westminster in 1672. Judith had never married, and Elizabeth was now a widow. Similarly, the Paulden sisters, 'aged virgins... about eighty years old', lived together at York, regaling visitors with stories of their long-dead brothers, cavalier officers during the civil wars half a century earlier.[32] Other sisters, equally close, lived together in the home of a married sibling. As we have seen, Frances and Winifred Blundell lived in their brother's household for most of their lives, and Frances became his wife's valued companion. But she also remained close to her

---

[27] Ibid., 266.

[28] Sara Mendelson and Mary O'Connor, '"Thy Passionately Loving Sister and Faithfull Friend": Anne Dormer's Letters to her Sister, Lady Trumbull', in Naomi J. Miller and Naomi Yavneh, eds, *Sibling Relations and Gender in the Early Modern World* (Aldershot, 2006), 206–15.

[29] John Fletcher, *The Womans Prize: or the Tamer Tamed*, in Francis Beaumont and John Fletcher, *Comedies and Tragedies* (1647).

[30] BL, Egerton MS 2715, f.5.

[31] *The Autobiography of Sir John Bramston*, ed. Lord Braybrooke, Camden Society, OS, 32 (1845), 351–2.

[32] *The Diary of Thomas Isham of Lamport*, ed. Sir Gyles Isham (Farnborough, 1971), 14; Joseph Hunter, ed., *The Diary of Ralph Thoresby FRS*, 2 vols (1830), ii.62.

sister, and Blundell paid tribute to her role as Winifred's 'husband', hinting at the emotional support she provided for a sister weaker in health and perhaps character.[33] Even married sisters sometimes dreamed of sharing a home, and a few found ways to contrive such an arrangement. Anne Lawrence and her sister provide one such example. Anne's husband was a royalist, while her sister's husband, John Bigge, came from a staunchly parliamentarian family. In the 1660s, when the Lawrences could not yet afford to maintain an independent household, Anne's sister secured her husband's grudging consent to let the couple live with them. Though the two men loathed each other, the arrangement survived for several years on the strength of the bond between their wives.[34] Rather more often, we find a married gentlewoman providing a home for a sister who had remained single. Thus Alice Carleton, who never married, found a home for many years with her sister Elizabeth Williams and her husband Alexander, a Jacobean official.[35]

Family visits made it possible for many gentlewomen to maintain ties with their sisters, even if they lived far away. If necessary, they would sometimes travel alone. Anne Oxinden was so desperate to see her sister that she insisted on going many miles on a bitterly cold and snowy day, and fell ill as a result.[36] Kind husbands would accommodate their wives' desires. When Frances Russell, Oliver Cromwell's daughter, went to stay with her sister Elizabeth in 1670, her husband wrote to say how much he was missing her. But, he added, 'When I consider that you are with a person that has so much love for you . . . I cannot but be satisfied.'[37] In August 1704, we find Elizabeth Middleton of Stockeld (Yorkshire) visiting her sister Frances Blundell of Crosby (Lancashire), and staying a week. She brought her daughter, but her husband had stayed at home.[38]

Gifts and letters supplemented such visits, or served as substitutes. Carefully chosen items of food and other small gifts were effective tokens of affectionate remembrance.[39] Letter writing could be more problematic, for women remained far less literate than men, and even in the late seventeenth century many elite women found writing irksome and daunting. Elizabeth Oxinden, penning a thank-you note to her brother in 1638, had felt obliged to add an apology. 'I would pray

---

[33] Margaret Blundell, ed., *Cavalier. Letters between William Blundell and his Friends 1620–1698* (1933), 55; *Flemings in Oxford*, iii.392n. For other female 'husbands' see Amanda E. Herbert, *Female Alliances. Gender, Identity, and Friendship in Early Modern Britain* (New Haven, Conn., 2014), 28–9; Eleanor Hubbard, *City Women. Money, Sex and the Social Order in Early Modern London* (Oxford, 2012), 246.

[34] *The Diary of William Lawrence*, ed. G. E. Aylmer (Beaminster, 1961), xvi, 1–4; Herbert, *Female Alliances*, 28; Rosemary O'Day, *The Family and Family Relationships, 1500–1900* (Basingstoke, 1994), 71.

[35] *The Letters of John Chamberlain*, ed. N. E. McClure (Philadelphia, 1939), ii.273, 326.

[36] *Oxinden Letters, 1607–1642*, 131–3.

[37] HMC, 52, *Frankland-Russell-Astley*, 36; cf. P. R. Seddon, ed., *Letters of John Holles 1587–1637*, Thoroton Society, 31, 35 (1975, 1983), i.2.

[38] J. J. Bagley, ed., *The Great Diurnall of Nicholas Blundell of Little Crosby, Lancashire, 1702–1728*, 3 vols, Record Society of Lancashire and Cheshire (1968–72), i.64–5; cf. iii.15, 20–1, 131; see also Isham, *Diary*, 103; *The Diary of a West Country Physician AD 1684–1726*, ed. Edmund Hobhouse (Rochester, 1934), 72; *The Diary of Bulstrode Whitelocke 1605–1675*, ed. Ruth Spalding (Oxford, 1990), 628, 646.

[39] Herbert, *Female Alliances*, esp. chaps 1–3; see e.g. *Barrington Family Letters 1628–1632*, ed. Arthur Searle, Camden Society, 4th series, 28 (1983), 78, 222–3.

you not to take it ill that you hear not from me,' she wrote, 'it is not for want of true love unto you but my bad writing.' Two generations later, Elizabeth North was making similar excuses. 'I am a very bad writer at best', she confessed, 'and very seldom do it but when I can't avoid it.'[40] Women too busy or disinclined to write would often send greetings via the letters that passed between their husbands, add brief postscripts, or ask husbands to relay a message. In 1632, for example, Elizabeth Masham was very anxious for some of her sister's 'water for the eyes', to treat an infection afflicting both her and her daughter. But instead of writing herself, she asked her husband to pass on her urgent request.[41] In the case of highly literate women, by contrast, letters often played a vital role in sustaining bonds over many years. Anne Dormer, cited earlier, sent a stream of letters to the sister she declared 'dearer than my own life'.[42] Muriel Bell referred humorously to the letters she exchanged with her sister as 'our weekly task', while Elizabeth Isham heard almost weekly from both her siblings when she was staying in London in the late 1620s.[43] The letters that passed between Barbara Hawtrey and her sister Anne de Grey clearly gave great pleasure to both. On one occasion, in 1654, Barbara told her sister that 'I was made well at the reading your letter, it moved me to laughter'. Having little news of her own, she closed her reply with the whimsical announcement that 'my stomach tells me that 'tis supper time'. The letter's significance lay in its reaffirmation of love, not its trivial content. Their bond also had a more serious dimension, however, as became evident when circumstances changed. Some years later Anne was considering marriage, and Barbara worried that her sister might be making a poor choice. She therefore took it upon herself to make enquiries about the character and circumstances of the prospective husband, and recruited her own husband to assist. Later still, with Anne now married (to a different man), we find Barbara looking forward eagerly to a visit: 'come as soon and stay as long as you please', she urged. Their correspondence continued over many years.[44]

Letters could provide practical support as well as sustaining emotional ties. Many addressed issues of family health and childcare, like the warm correspondence between Dorothy Lagoe and her sister Alice, in Restoration Lancashire. On one occasion Dorothy sent Alice some quinces that, she explained, physicians considered beneficial for infants' brain development. Living in Manchester, Dorothy was also able to shop for shoes and children's clothes for her sister, and arrange schooling for her daughter. Women often used their family networks to recruit nurses and servants, and Dorothy also set out to find a new chambermaid for her sister. One candidate, she reported rather engagingly, was honest 'but hath sweethearts, and is not mindful to take much pains'.[45]

---

[40] *Oxinden Letters 1607–1642*, 135; BL, Add. MS 32501, f.188; cf. fos. 88, 159, 206.
[41] Barrington, *Letters*, 232.
[42] Mendelson and O'Connor, ' "Thy Passionately Loving Sister" '; Herbert, *Female Alliances*, 21.
[43] Hughey, *Correspondence of Lady Katherine Paston*, 44–5; Isham, 'Rememberance', f.20v.
[44] BL, Egerton MS 2717, fos. 71, 156–7, 159, 161–3, 175, 191.
[45] HMC, 35, *Kenyon*, 78, 83, 89, 115, 122; cf. Barrington, *Letters*, 115; *Oxinden Letters, 1607–1642*, 112–13.

One of the most valuable forms of support, across the whole period and far beyond, was to care for a sister in childbed, and help manage the household during her lying-in. This was a common practice, and sisters (and mothers) were ideally equipped to provide both emotional and practical support.[46] Also common, and equally valuable, was for a woman to take in a sister's child. This would require her husband's consent, but she would bear most of the burden and in most cases the initiative would probably have been hers. In Jacobean Suffolk, we find Elizabeth Neville taking in the two youngest children of her sister Anne Woodhouse, who suffered poor health and was burdened with a feckless husband. Elizabeth's own children had died, and she became very attached to her spirited little niece Betty. She taught the child French, singing, sewing, and other appropriate skills, and years later set about finding her a good husband. Elizabeth also arranged a place at Eton for her young nephew Francis, and when she learned that he was miserable there she took steps to find him a better tutor. 'I will be as careful of him as I would be of my own', she promised.[47] Similar arrangements existed in many other families. Margaret Pulteney, a wealthy young widow, not only took in one of her sister's daughters, her namesake and god-daughter, but bestowed £900 on her.[48]

Assistance came in a multitude of other forms too. Anne Townshend (née Bacon) intervened in 1594 to help her unhappy younger sister Winifred, advising their stubborn father about a possible match. She also urged him to settle an annuity on her sister, to provide her with some measure of security and independence. Mary Whalley campaigned to secure the payment of her sister's portion, after their male kin had signally failed to help. And during the civil war we find a Cheshire clergyman's wife helping her sister, married to a royalist gentleman, by taking in some of their household goods. The aim was to protect them from marauding parliamentarian soldiers, and the sisters' solidarity outweighed family differences over politics and religion.[49]

MIDDLING-SORT SISTERS

Sisterly relationships in middling-sort families display several distinctive features. Thus, sisters would sometimes run shops and businesses in partnership, living and working together. Rachel and Hester Pinney ran a successful lace shop in London's New Exchange in the late 1670s to early 1680s, Alice and Jane Zains ran a linen-drapers' shop in Southampton in the 1690s, and two London sisters ran a starching business in the early 1700s, with a god-daughter as their assistant. There were many

---

[46] See e.g. A. Hassell Smith et al., eds, *The Papers of Nathaniel Bacon of Stiffkey*, 5 vols, Norfolk Record Society (1979–2010), i.61, 64–5, iii.332–3; Patricia Crawford, *Blood, Bodies and Families in Early Modern England* (Harlow, 2004), 188.

[47] Hassell Smith, *Papers of Nathaniel Bacon*, ii.211–12, 236–7, iv.26, 53.

[48] Verney, *Memoirs*, i.167, 288–9.

[49] Hassell Smith, *Papers of Nathaniel Bacon*, iii.279–80; Barrington, *Letters*, 156, 162–3; J. E. H. Bennett and J. C. Dewhurst, eds, *Quarter Sessions Records for the County Palatine of Chester 1559–1760*, Record Society of Lancashire and Cheshire, 94 (1940), 126.

similar arrangements.[50] Some other patterns of behaviour paralleled those of the gentry, with sisters providing a home or support for siblings in need.[51] In the case of Mary Windmill, it was not her sister but her young niece who needed help. Mary's drunken sister was mistreating her child, and Mary became so distressed that she took her away to raise herself, begging another sister for cast-off children's clothes.[52] Other middling-sort women found the means to go to the aid of siblings living far away. Rachel Pinney hastened down to Dorset in 1688 when another sister fell grievously ill, to help care for her and her children. Their brother promised to reimburse her expenses, whether she decided to travel by coach or hire a horse for the journey. He took it for granted that she could make the necessary arrangements, and undertake such a journey independently.[53] Ralph Josselin's daughters remained in regular contact with each other as well as with their parents, and helped one another in times of sickness and after childbirth.[54] His wife's sister lived much further away, and it was a special event when a letter arrived in July 1666. But Josselin records that she paid them a visit in July 1670, 'to our joy', and stayed almost three weeks.[55]

Few middling-sort women had the skills to sustain a close relationship through letters. Ties inevitably weakened over the years if sisters lived far apart and could neither visit nor write. If the need arose, they might hire a male scribe to write in their name. The diarist John Cannon helped many friends and neighbours in this way, sometimes trying to convey a client's voice as well as her message. In the case of a devout Presbyterian, he composed letters to her sister in what he called 'their own canting style'. For Cannon such ventriloquism was an amusement, but for the recipients it may have provided a gratifying sense of immediacy.[56] Despite the obstacles, even in quite modest families we find sisters able to maintain bonds of friendship and support over both time and distance. Ellen Harrison, a Lancashire yeoman's widow, paid a week's visit in 1718 to her sister near Ormskirk, about twenty miles away, and her sister returned her visit the following year. Leonard Wheatcroft records that in 1692 his daughter Anna, a farmer's wife in Yorkshire, 'sent for her sister Betty to be with her when she lay in', and she was there for the final month of the pregnancy. Betty appears to have stayed on, for five years later we

[50] Geoffrey F. Nuttall, ed., *Letters of John Pinney 1679–1693* (1939), 44–5; Pamela Sharpe, *Population and Society in an East Devon Parish. Reproducing Colyton 1540–1840* (Exeter, 2002), 98–9; Amy Froide, *Never Married. Singlewomen in Early Modern England* (Oxford, 2005), cf. 28, 55–6, 109–11; *OBOA*, 17120618; *The Autobiography of William Stout of Lancaster 1665–1752*, ed. J. D. Marshall (Manchester, 1967), 144.

[51] Ernest Axon, ed., *Oliver Heywood's Life of John Angier of Denton*, Chetham Society, NS, 97 (1937), 83, 102; Bagley, *Great Diurnall*, iii.50, 142.

[52] *The Chronicles of John Cannon, Excise Officer and Writing Master, 1684–1743*, ed. John Money (Oxford, 2010), ii.489, 506, 526, cf. 479.

[53] Nuttall, *Letters of John Pinney*, 61–2, 65.

[54] Josselin, *Diary*, 615–16, 622, 624, 634, 637, 639, 644; cf. *The Diary and Letter Book of the Rev. Thomas Brockbank 1671–1709*, ed. Richard Trappes-Lomax, Chetham Society, NS, 89 (1930), 275–6, 293–4.

[55] Josselin, *Diary*, 519, 554.

[56] Cannon, *Chronicles*, ii.288, 489, 506, 513, 526; cf. *The Diary of Roger Lowe*, ed. W. L. Sachse (1938), 46, 51, 53, 62. But for a scribe deliberately perverting the client's message see Sheila D. Thomson, ed., *The Book of Examinations and Depositions before the Mayor and Justices of Southampton 1648–1663*, Southampton Record Society, 37 (1994), 130–1.

find Wheatcroft and his daughter Sarah making a fifty-mile journey on foot to visit both Anna and Betty. Their reward for a trek that took three days each way was a 'very merry' stay for almost a week. Wheatcroft's daughter-in-law made similar visits to and with her own sisters.[57] In other cases our evidence for the survival of emotional bonds rests on no more than a passing remark by a third party. Thus in October 1672 Isaac Archer noted laconically in his diary, 'My wife was much troubled at the sudden death of her elder sister.' Nothing further survives to indicate the nature or strength of their relationship. Instead, Archer mused on whether her death might mean a larger portion for his wife. Similarly, Oliver Heywood mentions his wife Abigail's sister only once in his voluminous diaries and memoranda. The occasion was the news in September 1691 that she was dying, news that made Abigail desperate to hasten to Lancaster for one last meeting. Heywood had been finalizing arrangements for an extensive evangelical tour, and the issue triggered a fierce row between the couple. For once his wife prevailed, testimony to the strength of her feelings. They both travelled to Lancaster, with the preaching tour deferred.[58]

ORDINARY WOMEN, SERVANTS, AND THE POOR

For sibling bonds in the lower strata of society, we have to rely heavily on such fragmentary data. It was fairly easy to maintain contact when kin lived close by. Even maidservants would encounter friends and kin as they did their chores and ran errands. They might also meet at fairs, markets, and wakes, and usually enjoyed some leisure time on Sundays and holidays. At New Year 1611, Margaret Willshere, a servant in Worcestershire, was even able to devise an elaborate practical joke with her sister that must have taken considerable time to prepare. Dressed as men and armed with a dagger and pike, they knocked one night at the door of the illiterate village constable, and presented him with a paper they pretended was an order to raise a hue and cry. To their delight, he fell for the ruse.[59] Such an episode was exceptional, of course, but servants might return home between one period of annual service and the next, and many employers were happy for them to renew family ties at holiday times. On Christmas Day 1709, the Lancashire squire Nicholas Blundell noted in his diary that his cook had gone to visit her sister, a visit that was returned a week later. Blundell sometimes allowed servants to stay away overnight, or longer, and let their visiting kin stay under his own roof. Many employers also allowed servants to visit close family members who had fallen sick.[60]

[57] Bagley, ed., *Great Diurnall*, ii.228–9, 272–3; *The Autobiography of Leonard Wheatcroft of Ashover 1627–1706*, ed. Dorothy Riden, Derbyshire Record Society, 20 (1993), 97, 98, 101–2; cf. Cannon, *Chronicles*, 114, 276.

[58] 'The Diary of Isaac Archer 1641–1700', in Storey, ed., *Two East Anglian Diaries 1641–1729*, Suffolk Records Society, 36 (1994), 140; Heywood, *Autobiography*, iv.139–40.

[59] J. W. Willis Bund, ed., *Worcestershire County Records: Calendar of the Quarter Sessions Records, 1591–1643* (Worcester, 1900), 161.

[60] Bagley, *Great Diurnall*, i.196–8; cf. ii.46, 49, 85, 149; Alan Savile, ed., *Secret Comment. The Diaries of Gertrude Savile 1721–1757*, Thoroton Society, 41 (1997), 105.

Such evidence tells us little, of course, about the quality of such relationships. One employer described how her servant Moll and Moll's sister Betty had been 'passionately fond of one another', and that Betty's sudden death had left Moll so grief-stricken that she too had appeared likely to die.[61] Testimony of this kind, however, is vanishingly rare. Wills made by ordinary women, usually widows or young single women, provide more frequent if less graphic evidence of sisterly affection. Widows generally left most of their possessions to their children and grandchildren, but many also bequeathed treasured personal items to their sisters (and other close female kin), as tokens of affectionate remembrance. In early Elizabethan Essex, for example, Joan Crease left her sister her best petticoat, cap, and ring, while Agnes Mannying wanted her sister to have her 'best frock and a kerchief of holland'. Widows who left young children often asked a sister or brother to take them in. Jane Thayer specified in 1561 that she wanted her sister to look after her daughter Audrey, along with a stock of money the girl would inherit from her late father when she came of age.[62] Such wills hint at bonds that had been close or, at the very least, indicate a sense of trust. Amy Froide has shown that the wills of many single women reveal a similar pattern, with sisters outnumbering every other category of kin as legatees or executors. She suggests that while single women received material assistance mainly from their brothers, it was with their sisters that they enjoyed most companionship and emotional intimacy.[63]

Ordinary women were rarely in a position to provide financial support to sisters in need. The resources of married women were usually under their husbands' control, and few single women had money to spare. They might, however, provide support in many other forms. When young women migrated to London, in their teens or early twenties, they often lodged initially with an older sister and her husband while looking for a place in service. It seems likely that in most cases the older sister would have suggested the arrangement and persuaded her husband to agree. Even if the migrant had a brother also living in the capital, he would probably still be only an apprentice or a journeyman, unable as yet to provide such help.[64] In other towns and rural communities we can also find young women living with an older sister and brother-in-law. Some were urban migrants, while others had been orphaned.[65] In some cases

[61] Herbert, *Female Alliances*, 35.

[62] F. G. Emmison, ed., *Wills of the County of Essex (England). Volume 1, 1558–1565* (Washington, D.C., 1982), 14, 103–4, 113–14.

[63] Froide, *Never Married*, 47, 60; cf. Amy Louise Erickson, *Women and Property in Early Modern England* (1993), 212–13.

[64] Vivien Brodsky Elliott, 'Single Women and the London Marriage Market: Age, Status and Mobility, 1598–1619', in R. B. Outhwaite, ed., *Marriage and Society* (New York, 1982), 91–5; Hubbard, *City Women*, chap. 1; K. J. Allison, ed., 'An Elizabethan Village "Census"', *Bulletin of the Institute of Historical Research*, 36 (1963), 96, 99; *The Christian Progress of that Ancient Servant . . . George Whitehead* (1725), 292; Peter Earle, *A City Full of People. Men and Women of London 1650–1750* (1994), 201; Guildhall Library, London, MS 9065A/1A, f.43v.

[65] D. A. Gatley et al., eds, 'The Stoke-upon-Trent Parish Listing, 1701', *Collections for a History of Staffordshire*, Staffordshire Record Society, 4th series, 16 (1994), 206; WSRO, Ep.1/11/1, fos.28v–29.

such women remained for years in a sister's household, working as servants. Mary Clarke, giving evidence in 1720, said she had lived as a servant with her sister in Smithfield for eight or nine years.[66] Servants and former servants living in the same neighbourhood could also provide informal assistance and support. They might, for example, act as a point of contact for a sister seeking a new employer. Positions in service were generally filled by word of mouth, through informal networks, and a recommendation from a trusted servant would carry some weight. It was surely no coincidence that Rosamond Emery, nursekeeper to a London merchant's wife in 1706, was also the sister of one of her employer's maidservants. The maid had probably brought Rosamond to her mistress's attention—or possibly vice versa.[67] Other sisters provided both emotional and practical support at moments of crisis. Martha Doe, who alleged that she had been raped in December 1719, explained later that she had told her sister and shown her the bruises almost immediately, but had waited two months before informing her husband. The circumstances of the case were ambiguous, and she probably feared he would not believe her. Elizabeth Catlin, a servant accused of infanticide in 1720, had also turned to her sister at a moment of panic and danger. She had given birth in her employers' house, prematurely and alone, and sent for her sister to come and help her and clean the room, to remove all traces of the birth.[68]

Women might thus be able to provide assistance in forms that involved little if any financial burden. It cost nothing to lend a sister (or neighbour) household goods or clothes, or give away items they no longer needed, practices that remain as yet little explored. Household items and clothes could also be shared. Margaret Adams, a poor widow in Bury St Edmunds, left an intriguing will in 1632 in which she bequeathed five sheets, currently pawned, to her daughter Mary. If they could be redeemed, she continued, she wished 'that Mary shall lend the casting sheet to her sisters when they are in childbed'.[69] Other evidence throws further incidental light on lending practices. In one case, the rape of a little girl in 1684 was exposed only because her mother's sister had asked to borrow the child's 'worn shift'. Her own little girl was sick, and she did not want to dress her in clean linen. But when she looked at the borrowed shift she spotted some telltale signs of abuse, questioned the child, and soon uncovered the full story. While the circumstances were highly unusual, it may have been not uncommon for close kin to borrow or share children's or even adult clothing.[70] That is suggested by a case heard in the ecclesiastical court at York in 1622. Elizabeth Harrison of Pontefract, 23, a witness in a testamentary suit, explained that she lived with her mother and sister, the father having deserted them. They were extremely poor, and Elizabeth was promptly challenged on the good clothes she was wearing, with the insinuation that she had been bribed to give false testimony. Rebutting the smear, she retorted that the petticoat and waistcoat were prized possessions that she shared with her sister, 'one

[66] *OBSP*, t17200115-35.
[67] Bodleian, Rawlinson MS B382, f.468-v; cf. Savile, *Secret Comment*, 256–7.
[68] *OBSP*, t17200303-43; *OBSP*, t17201012-38.
[69] Nesta Evans, ed, *Wills of the Archdeaconry of Sudbury 1630–1635*, Suffolk Records Society, 29 (1987), 197.
[70] *OBSP*, t16841008-12.

wearing them one day and the other another'. Her mother, facing a similar challenge, explained that she had borrowed some of her clothes from her daughters. They had all wanted to look respectable on such an important occasion.[71]

Help of this kind paralleled the kinds of support often provided by friends and neighbours. The same applied to physical protection. Women escaping a violent husband sometimes found shelter with a sister, while a Norfolk widow fleeing an attempted rapist in 1604 similarly took refuge in her sister's house.[72] And though both kin and neighbours were generally reluctant to see a marriage collapse, they might be ready to confront and lecture the abusive spouse. In one such case, Ann Haslom of Bolton, desperately poor, was struggling to feed her small children, and her wastrel husband had provided nothing for the baby she was expecting. Lacking the credit to buy even a farthing candle, she was terrified of perhaps having to give birth in total darkness. After the baby arrived (fortunately in daylight), her sister railed at Ann's feckless partner, telling him that 'he was no husband, to provide nothing for her against such a time'. She might at least shame him into better behaviour.[73] Such interventions were not uncommon. A London woman tended her injured sister, beaten by a violent husband, scolded him, and then tried to mend the couple's relationship. Another woman, a servant in a similarly dysfunctional household, did all she could to help and protect a mistress who was also her sibling. And if an injured wife eventually sued for separation, the testimony of a sister would prove helpful in court proceedings.[74] Such testimony also had value in other circumstances. Women suing for defamation, for example, could sometimes call on family as well as neighbours for support. Margaret Smith's sister and mother both testified on her behalf when she sued an abusive landlord in 1608. Very occasionally we even find aggrieved sisters launching a joint defamation suit.[75] Close kin could be especially valuable in testamentary cases, where they might possess an intimate knowledge of the testator's wishes and relationships. And when Eleanor Baynes was charged with bigamy, two younger sisters were able to testify that her first husband had fled many years earlier, and was generally believed to be dead. They had both attended her second marriage, and could swear that it had been a legitimate ceremony. Though performed in her house, it had been conducted by a local minister using the prayer book.[76]

Among the poor, sibling support might often take a physical form, among women as well as men. The notebook of the Norfolk justice Robert Doughty records several instances of women employing violence on behalf of their families, and others may never have reached his ears. One woman had rescued a sister arrested for stealing geese; three sisters pursuing a family feud had assaulted a labourer's wife; and three others had assaulted a woman and seized the gleaning she

[71] BI, CP H 1499.

[72] Hassell Smith, *Papers of Nathaniel Bacon*, v.128; Earle, *City Full of People*, 236; Joanne Bailey, *Unquiet Lives. Marriage and Marriage Breakdown in England 1660–1800* (Cambridge, 2003), 33.

[73] Newcome, *Autobiography*, i.84–5; Hubbard, *City Women*, 164–70.

[74] Hubbard, *City Women*, 123–4, 166–7.

[75] SQSR, iii.365; Cambridge University Library, K6/33; LRRO, 1 D 41/4 Box 60/128–9.

[76] BI, CP H 363.

had gathered. In May 1665, the daughters of widow Yarne of Aylsham had also resorted to violence to defend their mother's good name. A labourer's wife claimed that Yarne had invited her to an alehouse to lie with a visiting gentleman, which cast Yarne in the role of a bawd. In middling-sort families, such a slur might have triggered a defamation suit. The sisters preferred a more direct response: they assaulted the labourer's wife and threatened to kill her. All these incidents occurred in one small part of Norfolk within the space of three years, and there is no reason to think them in any way exceptional.[77]

We have seen that support from close kin was still more important in the context of extreme poverty. Destitute men and women generally turned first to parents or adult children, and neighbours, but help might also be provided by lateral kin, including siblings of either sex.[78] Thus in 1646, Mary Spencer, heavily pregnant, struggled from London to the home of a poor sister in Hertfordshire to give birth. Mary's husband had been pressed into the army, and she presumably lacked the means and friends to feel safe having her baby in the capital. Richard Preece of Myddle, Cheshire, destroyed himself and his estate by drink, and it was his sister Jane who then stepped in and out 'of mere charity, maintained his widow'.[79] Those in precarious circumstances themselves would sometimes try to support still needier kin. The Norwich census of the poor in 1570 records Cicely Gose, abandoned by her husband, nonetheless providing a home for her sister's two children, probably orphans.[80] The heavy burden of such compassion becomes clear when it dragged down the donor too. A Lancashire woman took in her sick sister, and was then herself reduced to destitution. A similar fate befell a Worcestershire woman, deserted by her husband, who had attempted to maintain a 'poor innocent sister'.[81]

Few people in this period chose to live completely alone. Though elderly widows often found themselves in that situation, some were able to share a home with an unmarried daughter, pooling their meagre resources. At Norwich, for example, Rose Heywood was living with her two daughters, both in their late twenties, who maintained themselves by knitting hose.[82] The younger women might have found greater security by going into service, but living together gave them a degree of autonomy and maintained the family bond. Single women who had been living with their parents would also sometimes remain living together for a time after the parents died.[83] In towns, young women might choose to share a room and 'live at

[77] *The Notebook of Robert Doughty 1662–1665*, ed. James M. Rosenhem, Norfolk Record Society, 54 (1989), 27, 28, 41, 55.

[78] Steve Hindle, *On the Parish? The Micro-Politics of Poor Relief in Rural England c.1550–1750* (Oxford, 2004), 48–52; Jonathan Healey, *The First Century of Welfare. Poverty and Poor Relief in Lancashire 1620–1730* (Woodbridge, 2014), 146–52.

[79] William LeHardy, ed., *Hertfordshire County Records. Calendar of the Sessions Books, 1619–1657*, v, Hertfordshire Records Society (1928), 366–7; Richard Gough, *The History of Myddle*, ed. David Hey (Harmondsworth, 1981), 133.

[80] J. F. Pound, ed., *The Norwich Census of the Poor, 1570*, Norfolk Record Society, 40 (1971), 91; cf. 34, 54.

[81] Healey, *First Century*, 148–9; Willis Bund, ed., *Worcestershire County Records*, 248.

[82] Ibid., 84, cf. 64, 30.

[83] Froide, *Never Married*, 54–6; Cannon, *Chronicles*, i.197; Lawrence Stone, *Uncertain Unions. Marriage in England 1660–1753* (Oxford, 1992), 113.

their own hands', an arrangement that was strongly discouraged by the authorities, who feared they would sink into destitution or prostitution.[84] Such women were usually friends, but we sometimes find sisters making similar arrangements. Thus Philippa and Jane Peake, Quaker spinsters, were living together when they were prosecuted for Nonconformity in 1683. Officials seized their spinning implements, household utensils, and even the bed and blanket they shared. It may be that Nonconformist spinsters found it easier and safer to lodge together.[85] Cohabitation by older women raised little concern, for by sharing expenses they were less likely to need parish relief. Elizabeth and Alice Shakespeare, 'ancient' sisters sharing a home at Bidford (Warwickshire), entered the record when they were driven to petition for support, in 1671. Had they continued to scrape by, they would have been left in peace, and we would never have known of their domestic arrangements.[86]

RIVALRY AND INDIFFERENCE

Contemporaries were well aware, of course, that rivalry and resentment occurred between sisters as well as brothers. It is female tensions that drive the plot of *King Lear*, from the opening scene in which his daughters clash over the division of his lands. Goneril and Regan each claim to love him more, in a cynical attempt to win the largest share of his bounty, while Cordelia voices her contempt for their manoeuvres. Later in the play, the rivalry between Goneril and Regan takes on a sexual dimension as they are drawn into literally poisonous competition over the apparently alpha male Edmund. Goneril's hatred and ambition eventually lead her to commit the very rare crime of sororicide, and the tragedy ends with all three sisters dead.[87] In this play, sisterly bonds and gender solidarity count for nothing. The blood-soaked carnage enacted on the Jacobean stage bore little resemblance to the lives of the audiences, but it reflected domestic tensions that were all too familiar. In the 1630s, the Norfolk gentleman Thomas Knyvett playfully dubbed his wife Cordelia and her older sisters Goneril and Regan. In Restoration Cumberland, the unmarried Thomlinson sisters quarrelled so fiercely that their mother packed one of them off to Dublin, in despair, 'because sister Isabel made her fret and crossed her'. And in Restoration Wales, the close friendship between two sisters who had married two brothers turned into fierce resentment and rejection, to their father's dismay.[88]

The sources occasionally throw some light on the origins and nature of such rivalries and tensions. There was never any affection between Gertrude Savile, a

[84] Paul Griffiths, *Youth and Authority. Formative Experiences in England 1560–1640* (Oxford, 1996), 378–82.

[85] Norman Penney, ed., *Records of the Sufferings of Quakers in Cornwall* (1928), 115; Cannon, *Chronicles*, i.114.

[86] Healey, *First Century*, 151; S. C. Ratcliff and H. C. Johnson, eds, *Warwickshire County Records*, 9 vols (Warwick, 1935–64), v.158–9.

[87] *King Lear*, I.i, IV.ii, iv, vii.

[88] *The Knyvett Letters (1620–1644)*, ed. Bertram Schofield, Norfolk Record Society, 20 (1949), 79, 89–90, 105; 'The Diary of the Rev. John Thomlinson', ed. J. C. Hodgson, *Six North Country Diaries*, Surtees Society, 118 (1910), 153; Whitelocke, *Diary*, 643, 646, 737–8.

lifelong spinster, and her sister Ann, sixteen years older. Gertrude complained that 'from birth she did not love me and has always despised me (which is far worse than hating)'. Ann had enjoyed a far more comfortable life, and was preferred by both their brother and widowed mother. Yet she had allegedly always treated Gertrude coldly, resenting her as an 'intruder' and potential rival. Though we do not have Ann's perspective, their relationship was clearly plagued by rivalry and resentment throughout their lives.[89] Elizabeth Freke's relationship with her sisters, as we have seen, swung wildly between affection, gratitude, and resentment. The relationship between Elizabeth and Judith Isham was similarly conflicted. Elizabeth's autobiography reveals a mutual emotional dependency that oscillated between powerful love and competition for the affection of their parents and brother. Their parents admired Judith's lively mind and bookish tastes, and Elizabeth struggled to control her sense of inferiority. Judith made that no easier by declaring that she had more in common with her brother, and loved him more. Elizabeth claimed that she loved her sister 'never a whit the worse', but tensions are evident throughout her autobiography. Judith was just as emotionally conflicted, and once admitted having felt tempted to kill her sister as she slept.[90] The origin of the rivalry between the Mitford sisters is more obscure. We know that Isabel Mitford's four sisters shunned her wedding in 1717, an act of public humiliation that left her understandably angry and hurt. Isabel was the second youngest, and they may have resented her marrying before them, but other factors were almost certainly present. When another sister married, Isabel retaliated by making scathing comments about the bridegroom, and there are hints of sexual rivalry.[91]

Several tensions are apparent in the Pinney family, West Country lace-merchants, where all the siblings appear to have inherited something of their father's controlling temperament. They all did their best to block one another's marriage plans. When their father sent a reproachful letter to his daughter Sarah in 1685, Hester added a stern note warning Sarah that if she went ahead with her design to marry such 'a pitiful fellow', and at a time of family crisis, 'I shall disown you for a sister'. She herself, Hester added, was being courted by a nobleman's son, but 'for love to you all' would never think of marrying at such a time. Her appeal to family unity and loyalty barely concealed the competitive subtext.[92] Sexual rivalry is the key element in Lucy Hutchinson's brief account of her mother, another Lucy, the youngest daughter of Sir William St John. She had been the most beautiful of his daughters, and suitors who came to court her sisters would quickly transfer their attention to her. That triggered such friction that her parents eventually packed her off to Jersey, to restore family peace.[93] We can detect an element of sexual rivalry among the Verney sisters, too. When Mary Verney came to help her married sister

[89] Savile, *Secret Comment*, 15–16, 18, 63–4, 101, 136, 150, and *passim*.

[90] Isham, 'Rememberance', fos. 3v, 12v, 24v, and *passim*; Katharine Hodgkin, 'Elizabeth Isham's Everlasting Library: Memory and Self in Early Modern Autobiography', in Sally Alexander and Barbara Taylor, eds, *History and Psyche: Culture, Psychoanalysis, and the Past* (Basingstoke, 2012), 241–64.

[91] 'Diary of Thomlinson', 92–3, 119, 141–2.   [92] Nuttall, *Letters of John Pinney*, 32.

[93] Lucy Hutchinson, *Memoirs of the Life of Colonel John Hutchinson*, ed. John Sutherland (Oxford, 1973), 284.

Susan in 1649 during her lying-in, Susan accused her of being 'too familiar' with her husband.[94] In later years, the Verney women pursued their rivalry under a veneer of politeness, as they competed for the favour of their brother, Sir Ralph, and then his son, Sir John. At stake was the patronage of the family head, and the status and precedence it would confer. Who would receive financial help from Sir Ralph, and the best portions of venison, his favoured form of largesse? Who would receive visits from Sir John, how frequently, and in which order? And who would be allowed the use of his coach? Complex rules governed their world of polite sociability, and contemporaries were alert to every hint of favour or snubs. In 1695, we find Sir Ralph's surviving sisters squabbling over whose servant should take precedence riding in the funeral cortège of their late sister Penelope.[95]

Money and property were predictably often the issue in disputes at every level of society, linked, as in King Lear's troubled family, with jealousies over parental favouritism. A family feud in Jacobean Norfolk saw Mary and Prudence Hobart, gentlewomen, throw off all decorum as they punched, shoved, and spat at one another.[96] Many disputes originated in resentment over marriage portions perceived as unfair. A father's circumstances might improve over time, enabling him to give a younger daughter more than her sisters had received; equally, they might deteriorate, forcing him to be more sparing.[97] Portions, in any case, were generally related to the size of the jointure provided by the bridegroom's family. Tensions often ensued, and sometimes ended in litigation.[98] Similar conflicts erupted among the middling sort. A Southampton brewer explained in 1639 that he could not increase the portion he was offering with his daughter, but promised that should his estate ever improve he would make it up to 'as much as any other child of his should at any time after... have'. On his deathbed, thirteen years later, he was reminded of his promise and said he would honour it. Other men also tried to rectify differences between the portions they had given their daughters.[99] The minister Ralph Josselin was less judicious. Shortly before his death in 1683, he arranged portions of £500 apiece for his last unmarried daughters, far more than the £200 he had been able to give their sister Jane thirteen years earlier. Jane vented her anger both at him and at her sisters, resentful that younger siblings should be treated better than she had been. Such tensions were common over both portions and inheritance. Only rarely did they end with such an amicable settlement as one inheritance dispute in Lincolnshire in 1679: the two sisters and their husbands eventually agreed to share the lands and live together in the partitioned house.[100]

Alongside the histories of sibling affection and rivalry lies the almost invisible history of indifference. Sibling ties often weakened over the years, eroded by time

[94] Miriam Slater, *Family Life in the Seventeenth Century. The Verneys of Claydon House* (1984), 51, 86.
[95] Whyman, *Sociability and Power*, 24–5, 105–6.   [96] BL, Egerton MS 2715, f.55.
[97] Nesta Evans, ed., *The Wills of the Archdeaconry of Sudbury 1630–1635*, Suffolk Records Society, 29 (1987), 104.
[98] e.g. D'Ewes, *Autobiography*, ii.24–7.
[99] Thomson, ed., *Book of Examinations*, 147–8; Evans, *Wills of Sudbury*, 104.
[100] Josselin, *Diary*, 555, 643; Heywood, *Autobiography*, i.38.

and distance, with newer ties to spouses and children gradually taking priority. The point was made nicely by a Staffordshire gentlewoman, whose sister had asked her to pass on good wishes to their brother: 'she desires you to accept that, instead of a letter,' the writer added, 'for she is very busy playing with her boy Jack.'[101] Fading ties leave few traces in the record, almost by definition, but hints occasionally surface. Thus, while Ralph Josselin kept in touch with his sisters, there is little indication of close ties between the sisters themselves. On one rare occasion in October 1661, all three happened to visit him at the same time, and they all dined together. But Josselin noted that though his sister Anne stayed on for several more days, Mary, who had recently married (at 50) and was living close by, 'never came up to see us in all that time'. There is no mention of a quarrel. It may be that after living apart for many years, the sisters no longer felt any emotional bond. Mary had been living with a gentleman's family, and she may have felt superior now to her poorer sisters. Whatever the explanation, Josselin was saddened by her indifference. He was deeply disappointed too when two gentlewomen did not bother to come from London to attend their sister's funeral in his parish, despite having ample notice.[102] The ties of blood did not always endure.

---

[101] *Tixall Letters; or the Correspondence of the Aston Family and their Friends during the Seventeenth Century*, ed. Arthur Clifford (1815), i.106.
[102] Josselin, *Diary*, 483, 622.

6

Stepchildren, Half-Siblings, and the Illegitimate

Commentators agreed that stable, well-ordered families played a vital role in maintaining social order. Many families were, however, far from stable, and many children had lost at least one parent before reaching adulthood. The bereaved spouse would often remarry, and in 1688 over 30 per cent of the children in one Nottinghamshire parish were living with a step-parent.[1] And these were arguably the lucky ones, for a parent's death could easily lead a family to fall apart. Isaac Newton's widowed mother remarried when he was 3 years old, and moved to raise another family with her new husband, leaving the child to be raised by grandparents. He was disturbed and deeply resentful. When he drew up a list of his sins, at the age of 19, he recalled having threatened his stepfather and mother 'to burn them and the house over them'. Even among the gentry, a parent's death sometimes led to the break-up of the household.[2] This chapter explores parental loss and remarriage, the issues facing both adults and children, and their very mixed experiences and fortunes.

Harsh demographic facts shaped attitudes too. Edmund Harrold, a Manchester wig-maker, was bereft at losing his baby daughter in April 1713, after seeing her apparently well only the day before. He noted despairingly that death had now taken 'two dear wives and five sweet infants from me, and I for my part am likely to be next'. In the event, he survived another eight years, long enough to bury a third wife and marry a fourth. His diary reveals intense grief but also a recognition of life's practical demands. After the death of his second wife, Harrold had arranged for his two surviving children to live with their grandparents, with the new baby put out to nurse. He dreamt of his late wife on the first anniversary of her death, but by then he had already been married again for several months.[3] Contemporaries were all aware of the demographic facts, but differed widely in terms of emotional

---

[1] Peter Laslett and John Harrison, 'Clayworth and Cogenhoe', in H. E. Bell and R. L. Ollard, eds, *Historical Essays 1600–1750* (1963), 164–5, 170; cf. Vivien Brodsky, 'Widows in Late Elizabethan London: Remarriage, Economic Opportunity and Family Orientations', in Lloyd Bonfield, Richard Smith, and Keith Wrightson, eds, *The World We Have Gained* (Oxford, 1986), 128.

[2] Richard S. Westfall, *The Life of Isaac Newton* (Cambridge, 1993), 9–10; John Rogers, *Ohel, or Beth-shemesh* (1653), 409–10; *The Autobiography of Sir John Bramston*, ed. Lord Braybrooke, Camden Society, OS, 32 (1845), 107–8; Anthony Kenny, ed., *The Responsa Scholarum of the English College, Rome, 1598–1685*, Catholic Record Society, 54–5 (1962–3), i.67–71; *SQSR*, ii.15, 25; Ivor Slocombe, ed., *Wiltshire Quarter Sessions Order Book 1642–1654*, Wiltshire Record Society, 67 (2014), 213.

[3] *The Diary of Edmund Harrold, Wigmaker of Manchester 1712–15*, ed. Craig Horner (Aldershot, 2008), 67, 78, 86, 98.

resilience. In *The Witch of Edmonton*, for example, Thomas Dekker shows a newly wed husband deeply unsettled when a fortune teller predicts that he will have another wife. His bride, by contrast, recognizes that it was unlikely both would survive to old age, and remarks placidly that he might well live to marry several times. A young gentlewoman, equally pragmatic, wanted a marriage settlement that would maximize her chance of securing a good second match, should the first husband die without issue. Her friends thought this very reasonable.[4] But for any family with young children, the death of a parent was a heavy blow. In landed families, a father's death brought the perils of wardship, with the estate passing into the hands of outsiders likely to exploit it for their own profit. A tradesman's widow might lack sufficient expertise to manage the business, while the poor often needed two incomes to survive. At every level, parental death brought challenges over money, property, and the children's needs. And at every level remarriage was an option the bereaved were likely at least to consider.

Remarriage was common, especially for men, for both emotional and practical reasons. A widower needed someone to manage the house and care for his children, and would see a wife as more trustworthy than a housekeeper or servant. Widows often remarried too, both from inclination and through social pressure. But women's choices and options also depended on a range of other variables. Gentlewomen with financial independence sometimes chose to remain single, though others felt the need for a partner better versed in the law or financial affairs.[5] Some middling-sort widows could live on the interest of the money they had inherited, and a draper's or baker's widow might well have the expertise to carry on the business until her children came of age. That option was not available, however, to the widows of professional men, builders, miners, sailors, and many others. A tenant farmer's widow, who enjoyed a third of her husband's estate through the right of 'free bench', also knew that she might lose it by remarrying. Among the poor, by contrast, remarriage could help survival by pooling scarce resources, easing pressure on childcare, and saving on rent, fuel, and cooking. Poor and elderly widows were the most likely to remain single, yet even here we find matches that evidently made sense to those involved, however extraordinary they might appear now. The Norwich census of the poor recorded a blind man of 50 with a wife of 96, and a man of 95 with a wife of 40. While the ages given are unreliable, both parties had clearly been willing to ignore huge disparities.[6]

---

[4] Thomas Dekker, *The Witch of Edmonton*, ed. Etta Soiref Onat (New York, 1980), II.ii; Arthur Searle, ed., *Barrington Family Letters 1628–1632*, Camden Society, 4th series, 28 (1983), 104.

[5] For women craving advice and help, see e.g. Verney, *Memoirs* i.253; BL, Egerton MS 2715, f. 105; HMC, 23, *Cowper*, i.169. But for women confident in the law, see Tim Stretton, *Women Waging Law in Elizabethan England* (Cambridge, 1998).

[6] Eleanor Hubbard, *City Women. Money, Sex and the Social Order in Early Modern London* (Oxford, 2012), 241–4; Richard Smith, ed., *Land, Kinship and Life-Cycle* (Cambridge, 1984), essays by Tim Wales and B. A. Holderness; J. F. Pound, ed., *The Norwich Census of the Poor, 1570*, Norfolk Record Society, 40 (1971), 72, 90.

STEP-PARENTS AND CHILDREN

Those marrying again often brought children with them. A Halifax nailer who married a widow in 1678 became stepfather to her six children, and a widow in Stoke-on-Trent brought four into her new marriage.[7] More children were likely to follow if the woman was still fertile, so families might contain both step-siblings and half-siblings. High levels of child mortality often provided a brutal solution to the problems of space, maintenance, and compatibility, especially in London. Older children would go into service at the earliest opportunity, and others might be farmed out to relatives. Even so, many families had to navigate the tricky waters of step-relationships.[8]

Remarriage raised both emotional and material issues for a spouse who already had children. Would they be loved and cared for, or neglected and abused? Would their inheritances be at risk, especially if the surviving parent were also to die? Many parents felt deeply anxious on both scores. Some men left property and custody of their children to the widow only for as long as she remained single. If she remarried, other kin would inherit the property and responsibility for raising the children. One Essex villager stipulated that if his widow remarried, her new husband was to be bound over to perform the bequests to his children when they came of age.[9]

Remarriage among the poor also created potential problems for the local community. Would the new household be economically viable? What if the new husband was unable or unwilling to provide for his wife's children, or she abandoned them? We can find both men and women shuffling off their responsibilities, and leaving children to the care of the parish.[10] The inhabitants of Martham (Norfolk) reacted with fury in 1656 when a local widow married a Thetford man and moved there with him, leaving her young daughter behind. A fierce tussle ensued over who should maintain the child, ending with magistrates ordering Martham to take responsibility. The marriage may have been in the widow's interests, but hardly those of Martham's parishioners.[11] Magistrates had to adjudicate in many such disputes. John Harte wanted his wife's father to be made responsible for the two young stepchildren he was struggling to support. William Marten of Cheddar

[7] Heywood, *Autobiography*, ii.130; D. A. Gatley et al., eds, 'The Stoke-upon-Trent Parish Listing, 1701', *Collections for a History of Staffordshire*, Staffordshire Record Society, 4th series, 16 (1994), 203; cf. 209.

[8] For overviews see Stephen Collins, 'British Stepfamily Relationships, 1500–1800', *Journal of Family History*, 16 (1991); Patricia Crawford, *Parents of Poor Children in England, 1580–1800* (Oxford, 2010), 173–9.

[9] Barbara J, Todd, 'The Remarrying Widow: a Stereotype Reconsidered', in Mary Prior, ed., *Women in English Society 1500–1800* (1985); Laura Gowing, *Domestic Dangers. Women, Words, and Sex in Early Modern London* (Oxford, 1996), 170–1; F. G. Emmison, ed., *Wills of the County of Essex (England). Volume 1, 1558–1565* (Washington, D.C., 1982), 154.

[10] J. W. Willis Bund, ed., *Worcestershire County Records: Calendar of the Quarter Sessions Records, 1591–1643* (Worcester, 1900), 267, 457; SQSR, iii.14.

[11] D. E. Howell James, ed., *Norfolk Quarter Sessions Order Book 1650–1657*, Norfolk Record Society, 26 (1955), 34; cf. William Le Hardy, ed., *Hertfordshire County Records. Calendar to the Sessions Books 1658 to 1700* (Hertford, 1930), 224; S. C. Ratcliff and H. C. Johnson, eds, *Warwickshire County Records*, 9 vols (Warwick, 1935–64), v.73–4.

wanted his late wife's brothers, 'being very rich men', to maintain his little step-daughter. He had married a widow with a 3-year-old daughter, but his wife had died and he claimed the child might die of want. Did responsibility lie with him or with the child's uncles?[12] There was a host of such intractable problems.

Such problems, of course, affected only a minority. Most step-families coped financially and many appear to have adjusted adequately to their new circumstances. Some indeed flourished. The marriage of the Worcestershire squire Henry Townshend to Dorothy Dobbins, a second union for both, led eventually to another match, between Henry's son and Dorothy's daughter.[13] Elizabeth Angier, orphaned at 8, was similarly fortunate. Her devoted husband tells us that she had acquired 'a very tender [step]mother, that was very affectionate to her', and the pair had forged a bond 'sweeter and stronger than natural relation'.[14] Elizabeth Freke, also orphaned at an early age, with sisters still younger, recalled that their mother was 'not missed by us, we having so good and kind a father and an aunt of my mother's sister'. Two brothers had married two sisters, all living under the same roof, and the aunt had stepped into the maternal vacancy. When the aunt's husband died a few years later, the two fractured families effectively merged.[15]

It appears, indeed, that some children came to enjoy a better relationship with their stepmother than with their own father, and even occasionally better than the earlier bond with their natural mother. John Rastrick, a husbandman's son, recalled a difficult relationship with his mother but testified that his stepmother had been 'very kind and loving to me, and very careful and tender over me'.[16] In mid-seventeenth-century Kent, Henry Oxinden's second wife, Katherine, was much closer to his daughters and wayward son than any of them were to him.[17] The diary of the West Country physician Claver Morris reveals an especially close bond between stepmother and daughter. Morris broke off all contact with his only daughter, Betty, when she married secretly and against his express wishes. His wife sided with Betty, and later devised a successful stratagem to reconcile father and daughter. Betty was devastated when her stepmother eventually died. Rushing to the bedside she cried, 'Oh! my dear mother, I shall lose my best friend', and swooned. She had lost her birth mother while still an infant, so her stepmother was the only mother she would have remembered.[18]

---

[12] *SQSR*, i.93–4, ii.167. Cf. J. J. Bagley, ed., *The Great Diurnall of Nicholas Blundell of Little Crosby, Lancashire, 1702–1728*, 3 vols, Record Society of Lancashire and Cheshire (1968–72), i.305; Ratcliff and Johnson, eds, *Warwickshire County Records*, i.10–11.

[13] Stephen Porter, Stephen K. Roberts, and Ian Roy, eds, *The Diary and Papers of Henry Townshend, 1640–1663*, Worcestershire Historical Society, NS, 25 (2014), 15, 321–2; cf. *The Letters of John Chamberlain*, ed. N. E. McClure (Philadelphia, 1939), i.139.

[14] Heywood, *Autobiography*, i.59.

[15] *The Remembrances of Elizabeth Freke, 1671–1714*, ed. Raymond A. Anselment, Camden Society, 5th series, 18 (2001), 4–6, 40.

[16] *The Life of John Rastrick 1650–1727*, ed. Andrew Cambers, Camden Society, 5th series, 36 (2010), 39–40, 47.

[17] *Oxinden Letters 1642–1670*, 182–3, 243–4, 343; BL, Add. MS 28004, fos. 59, 111–15, 309, 318, 343; Add. MS 28005, fos. 111–17, 166, 197–231.

[18] Edmund Hobhouse, ed., *The Diary of a West Country Physician AD 1684–1726* (Rochester, 1934), 15, 66–8, 72, 117.

As these examples suggest, many step-parents took their responsibilities seriously. John Rastrick explained that his own children had been blessed with a loving stepmother, just as he had been, while a Quaker widow recalled that her late husband had been 'a tender husband and father to my children which I had by a former husband'. One very poor woman was still caring for a young stepson in Norwich in 1630 even though her husband had deserted both her and his child.[19] Men who had the custody of goods belonging to their young stepdaughters, for safe keeping, often stipulated in their wills that they must all be restored.[20] Some step-parents continued to provide support long after their spouse had died and the children had grown. We find an 80-year-old Sussex husbandman helping his stepdaughter in a protracted lawsuit. A widow in Southampton begged the town assembly to waive its rules and allow her stepdaughter to open a shop, while another continued to furnish her stepson with money after he had taken up an apprenticeship, against his master's express wishes.[21] Wills reflect other step-relationships that had clearly been affectionate. Elizabeth Blithman, a Newcastle widow who died in 1562, left all her goods to her stepchildren, the 'two wenches' she said had cared well for her. She commented tartly that her own kin had done nothing for her. Joan Hiche, a young pregnant widow, bequeathed her house to her unborn child, with a proviso that if it died the house was to be sold and the proceeds divided equally between her sister and her stepmother. Stephen Baker, a Suffolk husbandman, left all his goods to his second wife and thereafter to her daughter, Margaret, 'in consideration of the pains she has taken with me in my lifetime'. Similarly, George Sparrow, a baker, left all his houses, lands, and goods to his second wife, Mary, 'because she has faithfully vowed carefully to educate all mine and her children', and 'be a loving and careful mother providing for them'.[22] Other evidence sometimes incidentally reinforces this picture of harmonious accommodation. At the end of the period, for example, we find a London chambermaid inviting her stepmother and half-sister to tea on a Sunday afternoon.[23]

Such examples lend support to the claim that the cruel stepmother was no more than a 'cultural myth'.[24] But contemporaries emphatically disagreed. A gloomy pamphleteer commented in 1635 that:

---

[19] *Life of John Rastrick,*199; W. L. Sachse, ed., *Minutes of the Norwich Court of Mayoralty 1630–1631*, Norfolk Record Society, 15 (1942), 231, 233, 235; *Some Testimonies of the Life, Death and Sufferings of Amariah Drewet, of Cirencester* (1687), 3; cf. John Whiting, *Early Piety Exemplified* (1711), 5.

[20] See e.g. James Raine, ed., *Depositions and other Ecclesiastical Proceedings from the Courts of Durham*, Surtees Society, 21 (1845), 51.

[21] WSRO, Ep.1/11/9, fos.111v–114; Amy Froide, *Never Married. Singlewomen in Early Modern England* (Oxford, 2005), 30; R. C. Anderson, ed., *The Book of Examinations and Depositions 1622–1644*, 4 vols, Southampton Record Society (1929–36), iii.98–9.

[22] Raine, ed., *Depositions from Durham*, 66–8; Emmison, *Wills of Essex*, 12; Nesta Evans, ed., *Wills of the Archdeaconry of Sudbury 1630–1635*, Suffolk Records Society, 29 (1987), 69, 283.

[23] Alan Savile, ed., *Secret Comment. The Diaries of Gertrude Savile 1721–1757*, Thoroton Society, 41 (1997), 98.

[24] Heather Dubrow, 'The Message from Marcade: Parental Death in Tudor and Stuart England', in Betty S. Travitsky and Adele F. Seeff, eds, *Attending to Women in Early Modern England* (Newark, Del., 1994), 157.

> The rough-browed step-dame her young stepson hugs,
> Tempering for him (mean time) mortiferous drugs.

The image of the harsh stepmother, deeply rooted in proverbial wisdom, had passed down the centuries, and most people believed it was based on fact.[25] That view was held by women perhaps even more strongly than by men, especially when they were facing the perils of childbirth. The poet Anne Bradstreet, whose family had migrated to Massachusetts in 1630, addressed some heartfelt verses to her husband as she contemplated the possibility of dying in childbed. 'Look to my little ones, my dear remains,' she begged him,

> And if thou love thyself, or loved'st me,
> These O protect from step-dame's injury.[26]

Every mother knew that if she died in childbed, her husband would probably remarry. Would their children be cared for, or neglected and mistreated? Oliver Le Neve's wife, fearing she would not survive, asked him to retain a trusted nurse. Dorothy Moore, who died in 1673 (not in childbirth), left a poignant letter for her husband, anticipating his remarriage, begging him to be good to their children, and offering guidance on how best to secure each child's future welfare.[27] A widow contemplating remarriage would have similar worries. If she died first, could she be confident that her new husband would treat her children well? Married women rarely made wills, but Anne Sparke, who died in 1632, was determined to protect the interests of the children from her first marriage. She left a will that named her first husband's brother as executor, and asked him to take responsibility for the children. She granted her second husband permission to use her movable goods only if he gave security to pass them on to her children once they came of age. She evidently placed no trust in his reliability.[28]

Conduct books urged step-parents to cherish a new partner's children as their own. It was their duty 'to love them, to tender them, and to cherish them', one advised, 'as their own father and mother did'. Thomas Fuller argued that a mother should indeed be more indulgent to her stepchildren than to her own.[29] As William Gouge observed, 'If the world's proverb hold true (*love me and love my dog*), how much more true is this Christian rule, *love me and love my child?*' Instead, he lamented, it had always been common for men and women alike to resent their stepchildren, 'and cunningly seek to alienate the natural parent's affection from them'. And that inevitably bred resentment.[30] Another manual offered a similarly bleak assessment and claimed, moreover, that 'stepmothers do more often offend,

[25] Henry Goodcole, *The Adultresses Funerall Day* (1635), sig.A3 (I owe this reference to Robert Daniel). Maurice Palmer Tilley, *A Dictionary of the Proverbs in England in the Sixteenth and Seventeenth Centuries* (1950), D19, F609, H374, H592, M1207.

[26] *The Works of Anne Bradstreet*, ed. Jeanne Hensley (Cambridge, Mass., 1967), 224.

[27] BL, Egerton MS 2717, f. 163; HMC, 13, *Capt. Stewart*, 121.

[28] Evans, *Wills of Sudbury*, 183.

[29] John Dod and Robert Cleaver, *A Godly Forme of Household Governement* (1612), 239; Thomas Fuller, *The Holy State* (1642), 26.

[30] William Gouge, *Of Domesticall Duties* (1622), 580–2.

and fail in this duty than men, by reason that their affections be stronger than man's, and many times over-rule them'. It urged women to show 'motherless children no stepmother's friendship, but a right motherly kindness', and bolstered the message with a stark warning: the stepmother might also die young, and would she want to imagine her own children suffering at the hands of another 'rigorous, churlish and unkind' woman?[31]

Such reasoning rested in part on the traditional belief that women's constitutions rendered them more passionate and less rational than men. It reflected too the reality that women had the main care and oversight of children, especially in the early years. That made responsible widowers similarly anxious when they sought a new bride. The lawyer Bulstrode Whitelocke, twice widowed and reluctantly seeking a third wife, was mainly concerned to find someone who would be kind to his children. He was hugely relieved when the widow he chose proved as kind-hearted as he had hoped.[32] One London bride, warm-hearted or perhaps simply diplomatic, kissed her new husband's young child, and declared that she was marrying as much for love of the child as of its father.[33] If both partners had children, both might have concerns for their emotional, physical, and material welfare. A Leicestershire widower, wooing Elizabeth Stanbridge in 1590, asked if she could love his children 'as if they came from her own body'. She assured him that she could, and that she loved him too, but explained that she had sworn not to marry again until her own son had reached the age of 21, to protect his interests.[34] Widowers and widows alike were thus very conscious of the risks in remarriage. And if necessary, friends would remind them. When Mary Down, a comfortably off widow with eight children, was wooed by a poor young tenant farmer, friends were deeply suspicious and warned that he would try to alienate her from her children, to serve his own interests. She wailed that she felt torn 'between hawk and buzzard, hope and fear'.[35] Everyone knew, moreover, how easily appearances could deceive. John Fretwell, a timber merchant, was very solicitous for his three young daughters and determined to find a wife who would treat them kindly. He broke off one match when he suspected that would not be the case. Courting another woman, he asked her directly whether she liked his house and his children, and was delighted when she declared that she liked his children best of all. In the event, she turned out to be a disastrous partner. There were no guarantees.[36]

---

[31] Dod and Cleaver, *Godly Forme*, 240–1; *The Office of Christian Parents* (Cambridge, 1616), 132–3.

[32] *The Diary of Bulstrode Whitelocke 1605–1675*, ed. Ruth Spalding (Oxford, 1990), 253–4, 264; cf. Susan E. Whyman, *Sociability and Power in Late-Stuart England. The Cultural Worlds of the Verneys 1660–1720* (Oxford 1999), 119.

[33] Tim Reinke-Williams, *Women, Work and Sociability in Early Modern London* (Basingstoke, 2014), 28.

[34] LRRO, 1D 41/4/532; Hubbard, *City Women*, 243–4.   [35] Cannon, *Chronicles*, ii.323–4.

[36] 'Family History begun by James Fretwell', ed. Charles Jackson, *Yorkshire Diaries of the Seventeenth and Eighteenth Centuries*, Surtees Society, 65 (1875), 176–8; cf. HMC, 11, *Gawdy*, 54; W. L. Sachse, ed., *Minutes of the Norwich Court of Mayoralty 1632–1635*, Norfolk Record Society, 36 (1967), 75; Hubbard, *City Women*, 258–9.

Harsh or neglectful step-parents were far from figures of myth. Thomas Shepard recalled that his stepmother 'did seem not to love me, but incensed my father often against me'. When his father died, he was left in the sole care of his stepmother, until his older brother took him away and raised him in his own home.[37] Neighbours might also intervene if they became aware of abuse. When Margaret Clowes's young stepdaughter died in 1614, neighbours suspected her cruel parenting had been responsible, and said she had previously been reproved on that score. The girl's father, by contrast, claimed to have seen nothing amiss, perhaps reluctant to criticize his wife and jeopardize their relationship.[38] The case underlines the vulnerability of young stepchildren, who would spend most of their time under the supervision of the female parent. Stepdaughters were especially at risk, for girls were expected to be disciplined by their mothers. But boys could suffer too if a weak father proved unable to restrain a harsh stepmother. An eighteenth-century Lincolnshire farmer described in graphic detail the appalling abuse he had endured from the age of 6 at the hands of a sadistic stepmother. On one occasion, he had been flogged in the barn, naked and hanging upside down. His father he remembered as 'an easy, good-natured man', completely dominated by his wife.[39] Infants were still more vulnerable, and in rare cases neighbours felt compelled to intervene. They did so, for example, to save the infant daughter of Daniel Newcome, whose wife had died in childbirth in 1682. Daniel had remarried a few months later, and it was soon clear the infant was being badly mistreated. Its plight became so desperate that neighbours felt impelled to take it away, scandalized by such 'shameful abuse'.[40]

There were, of course, just as many bad stepfathers. Some cheated the children of their rightful inheritance. Others simply drove them away, like the man who had allegedly turned his wife's children 'out of doors, so that in a short time they either begged their bread or died in the streets with hunger'. Edward Randolph's children, also turned out by their stepfather, were more fortunate. An uncle was able to help and, capitalizing on his court connections, he urged Lord Burghley to intervene, and threatened to appeal to the Queen herself.[41] The children of the poor had no such saviours. Roderick Awdry, hanged at Tyburn at the age of 15, described how his father had died when he was very young, his mother had remarried, and he had been 'turned out of doors' by his stepfather. Sleeping rough and left to fend for himself, he had soon graduated from robbing orchards to burglary. Two of his brothers also turned to crime and similarly ended on the gallows.[42]

---

[37] 'Thomas Shepard's Memoir of his Own Life', in Alexander Young, ed., *Chronicles of the First Planters of the Colony of Massachusetts Bay* (Boston, 1846), 501–2.

[38] Anne J. Kettle, ed., 'Mathew Cradock's Book of Remembrance, 1614-15', *Collections for a History of Staffordshire*, Staffordshire Record Society, 4th series, 16 (1994), 106–8.

[39] [Charles Vario,] *The Modern Farmers Guide* (Glasgow, 1768), pp. v–xix.

[40] Newcome, *Autobiography*, ii.245, 248.

[41] *OBOA,* 16850506; Wood, *Life and Times*, i.425; HMC, 9, *Salisbury*, ii.206; cf. John Bruce, ed., *Liber Famelicus of Sir James Whitelocke*, Camden Society, OS, 70 (1858), 5–6.

[42] *OBOA,* 17140528; cf. 17141222, 17150511.

Only in extreme circumstances did abusive behaviour come before the courts. John Burt, an Oxfordshire villager, was accused in 1634 of making his stepdaughter, aged 19, strip naked, and of whipping her. He denied stripping her but told the court that as her stepfather he had the authority to punish her 'in what manner he pleaseth'. Neighbours remained sceptical. In this case, it was probably the whiff of sexual perversion that had triggered their concern.[43] Generally, it was only cruelty leading to a child's death that brought abuse before the courts, and we find a steady trickle of such cases. In 1560, Maud Smyth of Thurrock was convicted of shutting her young stepson in an oven, where he had suffocated. Richard Fyrmyn of Colchester was convicted of murder in 1601 for the brutal treatment of his 6-year-old stepdaughter, and the jury heard he had long wanted her dead.[44] Children were especially vulnerable when the remarrying parent had also died and they were left in the care of a resentful step-parent. Clemence Barnarde's father had married a second wife, Alice, and when he too died, Clemence followed her stepmother into her next marriage, now as a servant. A coroner's inquest heard that in July 1567 Alice had killed her with a hatchet, hiding the body near the kitchen and later dumping it in a pond. But trial juries often afforded step-parents the same benefit of the doubt they gave abusive employers. In this instance, they ruled that Clemence had been murdered by a fictitious 'John at Love'. Such verdicts were by no means rare.[45] In another disturbing episode, Abigail Pett, who had also lost both parents, died after a savage beating by her 'cruel' stepfather Thomas Nunn, a Suffolk clergyman. Nunn had the body hastily buried, but suspicious neighbours notified a magistrate, who ordered it to be exhumed. Nunn stood trial at Bury St Edmunds assizes in May 1599, and was found guilty of manslaughter.[46] Another woman, tried at the Old Bailey a century later for killing her stepdaughter, found witnesses to testify that '*though* she was mother in law [stepmother] to the deceased, *yet* she loved her well, and always gave her moderate correction'.[47] The reporter's language speaks volumes about contemporary attitudes and assumptions.

Despite Abigail Pett's fate, children in their teens were generally less vulnerable. Ralph Josselin disliked the 'sour spirit' of the stepmother he acquired in his mid-teens but his father remained kind, and he was able to cope.[48] The principal concern of older children was usually the material implications of their father's remarriage. Would his new wife's jointure eat into their inheritance? Would she alienate his affections, and persuade him to divert a sizeable part of the estate to her own children, or find some other way to undermine their inheritance? Josselin's own father died intestate, and like many others he felt aggrieved at the way his stepmother then treated him. John Newnham, an Elizabethan gentleman, published a vitriolic

---

[43] Oxfordshire Archives Office, Oxf. c12, fos. 203v–205.

[44] J. S. Cockburn, ed., *Calendar of Assize Records: Essex Indictments, Elizabeth I* (1978), 12, 519–20.

[45] Cockburn, *Calendar of Assize Records: Essex, Elizabeth*, 61–2; cf. 337; R. F. Hunnisett, ed., *Sussex Coroners' Inquests 1558–1603* (Kew, 1996), 38; Cockburn, ed., *Calendar of Assize Records: Kent Indictments, Elizabeth I* (1979), 82, 367.

[46] W. G. Perrin, ed., *The Autobiography of Phineas Pett*, Navy Records Society, 51 (1918), 12–13.

[47] *OBSP*, t16860707-12 (emphasis added).   [48] Josselin, *Diary*, 1–3.

attack on manipulative stepmothers in 1590, and complained that he had been plagued for twenty years by a malicious 'night-crow'. The result, he added, had been 'the spoiling me of my birthright'.[49]

Newnham was concerned only with the rights of elder sons, but every child was affected when a parent remarried. When William Edmundson, a Quaker widower, proposed to a widow in 1696, she agreed only on condition that both sets of children should give their consent.[50] If only a daughter had survived from a father's first marriage, her status as heiress was inevitably thrown into question by the arrival of a young stepmother. Anne Gawdy was the sole heiress of her wealthy father, and rumours in 1588 that his second wife was unexpectedly pregnant filled her husband's family with panic. 'What if my Lady cometh forth with a boy?' they fretted. What indeed—for then the inheritance would be lost.[51] Male heirs had reason to worry even when the estate was already settled on them. Sir Thomas Hutchinson, who died in 1643, chose to leave all his movables and everything not covered by his son's marriage settlement to his second wife and their children. That dealt a significant blow to his eldest son, and was perceived, if perhaps unfairly, as a deliberate slight. Robert Dormer went much further, disinheriting his eldest son and settling his entire estate on the eldest son of his second wife.[52] Other heirs were shocked when they discovered how much had been settled on the father's second wife and any children she might bear. Simonds D'Ewes was deeply worried when he learned that his widowed father was seeking a young bride. Simonds and his sisters urged him not to remarry, or at least to settle for 'some good and ancient widow, every way fit for him'. Their father was reluctant to relinquish his dream, but eventually settled for a suitably 'ancient' widow of 45. She had borne no children in her previous marriage and seemed unlikely to have any now. For his children, it was a triumph.[53]

Such material concerns were sometimes exacerbated by disquiet over the stepmother's character or social status. This might be merely a cover for self-interest, but was probably genuine if there was an extreme disparity in status. William Apsley, heir to a good estate in Sussex, was disgusted when his father made such a match and viewed his stepmother with contempt, along with the three sons she subsequently bore. Many years later, dying childless, William bequeathed his estate to his uncle and nephews rather than to these lowly half-brothers.[54] Sir Thomas Brathwaite, a Westmorland squire, did not even acknowledge his secret remarriage

---

[49] Josselin, *Diary*, 5; John Newnham, *Newnams Nightcrowe. A Bird that Breedeth Braules in many Families and Housholdes* (1590), sig. A2-v and *passim*.

[50] *A Journal of the Life of William Edmundson* (1837), 182–3, 203, 205.

[51] Isaac Herbert Jeayes, ed., *Letters of Philip Gawdy of Harling, Norfolk* (1906), 36–7, 40.

[52] Lucy Hutchinson, *Memoirs of the Life of Colonel John Hutchinson*, ed. John Sutherland (Oxford, 1973), 90–2; Sara Mendelson, 'Anne Dormer and her Children', in Naomi J. Miller and Naomi Yavneh, eds, *Gender and Early Modern Constructions of Childhood* (Farnham, 2011), 120.

[53] Dorothy Heighes Woodforde, ed., *Woodforde Papers and Diaries* (1932), 22; D'Ewes, *Autobiography*, 227–9; *The Diary of Sir Simonds D'Ewes (1622–1624)*, ed. Elisabeth Bourcier (Paris, 1974), 65–6, 123–4. His father retaliated by making his younger son, Richard, 15 his executor: *Autobiography*, ii.24.

[54] Hutchinson, *Memoirs*, 283.

to the daughter of one of his servants, despite the fact that she bore him eight children. The truth emerged only after his death, and his heir then contrived 'by various devices and suits at law . . . to deprive them of all provision and their mother of dower'.[55] We can find similar hostility towards low-born stepmothers in middling-sort families too. *The History of Myddle* records the story of a prosperous freeholder, Samuel Downton, whose wife had died leaving five underage children. Downton hired a maid to look after them, 'a young girl of obscure parentage, but somewhat fair'. His children were deeply troubled when he subsequently married her, and all left home as soon as they could. In this case, their misgivings proved justified. Downton and his new wife ran up heavy debts and eventually fled, abandoning their own four children to the care of the parish.[56]

Fewer issues were usually at stake when a widow remarried. The estate of her deceased husband would descend to his heirs according to manorial custom, his will, or a marriage settlement. The danger remained, however, that her new husband might squander her money and goods, gain possession of her land, and cheat her children of their inheritance. If she died before him, by the common law of 'curtesy' he had the right to enjoy for life all her real property, if they had had children. Fathers and mothers alike worried over such dangers. In 1618, the lawyer John Hoskyns, expecting shortly to die, told his wife of a bad dream in which he had seen her remarried to a roguish new husband who was 'pawning your plate, selling your leases, . . . and putting my boy to keep his hawks and dogs'.[57] Widows with comparable fears often chose to remain single, while those who did remarry increasingly insisted on settlements to place their estate beyond the reach of the new husband. One disgruntled fortune hunter, a younger brother, complained that this proved the law was biased against men.[58] These legal safeguards generally worked well. John Reresby, who was orphaned at 12 and lived with his mother and stepfather for some years, recalled that his mother ('a woman of great spirit') had held the purse strings until he came of age, and that his stepfather had treated him 'with all civility and respect'.[59] But when men died intestate, as was common in ordinary families, their children were more vulnerable. Phineas Pett complained that his father's death, and his mother's 'fatal matching with a most wicked husband', had brought the abrupt termination of his allowance and his university career.[60]

[55] Joseph Nicholson and Richard Burn, *The History and Antiquities of the Counties of Westmorland and Cumberland* (1777), i.127; *Flemings in Oxford*, ii.379.

[56] Richard Gough, *The History of Myddle*, ed. David Hey (Harmondsworth, 1981), 197–8.

[57] Amy Louise Erickson, *Women and Property in Early Modern England* (1993), 25; Louise Brown Osborn, ed., *The Life, Letters, and Writings of John Hoskyns 1566–1638* (New Haven, 1937), 81.

[58] Erickson, *Women and Property*, 132–7; Elizabeth Foyster, 'Marrying the Experienced Widow in Early Modern England: the Male Perspective', in Sandra Cavallo and Lyndan Warner, eds, *Widowhood in Medieval and Early Modern Europe* (Harlow, 1999), 114–18; *OBOA*,16850304; Francis Osborn, *The Works of Francis Osborn Esquire* (8th edition, 1682), Part 1, 31, 35–6.

[59] *Memoirs of Sir John Reresby*, ed. Andrew Browning (2nd edition, ed. Mary Geiter and W. A. Speck, 1991), 3–5.

[60] Perrin, *Autobiography of Phineas Pett*, 2–3.

We should not forget, of course, that step-parents also faced a major challenge of readjustment. Stepmothers, often living in a new home, had to forge a working relationship with children who were likely to be suspicious or openly hostile. Angel Harrington, who turned down a rich suitor in 1695, explained that she had vowed never to be a stepmother, having seen the unhappiness of so many. Anne and Elizabeth Cottrell never accepted a stepmother they branded 'the serpent', and formed a close alliance against her. Samuel Pepys, calling on a colleague's widow in 1667, found the house full of squabbling 'factions, she against the [step]children and they against one another and her'.[61] Stepfathers sometimes found that older children refused to accept them or their authority. Richard Dove was apprenticed to his stepfather, a London silversmith, but often stole from him. John Hunt proved utterly unable to control his stepdaughter Agnes, who had inherited a portion from her grandfather and was squandering it in wild living. In desperation, Hunt and his wife begged magistrates to intervene.[62] He was far from alone. A felon facing the gallows in 1685 lamented that his mother and stepfather had given him 'all the good counsel they could, but he would not be ruled by them'. A truculent young woman named Elizabeth Cranberry pushed defiance much further: when her stepfather threatened to turn her out of the house, after a quarrel, she took revenge by lacing his porridge with arsenic.[63] Friction between step-parent and child could easily breed tensions between the parents themselves. A fierce quarrel between a Leicestershire villager and his wife was triggered when she found him beating her child, whom he disliked. The friction between William Bedell and his wife reflected their very different ideas on child-rearing. Bedell was an austere clergyman, while his wife, an affluent widow with several children, had more fashionable values and tastes. His son commented tersely, many years later, that his father's 'will and authority bore the sway'. For his part, Ralph Josselin took some pride in the fact that, despite his stepmother's querulous nature, he had never caused any dissension between the couple.[64]

When a second marriage turned sour, most children predictably sided with their birth parent. If it broke down altogether and the wife sought a judicial separation, her children might testify to the cruelty she had suffered at their stepfather's hands. In one case, where the husband's son and the wife's son both testified, each supported his birth parent against the allegedly unjust step-parent.[65] Justinian Pagitt, a London law student, also took his father's part in a troubled household. Convinced that his father was being abused by his mean, selfish, and dishonest stepmother, Pagitt compiled a detailed dossier of her irresponsible behaviour, and her attempts to marginalize him and his younger brother.[66] In more serious cases,

[61] Whyman, *Sociability and Power*, 120–1; Sara Mendelson and Mary O'Connor, ' "Thy Passionately Loving Sister and Faithfull Friend": Anne Dormer's Letters to her Sister, Lady Trumbull', in Naomi J. Miller and Naomi Yavneh, eds, *Sibling Relations and Gender in the Early Modern World* (Aldershot, 2006), 207; Pepys, *Diary*, viii.476–7, x.22.

[62] *OBOA*, 17090518; *SQSR*, ii.218–19.   [63] *OBOA*, 16850304; *OBSP*, t17200427-43.

[64] LRRO, 1D 41/4, Box 30/81; J. E. B. Mayor, ed., *Life of Bishop Bedell by his Son* (Cambridge, 1871), 30; Josselin, *Diary*, 3.

[65] Foyster, 'Marrying the Experienced Widow', 119.   [66] BL, MS Harley 1026, fos.78v–82.

children might try to shield their mother from a violent stepfather, or alert neighbours. Adult children sometimes intervened more forcefully. One man complained that his angry stepdaughter had 'broken his head in several places', while the stepsons of a Yorkshire clergyman threatened to kill him, and contrived to have him imprisoned.[67]

Such tensions might continue far into the children's adult lives, in both elite and ordinary families. Sir Percival Willoughby and his wife both had fraught relationships with stepmothers, a breed 'from whom', Sir Percival wrote, 'God deliver us and ours'. A sharp-tongued woman in York was described as the 'utter enemy' of her stepson and his wife, and had brought numerous suits against them.[68] But family dynamics evolved over time, and a stepmother's position inevitably weakened if her husband died. A brother and sister in Wiltshire were accused in 1623 of using arson to drive their now widowed stepmother out of her house. If a husband had to be away for a long period, that too weakened the stepmother's position. In one such case, a Cheshire gentlewoman explained that her husband had handed control of his estate to his eldest son, directing him to maintain his stepmother and her family. Instead, she complained, he had 'obstinately and very undutifully refused' to support her, rendering her destitute.[69] For their part, successful men nursing old resentments took delight in the impotence of a once powerful stepmother. Sir Robert Paston, basking in royal favour in 1664, remarked smugly that his widowed stepmother would 'bleed to hear' of his good fortune, 'and that the king is so kind'.[70] Old animosities might never die.

HALF-SIBLINGS AND STEP-SIBLINGS

Any parent contemplating remarriage knew that a second brood might well create jealousies and concerns over inheritance. Some landowners opted to remain single, to protect the interests of their existing offspring, preserve the integrity of the estate, and maintain family harmony. Sir George Sondes remained a widower for twenty years to protect his sons' inheritance, and married again only after they both predeceased him. Richard Whalley, sick and ageing, explained apologetically that he had taken a new wife only 'to get a nurse to look after me'. He promised she would not seek to deprive his heirs of even a halfpenny.[71]

---

[67] Hubbard, *City Women*, 258; Froide, *Never Married*, 50; Heywood, *Autobiography*, iii.192.

[68] Cassandra, Duchess of Chandos, *The Continuation of the History of the Willoughby Family*, ed. A. C. Wood (Eton, Windsor, 1958), 24; BI, CP H4267; cf. Willis Bund, ed., *Worcestershire County Records*, 211.

[69] B. Howard Cunnington, ed., *Records of the County of Wilts.* (Devizes, 1932), 71–3; J. E. H. Bennett and J. C. Dewhurst, eds, *Quarter Sessions Records for the County Palatine of Chester 1559–1760*, Record Society of Lancashire and Cheshire, 94 (1940), 128–9; cf. Hubbard, *City Women*, 262–3.

[70] Jean Agnew, ed., *The Whirlpool of Misadventures. Letters of Robert Paston, First Earl of Yarmouth 1663–1679*, Norfolk Record Society, 76 (2013), 47.

[71] *Sir George Sondes his plaine Narrative to the World* (1655), 13, 27; Searle, ed., *Barrington Family Letters*, 29–30.

Fears that remarriage would create bitter family divisions over resources and inheritance often proved well founded. When William Blundell's daughter died in 1682, he urged his son-in-law, Richard Butler, not to remarry. As Butler was already heavily in debt, it would be folly to cripple the estate with 'the charge of a new and numerous breed of children'. His main concern, Blundell admitted, was to protect his grandchildren's interests, and his interference was deeply resented.[72] The remarriage of Sir William Guise (d.1642) of Elmore, Gloucestershire, proved still more divisive, and poisoned family relations for at least two generations. His grandson Christopher, compiling a family history many years later, told how Sir William had a son, also William, by his first wife, and numerous children by his second, a widow. Christopher damned her as an evil woman who had manipulated her husband to divert the estate and its resources away from his father. Christopher's father had been sent away to be raised elsewhere, and married off at the earliest opportunity to secure a portion which was then used to serve herself and her own children. Years later, penury forced him to send Christopher to be raised at Elmore by the now ageing grandfather, and the youngster found himself at the mercy of these uncles and aunts, his father's half-siblings. They had proceeded, he recalled, 'under the cloak of care and pretences religious, to wreak their malice upon every slight omission, and so punish my father, whom they hated, in me'. He had sunk into 'a great depression of spirit and melancholy', and commented bitterly that the physical and mental scars had lasted a lifetime. 'I cannot choose', he observed sourly, 'but note here the malice of cadets [junior branches], who are often the most unnatural enemies of their own house.' They should be loyal and deferential to the senior line, but all too often self-interest swamped such considerations.[73]

Guise did not address an important related issue: what responsibility, if any, did an heir have towards half-siblings? We have seen that William Apsley despised his low-born stepmother and her brood, and bequeathed his estate to other kin. Nevertheless, he still felt it proper to leave annuities of £30 to each of her sons, with an additional £100 a year to the eldest. He clearly felt some residual obligation to half-brothers he held in contempt, and primogeniture still resonated. Sir George Sondes also provided generously for six half-brothers and a half-sister he viewed with similar disdain, and Edmund Bohun, a Suffolk gentleman, took in the son of his widowed half-sister.[74] Isaac Newton resented his younger half-siblings, children of the stepfather he hated, but in later years provided some assistance to them and their own children.[75] Many heirs, however, were determined to challenge or evade the obligations laid down in their father's will. In 1579, Lord Keeper Bacon's elaborate will detailed what was to go to the two sons of his second marriage, but a

---

[72] Margaret Blundell, ed., *Cavalier. Letters between William Blundell and his Friends 1620–1698* (1933), 231–2, 238–40.

[73] G. Davies, ed., *Autobiography of Thomas Raymond and Memoirs of the Family of Guise of Elmore, Gloucestershire*, Camden Society, 3rd series, 28 (1917), 111–15, 120.

[74] Hutchinson, *Memoirs*, 283; *Sir George Sondes his Narrative*, 18; *The Diary and Autobiography of Edmund Bohun, Esq.*, ed. S. Wilton Rix (Beccles, 1853), 129.

[75] Frank E. Manuel, *A Portrait of Isaac Newton* (Cambridge, Mass., 1968), 34–5, 63.

lengthy dispute followed nonetheless, with both sets of half-brothers alleging bad faith.[76] Civility and good manners might quickly evaporate in such contests. During the course of an acrimonious tussle in 1719 over the estate of Sir Thomas Lorrain, a Northumberland baronet, a local diarist recorded bluntly that 'Mr Ed. Lorrain took K[itty] Lorrain's mantua from her mantua-maker and shit in it'. Calling her mother a bastard, he jeered that Kitty herself was no better, scoffing that her mother could not prove her marriage to his father. His infantile behaviour reflected resentment at the allegedly baleful influence of his stepmother and her brood. 'He says they cheated Sir Thomas when they kept his house', the diarist added.[77] Similar tensions surfaced among the middling sort. Phineas Pett, a young shipwright, bitterly resented the failure of his elder half-brother, Joseph, to provide any support. With both parents dead, Phineas's younger siblings were left at the mercy of a harsh stepfather, and Joseph apparently felt no responsibility towards them. 'God knoweth', Phineas exclaimed after the tragic death of his sister Abigail, noted above, 'he never disbursed [a] halfpenny to their bringing up, nor cared what became of them.' Phineas took his remaining young sisters and brother into his own home, and one of his half-sisters too.[78]

Relationships between half-siblings were often similarly strained. In some families step-siblings had almost no contact. Anthony Bacon took offence in 1595 when he learned that an older stepsister had married without even informing him of her plans. His mother, also left in ignorance, commented that 'your sister's nature is but unkind', though she urged him to avoid a quarrel.[79] But in other families, the children reached an amicable accommodation. In some, those born to the second wife were treated much like the younger children of the first, and appear to have accepted their place and obligations.[80] Rowland Lytton and his numerous siblings maintained a warm social friendship with their two maternal half-sisters and their husbands. Humphrey Coningsby, a poet and traveller who died abroad in 1610, left a will that named his half-sister Joyce Jeffreys sole executrix, and bequeathed her an annuity of 100 marks. Christopher Wandesford, briefly Lord Deputy of Ireland, placed a similar trust in his half-brother, making him executor, and guardian of his children.[81]

Real affection can be found in middling-sort families too. Betty and Will Morris, half-sibling offspring of the physician Claver Morris, enjoyed a warm relationship despite an age gap of twelve years. Elizabeth Jeake of Rye, a merchant's wife, visited

[76] A. Hassell Smith et al., eds, *The Papers of Nathaniel Bacon of Stiffkey*, 5 vols, Norfolk Record Society (1979–2010), ii.25–9, 77–107 *passim*.

[77] 'The Diary of the Rev. John Thomlinson', ed. J. C. Hodgson, *Six North Country Diaries*, Surtees Society, 118 (1910), 129.

[78] Perrin, *Autobiography of Phineas Pett*, 2, 3–4, 7, 9, 13–15, 76–7.

[79] Gemma Allen, ed., *The Letters of Lady Anne Bacon*, Camden Society, 5th series, 44 (2014), 226–9; cf. *Memoirs of Sir John Reresby*, 229–30.

[80] Alison D. Wall, ed., *Two Elizabethan Women: Correspondence of Joan and Maria Thynne 1575–1611*, Wiltshire Record Society, 38 (1983), 47–8.

[81] *Letters of John Chamberlain*, ed. McClure, i.118, 124, 289, ii.3, 174, 330–1 and *passim*; Judith M. Spicksley, ed., *The Business and Household Accounts of Joyce Jeffreys, spinster of Hereford, 1638–1648* (Oxford, 2012), 9–11, 77n., 280, 306; Thornton, *Autobiography*, 22.

her half-brother in Hastings in 1694, without her husband, and stayed for a month. John Johnson, a bachelor clergyman, proved 'kind and bountiful' to both his sister and half-sister when they fell on hard times.[82] Evidence from ordinary families is scarce, but here too some families clearly adjusted well. In the gregarious Wheatcroft family of Derbyshire, the half-siblings Martha and Titus appear to have had affectionate relationships with each other, with their stepbrother, and with their stepmother too.[83] Nehemiah Wallington, a turner, invited his half-sister to join a family visit to another sister, in 1635, 'to be merry together', and a Lancashire servant included his half-brother in a New Year family reunion.[84] Some half-siblings clearly felt a strong sense of responsibility towards such kin. Esther Hunt, who lived at Harwich with her father and his second wife, stayed on after her stepmother's death to keep house and look after her six or seven young half-siblings. And the ties of half-blood might endure. When William Craford, a penniless soldier, returned from the Low Countries in 1607, he turned to his half-brother for help and received 20s to cover his immediate needs. Edward Eade, returning similarly destitute from Virginia in 1634, found lodging in his half-brother's alehouse in Norwich for several months, and his half-brother helped him rebuild his life.[85]

Rather different factors shaped relationships between stepchildren. They could rarely expect to inherit more than a token legacy, so competing expectations were far less significant than in relationships between half-siblings. Even when men left no children of their own, stepchildren were unlikely to inherit. In 1560, John Croydon, a childless Essex mariner, bequeathed his estate to his widow and then his brother. Only if the brother died childless did he will £5 apiece to his wife's two children, with most of the estate passing to a friend or distant cousin. Another testator left his estate to his wife and children, with reversion to his brother's children should his own die without heirs. His stepchildren inherited only one sheep apiece.[86]

The most pressing issues for step-siblings were therefore discrimination in everyday life, and personal compatibility. Could they live with other family members in reasonable harmony? In some cases, the answer was emphatically negative. In 1625, the churchwardens of Selsey, Sussex, presented John Brookes and his wife for 'keeping house apart, by reason that their children which he had by a former wife and she by a former husband cannot well agree, making debate between them'. For 'a more quiet and contented living' they had been forced to

---

[82] Hobhouse, *Diary of a West Country Physician*, 66–7, 117, 119–20; Michael Hunter and Annabel Gregory, eds, *An Astrological Diary of the Seventeenth Century. Samuel Jeake of Rye 1652–1699* (Oxford, 1988), 247 and n.; *The Autobiography of William Stout of Lancaster 1665–1752*, ed. J. D. Marshall (Manchester, 1967), 112–13.

[83] *The Autobiography of Leonard Wheatcroft of Ashover 1627–1706*, ed. Dorothy Riden, Derbyshire Record Society, 20 (1993), 102–3.

[84] Paul S. Seaver, *Wallington's World. A Puritan Artisan in Seventeenth-Century London* (1985), 80; Bagley, ed., *Diurnall of Nicholas Blundell*, ii.85.

[85] Heywood, *Autobiography*, i.36; Hassell Smith, *Papers of Nathaniel Bacon*, v.280; Sachse, *Minutes of the Norwich Court of Mayoralty 1632–1635*, 157–8.

[86] Emmison, *Wills of Essex*, 32, 45; but cf. 93–4, 235 for exceptions.

maintain two homes.[87] Most families, however, appear to have reached an acceptable accommodation until the older children left home to enter service or an apprenticeship. And in some instances we can find a caring relationship between step- as well as half-siblings. In 1656, for example, Robert Meane of Bungay took in his sick stepbrother John Jay, a former soldier, and cared for him in his final illness.[88] Wills also occasionally suggest affection, or at least a sense of equity. Thus Agnes Andrewe, a young Essex spinster who died in 1563, bequeathed an identical sum of 20s to her sister and stepsister, both minors.[89] A few step-parents displayed a similar spirit. William Huntington of Chester told those gathered around his deathbed in 1559 that he wished to leave half his estate to his daughter. Asked to clarify, for he had both a daughter and a stepdaughter, he said that he meant his stepdaughter. Brushing aside his daughter's pleas, he said he had already provided generously for her. Similarly, William Kirkus of Durham, who died in 1570, told his wife that he trusted her to be as good to his children as to her own. Both these were nuncupative (orally delivered) wills, and both were challenged in the courts. The step-siblings evidently did not share the testators' equitable spirit.[90]

Wills provide, of course, only a snapshot at one moment. The dynamics within a family often fluctuated over time, and testamentary cases occasionally allow us to glimpse such shifts. The disputed will of Abraham Rigge, a Yorkshire villager, provides one such example. Rigge's second wife was a widow with a daughter named Mary, and when his wife died some years later, Rigge remained single with Mary now managing the household. This arrangement worked so well, witnesses agreed, that he had promised to leave her £10, in gratitude. But several witnesses claimed that Mary had grown stubborn, lazy, and disobedient. When he died in 1621, Rigge's will was found to contain a bequest to her with the figure of £10 altered to 10s. In the protracted lawsuit that ensued, his sons and their friends insisted that the change had been made on his instructions, reflecting disgust at her behaviour. Her friends countered that she had served him well, and that his sons had tampered with the will after his death. Most of the parties were poor and barely literate, and in their world £10 was a very substantial sum.[91]

ILLEGITIMATE SIBLINGS

Charles II notoriously showered titles and favours on his illegitimate offspring. Respectable men often preferred to keep such children at a distance, and unacknowledged. Elizabethan aristocrats, too, were less willing than their forebears to recognize

---

[87] Hilda Johnstone, ed., *Churchwardens' Presentments (17th century). Archdeaconry of Chichester*, Sussex Record Society, 49 (1950), 120.
[88] Howell James, *Norfolk Quarter Sessions Order Book 1650–1657*, 88–9, 91.
[89] Emmison, *Wills of Essex*, 166.
[90] E. K. M. Jarman, ed., *Justice and Conciliation in a Tudor Church Court: Depositions from . . . the Consistory Court of Chester, September 1558-March 1559*, Record Society of Lancashire and Cheshire, 146 (2012), 35–6; Raine, ed., *Depositions from Durham*, 212–15.
[91] BI, CP H1499.

illegitimate offspring. In *King Lear*, the Earl of Gloucester explains that he loved his illegitimate son and had paid for his education, but had kept him out of sight and had 'often blushed to acknowledge him'.[92] The issue was particularly sensitive if a man was nearing his end and had made no provision for such offspring. Naming them in a will would make their existence a matter of public record, embarrassing his family, whereas hitherto it might have been no more than rumour. Any legacy would almost certainly be resented by the legitimate children, and perhaps challenged. Sir Robert Brandling of Newcastle found himself in this predicament in the 1560s. He had a son he considered unsatisfactory and several brothers and sisters, most of them heavily in debt. His brother Henry urged him to make the will he had been putting off for years, and made several suggestions before touching on the most sensitive point: 'They say, in this town, if you had not so many bastards you would have made your will or [ere] now.' Sir Robert's reply underlines his reluctance to make any formal acknowledgement of paternity: 'If I have any I am able to find [i.e. provide for] them.' But his chaplain, sitting by the fire, commented that he had already been deputed to sound out Henry's wife to see if she would take one of them, and she had agreed. Brandling died with his affairs still in confusion.[93]

In most parts of England, respectable men preferred to make any provision for illegitimate offspring privately and informally. Sir John Oglander was disgusted by the behaviour of his neighbour, Sir Robert Dillington, who had got his own cousin with child and then, 'out of his miserable disposition, rather than to allow means for the keeping of it, suffered it to be known'.[94] Dillington had offended on three counts: he had ruined his cousin, failed to provide for her or the child, and failed to shield his family from embarrassment. Edmund Verney flouted convention still more brazenly, openly acknowledging the children he had fathered on the nurse-maids caring for his wife's own infants. His behaviour helped push her into a mental breakdown. Verney made a will leaving a house to one of his mistresses and her son, a will separate from the one that settled the affairs of his legitimate family. His brother John, more typical of his age and class, appears to have fathered one illegitimate child but took steps to conceal the fact from his family.[95]

Exceptional circumstances sometimes produced very different arrangements. Sir Nicholas Bacon, Elizabeth's Lord Keeper, was happy to marry his younger son to the illegitimate daughter of the wealthy financier Sir Thomas Gresham. The bride predictably brought a very large portion, and there were already close links between the two families.[96] Occasionally, too, a landowner without a lawful heir would acknowledge an illegitimate child and leave his estate to him or her. Sir Edward Hoby surprised contemporaries in 1617 by making his illegitimate son Peregrine his heir, 'not so much as once remembering his brother Sir Thomas

---

[92] *King Lear*, I.i.   [93] Raine, *Depositions from Durham*, 121–5.

[94] Francis Bamford, ed., *A Royalist's Notebook. The Commonplace Book of Sir John Oglander Kt. of Nunwell* (1936), 50–1.

[95] Whyman, *Sociability and Power*, 113, 116–17.

[96] Hassell Smith, *Papers of Nathaniel Bacon*, i.10, 290–1.

Hoby with anything which he could take from him'. Sir Edward certainly loved his son, and presumably hated his brother. Peregrine went on to sit in both the Long and Cavalier Parliaments. Sir Francis Wortley similarly made his illegitimate daughter a wealthy heiress, and her guardian, the Earl of Sandwich, was delighted to match her with his younger son.[97]

For most, however, illegitimate children remained a sensitive issue. John Smyth, a wealthy merchant and former mayor of Bristol, left 40 marks in 1555 to an illegitimate daughter in London. It was a tiny sum in the context of his huge estate (with money and goods totalling over £2,000, besides landed property), and he minimized embarrassment for his family by concealing her name and address. A friend was appointed to handle the matter.[98] At the other end of the social spectrum, John Reade, an Essex smallholder, bequeathed most of his little estate to his wife and their son in 1560, but was also concerned for the welfare of his 'base son John'. So he left 40s to his sister Elizabeth, directing her to see the boy brought up honestly, and also left him four ewes, to take possession of their increase when he came of age. Reade made his wife executrix, but clearly thought that his sister was more likely to protect the child's welfare. Of the thousand Essex wills proved between 1558 and 1565, this was the only one to mention illegitimate offspring. Similarly, only one of almost nine hundred Suffolk wills in the early 1630s mentioned the subject, and then in guarded terms. A yeoman asked his executor to raise 'the supposed daughter of my [apparently deceased] son John'.[99] There were, however, striking geographical variations. In north-eastern Lancashire, where illegitimacy rates were far higher than in southern England, testators were far readier to acknowledge illegitimate children. In the period 1600–40, 17 per cent of testators made some provision, often quite generous, for such children. Most bequests were in cash or kind, but if the legitimate children were all daughters, a testator might also leave land to an illegitimate son, specifying what financial support he was to give his half-sisters.[100] Illegitimate children had no claim in law, of course, if a parent died intestate. Their welfare depended on any informal arrangements made earlier or, failing that, on whatever the lawful heirs might agree. Such agreements were difficult to secure, and equally difficult to enforce.[101]

Roughly 7 per cent of women in early modern England bore their first child outside wedlock.[102] A destitute single mother without friends might be whipped and incarcerated, with her infant sometimes removed and put out to nurse. In many other cases, the mother's or father's kin provided financial support and arranged temporary safe accommodation. Some women found a refuge with their

[97] *ODNB*, Hoby; John Maclean, ed., *Letters from George Lord Carew to Sir Thomas Roe*, Camden Soc, 76 (1860), 91; Frank R. Harris, *The Life of Edward Mountagu* (2 vols, 1912), ii.234–5.

[98] J. H. Bettey, ed., *Calendar of the Correspondence of the Smyth Family of Ashton Court 1548–1642*, Bristol Record Society, 35 (1982), pp. xi–xii.

[99] Emmison, *Wills of Essex*, 42; Evans, *Wills of Sudbury*, 167.

[100] John T. Swain, *Industry before the Industrial Revolution. North-East Lancashire c.1500–1640*, Chetham Society, 3rd series, 32 (1986), 25–6, 78–9, 97–8, 101, 140.

[101] See e.g. Jarman, *Justice and Conciliation*, 38–40, 53–4, 82–3.

[102] Adrian Wilson, *Ritual and Conflict. The Social Relations of Childbirth in Early Modern England* (Farnham, 2013), 13.

parents or a sibling, and such arrangements could sometimes become permanent. In 1701, for example, one household in Stoke-on-Trent comprised a brother and sister, both single, and the sister's illegitimate daughter, aged 10. The sister, several years older than her brother, was presumably acting as housekeeper, making this an arrangement convenient for them both. A married householder in the town had also taken in his sister and her illegitimate child, and in this case the blood tie must have been the main factor.[103] Bearing an illegitimate child did not necessarily destroy the mother's prospects of marriage, either to the father or more often, after a longer gap, to a different man. And some women proved able both to keep the child and find a husband. Thus at Stoke, Henry Astbury's household included his wife, their daughter aged 4, and his wife's illegitimate son, now aged 20.[104]

Irregular families might be tolerated if they could pay their way. If they ran into difficulties, however, financial responsibility was fiercely contested, even more than in the case of stepchildren. When George Bursie sank into poverty in 1627, did responsibility for the child his wife had earlier borne out of wedlock rest with him, the parish where the child had been born, or the parish where they now lived? Humfrey Langier had provided a home to his wife's younger sister and was understandably dismayed when some years later she bore a child. With no father identified, was Langier or the parish responsible for its maintenance? Magistrates settled on Langier, a ruling he vehemently disputed.[105] The case of Dorothy Codner raised still more questions. Dorothy had fallen pregnant at Cullompton, Devon, where she was settled, had given birth somewhere in Wales, and had then returned to Cullompton with her child. Several years later, she left the child with her sister and brother-in-law in Somerset, to make a short visit to Ireland. When she failed to return, maintenance became a problem for magistrates in two and potentially three counties.[106] Siblings did occasionally find themselves shouldered with such unwelcome burdens. Christopher Smith, for example, was bound over to provide for an illegitimate child fathered by his brother, and did so for seven years, until the boy was old enough to be apprenticed. An unusual case saw Mathew Reeves ordered to maintain his illegitimate infant half-brother, the posthumous offspring of his own father.[107]

The murderous rage of the bastard Edmund in *King Lear* is hard to document in real families, but only rarely do we find a warm relationship between legitimate and illegitimate siblings. One possible exception comes from the Chester consistory court in 1558. When Thomas Highton, gentleman, charged his wife Kathryn with adultery, the defence proctor objected that two of his witnesses were Highton's illegitimate sisters, one of them his 'great and near friend'. Kathryn fought back by

[103] Gatley, 'Stoke-upon-Trent Parish Listing', 195, 211.

[104] Richard Adair, *Courtship, Illegitimacy and Marriage in Early Modern England* (Manchester, 1996), 79–83; Wilson, *Ritual and Conflict*, 48–54; Laura Gowing, 'Secret Births and Infanticide in Seventeenth-Century England', *Past and Present*, 156 (1997), 87–8, 102; Gatley, 'Stoke-upon-Trent Parish Listing', 204; cf. 191.

[105] *SQSR*, i.225, ii.56, 153–4.   [106] *SQSR*, ii.284–5.

[107] John Lister, ed., *West Riding Sessions Records 1611–1642*, Yorkshire Archaeological Society, 54 (1915), 177; *SQSR*, iv.215–16.h.

suing her husband for defamation, which makes this an exceptional case indeed.[108] The Somerset diarist John Cannon provides a later and much happier example. Cannon's father had an illegitimate child in 1681 by his maidservant, Margaret White, during a period when his wife lay bedridden for a year. The servant moved back to her parents' village before the birth, and the Cannons' marriage survived the acrimonious fallout. Margaret was still alive sixty years later and her illegitimate child, Edith, had married and raised a large family. What makes the story unusual is that the diarist (born in 1684) maintained a friendly and enduring relationship with his illegitimate half-sister. She was always affectionate towards him and his children, he remarked, and 'both acknowledged each other as brother and sister, their children respectively calling uncle and aunt'.[109]

SIBLING INCEST

Incest was a spiritual offence that fell within the remit of the ecclesiastical courts. The Church's broad definition prohibited sexual relations or marriage between cousins, in-laws, and many other kin by blood or marriage. Most contemporaries were more relaxed, but sexual relationships between siblings were viewed as unnatural and disruptive, and the issue featured prominently in the revenge tragedies of the late Elizabethan and Jacobean period.

Among the elite, incest might also provide titillating material for gossip. There were enduring rumours, for example, that Sir Philip Sidney and his sister Mary, countess of Pembroke, had been lovers.[110] *The Twins*, a tragi-comedy performed at the Salisbury Court theatre, told the fanciful story of an Italian woman married to a nobleman but lusting after his identical twin brother. She vows to kill herself unless he sleeps with her, so he reluctantly agrees, but he tells his brother and, in a predictable plot device, the night-time assignation sees the twins swapping places. The husband graciously forgives his wife's incestuous appetites, commenting that 'it is the general disease of Italy, not thine'. That would have raised an easy laugh.[111] Lady Fanshawe, passing through Canterbury in 1663, was both shocked and thrilled by gossip about a Colonel Culpepper, whose sister had 'lived with him, as the world said, in too much love'. After the sister died, earlier that year, her brother had allegedly kept the body in his buttery, declaring that he too was dying and wanted to be buried with her. Her ghostly head was rumoured to appear and lie by him in bed every night, wherever he slept.[112] This was not only a world of salacious gossip, however. The diarist Anthony Wood recorded the melancholy case of a young gentleman of Lincoln's Inn, who had been passionately in love with his sister. Their father had tried to break the liaison by sending her to Ireland, but he

---

[108] Ibid., 21.   [109] Cannon, *Chronicles*, i.17–18; cf. Adair, *Courtship, Illegitimacy*, 89–90.

[110] John Aubrey, *Brief Lives*, ed. Kate Bennett, 2 vols (Oxford, 2015), i.252, ii.1094.

[111] W. Rider, *The Twins. A Tragi-Comedy* (1655). Rider styles himself Master of Arts, and may be the Oxford namesake awarded that degree in 1648. If so, the play possibly dates from the 1640s.

[112] *The Memoirs of Anne, Lady Halkett and Ann, Lady Fanshawe*, ed. John Loftis (Oxford, 1979), 150–1.

had followed and brought her back. When the father did eventually succeed in separating them, the young man shot himself.[113]

Incest cases appear in most ecclesiastical court records, though the numbers are always small and parish officers often turned a blind eye. Most prosecutions involved liaisons between men and their stepdaughters or sisters-in-law.[114] In one unusual case, however, parents had allegedly condoned an incestuous relationship between their son and daughter. After finding them in bed together, they had kept their counsel and made themselves 'bawds unto their children'.[115] Several cases came before the ecclesiastical High Commission of Durham in the 1630s, which possessed far greater punitive powers than the lower courts. William Hall of Newcastle and his widowed stepmother, convicted of incest in 1632, were both sentenced to perform public penance and fined £500. Such impossible fines were designed to cow offenders, and generally waived once they submitted.[116] Penalties were heaviest when a child had resulted. That had exposed a long-term liaison between William Carlell and his sister Jane, and they both received harsh sentences: public penance in Durham cathedral, their local church and chapel, and three market places, and seven years imprisonment.[117] Incest became a criminal and capital offence in 1650, when England was briefly a republic, but again only a handful of prosecutions are recorded.[118] The church courts regained jurisdiction after the Restoration.

Illegitimacy and incest both carried a stigma in early modern England. Step-families did not. They were common, and one scholar has suggested that children growing up in them would not have been considered 'deprived'.[119] Nonetheless, those affected faced many of the same challenges of re-adjustment that adults and children face today. The tensions raised by step- and half-sibling relationships added a further dimension to ordinary sibling rivalries. For the propertied, a father's remarriage might pose a significant threat to the material interests of his children. In the case of young children, at every level of society, the arrival of a step-parent brought fears of neglect, discrimination, or abuse. And if such fears often proved unwarranted, there were clearly also many cases when they did not.

---

[113] Wood, *Life and Times*, ii.298. For the victim, Peter Woodcock, see J. and J. A. Venn, *Alumni Cantabrigenses... to 1751* (Cambridge, 1922–7), iv.457.

[114] Martin Ingram, *Church Courts, Sex and Marriage in England, 1570–1640* (Cambridge, 1987), 245–9.
  LRRO, 1D 41/4, Box 4/19–21; Cambridge University Library, EDR, D2/11, f.232; LRRO 1D 41/4, Box 80/36–7; WSRO, Ep.1/11/9, fos. 104v–105v; cf. Adair, *Courtship, Illegitimacy*, 160–2.

[115] G. R. Quaife, *Wanton Wenches and Wayward Wives* (1979), 177–8, 193.

[116] James Raine, ed., *The Acts of the High Commission Court within the Diocese of Durham*, Surtees Society, 34 (1858), 28–9, cf. 31–2, 107–8, 123.

[117] Raine, ed., *Acts of the High Commission*, 76–7; cf. 146 (sister), 100–1 (sister-in-law).

[118] J. A. Sharpe, *Crime in Seventeenth-Century England. A County Study* (Cambridge, 1983), 68–70; Bernard Capp, *England's Culture Wars* (Oxford, 2012), 139–40. On eighteenth-century attitudes see Amy Harris, *Siblinghood and Social Relations in Georgian England* (Manchester, 2012), 98–102.

[119] Miranda Chaytor, 'Household and Kinship: Ryton in the late 16th and early 17th Centuries', *History Workshop*, 10 (1980), 29.

7

Siblings and Salvation

A book on sibling relationships today would be very unlikely to include a chapter on religion. But the upheavals triggered by Henry VIII's break with Rome disrupted individual families as well as the nation at large. Each of Henry's children imposed a radically new settlement, and religion proved equally divisive in the Stuart century. Allegiances and identities long remained fluid, and only after several generations did most of the nation feel firmly Protestant. In the mid-Tudor decades, and for some time later, it was impossible to know which faith would eventually emerge as the official orthodoxy. Most families conformed to the church order prescribed by the state, at least outwardly, and in matters such as marriage arrangements gave priority to property and other worldly considerations, overlooking religious differences.[1] But other families were torn apart. The spread of early Protestantism created a generational clash, with many young people drawn to the new ideas while their parents clung to traditional beliefs and practices.[2] The Elizabethan settlement of 1559 failed to satisfy the more deeply religious, creating another fault line. Some espoused the 'hotter' puritan cause or, in later generations, joined radical sects such as the Baptists or Quakers. Religious divisions were not only generational. Zealous brothers or sisters were often appalled by their siblings' worldliness, while in other families the worldly tried to dissuade or obstruct converts, or played a mediating role. All these scenarios were re-enacted many times across the period. Yet a passionately shared faith could also create a powerful sense of spiritual kinship, superseding and surpassing the ties of blood. The puritan preacher John Dod proudly 'testified from his own experience, that for the loss of one carnal brother he had two hundred spiritual brethren'. And when Sir Francis Hastings, another puritan, wrote to a cousin in 1583, he described himself as 'your kinsman by marriage, and your brother by profession'. Nonconformists routinely referred to each other as 'Brother' and 'Sister', and one convert could hail the Quaker leader George Fox as 'our elder brother and father in Israel'.[3]

---

[1] Norman Jones, *The English Reformation. Religion and Cultural Adaptation* (Oxford, 2002), chap. 3.

[2] Susan Brigden, 'Youth and the English Reformation', *Past and Present*, 95 (1982); Alexandra Walsham, 'The Reformation of the Generations. Youth, Age and Religious Change in England, c.1500–1700', *Transactions of the Royal Historical Society*, 6th series, 21 (2011).

[3] Claire Cross, ed., *The Letters of Sir Francis Hastings, 1574–1609*, Sussex Record Society, 69 (1969), 25; Samuel Clarke, *The Lives of Two and Twenty English Divines* (1660), 207; *Some Account of the Life of Joseph Pike*, ed. John Barclay (1837), 39.

SUPPORT, EXHORTATION, AND SOLIDARITY

The most common religious divisions were not in fact between competing faiths but between the committed and the easy-going or apathetic. Parents bore primary responsibility for the Christian upbringing of their children. While siblings often acted as godparents for a nephew or niece, they appear to have seen this role as essentially secular, an affirmation of kinship. There is little evidence of godparents playing much part in children's religious education.[4] Pious parents, by contrast, were naturally anxious for children to follow in their footsteps. They tried to instil firm moral values from an early age, and to encourage a spiritual awareness as the children grew older. Older siblings would help in this process, monitoring and guiding their younger brothers and sisters. At the most basic level, Oliver Heywood recalled his sister chiding him for bad language when he was playing in the street. John Whiting, whose mother died when he was 10, similarly recalled that his sister Mary 'would reprove me (being younger than her) if she observed I spoke or did anything amiss; so that she was an awe and check upon me, when I was any ways light, or wanton'. Little Mary Walker would turn to an older sibling for help during Bible readings in the family. Attending closely, she would 'ask her sister the meaning of some passages she understood not', and discuss her thoughts as they sat sewing together.[5] The lawyer John Hoskyns wanted such instruction to become part of the routine arrangements of his household in Herefordshire. So 'let your girls hear the youngest children's words', he wrote in 1629, 'and let them teach them or read to them the principles of religion'. The Elizabethan poet Isabella Whitney had also guided her sisters and later, when they were employed as servants in London, she exhorted them to behave honestly and diligently, 'Forgetting not to pray as I before you taught'.[6]

Older siblings sometimes carved out for themselves more ambitious spiritual roles. The Dissenter Gervase Disney remembered how forcefully his elder brother Cornelius had discharged his self-appointed duties. On Sabbath evenings, he recalled, Cornelius would take one of his little brothers or sisters 'to walk with him in the garden, where he would always commune with us of heavenly matters'. His vivid picture of the joys of heaven made Gervase long to be there already, while his descriptions of hellfire terrified his listeners.[7] Mary Bewley, eldest child of

[4] Will Coster, *Baptism and Spiritual Kinship in Early Modern England* (Aldershot, 2002), esp. 203–10. Sibling godparents are found at most levels of society, for example in the Blundell, Brockbank, Isham, Jeffreys, Lowe, Paston, Pett, Thornton, Wheatcroft, Whitelocke and Yonge families. See also David Cressy, *Birth, Marriage and Death. Ritual, Religion and the Life-Cycle in Tudor and Stuart England* (Oxford, 1997), 149–61.

[5] Heywood, *Autobiography*, i.153–4; John Whiting, *Early Piety Exemplified, or the Life and Death of Mary Whiting* (1711), 9; Anthony Walker, *The Vertuous Wife, or the Holy Life of Mrs Elizabeth Walker* (1694), 97.

[6] Louise Brown Osborn, ed., *The Life, Letters, and Writings of John Hoskyns 1566–1638* (New Haven, 1937), 96; Isabella Whitney, *A sweet Nosgay, or pleasant posye* (1573), sig. D.

[7] *Some Remarkable Passages in the Holy Life and Death of Gervase Disney, Esq.* (1692), 17–18, cf. J. E. B. Mayor, ed., *Nicholas Ferrar. Two Lives, by his Brother John and by Doctor Jebb* (Cambridge, 1855), 11–12.

a Quaker family in Cumberland, provided more sober guidance. As her brother George recalled, she was 'a very good example to us that were younger in piety and virtue, in true humility and obedience to our parents; she also wrote to me, being thoughtful of my welfare'. George had moved to Dublin in 1698 to take up an apprenticeship, at the age of about 14, and he treasured Mary's letters. Many years later he copied one into his memoirs, hoping it would guide and encourage his own children.[8]

Most families contained members with differing levels of religious commitment, and the devout often sought to awaken their more worldly siblings to the hellfire awaiting them. This sense of mission was particularly strong among puritans and Nonconformists. John Janeway, a puritan minister's son, had a conversion experience at the age of about 18, and thereafter monitored closely the spiritual health of his siblings. One poor youngster, a boy of 11, fell asleep one day during family prayers, and found himself immediately the focus of an intense programme of admonition and exhortation.[9] The minister Henry Newcome felt a similar sense of responsibility. Visiting London after the Great Fire, he was dismayed by the waning zeal of his brother Thomas, and embarked on a mission to re-establish a godly household regime. Newcome felt still greater dismay when his own wayward son, Daniel, fell dangerously ill and refused to acknowledge his sins or prepare to meet his Maker. Newcome's appeals and warnings proved fruitless, and eventually, in desperation, he summoned Daniel's elder brother 'to deal plainly and home with him'. It was sibling not parental exhortation that finally brought Daniel to a suitably penitential frame of mind.[10]

Many godly laymen and women felt similarly responsible for the spiritual welfare of their close kin.[11] The Lancashire puritan Richard Hardiman, for example, was annoyed when his worldly sister and her husband descended on him one day to enjoy some 'mad revelling and feasting' at Ratcliffe Wakes, near Manchester. He told them frostily that they would have been more welcome at another time. But he somehow persuaded them to attend a sermon by the fiery puritan minister John Angier, and this proved to be the first step in his sister's conversion. She went on to become a puritan enthusiast.[12] The apprentice Roger Lowe also felt it his duty and right to guide less pious siblings. When his older sister Ellen called at his shop one day to buy provisions, he told her sternly that she should 'go to church and labour to instruct her children in the ways of God, and in so doing God would bless her and make them comfortable to her'. He lectured his other sister, Katherine, too, though in her case his counsel proved less acceptable. Calling on her one day in 1669, he urged her 'to bethink herself and live godly, considering she had but a

---

[8] George Bewley, *A Narrative of the Christian Experiences of George Bewley* (Dublin, 1750) 11–14.

[9] James Janeway, *Invisibles, Realities, Demonstrated in the Holy Life and Triumphant Death of Mr John Janeway* (1673), 21–3.

[10] Newcome, *Autobiography*, i.164–5, 178, ii.252–4.

[11] e.g. William Hinde, *A Faithfull Remonstrance of the Holy Life and Happy Death of Iohn Bruen* (1641), 98; cf. 110–12.

[12] *Oliver Heywood's Life of John Angier of Denton*, ed. Ernest Axon, Chetham Society, NS, 97 (1937), 58–9.

short time to live here'. But, the diarist records plaintively, 'she was highly offended, so I came home'.[13]

Like preachers, pious siblings recognized that the most effective weapon against complacency was the ever-present danger of death, for young and old alike. In 1672, Elizabeth Martindale, sick and close to death, used her situation to urge her brother Thomas 'to make haste with repentance, and not to leave it to his death-bed'.[14] When close kin fell ill, the pious would exhort, counsel, or reassure them, with women often proving as effective as men as spiritual counsellors. One young woman, who had visited her brother in London during the terrifying plague outbreak of 1625, sent him a letter of spiritual comfort and exhortation as soon as she arrived back home. It quickly found its way into print to edify and encourage other families in danger.[15] A generation later Elizabeth Chambers, an officer's wife, told how she had tended her dying sister, and 'often spoke to my sister of Christ within, and did often pray by her, and was (through grace) made an instrument to do her great good'.[16] Dorothy Wilson of Wolverhampton played a still more decisive role, recorded in a vivid account that also found its way into print. Raised in a Nonconformist family, Dorothy lived with her widowed mother and her brother James, aged 24. James had rejected the family's values and become addicted to drink and loose company, and he and his friends would jeer at Dorothy as she went to her meetings. But when he fell dangerously ill in February 1669, he was seized by the terrors of hell, and turned to her in desperation for comfort and guidance. 'Oh sister, is there any mercy for me?' he asked piteously. Dorothy had her answer ready: 'She told him, that if he did now repent from the bottom of his heart for his sin, there is hope. He fell a-weeping grievously.' She read to him from scripture, and told him that God had waited until this final crisis in his sinful life to demonstrate his divine power and mercy, 'at which his heart seemed to be wonderfully broken'. A Nonconformist minister visited too, but the narrative emphasizes that it was Dorothy who had secured her brother's conversion. And when he lay dying it was Dorothy he asked to 'sound out his repentance throughout the town'.[17] Inevitably, such efforts did not always succeed. The story of two highwaymen, the Grady brothers, records one poignant failure. After their capture early in 1680, Timothy Grady was quickly filled with remorse for his crimes, and spent his time awaiting trial praying, reading, and listening to the ministers who came to exhort the prisoners to repent. His brother Edward, by contrast, proved impervious to every appeal and to his impending death on the gallows. Timothy was so distressed that he pleaded for his brother to be given a reprieve, 'saying, that he feared he was not in a

---

[13] *The Diary of Roger Lowe, of Ashton-in-Makerfield, Lancashire 1663–74*, ed. William L. Sachse (1938), 55, 122.

[14] *The Life of Adam Martindale*, ed. Richard Parkinson, Chetham Society, 4 (1845), 209.

[15] A. H., *Another godly Letter, lately written to the same H.H. by his owne Sister out of the Countrey* (1625).

[16] John Rogers, *Ohel, or Beth-shemesh* (1653), 408.

[17] *The Repenting Sinner Pardoned: Being a brief Relation of the wicked Life and penitent pious Death of James Wilson of Wolverhampton* (1669), 10–12, 14, 27 and *passim*.

fit condition to die'. The court remained unmoved, and the brothers were hanged together at Tyburn.[18]

Most striking to modern readers are the accounts of young children who appear to have been at some level already spiritually aware. Some were perhaps merely role-playing, imitating the godly ministers they had seen. Ralph Josselin admitted that from childhood he had been filled with 'delight and admiration and desire to imitate them', and 'would be acting in corners'. Henry Newcome, a minister's child, had also loved playing the role among his friends, as had Oliver Heywood.[19] But some of the children raised in godly families seem to have internalized the concerns as well as the language and behaviour of their elders. In 1672, the Nonconformist James Janeway published a set of idealized accounts of the conversion, holy lives, and 'joyful deaths' of thirteen children who had died before reaching adolescence. Aimed at young readers, the narratives focused on the children's assurance of salvation, but they reveal too how many had developed a childish sense of mission, directed primarily at their siblings. Thus Sarah Hawley, moved by a sermon at 8 or 9, 'got her little brother and sister into a chamber with her, and told them of their condition by nature, and wept over them, and prayed with them and for them'. On her deathbed, she bade farewell to them with edifying words of exhortation to each in turn.[20] Another young girl seized the opportunity one day, when her parents were at church, to conduct an impromptu service at home. Gathering her siblings and some neighbours' children, she told them that the Lord's Day must be strictly observed, and prayed with them.[21] Some of these children had also felt it their duty to rebuke less pious siblings. John Sudlow, for example, 'was very watchful over his brothers and sisters, and would not suffer them to use any unhandsome words or to do any unhandsome action'.[22] Some had also tried to comfort a grieving parent, or even took it upon themselves to counsel parents whose own behaviour had fallen short.[23]

These children were obviously mirroring the language and behaviour of their parents. At one level their actions were simply a form of play, yet they would also have absorbed their elders' beliefs, within the limits of their capacity, and there seems little reason to doubt their sincerity. Most children would have witnessed a sibling's death and realized life's fragility at a very early age. In August 1712, the Catholic squire Nicholas Blundell noted in his diary that his two young daughters, aged 8 and 6, had buried one of their dolls 'with a great deal of formality'. They had a garland of flowers carried before it, and twenty playfellows attended their elaborate make-believe ceremony.[24] For others it was more than play. John Sudlow

---

[18] *Fair Warning from Tyburn* [1680], 2.

[19] Josselin, *Diary*, 1; Newcome, *Autobiography*, i.7; cf. Heywood, *Autobiography*, i.157.

[20] James Janeway, *A Token for Children: Being an Exact Account of the Conversion, Holy and Exemplary Lives, and Joyful Deaths, of several young Children* (1673). 2, 5, 13–15; Ralph Houlbrooke, 'Death in childhood: the practice of the "good death" in James Jameway's *A Token for Children*', in Anthony Fletcher and Stephen Hussey, eds, *Childhood in Question. Children, Parents and the State* (Manchester, 1999), 37–56.

[21] Janeway, *A Token*, 31.   [22] Janeway, *A Token*, 28; cf. 45, Part 2, 8–9, 75–6.

[23] Janeway, *A Token*, Part 2, 17, 75–6; cf. Thornton, *Autobiography*, 262–3.

[24] J. J. Bagley, ed., *The Great Diurnall of Nicholas Blundell of Little Crosby, Lancashire, 1702–1728*, 3 vols, Record Society of Lancashire and Cheshire (1968–72), ii.29.

was only 4 when he saw his little brother lowered into the grave, and it was this distressing event that had prompted him to ask questions about death and the hereafter. Similarly, it was the death of a little sister in 1669 that triggered Elizabeth Walker's religious crisis, at the age of 11. Her parents found some comfort in reflecting that the death of one beloved child had brought the 'spiritual birth of another, not less dear to us'.[25] Most children understandably reacted to the death of a sibling or parent, or the approach of their own, with fear and distress. But others had clearly internalized what they had been told, and could look forward to a reunion with their loved ones in heaven. Mary Martindale, who died at the age of 4, had been deeply affected by the death of her baby brother, and thereafter would often talk of heaven and wanting to be buried by him.[26]

Few children, of course, would have matched Janeway's idealized paragons, and their assertive piety had sometimes irritated their siblings. We learn that when John Harvy rebuked his brother and sister for taking a sinful pride in their new clothes, he found that 'his reproof signified little'. And when they scoffed their food without waiting for a blessing, he could only protest lamely, 'that is just like a hog'.[27] Even so, Janeway's collection has been called 'probably the most influential children's book ever written', and it had a significant impact on generations of children as they came to terms with the reality of death.[28] One early example was Cartaret Rede, daughter of Wiltshire Nonconformists, who died in 1701 shortly before her seventh birthday. Her mother had kept a record of the little girl's pious expressions and actions, and noted one day that 'I found her reading Mr John Janeway's *Life and Death*, she was all in tears. She said to me, Oh! that I were such a worm as this was! . . . Oh! that I were in the bosom of Jesus.' When she first realized that she might die young, she had remarked calmly that 'when I am with God and good angels, I shall not want neither food nor raiment, for God will give me all I want'. Her short life and pious death became in turn another model for children, reflected by the wholesale price also being supplied on the title page.[29]

It is hardly surprising that parental attempts to raise pious offspring drove other children to rebel. Little Cartaret Rede had been distressed that her brother Charles showed no interest in religion, and had sent him a letter of stern exhortation. 'I hope God will take away that heart of stone in you,' she wrote (surely with parental assistance), 'for it is a dismal thing to die in your sins and go to hell for ever.'[30] But when parents succeeded, their children often enjoyed a lifelong sense of spiritual solidarity.[31] Typical was the close bond between Daniel Dyke (d.1614)

---

[25] Janeway, *A Token*, Part 2, 2–3; Walker, *Vertuous Wife*, 97–102; cf. *Strength in Weakness Manifest in the Life of Elizabeth Stirredge* (1711), 4–8.

[26] *Life of Martindale*, 209; Thornton, *Autobiography*, 94; Houlbrooke, 'Death in childhood', 41, 44–5.

[27] Janeway, *A Token*, Part 2, 75–6, 78.

[28] Gillian Avery, 'The Puritans and their Heirs', in *eadem* and Julia Briggs, eds., *Children and their Books* (Oxford, 1989), 109–13 (quotation at 113).

[29] Sarah Rede, *A Token for Youth: or, Instruction to Children* (1760), 6, 13 and *passim*.

[30] Rede, *A Token*, 9, 23.

[31] Mary Prior, 'Reviled and crucified marriages: the position of Tudor bishops' wives', in *eadem*, ed., *Women in English Society 1500–1800* (1985), 131; cf. 125; Patrick Collinson, *Godly People: Essays on English Protestantism and Puritanism* (1983), chap. 10.

and his brother Jeremiah (d.1639), who published Daniel's works after his death. Their bond was typical in other ways too: Jeremiah modestly identified himself as the 'younger and inferior' brother, proud to publish the work of 'his elder, and superior' sibling.[32] The children of the Nonconformist minister Philip Henry provide another striking example. Matthew Henry sometimes preached at the lecture his sister Sarah and her husband had established, and several kept spiritual diaries. The sisters corresponded regularly on both spiritual and family matters, sharing experiences and offering mutual comfort and guidance. They all gathered whenever the opportunity arose. When Sarah lost her first child in 1688, a few days after its birth, she described finding comfort from her loving husband and from 'parents, brothers, sisters—all joining with me in singing to God, both of mercy and judgement'.[33] Many other families maintained similar networks of spiritual comfort and support, in what Diane Willen has described as a 'self-fashioned community'.[34] Support might also take the form of cooperation to promote the godly cause. In 1587, for example, Elizabeth Nonne was eager to advance a puritan minister she favoured to a vacant living in the Gawdy family's gift. The patronage belonged to the head of the family, Sir Bassingbourne Gawdy, but she calculated that an indirect approach through her sister, Gawdy's wife Anne, offered a better prospect of success. The minister was duly appointed, thanks to the women's alliance.[35]

Quaker families provide still more striking examples of solidarity and support. John Whiting accompanied his precocious older sister, Mary, on some of her preaching tours, and after her death at the age of only 21 he published an admiring account of her short life.[36] Another Quaker begged to be allowed to take his brother's place in prison, because his brother was distressed at the prospect of his wife giving birth alone and penniless.[37] At Bristol, where a wave of persecution in 1682 saw most adult Friends thrown into gaol, it was reported that 'the children kept up the meetings regularly and with a remarkable gravity and composure'. By August, many of the children had also been imprisoned or sent to Bridewell, some as young as 7 or 8. Some were still there in October, including Patience and Mary Horne, sisters aged 11 and 7, and Mary and Elizabeth Jaques, aged 13 and 11. It was an astonishing demonstration of solidarity, and by no means unique. Three young Quaker sisters, arrested in Cornwall in 1683, languished together in prison for three years.[38]

Close spiritual ties between siblings generally reflected a shared godly upbringing. When parents died while the children were still young, the older siblings had to take their place as best they could. It was a formidable challenge. One struggling girl

---

[32] Daniel Dyke, *The Mystery of Selfe-Deceiving* (1617), sig. A2-v, A5; William Haller, *The Rise of Puritanism* (New York, 1938), chap. 2.

[33] J. B. Williams, *Memoirs of the Life and Character of Mrs Sarah Savage* (1829), 70–1 and *passim*; Patricia Crawford, *Blood, Bodies and Families in Early Modern England* (2004), chap. 6.

[34] Diane Willen, ' "Communion of the Saints": Spiritual Reciprocity and the Godly Community in Early Modern England', *Albion*, 27 (1995), 20, 33–5.

[35] HMC, 11, *Gawdy*, 26.   [36] Whiting, *Early Piety Exemplified*, 24, 33–4. She died in 1676.

[37] Joseph Besse, *The Sufferings of the Quakers*, 2 vols (1753), i.331–2.

[38] Besse, *Sufferings*, i.66–8, 126.

wrote for advice to the Nonconformist Elizabeth Bury, who offered some practical suggestions. In the case of her little brother, Bury advised, she should try to guide his behaviour with frequent but short interventions, adapting her language to his limited capacity. 'If God makes you instrumental in the conversion of your brothers and sisters,' she urged, 'it will be a great honour and comfort, and make the strongest union amongst you. Take special care of them that are in the greatest danger. Imitate your godly, impartial mother.'[39]

In the case of Elizabeth Isham and her brother and sister, growing up at Lamport Hall in Jacobean Northamptonshire, the spiritual influence of parents and siblings proved almost overwhelming. The children were raised in an intensely religious atmosphere, steeped in puritan piety from early childhood by their mother and grandmother. They lost both these powerful guides in their early teens, and thereafter Elizabeth and her younger sister Judith looked to each other, sharing their spiritual experiences, joys, and fears. For years, Elizabeth wrote, 'we bore one another's burthen', offering mutual comfort and reassurance. Judith's chronic ill health and brittle bones made her burdens physical as well as spiritual, and both sisters endured bouts of despair. Elizabeth sometimes felt the devil tempting her to curse God and her father, and both sisters experienced suicidal urges. For the most part, they battled their spiritual demons together, and Elizabeth thought that no one understood her dark temptations better than Judith. But their bond was sometimes disfigured by a sibling jealousy that could generate spiritual rivalry. Judith would describe the raptures of joy she sometimes experienced, transports that Elizabeth never enjoyed. She fretted that she did not deserve them, for she had never suffered the physical torments that were also Judith's lot, but she found ways to assert her own claims. During one period, when their mother lay bedridden and depressed, Elizabeth would whisper comforting passages from scripture into her ear and, as she recalled years later, 'by this means I had got the better hand of my sister'.[40] Judith, though generally the more favoured, also harboured powerful jealousies. On one occasion, she admitted, she had even been tempted to kill her sister as she lay sleeping beside her. She also told Elizabeth, unkindly, that she found more spiritual comfort from their brother Justinian than from her. Justinian tried to help both sisters with their spiritual torments. He too experienced doubts and temptations, but Elizabeth believed that 'being a man [he] had more strength and learning to withstand them', and his support and guidance were clearly important for both sisters. Elizabeth used a prayer he had composed in her own private devotions. To alleviate her melancholy he also lent her books, such as *The Cure of Cares* and poetical works by Sidney and Spenser, hoping they would provide relief from Foxe's 'Book of Martyrs'.[41] Spiritual support involved reassurance as well as exhortation.

---

[39] Samuel Bury, *An Account of the Life and Death of Mrs Elizabeth Bury* (1720), 186.
[40] Isham, 'Rememberances', fos, 3v, 12v, 22-v, 28 and *passim*; Peter Lake and Isaac Stephens, *Scandal and Religious Identity in Early Stuart England* (Woodbridge, 2015), 298–315.
[41] Isham, 'Rememberances', fos. 24v, 25v, 26, 27v; 'Diary', fos. 25, 28, 29.

Very occasionally, such claustrophobic 'spiritual bonding' took the still darker form of demonic possession. Contemporaries were fascinated both by child prophets, apparently inspired by the spirit, and by children apparently possessed, who often displayed very similar symptoms.[42] In one notorious case, five sisters aged between 9 and 15, daughters of Sir Robert Throckmorton of Warboys (Hunts.), all claimed to be possessed by demonic spirits. From 1589, first Jane, aged about 10, and then her younger and older siblings experienced violent fits which continued periodically for several years. They convinced their parents and local ministers, and pointed the finger of blame at a poor neighbour, Mother Samuel, and her family, urging her to confess and repent. Children were normally on the receiving end of religious exhortation, and the girls must have found it hugely exciting to be preaching at others, in the presence of admiring parents and other adults. They achieved their goals: the Samuels were eventually worn down and confessed, and were then tried and condemned, despite withdrawing their confessions. They died defiantly. Whether the girls had come to believe their own claims is impossible for us to know. A 'possessed' child enjoyed a freedom of speech and behaviour that was unthinkable in normal circumstances. She (or occasionally he) could shout and swear, and abuse and contradict parents, ministers, and other authority figures. The temptation to stand by their claims, and eventually believe them, must have been strong.[43]

We can also find witchcraft and siblings linked in several other contexts. A court in Essex was told in 1582 that John Sellis, aged 6, had cried out to his father one night, screaming that he was being tormented by a spirit that 'was like his sister but that it was all black'. His older brother confirmed his story, and both testified that their father had railed at his wife as a whore and witch sending her imps to plague his children. Their father denied the whole story. Whatever the tangled web of child and adult relationships in this troubled household, it is clear that child alliances could exert significant influence. Cicely Sellis, the mother, was condemned to death as a witch.[44] Siblings were occasionally linked with demonism in other ways. In one Jacobean case, a gentleman who came to the aid of his bewitched sister was then himself bewitched.[45] In County Durham, a distracted and violent woman became the focus of a collective family response. Her husband, convinced she was possessed, called for her sister to help restrain her while he and his brother laid their hands on her and charged the devil to depart. In other cases, we find sisters themselves condemned as witches—not surprising, perhaps, when witchcraft was believed to run in families. By contrast, Lawrence Kemp of St Osyth

---

[42] Alexandra Walsham, ' "Out of the Mouths of Babes and Sucklings": Prophecy, Puritanism and Childhood in Elizabethan Suffolk', in Diana Wood, ed., *The Church and Childhood (Studies in Church History, 31)* (1994), 285–99.

[43] *The most strange and admirable Discoverie of the three Witches of Warboys* (1593); cf. James Sharpe, *Instruments of Darkness. Witchcraft in England 1550–1750* (1996), chap. 8; Keith Thomas, *Religion and the Decline of Magic* (1971), 477–92.

[44] Barbara Rosen, ed., *Witchcraft in England 1558–1618* (Amherst, Mass., 1991).132–5, 156.

[45] Rosen, *Witchcraft*, 346–8; *Most Fearefull and Strange Newes from the Bishoppricke of Durham* (1641).

blamed his wife's death on witchcraft by his sister Ursula, an extreme example of the tensions that could arise between siblings and in-laws.[46]

A DIVIDED NATION: THE CATHOLIC EXPERIENCE

Post-Reformation Catholic families played a key role in the survival and rebirth of the faith. Family solidarity and support were vital for a faith that endured fierce persecution over several generations. Committed recusants raised their children in traditional beliefs and practices, and in the absence of a priest Catholic women kept the flame alive by maintaining the religious calendar within their household. Many families with sufficient means sent their sons to be educated abroad in Catholic schools and seminaries. Many of them, including numerous brothers and half-brothers, subsequently found their way into the priesthood.[47] When William Hance was arrested at Leicester in 1582, he was carrying several holy relics, one of them 'a drop of his brother's blood that was hanged for the Catholic religion'. His brother Everard, a fellow priest, had suffered at Tyburn the previous year.[48]

Catholic survival also owed much to the work of missionary priests, who in turn depended on support from lay men and women ready to shelter them at the risk of their own lives. Here too we often find a family dimension. For several decades from the 1580s, Anne Vaux and her sister provided a refuge for the Jesuit leader Henry Garnet, safe meeting places for other priests, and funding to sustain the early mission. A century later, two sisters at Oxford devoted their lives to sheltering the Jesuit priest William Wolfe, who secured numerous conversions within the university.[49] Other priests found shelter with their own siblings, such as the Lancashire Jesuits who stayed with their recusant sister Dorothy Birtwhistle in the early seventeenth century. Dorothy's commitment went further; it was her attempt to convert the wife of the local curate that brought her to the attention of the authorities. The sister of Nicholas Sanders, a prominent Catholic exile, was a similarly forthright woman. In 1585, the bishop of Winchester branded her 'very obstinate', and insisted that she must remain a prisoner in London. If allowed to return home to Hampshire, he warned, her dangerous influence would outweigh the effects of ten Protestant sermons.[50]

For over a century, lay Catholics faced heavy fines and imprisonment, with the terrifying threat of the gallows if they dared to shelter priests. These dangers created powerful pressure on families to conform, at least outwardly, and many did so,

[46] Rosen, *Witchcraft*, 94, 111, 115, 127–8, 144.
[47] John Bossy, *The English Catholic Community 1570–1850* (1975), 152–8; Godfrey Anstruther, *The Seminary Priests. A Dictionary of the Secular Clergy of England and Wales 1558–1850*, 4 vols (Great Wakering, Essex, 1969–77), i–ii, *passim*.
[48] Cross, *Letters of Sir Francis Hastings*, 25.
[49] *ODNB*, Ann Vaux, Eleanor Brooksby; Bossy, *English Catholic Community*, 233–4; Marie Rowlands, 'Recusant Women, 1560–1640,' in Mary Prior, ed., *Women in Early Modern Society 1500–1800* (1985), 158; *ODNB*, William Wolfe; Wood, *Life and Times*, ii.269n–270n.
[50] HMC, 35, *Kenyon*, 18; TNA, SP 12/185/17; Anstruther, *Seminary Priests*, i.172–3.

especially family heads and their heirs. Many, dubbed 'church-papists', practised a minimal outward conformity that often proved sufficient to save them from prosecution.[51] Self-interest, ignorance, or indifference saw many Catholics gradually drift away. Like their Protestant equivalents, many Catholic and Catholic-leaning families included members with widely differing levels of commitment. Here too, the zealous longed to reclaim their lapsed or worldly kin. 'Conversion' in this context generally meant winning back those who had fallen away and persuading them to seek formal 'reconciliation' with the Catholic Church. Many of the young Catholics trained at the English College in Rome, usually planning to enter the priesthood, had been raised in 'schismatic' families, Catholic in sympathy but not in communion with the Church, or in families that were split between Catholics, schismatics, conformists, and Protestant 'heretics'. In brief accounts of their early lives, recorded in the *Responsa Scholarum*, many paid tribute to the decisive influence of close kin in converting them from schism, ignorance, or indifference. And those who had converted before reaching adulthood often identified siblings as well as parents and other kin as having played this role.[52] Thomas Beveridge, raised by schismatic parents, recalled having been deeply impressed, aged 8, by a 'beloved' elder brother who had made a pilgrimage to Rome. Sent to London at 15 to be apprenticed, Beveridge persuaded another brother to arrange his passage to the Continent to pursue a Catholic future.[53] In most such cases, as we would expect, it was an elder brother or half-brother, sometimes already in the priesthood, who had made the crucial intervention. For Richard Fisher, it had come when he visited an older brother at Wisbech Castle, where many priests were incarcerated under Elizabeth. Their encounter proved a decisive turning point in his life.[54] Peter Curtis, born in 1595, had been converted at the age of 14 or 15 by his elder brother, a Jesuit, who had then sent him to be educated at St Omer. Curtis said he had previously been a 'heretic', but seven of his ten siblings were Catholics, two of them Jesuit priests, and his mother had died a Catholic. This was clearly a family with a deeply Catholic spirit, even if his parents had conformed for a time.[55] Not every account matched this pattern, however. In the case of Brian Cansfield, converted at 15, inspiration had come from a younger brother. Richard Cornwallis, a much older convert, had been won over at 26 by his half-brother, a priest, after having studied at Cambridge for ten years.[56] A few converts acknowledged the role of a sister. One had been moved by his

---

[51] Alexandra Walsham, *Church Papists. Catholicism, Conformity and Confessional Polemic in Early Modern England* (1993).

[52] Anthony Kenny, ed., *The Responsa Scholarum of the English College, Rome,* Catholic Record Society, 54–5, (1962–3); Lucy Underwood, *Childhood, Youth and Religious Dissent in Post-Reformation England* (Basingstoke, 2014), 35–44 and *passim*.

[53] Kenny, *Responsa,* i.72–4.

[54] Kenny, *Responsa,* i.15–18; cf. i.4–5, 174–5, 193–5, 221–2, 233–7, 240–1, 277–80, 294–5, 331–2, 345–6.

[55] Kenny, *Responsa,* i.345–6; Anstruther, *Seminary Priests,* ii.78–9; cf. Michael Questier, 'Clerical Recruitment and Conversion to Rome', in Claire Cross, ed., *Patronage and Recruitment in the Tudor and Early Stuart Church* (York, 1996), 87.

[56] Kenny, *Responsa,* i.4–5.106–7.

sister's piety and devotion, while an Oxford student had been ashamed to find a younger sister far better informed than himself.[57] Some sisters were ready to proselytize openly within their families. A contemporary reported in 1602 that Lady Bridget Norris, a widow, 'is become a great Catholic, and takes great care and pains to convert her sisters'.[58]

Family ties were inevitably weakened when young men moved to seminaries abroad, especially if they had left without parental consent. Even supportive families found it difficult to maintain contact during the years when religious conflict was at its most intense. Many of the new entrants at the English College in Rome were poorly informed about the situation of their families back in England. Robert Forster, who had left England at the age of 13, explained in 1606 that he did not know how his family in Norfolk was faring, or even the names of the siblings born after his departure.[59] Those living in Flanders or France generally found it easier to maintain contact, at least in peacetime. Young women who entered schools or convents abroad almost always enjoyed the support of their families and, especially in the second half of our period, found it relatively easy to sustain family ties. Some nuns exchanged letters with close kin over many years, and received occasional visits. Such ties might be reinforced by a niece arriving to become a novice. The English houses depended on financial support from families back in the homeland, and this made some level of contact essential.[60]

In an age of religious persecution and sedition, it was predictable that sibling bonds would also find more dramatic and sometimes violent expression. German Pole, a priest arrested in Derbyshire in 1610, was rescued by his Jesuit brother. Nicholas Titchborne, a lay Catholic, staged the still more daring rescue of his brother Thomas, a seminary priest, as he was being conveyed under guard through the London streets. Nicholas had arranged money, clothes, and a horse for their escape, but the brothers paid dearly for their bravado: they were both captured and hanged at Tyburn.[61] Siblings might also be drawn into treason and rebellion. Among the leaders of the Lincolnshire rising of 1536, which immediately preceded the Pilgrimage of Grace, were the three Leech brothers, one a priest. All three were hanged.[62] In 1605, the leading Gunpowder Plotters included the brothers Thomas and Robert Winter and Christopher and John Wright. All four were involved in the bloody shoot-out at Holbeach House, where the Wrights were killed and the

[57] Kenny, *Responsa*, i.74–8, 185–7, 197–8.
[58] *The Letters of John Chamberlain*, ed. N. E. McClure (Philadelphia, 1939), i.170.
[59] Kenny, *Responsa*, i.177–8.
[60] Claire Walker; 'Recusants. Daughters and Sisters in Christ: English Nuns and their Communities in the Seventeenth Century', in Stephanie Tarbin and Susan Broomhall, eds, *Women, Identities and Communities in Early Modern Europe* (Aldershot, 2008), 62–76; Isobel Grundy, 'Women's history? Writings by English Nuns', in *eadem* and Susan Wiseman, eds, *Women, Writing, History 1640–1740* (1992), 126–38; Bagley, ed., *Great Diurnall of Nicholas Blundell*, ii.165–80, iii.107–12.
[61] Anstruther, *Seminary Priests*, ii.249; HMC, 39, *Eliot Hodgkin*, 270–2.
[62] M. E. James, 'Obedience and dissent in Henrician England: the Lincolnshire Rebellion 1536', *Past and Present*, 48 (1970), 21, 25. Robert Kett and his brother William, a butcher, played a comparable role in the Norfolk Protestant rebellion of 1549.

Winters captured and subsequently executed.[63] We can find other siblings implicated in the Popish Plot in 1678, and in Jacobite plotting after the Glorious
Revolution, with their sisters sometimes drawn into the margins of their activities.[64]

FAMILY CONFLICTS

Against the narratives of solidarity and support, both Catholic and Protestant, we
must set the counter-narrative of families divided by faith. Until the civil war, the
main fault line lay between Protestant and Catholic, a fault line that remained
central throughout the period. Especially in its earlier part, we find committed
Catholics reacting with horror when a child was drawn away to the Protestant
cause. Early in Elizabeth's reign Laurence Chaderton, a Cambridge student from a
staunchly Catholic family in Lancashire, informed his father that he had converted
to Protestantism, at the same time rather naively requesting financial support to
further his studies. The response was brusque; his father disinherited him and sent
him a bag 'with a groat in it, to go a begging withal'. In the event, Chaderton went
on to a successful career, becoming eventually the first Master of Emmanuel
College.[65] Some Protestant fathers responded with similar outrage. One disinherited a 'lost son' who had turned to Rome, damning his apostasy as undutiful, disloyal
to the state, and irreligious.[66] In the most extreme cases of parental rejection,
converts returning to England as Catholic priests were betrayed to the authorities
by their own fathers. John Maxey suffered this fate in 1616, and died in prison the
following year. His embittered father wanted him to be buried in the prison
rubbish heap.[67]

Protestant families knew that conversion to Rome brought the risk of imprisonment and financial ruin for the convert, and would call into doubt the loyalty of
every member. It also created a painful tension between the loyalty due to the
family and to the sovereign. Thomas Ithell, Master of Jesus College, Cambridge,
was so alarmed by the activities of his brother Ralph, a Jesuit priest, that he felt it his
duty to inform Lord Burghley. Robert Markham, younger son of a Nottinghamshire gentleman, dismayed his family by converting to Rome in the 1590s. When
he announced his plan to seek a military career abroad, his father made him pledge
never to fight for Spain against the Queen, and his elder brother urged him to turn
his arms instead against the Ottoman Turks.[68] Margaret Eure's family responded
with outrage when she married a Catholic in 1639. Her mother said the news had

---

[63] See *ODNB* for all these; Mark Nicholls, *Investigating Gunpowder Plot* (Manchester, 1991),
12–13 and *passim*.

[64] HMC, 32, *Fitzherbert*, 128–9, 158; HMC, 35, *Kenyon*, 226; HMC, 9, *Salisbury*, xviii.34.

[65] Clarke, *Lives of Two and Twenty English Divines*, 168–9.

[66] Kenny, *Responsa*, i.121–2,168; Anstruther, *Seminary Priests*, ii.73–4; HMC, 9, *Salisbury*, i.298;
Walsham, 'Reformation of the Generations', 103, 111.

[67] Anstruther, *Seminary Priests*, i.3, ii.213–14.

[68] Anstruther, *Seminary Priests*, i.184–6, 235–6; Sir Clement Markham, ed., *Markham Memorials*,
2 vols (1913), i.103–7.

almost killed her, though she admitted he would have been acceptable in every other respect. Margaret's brother urged her to conceal the marriage as long as possible, to avoid 'perpetual shame'. She was confident that she could soon convert her husband to Protestantism, though in the event it was she who converted to Rome. The final outcome proved more satisfactory, at least for her family. Her husband was killed in the civil war, and her brother reported in 1645 that she was now about to remarry, 'and (which is my comfort) to a Protestant this time'. Her return to the Protestant fold soon followed.[69]

Throughout the period, the mere rumour of conversion was sufficient to raise deep alarm among other family members. Thomas Coke had aroused suspicions by travelling to Italy in the company of the Catholic Earl of Arundel, and his death abroad in 1621 prompted persistent rumours that he had died a Catholic. His brothers mourned the loss of their 'beloved brother', but they remained deeply troubled until news finally arrived that he had after all died a 'true [i.e. Protestant] Christian'.[70] Such rumours were even more alarming for the individuals who found themselves under suspicion. William Foulis, the son of a Yorkshire baronet, was living in Paris when he learned that 'some cursed rogue' had convinced his father that he had converted to Rome. He feared his father would disinherit him. Anthony Wood, the Oxford antiquary, reacted with dismay in 1673 when his brother told him of a general report that he was a secret Catholic. Sir John Bramston described his horror at similar rumours about himself, which the Earl of Oxford had passed on to Bramston's brother, Moundford, in strict confidence. Knowing their potentially disastrous consequences, Moundford told his brother at the earliest opportunity and Sir John immediately launched a determined campaign to clear his name.[71]

Despite these starkly polarized attitudes, we should not forget that religious loyalties and identities had long remained fluid and confused. For much of Elizabeth's reign, many men and women found it hard to achieve any sense of spiritual certainty, torn between the fiercely competing claims of Reformers and Catholics. At Oxford, the six Rainolds brothers, five of them college fellows, wrestled for years over the identity of the true Church. According to several early accounts, William and John Rainolds argued with such passionate conviction that each eventually converted the other. William renounced his Protestant ordination, abandoned England, and went on to become a prominent Catholic priest and polemicist. John, by contrast, abandoned Catholicism to become a strict Calvinist, a leading puritan figure in the university, and a fierce anti-Catholic polemicist.[72] Many lay Catholics oscillated between recusancy and church-papism, torn between conscience and fears for their safety and the welfare of their families. The Jesuit

---

[69] Verney, *Memoirs*, i.276–96.   [70] HMC, 23, *Cowper*, i.114, 116.

[71] Sir Gyles Isham, ed., *The Diary of Thomas Isham of Lamport* (Farnborough, 1971), 51; Wood, *Life and Times*, ii.275; *The Autobiography of Sir John Bramston*, ed. Lord Braybrooke, Camden Society, OS, 32 (1845), 127–9.

[72] *ODNB*, William and John Rainolds; Anthony Wood, *Athenae Oxonienses*, 4 vols (1813, repr. 1967), i.613–15; Jennifer Loach, 'Reformation Controversies', in James McConica, ed., *The History of the University of Oxford: III. The Collegiate University* (Oxford, 1986), 382.

William Weston told the cautionary tale of one timid conformist who had kept his brother, a priest, close at hand, so that if taken dangerously ill he could be received hastily back into the fold. But God was not to be mocked; the faint-heart fell ill while away from home, and died before his brother could arrive.[73]

As we have seen, many of the young men recorded in the *Responsa Scholarum* came from families that had included Catholics, schismatics, conformists, and in some cases Protestant 'heretics'. John Curtis explained, around 1608, that while one of his brothers was a Jesuit, another was a minister in the Church of England. After many years as a Protestant, Curtis had been converted by the Jesuit and went on to become a priest himself.[74] Zealous Catholics who knew that some of their close kin were committed 'heretics' often felt a strong desire to save them.[75] The story of Edmund Geninges, a martyr later canonized, offers perhaps the most famous example. A young Jesuit trained in Spain, Geninges arrived in England in 1591 and promptly headed for London in the hope of tracking down and converting his family, whom he had not seen for many years. He discovered that only one younger brother, John, was still alive, and neither initially recognized the other. When Edmund revealed his identity, his brother reacted with dismay. Viewing Catholics as traitors, he told Edmund to stay well away. Geninges refused to abandon his dream and soon returned to London, where this time he was almost immediately captured. John refused to visit him in prison, and stayed away from his trial and grisly execution. But ten days later he was suddenly overwhelmed by his brother's self-sacrifice, and experienced an emotional conversion that he attributed 'wholly (next after God) to the intercession of his blessed brother'. He went on to a long and prominent career as a Franciscan.[76] Other Catholics felt a similar mission to save their 'lost' siblings. In 1625, we find William Purnell, a convert and priest in Seville, sending an emotional appeal to his Protestant brother in England, laying out the considerations that had led him to embrace Catholicism, after many 'prayers, tears, sighs'. He told his brother that the Protestant road led only to hell, and begged him to return to the truth while there was still time.[77]

Conversion was a complex phenomenon, however, and might be neither permanent nor complete. Some people wavered, for months or even years. Bridget Carleton flirted for months in 1602–3 with the idea of converting to Catholicism, demanding advice and support from her siblings and friends. They grew exasperated by her behaviour, 'irresolute and inconstant, and yet peevish and wilful', and suspected she was simply seeking attention and 'loves to hold her friends in suspense'.[78] Some of those who did convert remained uncertain, while fear of imprisonment, torture, or execution led others to fall away. And brothers could

---

[73] Philip Caraman, *William Weston. The Autobiography of an Elizabethan* (1955), 37–8.
[74] Kenny, *Responsa*, i.221–2.   [75] Questier, 'Clerical Recruitment', 83–7.
[76] John Geninges, *The Life and Death of Mr Edmund Geninges* (St. Omers, 1614; facsimile reprint Menston, 1971), 47–61, 96–100, quotation at 100; *ODNB*, Geninges; Underwood, *Childhood*, 119–23.
[77] TNA, SP16/4/65; Anstruther, *Seminary Priests*, i.83, ii.259; cf. ii.107–8.
[78] *Letters of John Chamberlain*, ed. McClure, i.140–1, 147–8, 157–8, 164. Her sister Alice wavered too.

occasionally lead siblings out of the Catholic fold as well as into it. John Salkeld and his younger brother Henry, for example, were both Jesuit priests, trained at Seville and sent as missionaries to England. After his arrest, John quickly returned to the Church of England and Henry promptly followed his lead. The brothers received royal pardons on the very same day, in March 1615.[79]

Some families tried to dissuade potential converts, whether on grounds of principle or to shield them from danger. William Williamson, born into a schismatic family, described how his elder brother and parents had obstructed his longing to be received into the Church. Henry Pole, aged 17, recalled his mother's desperate attempts to dissuade him from going to St Omer. Though her tears had distressed him, he chose to disobey a parent rather than lose his soul. Francis Miles, born into a Protestant family and converted at 14 through the influence of a friend, told how his mother and elder brother had burnt his Catholic books and pressured him into returning to the established Church. For several years he had floundered, until new friends brought him back into the Catholic fold, in defiance of both threats and bribes from his family.[80] The Laythwaite family saw another attempt to reclaim a Catholic sibling. Edward Laythwaite had been a London apprentice when he learned that his elder brother Thomas, a missionary priest, had been captured and gaoled at Exeter. Abandoning his master, Edward hastened there, apparently to urge him to save his life by abjuring. Instead, Thomas persuaded him to convert to Rome.[81]

Divisions within Protestant families could prove equally stressful, especially following the rise of separatist movements from the mid-seventeenth century. Laurence Clarkson of Preston, later notorious as a Ranter, tells how in 1630, at the age of 15, he had become a follower of radical puritan preachers, drawn away by older brothers 'more gifted in the knowledge of the Scriptures than myself'. The local minister warned their father of 'the danger of his children going into heresy', a prospect 'which did much incense our father'. But parental attempts to win Clarkson back to the established Church proved vain; he decided it was his duty 'to obey God before man'.[82] In some families, siblings were able to exchange ideas and doubts in an open-minded spirit. Early in 1645, for example, a separatist army ensign set out his thoughts on family prayers, and asked his sister for her opinion. She replied with a friendly exposition of her own position.[83] In other families, by contrast, the sibling bond was torn apart. When John Cosens, an apprentice or journeyman at Chatham, discussed religious issues with his brother Robert, also in 1645, he was scandalized by his brother's blasphemous dismissal of Christ and his

---

[79] Michael Questier, *Conversion, Politics and Religion in England 1580–1625* (Cambridge, 1996), 47; cf. 52, 118 and n.; *ODNB*, John Salkeld.

[80] Kenny, *Responsa*, i.209–10, 264–5, 295–6; cf. Anstruther, *Seminary Priests*, ii.102–3; *ODNB*, George Fisher.

[81] Questier, *Conversion*, 96; Anstruther, *Seminary Priests*, ii.181. For Edward's rather different account see Kenny, *Responsa*, i.203–4.

[82] Laurence Claxton [Clarkson], *The Lost Sheep Found* (1660), 4–5.

[83] Thomas Edwards, *Gangraena* (1646: facsimile edition, Exeter, 1977), iii.59–60.

teaching. Robert was subsequently charged with blasphemy, and John gave evidence against him.[84]

Young converts still living in the parental home faced particular difficulties, both practical and psychological. With little personal autonomy, they had to wrestle with the incompatible duties they owed to God and to their parents. Agnes Beaumont, a farmer's daughter in Bedfordshire, penned a vivid account of the tensions inherent in such a situation. Agnes, who kept house for her widowed father, had become a committed disciple of the Nonconformist, John Bunyan, despite her father's disapproval. When she defied his order to leave the congregation, her father retaliated by locking her out of the house, in midwinter. She passed a miserable night in the freezing barn, tormented by the impossibility of reconciling her family and spiritual duties. Her older brother, who farmed nearby and shared her faith, offered some moral and practical support, and without it her plight would have been still worse.[85] The pressures were most intense when a convert had no ally within the family, especially if the others combined to force the apostate back to the 'truth'. That was the situation facing Anne Upcott of St Austell, whose conversion to Quakerism outraged her three brothers and her father, the town's minister, who would have viewed it as a double betrayal. Anne's sister found her mending a torn waistcoat one Sunday in 1658 and told their brother John, who as parish constable secured a warrant to set her in the stocks for profaning the Sabbath. There she remained for several hours in the rain, surrounded by a crowd of jeering boys, and with her brothers and father looking on with crude jests. One of her brothers told her later that he would be constable the following year, and would be ready to whip her to the next town and back, adding sadistically that 'he had a good strong arm for the purpose'. Anne remained defiantly steadfast in her faith.[86]

Beaumont's story illustrates sibling solidarity against a hostile father, while Upcott's shows a convert facing hostility from both parent and siblings. Other families present a third scenario, with siblings attempting to mediate. The autobiography of Thomas Ellwood, a young Quaker convert, provides a vivid account of this situation. His father, a short-tempered magistrate, was enraged by his son's conversion and his refusal to perform conventional gestures of deference, such as doffing his hat in his father's presence. Ellwood's younger sister sought to defuse the situation and restrain their father's violent anger. On one fraught occasion, she found him beating her brother so fiercely about the head with his cane that she feared he would be killed. In desperation she threatened to throw open the window and cry murder. Her intervention succeeded; her father stopped, Thomas retreated to his chamber, and she followed to dress his wounds. Another sister, who had been staying in London, responded to his new faith with puzzlement and pity rather than hostility. Both sisters,

---

[84] Ibid., ii.115–20.

[85] Bernard Capp, 'The Travails of Agnes Beaumont', in Bronach Kane and Fiona Williamson, eds, *Women's Agency and the Law, 1300–1700* (2013), 111–24. The most accessible text is now *John Bunyan: Grace Abounding and other Spiritual Autobiographies*, ed. J. Stachniewski and A. Pacheco (Oxford, 1998).

[86] Norman Penney, ed., *Records of the Sufferings of Quakers in Cornwall 1655–1686* (1928), 17–19, 22; Besse, *Sufferings*, i.116.

Ellwood recalled gratefully, 'carried themselves very kindly towards me, and did what they could to mitigate my father's displeasure against me'.[87]

Though Thomas Ellwood does not appear to have tried to evangelize his own family, many converts were understandably eager to explain their new faith and convince their families. Whole families sometimes converted to the Quakers, like Thomas Bagg of Bridport, his wife, and their four daughters. Thomas Aldam's sister followed his lead, married another Quaker, and became an evangelist herself.[88] The evangelist George Whitehead described many similar cases, including that of John Lawrence, a former army captain. Lawrence heard him speak in 1654, and invited him to a meeting at his home. Quickly converted to the Quaker faith, he was soon followed by his brother, their wives, his wife's sister, and her husband.[89] But the explosive growth of the Quakers triggered fear, anger, and persecution too, and we can also find sibling solidarity taking the diametrically opposite form of alliances directed against them. Brothers occasionally acted as informers, and sibling ministers and justices sometimes combined to report and prosecute Dissenters. Resolute sisters occasionally took still more direct action. When Richard Davies, an apprentice felt-maker, became a Quaker in the late 1650s, his master proved sympathetic but his 'cruel mistress' was appalled. Davies described later how she often beat and threatened to kill him. One day she had appeared with her sister, both women brandishing staffs, and 'the sister began to beat her brother my master', while his wife beat another young convert.[90]

Religious divisions frequently bred family tensions and conflict, but we should not forget that the ties of blood might also prevail. In the case of recusants, an influential Protestant sibling often proved an invaluable asset. It was the protection of a Protestant brother that allowed Richard Stanton, an Elizabethan Catholic lawyer, to follow his profession.[91] Catherine Everard, whose recusant husband was imprisoned in 1579, begged her brother Bassingbourne Gawdy to lobby courtiers on his behalf. Gawdy obliged by petitioning the Privy Council, and secured his release. Francis Miles, who complained that his family had tried to obstruct his conversion to Catholicism, had to acknowledge that it was his brother who had secured his release from prison, by appealing to the bishop of London on his behalf.[92] Other siblings used their connections to secure the release of imprisoned priests, or reverse an outlawry.[93]

The intervention of close kin could be important for persecuted Protestants too. In the civil war period, we can find puritan ministers coming to the aid of clerical

---

[87] *The History of the Life of Thomas Ellwood*, ed. G. C. Crump (1900) 3–6, 40–1, 50, 100.

[88] Norman Penny, ed., *The First Publishers of Truth* (1907), 78, 79–82, 165, 255.

[89] *The Christian Progress of that ancient servant and minister of Jesus Christ, George Whitehead* (1725), 24, 29, 244; cf. Henry Kettle, former mayor of Thetford, with his wife, son, and daughter: ibid., 251–4.

[90] Elias Osborn, *A Brief Narrative of the Life, Labours and Sufferings of Elias Osborn* (1723), 42–3; Besse, *Sufferings*, i.338; Richard Davies, *An Account of the Convincement, Exercises, Services, and Travels of Richard Davies* (1794), 33.

[91] Anstruther, *Seminary Priests*, ii.309.   [92] HMC, 11, *Gawdy*, 11; Kenny, *Responsa*, i.264–6.

[93] Anstruther, *Seminary Priests*, ii.177, 221–2; A. Hassell Smith et al., eds, *The Papers of Nathaniel Bacon of Stiffkey*, 5 vols, Norfolk Record Society (1979–2010), iii.276; HMC, 9, *Salisbury*, xviii.211.

siblings ejected by the parliamentarians.[94] Quakers sometimes received help from non-Quaker kin. A Cornish Quaker gaoled in 1658 for refusing to pay tithes was freed when his brother paid them on his behalf. Kin quite often paid such fines, generally without the knowledge or consent of the Quakers themselves. At Bristol, a councillor tried to secure the release of his Quaker sister by pleading that she was heavily pregnant and seriously ill.[95] Two Welsh Quakers enjoyed the assistance of a non-Quaker brother, employed in the Court of Chancery in London, who was ready to provide legal advice to Welsh Quakers facing prosecution.[96] In the later seventeenth century, kinship sometimes also prevailed among Anglicans and Nonconformists. In one such case, Seth Ward, bishop of Salisbury, found himself badgered by a Nonconformist sister who ignored their religious differences. 'Brother,' she wrote bluntly (disdaining to use his episcopal title), 'since there is corn in Egypt, it is not meet that the children of Israel should want.' Ward responded to this self-serving appeal by providing some assistance, no doubt through gritted teeth.[97] In the case of the Sampson brothers, both ministers in the 1650s, it was surely genuine affection that triumphed over denominational differences. Henry, the elder, was ejected at the Restoration and forged a successful new career in medicine, while remaining a firm Independent. His brother William conformed, and officiated for many years as the staunchly Anglican Rector of Clayworth (Nottinghamshire). Yet the brothers remained close. William, who was childless, invited Henry's son to live with him and made him his heir; and when Henry fell terminally ill, he chose to leave London and end his life at Clayworth.[98]

The sources for religious history generally steer us towards the themes of either zeal or conflict. Almost by definition, peaceful coexistence leaves few traces. So it is also well to remember that many individuals who considered themselves good Christians adopted a more tolerant stance, especially in the unsettled early Elizabethan period, and after the Restoration. Many Anglicans had no wish to see Nonconformist neighbours harassed and imprisoned. One aggressive informer was even scolded by his mother, who told him that she and his brothers and sisters felt 'deep grief and trouble' over his activities, and urged him to stop.[99] In Lancashire, we find the prosperous maltster John Johnson, a 'wholly conformable' Anglican, marrying a Catholic wife and later, after her death, a 'zealous Presbyterian'. When Johnson himself died, he chose a Quaker friend and executor to arrange the board and education of his younger children. Johnson and his circle clearly lived in a spirit of mutual tolerance.[100] Other families, though less easy-going, gradually came to

---

[94] Fiona McCall, *Baal's Priests. The Loyalist Clergy and the English Revolution* (Farnham, 2013), 185, 212–13. But for a counter-example see ibid., 216–17.

[95] Besse, *Sufferings*, i.52; cf, i.632, ii.20–2, 112–19; Penney, *Record of the Sufferings*, 12.

[96] Davies, *An Account*, 59–60, 131.

[97] Walter Pope, *The Life of Seth, Lord Bishop of Salisbury* (1697), 6.

[98] *ODNB*, Henry and William Sampson; cf. Amy Harris, *Siblinghood and Social Relations in Georgian England* (Manchester, 2012), 125.

[99] Besse, *Sufferings*, i.602.

[100] *The Autobiography of William Stout of Lancaster 1665–1752*, ed. J. D. Marshall (Manchester, 1967), 110–12, 258.

terms with their religious differences. Charles Doe, a London apprentice in the late 1660s, recalled how his stepfather had initially tried to stop him attending a Baptist congregation. His stepfather was a staunch Presbyterian, so Doe pointed out that he was only seeking the same liberty of conscience that his stepfather wanted for himself. The argument struck home, and the pressure ceased.[101] Other contemporaries viewed all zealots with distaste, and kept their distance. Muriel Bell and her sister Abigail Moundeford were both widows in the 1620s, and Abigail proposed that they should set up home together. Muriel firmly rejected the suggestion, for her sister was a dour and troubled puritan. High-spirited and cheerful by nature, Muriel preferred to move in with her firmly anti-puritan nephew and his family.[102]

---

[101] Charles Doe, *A Collection of Experience of the Work of Grace* (1700), 29–30.
[102] *The Knyvett Letters (1620–1644),* ed. Bertram Schofield, Norfolk Record Society, 20 (1949), 26.

PART II

FAMILY STORIES

8

William Stout

Solidarity and Support

William Stout (1665–1752) was a successful Quaker businessman in Lancaster. The son of a hard-working and canny yeoman at nearby Bolton-le-Sands, Stout was apprenticed to a Quaker tradesman, and for many years thrived as a retail and wholesale grocer and ironmonger. He converted to Quakerism towards the end of his apprenticeship, and went on to become a significant figure in the Lancashire branch of the movement. His autobiography, composed towards the end of a long life, covers almost eighty years.[1] Stout was part of a close-knit family, not given to effusive language but deeply concerned for the welfare and interests of each member. His autobiography is a valuable source for the strength of sibling relationships, and the significance of reciprocal responsibilities.

William was the thirdborn of seven siblings, one of whom died in infancy. He never married, and neither did his older sister Ellen. His younger brother Leonard married at 29, but his older brother Josias not until the age of 47; this was a family in which blood rather than marital ties had priority. Their father died in 1681, leaving children who ranged in age from 5 to 20. Stout's mother, Elizabeth, moved to secure his future by binding him apprentice to a prosperous grocer and ironmonger in Lancaster. (74) Only a few months later he lost his two youngest brothers to smallpox. One of them, Richard, almost 10, had been a bright boy, quick to learn, and Stout was deeply distressed by his death. He had already formed hopes that in years to come Richard 'might have been assistant to me, or I to him, if he had lived till I had performed my apprenticeship'. (76) It is a characteristic example of the blend of affection, family solidarity, and business sense that shaped his outlook and behaviour. Ellen was even more devastated by losing her young brothers and her father, and was reduced to a very low condition. Her mother sent her to stay with relations in Kendal to recover her health and spirits. (76)

Stout's career progressed with very few setbacks. He was hard-working, cautious, and a good judge of men and of business risks and opportunities. After completing his apprenticeship he set up in trade in 1687, with a working capital of £120, most of it coming from his share of his late father's estate. Part he had raised by selling a parcel of land to his brother Josias, and Josias lent him a horse for a journey to London to buy stock for the shop. While this was not a family business, the family

---

[1] *The Autobiography of William Stout of Lancaster 1665–1752*, ed. J. D. Marshall (Manchester, 1967). Numbers in brackets refer to this work.

played a significant role from the start. William's sister lent him £10 from her own share of the inheritance, and came over at Midsummer Fair and on market days to help in the shop. (89–90) Moreover, he recalled, when he fell seriously ill in 1688, his 'dear sister Ellen attended me and the shop, all the time of my weakness'. (91) The family came to his aid again in 1690, when he went to Sheffield to buy more stock. Josias and a cousin acted as sureties for a loan he took out, and Ellen managed the shop during the six days he was away. (96) The business thrived. Each year Stout cast up his accounts, and by 1703 he calculated that he was worth £1,142. By 1722, it had grown to £4,350. (142, 187) William Stout was the epitome of the Weberian puritan stereotype, pious, ascetic, industrious. He rose early, lived frugally, and possessed an iron constitution. He was so inured to cold that he chose to sit away from the fire even in the harshest winters. (80–1, 105) Though heavily involved in the affairs of the Quaker movement and the town's mercantile community, Stout remained essentially a private man. His main recreation was walking in the fields at sunrise, and on moonlit nights in winter, either alone or with his friend Richard Greene. After Greene's early death, the walks were solitary. (96, 99, 140, 196, 201) Stout strongly disapproved of loose talk, loose behaviour, idleness, and drink, and his autobiography was in part a moralizing chronicle of the dangers of drink and extravagant living. (100, 104–5, 140, 144, 150) Sober, efficient, and responsible, Stout was often asked to pick up the pieces and sort out the financial mess left by those who had fallen by the wayside. His faith was deep and apparently unproblematic. There was no dramatic conversion experience, and there is no evidence of spiritual crises or doubts thereafter. (82–5)

Stout never married, despite several opportunities. The only time he was seriously tempted was when Bethia Greene, who belonged to a local Quaker family, returned from London in 1702 following the death of her brother Richard, Stout's friend. Bethia was a lively young woman of 26, twelve years younger than Stout. Despite the family's religion, she had been brought up 'in a genteel manner under a very indulgent mother', and loved 'light and airy company'. Stout was captivated, and decided that 'if ever I married, it must be to her'. At the same time, he was painfully conscious of the difference in age and the huge disparity in personality and tastes. Bethia looked askance at his sober clothes and austere life, and tried to avoid his company. Nothing came of the tentative negotiations, and he was almost certainly right that marriage would have proved deeply unhappy for them both. (140–2)

When he first opened his shop Stout took meals at a neighbour's house, and slept in a small room in his shop, sparsely furnished with only a bed, table, and small light. (90) In 1690, with his business growing, he decided to keep house himself, a plan he first discussed carefully with his mother and sister. Ellen offered to act as housekeeper in the rooms he now rented. (102) She was already an important figure in his life, and they forged a very successful partnership. Though Ellen was the firstborn of the family, the gender norms of the age and her father's death consigned her to a life of service and support. All the children began their education at a dame school at Bolton-le-Sands, and the boys then moved on to a free (grammar) school there. Ellen's schooling was much briefer. With their mother heavily engaged on the farm, dressing corn for market and helping at haymaking and harvest, she was taken from school and 'early confined to wait on her brothers, more than she was well able.'[2] She proved 'a good and diligent assistant to her mother, in waiting upon and providing for the younger children in knitting, sewing and spinning'. (68–9) Contemporary attitudes were perhaps also reflected in their father's will, for he left her less than any of her brothers, even the 5-year-old. These provisions may, however, also reflect the fact that he had laid out considerable sums in sending her to several doctors, in fruitless attempts to relieve her medical problems. Perhaps he did not expect her to live long. (68–9, 72–3) After his death, his widow kept on the farm, with Ellen now playing a still larger role in managing the house and caring for the younger children. Over the next few years, she received several offers of marriage from local yeomen, but her mother advised her to remain single. Given her fragile health and the 'hazard of happiness' in any marriage, her mother argued, spinsterhood was a more sensible option. (87) Ellen complied, and it is difficult to imagine her surviving the rigours of childbirth. But she was certainly no valetudinarian. As well as running the home, she had helped in Stout's shop from the beginning, and managed it when he was away. (99) Brother and sister developed an enduring bond that appears never to have frayed. Stout described her as always 'careful and diligent to serve me as much or more than if I had been her own son. And I was tender to her.' She was four years his elder, and his description of her quasi-maternal care may carry an echo of their childhood relationship. He always refers to her as his 'dear sister', was solicitous over her health, and hired a good maidservant to spare her the heaviest domestic chores. (142) He was highly impressed by Ellen's value in the business. She took charge on market days, and Stout considered her as capable as his apprentice in the retail side of the trade. (150–1) It was the closest relationship either ever enjoyed, characterized by affection, trust, and a genuine concern to protect and advance the interests of the other. Ellen eventually became a Quaker too, though, as Stout stressed, without any pressure or persuasion by him. (127)

Theirs was a household very different from the conduct book or demographers' norm. Its core members were Stout and his sister, with an apprentice and maidservant. Their mother, Elizabeth, joined them when she grew too frail to manage the patrimonial farmstead, and they lived harmoniously together until her death, about eight years later. She was not a Quaker, and Stout put no pressure on her to become one. Years earlier, when he had first converted in his late teens, he was deeply relieved that his mother took the news calmly, and respected his decision. (84–5, 159, 175–6) There were usually also small children in the household. His younger brother Leonard, who farmed at Hatlex, near Bolton-le-Sands, had a large brood of nine children, all but one of whom survived to adulthood. Providing for them strained his resources, and William and Ellen helped out by taking in their young nephews and nieces in turn, from the age of 2, and looking after them until they

---

[2] The text has singular 'brother', presumably a slip.

were 6 and old enough for school. Ellen 'was as careful to nurse and correct them as if they had been her own children'. (142)

Stout's narrative also provides a valuable account of relationships between the three surviving brothers. Josias, the eldest, inherited the farm. He was 18 when their father died, and showed both aptitude and commitment. Their mother hired an experienced manager for a few years until he was old enough to run the farm himself. Josias and his mother proved a successful team, and it prospered in their care. Josias shared the family's sense of mutual responsibility, and improved the small estate their father had bought for Leonard at Hatlex. (75–6, 87) Their mother bought some land lying between the family's main holding and Hatlex, and gave half each to Josias and Leonard. As part of the transaction, the sum of £100 was made chargeable at her disposal, and she chose to give £60 of it to her daughter Ellen and the balance to William. (102–3) Josias showed little inclination to marry, and did not want to hire a housekeeper, so he and his mother ran the farm together until in her late sixties she felt too old to continue. The family then devised a new arrangement. Josias let the farm to a tenant and went to live with his brother Leonard, with their mother staying sometimes there and sometimes with William. But when the tenant proved unsatisfactory, Josias and his mother resumed their former joint operation, assisted now by a man and a maidservant. They prospered once more, 'to the satisfaction', Stout relates, 'of me, my sister and all our friends and relations'. (131–2) By 1709, however, Elizabeth was in her mid-seventies and increasingly infirm, which made the arrangement no longer sustainable. She accordingly persuaded Josias to marry at last. He was 47, and his new wife, Sibill, about 30. She had previously kept house for her father, and predictably friction arose between the two women over domestic management. Elizabeth moved out to live with Stout, as we have seen, and remained there till her death. Josias, according to his brother, was always 'a quiet and modest man, his wife being of a resolute disposition, and he was very condescending for peace sake'. They lived together for twenty-eight years, but had no children. (159) When Sibill died, in 1738, Josias persuaded Leonard and his family to come and live with him, though in the event he survived his wife by only a few weeks. (223–4)

Josias had made a will some years earlier. Following William's advice, most of his estate was left to him, as the natural heir, but charged with payments totalling £352 to Leonard's children as and when they reached maturity. William also allowed Leonard to occupy the family farm, rent-free, as well as other lands that William had bought, also rent-free. Stout had wanted nothing from this inheritance, and gained nothing. He and Josias had set out to devise the best possible arrangements for their less astute younger brother and his children and grandchildren. (224–5, 239)

Leonard's fortunes and misfortunes, and those of his children and grandchildren, feature prominently in Stout's narrative. Though Leonard had very limited skill in writing and arithmetic, he became a diligent and moderately successful farmer. (75–6, 102–3) That had not always seemed likely. In the mid-1690s, Stout records, 'my mother and sister and self were in great concern for our brother Leonard', who was keeping dubious company and dabbling in risky ventures buying and selling cattle. The family decided that it would be best to have him married, to keep him away from bad company. Leonard's choice, however, was an underage orphan named Ellen Benison, whose estate lay under the control of a wasteful guardian. The family urged Leonard to defer his courtship till she came of age. But when the guardian died, Leonard renewed his suit and married her in 1697, selling her land and using it to buy more lands near his own. His young bride knew little of housekeeping, so his mother sent an experienced maidservant of her own to serve them, and provided advice and assistance to help the couple establish a competent domestic regime. (116, 119) In 1698, when Stout gave up housekeeping for a time, his sister also went to live with Leonard and his bride, 'where she was of good service and company to his young wife in her house keeping'. (121–2) The Stout family was a highly cooperative and interdependent enterprise, with individuals regularly moving from house to house to meet the needs of other members.

Stout himself, childless, developed a strong sense of responsibility towards Leonard's numerous offspring. From his mid-fifties he often thought of retiring from business, and continued in trade primarily in the interests of his nephews and nieces, and later his great-nephews and -nieces. (171, 178–9, 192, 200) As young children, his nephews and nieces had each lived for some time with him and Ellen, and he hoped that as they grew older they would be guided by his advice. (178) In that, he was to be repeatedly disappointed. When the sickly eldest daughter, Elizabeth, was about 19, she married an equally young tradesman, who kept a shop at Cartmel. Stout strongly disapproved, judging them too young for either marriage or business, and refused to help. They were 'thoughtless at first in marriage', he complained, and 'they continued so ten years'. (178–9) The husband died in 1732, in debt, leaving an 'indolent and thoughtless' widow and twins aged about 10. Stout sorted out and wound up the business; Elizabeth and the twins moved back to live with her parents, and Stout promised £10 a year to help maintain the children. (211–12, 218–19)

Far more troubling was the saga of his nephew and namesake William, whom he had raised and educated from the age of 2. In 1721, young William was 15, and his parents wanted Stout to take him on as apprentice. While that had been the original plan, Stout judged him unsuitable, and urged his parents to take the lad back home to work on the farm. But when Leonard and his wife persisted in their dream, he gave way, 'considering natural affection, and my desire to promote his children'. (184–5) His anxieties proved well founded. On one occasion, his nephew put some gunpowder in a friend's pipe, as a practical joke, and triggered an explosion that might easily have killed them both. (190–1) When young William completed his apprenticeship, in 1728, Stout generously made over his shop, trade, and stock to him, at the parents' request. He offered help and advice too, gradually withdrawn when he found his advice always ignored. And in 1730, he gloomily noted that William had married an unsuitable wife, 'without the advice, knowledge or consent of any of his relations'. (205) The business went rapidly downhill, and in 1731 Stout had to step in, resume control, and set about paying off the debts his nephew had amassed, amounting to over £900. (208–9) He had cleared them within a year or so. But he was now so weary of business that when his nephew promised to reform, he allowed him to take over his business once more. Stout had few expectations that it would prosper, and observed that his nephew's wife, bred as a gentlewoman, 'knew nothing of business or housekeeping'. (209) Stout now lived in rooms over the shop, with two of Leonard's younger daughters keeping house for him. In 1737, his nephew broke again, and again Stout had to sort out the mess. His penniless nephew and wife took a little house, with Stout giving them £40 a year to live on. (225–6) Predictably, they were soon in debt again, and by 1742, their family was on the point of breaking up. Stout was minded to abandon them as beyond redemption, but at his brother's 'earnest request' he agreed to pay them £50 for another year—payable now on the strict basis of 5s a week for 'market money', allowances for fuel, malt, meal, and rent, and £10 for clothing. Tradesmen knew not to give them credit, and this 'tough love' appears to have worked. (232)

Stout considered his other nephews and nieces similarly lacking in both gratitude and judgement. Leonard's youngest son, John, did not flourish at school, and Stout, thinking he would do best at husbandry, offered to buy him an estate worth £40 p.a. But John wanted to be a draper or mercer, and his parents arranged an apprenticeship to a draper in Kendal, expecting Stout to pay the £40 required to bind him. Stout did so, unwillingly, and provided most of John's clothes during his apprentice years. (206–7) Once they were over, John wanted to move back to Lancaster and take over Stout's shop premises. Stout advised against the plan, pointing out that John knew no potential customers in Lancaster and would face considerable competition from existing businesses. But John had the strong support of his parents and siblings, and eventually Stout gave way. He even advanced the young man £300 to buy stock to set up in trade. (222–3)

The nieces proved equally problematic, in different ways. After his sister Ellen died in 1724, Stout arranged for his niece Jennet to keep house for him. Perhaps inevitably, she did not match up to Ellen's high standards. Stout thought her too easily led into bad company, despite his best efforts to control her. Three years later, she married a yeoman in Westmorland, with her parents' consent. Her father promised a portion of £300, of which Stout somewhat grudgingly contributed almost half. (192, 196, 198–9) When he passed on his shop to his nephew in 1728, Leonard's third daughter Ellen moved in to act as housekeeper for them. (201) She too proved difficult to handle. Stout managed to block a relationship she struck up with a young chandler, Thomas Cort, whereupon she began a far more unsuitable liaison with an Irish dragoon quartered in the town. Stout rushed to warn her parents, who packed her off to stay with her sister in Westmorland until the dragoons had moved on. But when she returned, Ellen renewed her liaison with Cort, and they eventually married. Stout strongly disapproved, but was nonetheless typically generous to the young couple. He gave them £20 on their marriage, along with bedding and other household goods, and later added another £50. Moreover, after buying and rebuilding a house in Penny Street, he settled it on them and their heirs forever, at an annual rent of £5. He later accused Cort of ingratitude, but conceded that he was a diligent and successful tradesman, 'which was to my satisfaction'. (203, 207–8)

In 1730, Stout took in Margaret, Leonard's fourth daughter, who had been sent to help the younger William in his shop. History soon repeated itself when she struck up a relationship with a 'loose' young grocer. Stout urged her parents to take her home, and they eventually did. It was a lucky escape, for a few weeks later the grocer, deeply in debt, abandoned his shop and fled. (204–5) Stout must have had misgivings when he took her back in 1734, along with Leonard's youngest daughter, Mary, to act as joint housekeepers. Margaret soon developed attachments to other young men Stout considered unsuitable, and he resolved to send her home again. But this time she outmanoeuvred him; one day when he was away on business she was married privately to one Walter Burnskill, without the knowledge of either Stout or her parents. Her devious behaviour triggered some bitter reflections on the ingratitude of the nephews and nieces he had helped to raise. Her sister Mary was infirm, so Stout now abandoned housekeeping. (215–16)

Happily, the family history ended on a far more positive note. Despite her wayward behaviour, Stout gave Margaret £10 to buy household goods, and planned further help if she acknowledged the hurt she had done him. It is unclear whether she ever did so. Nonetheless, when her husband set up in trade, Stout offered to rebuild his dilapidated shop and houses, 'in respect to his wife', and laid out almost £200 on the project. (218, 219–20) Ellen and her husband, Thomas Cort, prospered, and when Cort planned to build a new house in Pudding Lane, Stout gave £50 towards the costs, along with building materials to the same value. (229–30) Nephew William remained a ne'er-do-well, but nephew Leonard prospered, and married with parental approval. (217, 218–19) Nephew John, the draper, flourished too, and indeed went on to become mayor of Lancaster. (277, 279) And in 1742, Stout's niece Mary married a young apothecary and surgeon, a man he respected and admired. For once, he was pleased by the match, and provided financial assistance to equal what he had given his other nephews and nieces. (235–6) In the closing years of the narrative, Stout had his orphaned great-niece Mary Hall (Leonard's granddaughter) living with him. He had taken her in, he wrote, 'free, in order to improving herself in learning', but she gradually came to share and then take over the housekeeping, to his great satisfaction. A woman came in every week or two to wash, brew, and clean. (226, 229, 232–3, 236)

This was a family story full of vicissitudes, told by an austere, demanding, but also caring and generous narrator. The Stouts are an excellent example of a family that viewed itself as a common enterprise, and acted accordingly. Stout and his siblings remained close and mutually supportive throughout their lives, bound together by affection and a powerful sense of mutual responsibility. Stout repeatedly emphasized the 'unity' and 'concord' with which they and their mother lived together. (87, 102) This was a family ethos far removed from the individualism that Alan Macfarlane has identified as the norm in early modern England.[3] Though Stout's wealth set him apart from the other members, this was also a story of interdependence. He always acknowledged his immense debt to his sister Ellen, who devoted

---

[3] Alan Macfarlane, *The Origins of English Individualism* (Oxford, 1978).

her entire life to him, her other brothers, and her nephews and nieces. Ellen left no will, but asked for her modest estate to be shared among her brother Leonard's daughters. (192) Though the next generation proved far less responsible, Stout behaved with remarkable generosity and tolerance towards them, swayed by his affection for Leonard. They in turn displayed a sense of family responsibility at least towards one another. When John the draper moved to Lancaster to open a shop, he boarded with his sister, Margaret Burnskill, and her husband, John. (222–3) Burnskill had earlier taken on as apprentice the orphan William Hall, son of Leonard's daughter Elizabeth, with encouragement and support from both grandfather and great-uncle. (220) And when Stout's feckless nephew William finally broke, his younger brother, Leonard junior, took in his young son (yet another William) and provided his food, clothing, and schooling. (232) Similarly, when Stout's niece Ellen was in danger of throwing herself away on the young dragoon, her married sister Jennet was ready to take her in, at Kendal. (203) Stout, his parents, and his siblings showed a deep concern for the welfare of the whole family. The older and wealthier members provided for those in need, and most family decisions were reached collectively. Stout himself was a controlling personality, yet he repeatedly allowed himself to be overruled by the collective wishes of other family members. And he would then fund the arrangements they desired, even when he thought them misguided. Austere and rigorously self-disciplined as he was, William Stout could never long resist or ignore the ties of blood.

9

Samuel Pepys

Care and Control

Samuel Pepys (1633–1703) is the most celebrated diarist in English history, and deservedly so. He enjoyed a successful career, launched through the patronage of his kinsman Edward Mountagu, later Earl of Sandwich, and had an unquenchable zest for life. He loved women, the theatre, music, books, and good company.[1] Yet when he summed up his life at the close of 1661, we find him writing that 'My chiefest thoughts is now to get a good wife for Tom', his younger brother. (ii.242) Pepys had two younger brothers and a younger sister, and his sense of a moral obligation to see them all settled and secure took up much of his time and energy throughout the diary period and beyond.

As the oldest and by far the most successful of the siblings, Samuel felt a double responsibility to help guide them through life. In return, he demanded their gratitude, deference, and obedience. He viewed all three siblings as troublesome and unsatisfactory. He needed to provide for his sister Pall (properly, Paulina) until she could, if possible, be found a husband; Tom, a tailor, brought endless worries over both his business and marital prospects; and John, the youngest, had to be helped through school and university and into a career. Personal affection played only a small role in the family dynamics. He did not warm to any of his siblings and, as he eventually discovered, their gratitude was mixed with deep resentment. What makes this sibling story of particular interest is his characteristic frankness about the emotions and motivations that guided his actions. His sense of obligation was all the more striking for he was an ambitious young man, still making his way, and with his father still alive. Samuel took on responsibilities that society generally placed at a father's door and became, in effect, the family's head. And as his diary reveals, he felt considerable resentment at his burden, and at his siblings' failure to discharge their own responsibilities. The chapter begins with Samuel's assessment of his siblings.

PALL THE UNWANTED

Pall, born in 1640 and seven years his junior, presented perhaps the greatest challenge. In 1660, when the diary begins, she was living with her parents and

---

[1] For his life and career, see Claire Tomalin, *Samuel Pepys: the Unequalled Self* (Harmondsworth, 2003). Figures in the text refer to *The Diary of Samuel Pepys*, ed. R. C. Latham and W. Matthews (1971–83).

the two younger brothers in the family home off Fleet Street, in the parish of St Bride's. She had few prospects of making a good marriage. As Samuel often ruefully reflected, none of his extended family had been blessed with good looks, and Pall too was 'ill favoured'. Her father, a tailor, could not offer a substantial dowry, and Samuel himself was not yet in a position to provide one. Pall's personality presented a further problem. Samuel thought her ill-natured, her parents found her a burden, and in January 1660 father and son had to reprimand her sternly for pilfering. (i.27) Her future looked problematic. Towards the end of the year, Samuel and his wife, Elizabeth, suggested a possible way forward: Pall should come and live with them, not as a guest but earning her keep as a servant. Pall wept for joy at the proposal, which suggests how fraught her situation had become at home. Though certain this arrangement would be in Pall's best interests, Samuel was far from sure it would work. When she arrived in January 1661, he underlined her menial status by not allowing her to sit down with them at dinner, 'that she may not expect it hereafter'. (i.288, 291, ii.4) She would eat with the other servants. Even so, his doubts proved well founded, and by July he had decided that his 'proud and idle' sister would have to go. (ii.139) His parents received the news with dismay. They were on the point of retiring to the small family estate at Brampton, Huntingdonshire, which John Pepys had recently inherited from his brother, and they had hoped to be rid of Pall. The storm burst on Sunday 25 August when Samuel called up Pall to his chamber, and 'in great anger told her before my father that I would keep her no longer; and my father, he said he would have nothing to do with her'. Pall flew into a rage. Eventually, after they had brought down her 'high spirit', Samuel persuaded his father to let her accompany them to Brampton, 'and stay there a-while to see how she will demean herself'. Pall and her mother left by wagon on 5 September, with Pall 'crying exceedingly'. Samuel saw them off, after delivering a stern lecture on her behaviour. (ii.153, 161–2, 172)

Visiting Brampton a year later, he found his sister little changed. 'I find her so very ill-natured that I cannot love her,' he confided in his diary, 'and she so cruel an hypocrite that she can cry when she please.' (iii.223) But for Pall to be buried in the country, living acrimoniously with her parents, was hardly a long-term solution. Early in 1663, his wife floated a new idea. With Samuel's career now progressing well, Elizabeth wanted a live-in companion, and Pall might fill the role. Samuel was doubtful, though he reflected that she would at least be cheap. In the event, Elizabeth changed her mind, and the idea was dropped. (iv.3, 15) At the year's end he summed up the situation in bleak terms: 'Pall with my father, and God knows what she doth there or what will become of her, for I have not anything yet to spare her, and she grows now old and must be disposed of one way or another.' (iv.439) Pall was 23!

The following year saw a radical shift in approach. In January 1664, Samuel calculated that he was worth £858 'clear' and began to look out for possible husbands for Pall, willing now to provide a modest dowry from his own resources. A widowed naval captain was the first potential candidate, with Samuel and his wife both 'mighty earnest' to promote a match. (v.31, 42–3) When nothing came of this, he proposed that Pall should come to London 'for her preferment, if by any

means I can get her a husband here'. Characteristically, his thinking was simultaneously generous and self-interested. Finding a husband would be time-consuming
and difficult, 'yet it will be better than to have her stay there [at Brampton] till
nobody will have her, and then be flung upon my hands'. (v.151–2, 183) Elizabeth
spent some time at Brampton that summer, and her 'sad stories of the ill,
improvident, disquiet, and sluttish manner' in which Pall and her parents lived
reinforced the urgency of the problem. To secure a husband Pall would need to be
at least presentable, and in September we find Elizabeth buying her new clothes.
(v.234, 274) In the event, Pall's visit was deferred, but from 1665 the couple were
assiduous in searching for a suitable spouse. One proposal was their neighbour
Philip Harman, an upholsterer, whose wife had recently died in childbed, but
the mooted dowry of £500 was more than Samuel felt he could afford. (vi.163–4,
170) It was also more than Elizabeth would accept. While Samuel was master of his
household, he was by no means an absolute sovereign, and knew from painful
experience the storms that erupted when he overplayed his hand. Elizabeth was,
throughout, an active partner in the quest to settle Pall, and she indicated £400
as the figure she considered acceptable. (vi.252) Nonetheless, Samuel pursued the
match for a year, with his cousin Antony Joyce acting as intermediary. He did
eventually offer a larger dowry, only for Harman to torpedo the negotiations by
raising his demands further. (vii.15, 23, 73, 78, 81–2) Several other names were
canvassed, including a younger son of the navy victualler Denis Gauden. The main
beneficiaries would have been Gauden and the diarist himself. Such a close
connection would steer naval contracts towards Gauden, with Samuel enjoying
sweeteners. He was strongly attracted to the idea, until warned that it would lay
him wide open to allegations of corruption. (vii.88–9)

Meanwhile, John Pepys senior had written to suggest yet another candidate:
Robert Ensum, a Huntingdonshire farmer and heir to a considerable estate.
Samuel's initial positive response was shaken when Elizabeth dismissed Ensum as
'a drunken, ill-favoured, ill-bred country fellow', but he thought the possibility
worth exploring. (vii.78) Elizabeth agreed to go down to Brampton to reassess
Ensum, and Samuel resolved to go ahead if she signalled her approval, another
indication of the significant role she was playing. (vii.86, 91) Elizabeth returned
with a positive verdict, and in late May 1666, Pall and her father came to London to
discuss the match. Samuel thought his sister looked at least passable: 'a pretty good-
bodied woman and not over thick', though 'full of freckles and not handsome in
face'. He agreed to offer a £500 dowry, with Elizabeth's consent, and Pall and her
father returned home content. (vii.104, 138, 170, 175) But Ensum's death a few
months later brought the negotiations to an abrupt end. (vii.405)

Fresh ideas were needed. Elizabeth took it upon herself to sound out Samuel's
colleague Will Hewer, who was polite but uninterested. (viii.17) Samuel preferred
the idea of a match with his 'old good friend' Richard Cumberland, a Cambridge
contemporary, who had just come to London and renewed their acquaintance.
Cumberland was as yet only a parish minister in Northamptonshire, but good
company and 'a most excellent person'. To have him as a brother-in-law, Samuel
mused, he would gladly add another £100 to Pall's dowry, and he eagerly pursued

the dream. (viii.118, ix.17) Another visit to Brampton, in October 1667, under-lined the urgency of the situation, for Pall, he thought, 'grows old and ugly' and remained as cantankerous as ever. 'God forgive me,' he wrote, 'I have no great love for her; but only, is my sister and must be provided for.' (viii.474–5)

A solution finally emerged only a few weeks later. John Pepys proposed a young Huntingdonshire farmer named John Jackson, to whom Ensum had left part of his estate. (viii.539, 585) Negotiations progressed rapidly, with much of the business left to their cousin Roger Pepys, a lawyer. Samuel wanted to judge Jackson for himself, and early in February, his cousin brought the young man to London, where they dined together. He was underwhelmed. Jackson was 'a plain young man', he decided, 'of no education nor discourse', but good and 'handsome enough for her'. Though he expected 'no pleasure nor content in him, as if he had been a man of breeding and parts like Cumberland', they quickly agreed terms: Samuel would provide a dowry of £600, and secured a jointure of £60 a year should Pall be left a widow, good terms by the standards of the day. (ix.16–19, 55–6, 97; x.322) Elizabeth wanted a 'merry wedding' in London. Samuel did not, and the couple were wed at Brampton in February 1669, with neither the diarist nor his wife attending. (ix.58, 100) For Samuel, it was an occasion for relief rather than celebration, with Jackson merely an acceptable match for a sister he had never liked. Visiting the couple at Brampton the following spring, he found Pall 'growing fat' and 'comelier than before. But a mighty pert woman she is, and I think proud, he keeping her mighty handsome, and they say mighty fond.' (ix.210–11)

Pall's problems had hung over him for almost a decade, and it had taken five years to find her a husband amidst the distractions of plague, fire, and war. Despite feeling no affection, Samuel had never shirked what he saw as his responsibilities. He genuinely wanted to see Pall settled, and felt it his duty to bring this about. Ideally, he would have liked a marriage that would also bring tangible benefits to himself, whether financial (with Gauden) or intellectual (with Cumberland). Pall probably never met, or even knew about, these prospective suitors. In the event, he settled for a prosaic match that would satisfy her and relieve his burden. He reflected that it might also prove useful to have a brother-in-law in Huntingdon-shire, to protect his interests there should his father die. (ix.19) He had discharged his fraternal duty, and there was no obligation to put on a show of celebration. Pall always expressed her love for her brother, though he rarely believed her. She named her firstborn Samuel, in his honour, a gesture he probably viewed as prompted by calculation. In a surprising twist, he admitted feeling troubled when news arrived that his sister was pregnant. Perhaps he was jealous that in fertility at least she could outmatch him. (v.553 and n.)

TOM THE TAILOR

Tom, born in 1634 and only a year younger than the diarist, also proved prob-lematic. Samuel felt rather more affection towards him, at least intermittently, but little trust or respect. Tom was easy-going, good-humoured, and feckless. He had little in the way of education or brains, and none of Samuel's self-discipline or drive. In 1660, he was working as a tailor alongside his father. When John Pepys retired and moved to the country in 1661, he let Tom take over his house and trade. Taking in lodgers to help pay his way, Tom set up in business with two apprentices and a maidservant to keep house. (ii.167, x.324) Samuel worried about him on many scores, both business and personal, and when Tom hired an attractive new maidservant, prayed that his brother would not 'play the fool with her'. His fears, on all these grounds, were to prove well founded. (iv.80)

Samuel provided his brother with support and advice on numerous occasions. Tom was a frequent visitor, often coming for Sunday dinner. In March 1661, we find Samuel looking through his wardrobe and presenting Tom with 'a suit of black stuff clothes', a hat, and some shoes. He regularly employed his brother to make new clothes for him or alter old ones, and was happy to pay over the odds. (i.186, 267, ii.60, iii.47, 84, iv.124) Tom was duly grateful. On one occasion he brought a pair of fine slippers as a present, and on another sent a velvet riding hat, apparently as a peace offering. (ii.39, iv.360) Samuel lent him money, and devised various schemes to boost his income. (i.186, iii.69, 103, 117)

In return, as elder brother, Samuel expected Tom to provide services as and when required. He and Elizabeth stayed at Tom's house on several occasions when builders or decorators were at work in their own home. And when some alterations were in progress, he called on Tom's men to help him shift goods. (iii.184, 234, 252–5) Tom could also be directed to undertake errands, such as booking a coach place to carry Elizabeth to Brampton—and scolded when he failed to do so. (iii.144) We find Samuel repeatedly delivering advice, lectures, warnings, and commands, and making plain his anger if they were not heeded.

The fruits of all this support and guidance were disappointing. Tom's feckless character was never in much doubt. On 2 October 1660, he had turned up crestfallen with a tale of woe; his father had thrown him out for staying out all night, without permission. Samuel scolded him, and gave him a bed for the night. When Tom apologized, Samuel interceded and persuaded their father to take him back. A year later, with John Pepys about to hand over his business to his wayward son, Samuel doubted that it would survive long in Tom's hands, 'for want of brains and care'. (i.256–7, ii.167) Over the next few years, he occasionally took a more positive view. Once, calling on his brother, he was pleasantly surprised to 'find him a man like to do well, which contents me much', and in June 1663 he judged that Tom now 'grows a very thriving man, as he himself tells me'. (iii.2, 55, iv.183) But such optimistic moments were rare. Tom's behaviour more often generated disappointment, alarm, or anger. Samuel was angry when he found Tom lying about his work, or botching it. (iii.82, iv.112) He was alarmed when he called one day to find the door and hatch open, Tom away, and no one answering when he knocked. Eventually the maid appeared, and complained about Tom's failure to control the apprentices who should have been minding the shop. Samuel was furious. 'I am resolved to school him soundly for it', he vowed, and returned next day to vent his anger. (iii.194–5) When Tom was away again a few weeks later, Samuel made sure the house was properly looked after. (iii.214)

Samuel was always conscious that his siblings' financial security, and his parents' too, rested on his own survival and prosperity. On 1 May 1663, he sat down with Tom and his father to devise a course that might shield them from financial disaster. It was a stressful occasion that reduced them all to tears. (iv.119) But only a few weeks later he found Tom breezily outlining plans to rebuild part of his house, oblivious of cost, and the work went ahead despite Samuel's disapproval. He was understandably annoyed when Tom wrote begging for another loan, and sceptical of his claim that his business was thriving. He demanded to see the accounts, refused to see Tom again until he produced them, and resolved to lend him nothing more. (iv.236, 271, 291, 292)

Yet though the accounts never materialized, the brothers continued to meet. Samuel inspected and even admired the rebuilding, and continued to commission tailoring work. (iv.341, 369) Predictably, Tom never changed his ways. Samuel fumed that he always arrived late ('which doth vex me to the blood'), and was 'sluggish' in all his affairs. He was bewildered when Tom delivered some new clothes without bothering to send the bill to accompany them. How could he be so unprofessional? (iv.342–3, 356) And when Samuel called some months later, he was appalled to find that Tom had gone out leaving his books, papers, and bills strewn over the parlour table. That triggered another lecture. (v.39–40)

Debt-laden gentlemen often dreamed of a rich wife to solve their problems, and such dreams were not confined to the elites. Tom's family judged that his only hope of ever achieving financial security would be through a good marriage. The search for a bride began as soon as Tom took over the business, and Samuel, his father, their cousins, and friends all became involved. It would not be easy, for Tom had little education, nondescript looks, and a speech impediment, and had only the house and business to bring to the table. One girl's portion was considered too small, another's too large for a match to have any chance of success. (ii.158–9, 163, 165) By the close of 1661, the diarist notes, finding Tom a good wife had come to occupy his 'chiefest thoughts'. A young woman related to his cousins the Joyces, 'worth £200 in ready money', looked potentially promising, and Samuel set about trying to shore up his brother's position. But he soon came to think Tom could do better. After all, he reflected, it seemed unlikely he would ever have children himself, so Tom would become both his and their father's heir. Thanking the Joyces for their goodwill, he asked them to proceed no further. It was perhaps a misjudgement. (ii.225, 230, 242, iii.2, 3, 16, 69)

The story took a new twist a few months later, when Samuel learned that his brother had disappeared for a week, pursuing a bride near Banbury, and accompanied by their cousin Dr Thomas Pepys, a Cambridgeshire physician. Neither had breathed a word of this project, and he was furious at the snub. But the young woman sounded an ideal prospect: a well-educated gentlewoman who would bring £500 in return for a jointure of £40 p.a. Tom had liked her, and had been well received by her family. So, swallowing his pride, Samuel threw himself into the business. He wrote on Tom's behalf to the man who appears to have initiated the match, a Mr Cooke, and to the young lady herself, for Tom was no penman. He even composed a love letter in his brother's name. (iii.166, 176–8, 183, 185,

187, 192, 201–5) He also wrote to her mother, Mrs Butler, and Tom and Cooke took the letter with them on a second visit to Banbury. Mrs Butler came to London to complete the negotiations, and Elizabeth stayed overnight at Tom's house to guide him on how to entertain his visitor. Samuel lay awake all night at home, his head full of Tom's business. (iii.208, 210, 226–8) But after such a promising start, the negotiations proved disastrous. Tom and Cooke offered recklessly generous terms that would have left Tom with little benefit from the match. Samuel was 'stark-mad' at such folly, and vowed that the match would never go ahead on such terms. The negotiations, in any case, soon faltered. Mrs Butler and her agent dropped the portion on offer to £400, commenting on Tom's small house and his speech impediment. Samuel felt that both parties had been misled, and the match was abandoned. (iii.228, 231–3, 235–6) Bitterly disappointed, Tom long dreamed of reviving it. (iii.287, iv.12, 253) Samuel preferred to explore other options. He reopened negotiations with a London merchant, but was told that the young woman in question 'could not fancy my brother because of his imperfection in his speech'. (iv.19, 21)

Poor Tom was never to find a bride. Early in 1664, he fell seriously ill with consumption, and was given only two months to live. (v.9–10, 20, 22, 29) On Sunday 13 March, a messenger reported that he was dying, and from the pox, not consumption. Samuel rushed to his bedside, to find him barely conscious. He returned on Monday and Tuesday, stricken with grief and shocked at the imminence of such a shameful death. Moreover, the maid confided that Tom was also heavily in debt and had been constantly harassed by strange men 'for money or something worse'. 'Upon the whole', Samuel reflected bitterly, 'I do find he is, whether he lives or dies, a ruined man.' More selfishly, he was also conscious of 'the trouble that would arise to me by his death or continuing sick'. One concern was soon dispelled. A doctor examined Tom's body a few hours before he expired, on the Tuesday, and declared that, after all, there was no evidence that he had, or had ever had, the pox. That brought Samuel such huge relief that he sent out for a barrel of oysters to celebrate. Scandal, already spreading, could be halted in its tracks. (v.79, 81–2, 84–6) He organized a decent funeral for his brother, arranging for burial in the church rather than churchyard, and invited 120 mourners. Afterwards there were more oysters, cake, and cheese back at the house. Even at such a time his sharp eye missed nothing: the gravedigger's self-importance, and the guests' jocularity once the funeral was over. 'Lord,' he reflected, 'the world makes nothing of the memory of a man an hour after he is dead.' Nor did he spare himself. He had felt real grief as he watched his brother dying, but recognized that 'presently after and ever since, I have had very little grief indeed for him'. (v.88–91) Tom had always brought problems, and Samuel feared more might yet emerge.

His fears were soon realized. Going through Tom's papers, he discovered that his brothers had been 'carrying on plots against me to promote Tom's having of his Banbury Mistress'. The conspiratorial language reflects his claim to a natural authority over their affairs. More important, his father arrived to examine Tom's business papers and found that he had been even more negligent than they thought, with debts of over £300. (iii.85 and n., 91–2, 97) Still worse was to follow. One of his father's old servants, John Noble, arrived and revealed that Tom had fathered twins by a former maidservant. One had survived, and the affair had been hushed up, with Tom paying a poor man named Cave £5 to take her. The plan had soon unravelled; the parish had prosecuted Cave, who landed in gaol for a time. Noble and Cave were now demanding money for their silence. Dismayed at this new threat of public shame and fresh expense, Samuel was 'vexed to think what a rogue my brother was in all respects', and was reduced almost to despair. 'I know not what in the world to do', he lamented. Noble turned up at the office one day to say that he now had Cave back in prison, and offered to silence him permanently in return for a fee. When Samuel spurned the proposal, 'the rogue' then vowed to ally with Cave and sue him. (v.113–15, 142, 154, 158, 167–8, 252–3) The threat seems not to have materialized, but months later Samuel was still fuming over the 'vexations', 'disgrace and discontent' that Tom's death had brought to him and his family. (v.360)

JOHN THE STUDENT

John, the youngest brother, born in 1641, was still at school when the diary begins, and the age gap made this a very different relationship. John was much brighter than Tom and Pall, and Samuel had high hopes of him. But many of the familiar sibling tensions were to resurface. Samuel dispensed heavy-handed advice, instructions, and reprimands alongside his support, and demanded diligence and gratitude from his young brother. When John failed to live up to these require-ments, Samuel made plain his anger and disappointment. John chafed at his overbearing manner, and when Samuel accidentally discovered the depth of his resentment, their relationship came close to collapse.

The early years had been more auspicious. In January 1660, we find Samuel helping his brother prepare a crucial public exercise at his school, St Paul's. He went in person to see John's performance, and was delighted to see the school reward it with an exhibition to Cambridge, where Samuel himself had studied a decade earlier. (i.11–12, 27, 42, 44, 46) He provided John with textbooks and other necessaries, and spent several days at Cambridge in February, helping to see John settled in at Christ's College. (i.61, 63–9) A few months later he was pleased to receive a letter penned in Latin. He supplied more books, and was delighted when John was elected to a college scholarship. (i.137, 222, 243, ii/44) But matters did not always proceed so smoothly. Paying a surprise visit in July, Samuel was disgusted to find his brother still in bed at 8 o'clock on a summer morning. He was irritated, too, that John proved a poor correspondent. (ii.73, 95, 135, iii.21) These were minor matters, of course. He sent John more books, and when the family gathered at Brampton in October 1662, he made a point of inviting him into his chamber each evening after supper, 'for discourse sake'. (iii.33, 220) Early in 1663, he was delighted when John was awarded his BA, though saddened that he had developed symptoms of the stone, the crippling disease that some years earlier had brought the diarist himself close to death. (iv.27) A few months later, with

John now back at Brampton, Samuel looked to him as an ally in holding together their parents' rocky marriage. (iv.90, 96)

The sibling relationship deteriorated once more when John came to stay in August 1663. Samuel was initially impressed by his familiarity with the exciting new ideas of Descartes, of which he himself knew nothing. But when he grilled John on traditional learning, including Aristotle, he found him lamentably deficient. He took it upon himself to set John informal tests in Latin and Greek, with disappointing results, and after a minor tiff dismissed his brother as an 'ass and coxcomb'. Elizabeth, for her part, made clear that she disliked having John in the house. (iv.263, 267–9, 271, 282, 293) Samuel's disillusion ran deep. 'I am troubled', he confided to his diary, 'to see how, contrary to my expectation, my brother John neither is the scholar nor minds his studies as I thought he would have done—but loiters away his time, so that I must send him soon to Cambridge again.' (iv.291–2) Before leaving, John had to endure 'a most severe reprimand', sustained for two hours and delivered 'with great passion and sharp words'. In future, he was warned, there would be no more support unless he applied himself more energetically. (iv.316–17, 439)

The chill deepened into a freeze the following spring. Sorting through Tom's papers after his funeral, Samuel stumbled upon letters from John that were full of scurrilous abuse and complaints about the way he had been treated, and 'crafty designs' to thwart Samuel's wishes over family affairs. Mortified by such ingratitude and betrayal, he vowed to make John pay for his behaviour. When he arrived in London only a day or two later, with his father, Samuel read the letters aloud to them, and his anger swelled at John's 'silly and churlish' response. He vowed never to give him money again, and never to forget the injury. (v.91–3) The breach proved bitter and prolonged. Samuel rejected his parents' pleas to forgive him, and drew up a will that excluded John from any share of his estate. (v.135, 137, 298, vi.134, vii.134) But his fury gradually subsided. He brought himself to write to John in April 1666, and though his language was sharp, he was already planning to invite him to London after taking his MA, to launch the career he was planning in the Church. He took soundings, and reflected that 'if he be good for anything, [I] doubt not to get him preferment'. The hurt was not forgotten, however; he would give John board and lodging, but any money would be provided only as a loan. (v.261, vii.50, 111–12, 170)

In the event, John appeared unannounced in September, just after the Great Fire, to make sure they were all safe. Samuel was touched by his concern, and despite his vows, gave him 40s 'for his pocket' when he left. (vii.281–3) The visit smoothed their fractured relationship, and just over a week later, Samuel invited him back to London. During the Fire, he had turned most of his estate into gold and silver and hidden it in his house, and he wanted another pair of eyes to watch over it. He was also planning to convey some of it into the country, for greater safety, and wanted John to accompany it. (vii.293, 344, 367) The visit proved remarkably harmonious. Samuel was pleasantly surprised to find his brother a 'sober' young man, and noted that Elizabeth now 'loves him mightily'. To his delight, John took up the viol, and they were soon happily playing together. John accompanied the couple to the theatre, and catalogued the diarist's library. (vii.327, 398, viii.8, 40, 49) Samuel had already bought the clerical vestments his brother would need for an ecclesiastical career, but he grew increasingly doubtful that it was the right choice. John showed little sense of vocation, his voice was poor, and he was a mediocre scholar. (vii.310, 313, 327, 346) He remained in London for several months, but no career materialized. His visit almost ended in disaster. On 7 February 1667, the day before he was due to leave, John suddenly collapsed and lay unconscious 'as pale as death'. He soon recovered, but the episode made Samuel realize, to his surprise, that he was growing to love his brother again. He and his father decided that John should return to Cambridge, and that Samuel would support him there for a further year while trying to find him a parish living or a naval chaplaincy. (viii.48–9, 471)

When Samuel Pepys abandoned his diary at the end of May 1669, John had still to find a living. Their relationship, however, had remained amicable. John had visited him and his wife again that month, and the three of them had enjoyed boat trips, a picnic, an outing to Hyde Park, and another visit to the theatre. (ix.553, 555, 556, 563) John abandoned the idea of a career in the Church, and in 1670, Samuel secured him a position as Clerk of Trinity House, which proved the start of a successful administrative career. Three years later, he was appointed joint Clerk of the Acts in the Navy Office, holding the two posts in tandem. (x.319–20) Despite their mutual frustrations and resentments, Samuel and John proved able to develop a friendly relationship. They had more in common than either had with Tom or Pall.

THE LATER YEARS AND THE LETTERS

Samuel Pepys's diary is inevitably highly subjective. We see relationships always through his eyes. The diary provides only limited information on how his siblings felt towards him, or their relationships with each other. Samuel remarks in passing that Tom shared his low opinion of their sister, condemning her 'ill nature and lazy life', but that he too felt disgusted by John's 'base' comments about her. (v.54, 91–2) To hear their own voices, and for sibling relationships in the post-diary period, we must turn to the family correspondence.[2] Though much has been lost, the letters that survive provide a perspective that significantly modifies the picture painted by the diarist. He knew that his siblings found him overbearing and hypercritical, but was often unaware of their attempts to escape his control. After Tom's death, he was furious to discover letters that showed they had forged 'crafty designs' to bypass and thwart him. (v.91–3) Tom had struck out independently in pursuing his 'Banbury Mistress', and continued the pursuit even after Samuel had broken off negotiations. John and Pall were complicit, and Tom told them he would conclude the match quickly if all went well. He would seek his father's approval but

---

[2] Helen Truesdell Heath, ed., *The Letters of Samuel Pepys and his Family Circle* (Oxford, 1955); cited as '*L*' in the text.

made no reference to Samuel. The rest of the family were clearly planning to present him with a fait accompli. (iv.12, v.91–3; *L*, 6–7) Tom also concealed the fact that he had fathered illegitimate twins, turning to one of his father's old servants rather than his brother for help.

The letters also modify the picture in another significant respect. The diary shows Samuel as the sole benefactor to his needy siblings and parents. The letters, however, reveal that his brothers also provided support to other family members, as and when they could. Tom gave some financial assistance to his sister, and £20 to his brother John to support him at Cambridge. (*L*, 5, 8) John was a student for most of the diary period, but once installed at Trinity House he quickly became a generous-spirited benefactor to his sister and her struggling husband, and also to his father. He sent his father gifts of wine, and was far readier than Samuel to provide support without imposing conditions or delivering lectures. 'As for the money,' he wrote breezily to his father in 1674, 'pray draw a bill on me for two hundred and fifty pounds, I will pay it here on sight.' (*L*, 29–30) When Pall's husband, John Jackson, sank into debt, John took over the lease of their house and estate at Ellington in 1675. Pall was hugely grateful, and sent a message via their father that she would ensure he was repaid in full. If necessary, she wrote, 'I will sell all that ever I have before I will disoblige such a real friend as he is, or let him lose any part what I am indebted to him.' (*L*, 36, 38–9, 41–3)

By 1670, not long after the diary ends, Samuel Pepys must have felt that his family responsibilities were largely over. Tom had died, John was settled in a career, and Pall was satisfactorily married and providing a home for their father, now a widower. In the event, his duties proved far from over. Pall's marriage descended into acrimony, as her husband sank ever deeper into debt. In 1676, we find Samuel and John working together on plans to limit the damage, and save their sister from the threat of destitution. Much of Jackson's estate was conveyed by deed of settlement to Pall and her children. (*L*, 46, 51–4) In 1680, with his creditors clamouring for payment, Jackson begged Samuel to buy most of his remaining lands in Brampton. Samuel was reluctant, and agreed eventually only because his father was desperate to keep all the Brampton lands within the family. Even then, he drove a hard bargain. He made it clear that he would expect 'a penny-worth for a penny'. He also wanted Pall's future to be guaranteed 'against any further new difficulties that his [Jackson's] folly or ill-husbandry can contract upon her'. He suspected, rightly as it transpired, that the £200 he had agreed to pay would not be sufficient to cover all Jackson's debts, and feared he would soon be asked for more. Damning his brother-in-law's 'incorrigibleness', he told himself that he had 'already done too much to have any more flung away upon him'. Jackson was indeed soon begging Samuel for more, explaining that he would need £350 to satisfy all his creditors. In return, he made an abject offer to settle his entire remaining estate, both personal and real, on Pall and the children, retaining only a tiny yearly allowance of £10. Samuel was still considering the offer when Jackson died in September 1680. (*L*, 158–64)

One of the more unusual features of the family dynamics is that Samuel had come to act, in effect, as elder brother to his parents as well as his siblings. This too continued beyond the diary years. John Pepys senior, a kindly man, was ineffective in financial matters and increasingly dependent on his son's support and advice. In this relationship, as elsewhere, Samuel adopted a somewhat overbearing manner. The Brampton estate his father had inherited brought with it very considerable debts and charges. When Samuel did the arithmetic in 1663, he found these would leave no more than £29 a year for his parents to live on, 'a very sad consideration'. He generously offered a supplement to guarantee his parents £50 a year, but in return for this 'unwelcome burden' he demanded a price: his parents must stop squabbling and turn 'to the study of thrift and quietness, that I may hear no more of those differences'. He laid down a set of strict housekeeping instructions they must follow, and told them to expect no more supplements. If they considered £50 too little to live on, they could return to the London house and send Pall into service. And if their behaviour failed to improve, he threatened to withdraw all support. (*L*, 1–2; ii.183, iv.87) In the event, Samuel proved considerably more generous than this would suggest. We find him sending glass, wine, sugar, and other gifts to Brampton. He sent old clothes too, and even six pairs of old shoes, though he found this a distasteful inversion of normal father–son relationships. (iii.33, iv.6, 87, v.261, 344, 346, vi.149, viii.565, x.318–19)

John Pepys senior was genuinely grateful for his son's help and fully acknowledged his debt. When Samuel fell ill in 1663, his father asked anxiously, 'in what a sad condition should your poor old father and mother be in if the Lord should take you before us?' (*L*, 10–11) But, like the younger siblings, he resented his dependency, and as Samuel's career blossomed, he encouraged their belief that he could and should be doing more for them all. He said so bluntly, which made Samuel angry at what he saw as presumption and ingratitude. (iv.308) Samuel was mortified when he learned that his father had begged the Earl of Sandwich, his patron, to press him to provide more generously for Pall. His father also wrote, more than once, to their cousin Roger Pepys, the lawyer and MP, on behalf of both Pall and John. Samuel deeply resented all such meddling. (iv.366, v.44–5, 48, 66, 135, 137) But despite their differences, he retained a deep affection for his father, judging him 'one of the most careful and innocent men in the world'. When his father arrived in London, following Tom's death, Samuel was very glad to see him, 'my heart never being fuller of love to him, nor admiration of his prudence and pains heretofore in the world'. His father had always been diligent and careful in his trade, and unwavering in his concern for all his children. In 1666, Samuel promised to cover the £30 his father was paying each year in taxes and other charges, 'at which the poor man was overjoyed and wept'. (vii.169) Samuel also sympathized with his domestic plight, trapped in a marriage that had become desperately unhappy. As early as 1661, he commented that his mother was now so quarrelsome and 'unsufferably foolish and simple' that he did know how his father could bear it. The tears he shed on hearing of her death in 1668 quickly dried. (ii.111, v.120, vii.151, 164, ix.134)

John Pepys senior and his son John both died in 1680, only a few months before Jackson. Pall fell gravely ill, so Samuel was left alone to confront the tangled web of family affairs. He found to his dismay that his brother, casual about money, had died owing substantial debts to Trinity House. Samuel agreed a down payment of £300, and promised to pay whatever more might be owed. (*L*, 54, 61–3) A few years earlier, investigating the Brampton properties, he had discovered that there were still claims against Tom's estate, thirteen years after his death, and that they were now his father's responsibility as the administrator. He promised that if necessary he would clear them himself. (*L*, 51–4) After Jackson's death, he also provided carefully for Pall and her children, both during and after her long illness and convalescence in London. He found her elder boy a place in the navy, while the younger, more scholarly, went to Cambridge and eventually inherited Pepys's estate and collections. (*L*, 170–4, 180–2, 190–6, 210, 212–13) Throughout the 1670s and 1680s Samuel also provided support for his late wife's brother, Balty (Balthasar St Michel), and his wife, Ester.

Each member of the Pepys family accepted contemporary ideas on the reciprocal rights and responsibilities of siblings, which should guide behaviour irrespective of affection or dislike. Samuel felt bound to help and support his siblings (and parents), and in return demanded their respect, compliance, and gratitude. The sibling relationships were severely tested and often strained, but he discharged his duty conscientiously and to his own satisfaction. He saw John settled in a career, Pall married, and his parents supported in their old age. Tom had received generous help and support, which would almost certainly have continued had he lived longer.

In many respects, the siblings' behaviour and attitudes were typical of elite and middling-sort relationships. Like many elder brothers, Samuel saw his siblings (and other close kin) as both demanding and irresponsible. His brothers and Pall's husband all died heavily in debt, his parents had little financial sense, and Balty and his wife were always clamouring for help and on the brink of disaster. He thought them all ungrateful, and whenever they fell short of his expectations he responded with sharp rebukes and reproofs. His vow to 'school' Tom on his failings reflected his sense of superiority and authority. (i.256, iii.194) For their part, his siblings and kin were grateful but saw him as controlling and tight-fisted. They too had some justification. A striking example, after Tom's death, was Samuel's determination to recover the £87 he had earlier lent his brother. Their father was now liable for this debt, as administrator of Tom's estate, and a decade later we find Samuel making his hard-strapped parent sign a promissory note acknowledging that the money was still owed. Thirty pounds were indeed repaid shortly afterwards. (*L*, 10, 23) Samuel's attitude towards his brother-in-law Balty and his wife provides another revealing example. In 1681, when Balty was working abroad, Samuel installed his wife, Ester, and her children at Brampton, rent-free, with a weekly allowance of 20 shillings. Ester complained that she could not survive on such a sum, which prompted stern letters on the duty of thrift. Samuel insisted that provisions were cheap in the country, and told how, in the 1650s, he and his wife had managed to live in London for several years on 20s a week. And he told her, moreover, that he could prove it: his wife had kept daily kitchen accounts, recording her outlay on every bunch of carrots and washing-ball, 'which I have under her own hand to show you at this day'. He had kept his wife's kitchen accounts, carefully filed, for twenty-five years. (*L*, 183–90)

Samuel Pepys's controlling nature shaped his sibling relationships as well as his marriage. He took his responsibilities seriously, and though he resented the burden, devoted time, effort, and money to his siblings' support. Their gratitude was tempered by resentment at his overbearing manner. That sometimes led them to conspire against him, which in turn exacerbated his own sense of grievance. Yet in many respects, this was overall a positive story. Samuel had honoured his moral obligations, and the relationships between the siblings had played a central role in the lives of them all. And in the case of John, fraternal support had enabled a younger brother to evolve from supplicant to co-benefactor.

10

Alice Thornton and Dorothy Osborne
Troubles with Brothers

ALICE THORNTON (1626–1707)

Alice Thornton's sprawling autobiography presents an emotional narrative of her sufferings with a spirited vindication of her actions. Her passive-aggressive tale of female weakness, isolation, and sorrows is punctuated by outbursts of angry defiance and determination. Many of her woes she blamed on her brother Christopher, and she recognized that to justify her own life and actions she would have to expose the cruel behaviour of other family members. To do that without compromising family honour presented a tough challenge.

Born at Kirklington, Yorkshire, Alice was the fifth child of the lawyer Christopher Wandesford. Her father, a close friend of Sir Thomas Wentworth, sat in all the parliaments of the 1620s before moving to Ireland, where he served as Master of the Rolls. In 1640, he succeeded Wentworth (now Earl of Strafford) as Lord Deputy of Ireland, but his term in office proved brief, for he fell sick and died in December 1640.[1] His death dealt a devastating blow to the family, and the outbreak of the Irish Rebellion nine months later threatened their lives. They found temporary refuge in Dublin Castle until his widow could arrange a passage to Chester, with such plate and household goods as she could carry. (31)

Alice idealized her parents. Her father, she wrote, had been a pious man and a diligent, just magistrate. She emphasized too his sense of responsibility towards his immediate family and wider kin. He was 'a dear and loving brother to his brothers and sisters, taking care for their advantage in education and preferment, as branches from the same stock with himself'. To all his children he gave 'a wise and prudential love', ensuring they received a good education, and made 'fair and noble provisions for them in his last will and testament'. (20–1) This last point was to have particular significance for her narrative. Alice described in careful detail how her father on his deathbed had called for his will to be read out in the presence of a large and eminent company, and had confirmed its terms. (22) In listing her father's virtues, Alice was not merely expressing filial duty and affection. She was creating a benchmark against which, over the years, the behaviour of many of her close kin could be measured and found wanting.

---

[1] For his career, see *ODNB*, Christopher Wandesford. Figures in the text refer to *The Autobiography of Alice Thornton*, ed. Charles Jackson, Surtees Society, 62 (1873).

Her mother was now responsible for the family's survival. Alice's three brothers were all still under age, though her sister Catherine was much older and long since married. When civil war broke out in England, Chester was no longer a safe refuge. Alice's mother (also Alice) possessed a small estate at Hipswell, near Richmond, as part of her widow's jointure, but this too was vulnerable to marauding soldiers. So in 1643, she took the three youngest children to lodge with Catherine, a few miles away at Snape. They found a warm welcome, though Catherine's husband, Sir Thomas Osborne, was mostly away, fighting for the king. (38–9) The younger boys, Christopher and John, were entered into school in York. George, the eldest, was packed off to France with his tutor, for greater safety and to further his education. When his money ran out, however, he had to return, and he narrowly escaped arrest as a suspected cavalier officer after the Battle of Marston Moor. The battle gave parliamentary forces firm control of the region, which made it safe for the family to move to Hipswell. Even so, life remained unsettled. They had to provide free quarter for a troop of Scottish soldiers, Alice was almost abducted by an obstreperous Scottish officer, and George had to go into hiding after refusing to take the oath required under the Solemn League and Covenant. (42–7) Alice also suffered a huge personal loss in September 1645 with the death of her beloved sister, Catherine, a few weeks after the birth of her sixteenth child. She had spent a week at her sister's bedside, and was deeply affected. (49–53)

The end of the war brought little comfort to this staunchly royalist family, and any relief that the fighting was over proved short-lived. Wandesford had appointed his wife and her half-brother, Sir Edward Osborne, as joint guardians of his eldest son and heir, and Osborne discharged his responsibilities with exemplary dedication. 'He had so fraternal a love for, and parental care over, my dear mother and us all', Alice recalled, that the family had lived in harmony and as much tranquility as the times could afford. As an executor of the will, he made sure 'that each party had its right and dues'. So when Osborne died suddenly in 1647, she lamented, 'I suffered the loss of a father, and my mother a husband.' Here was another benchmark against which to judge her other kin. William Wandesford, her father's half-brother and one of his executors, now managed the estate, and through poor management and bad luck its entire income was swallowed up to pay off her father's debts. (54–5) More troubles followed. Enemies contrived to have her brother George declared a delinquent, though he was still a minor, and the estate was sequestered. Total ruin was averted only by a deal that was to shape the rest of Alice's life. Her uncle William negotiated her marriage into a local parliamentarian family, in return for which it would use its influence to lift the sequestration. Alice and her mother were not consulted until the negotiations were complete, and then told this was the only way for the family to escape disaster. Alice had no wish to marry, certainly not into a puritan, parliamentarian family, but submitted when her mother was persuaded that this offered the family's only hope. A daughter's sacrifice was the price that had to be paid. The sequestration was lifted. (57–62)

Remembering her early life, Alice emphasized the family's happiness in Ireland in the 1630s, and its solidarity during the perils of the civil war. The value of her autobiography for this study lies in the sibling feuds that became a dominant theme thereafter. The first painful breach came between her brothers George and Christopher. From the hints she provides, it appears to have originated in tensions familiar between elder and younger brothers. George's servant had fed him malicious stories that caused a rift between them. It became so bitter that George vowed to cut his brother out of the inheritance, should he die without children, and leave the estate to his younger brother John and Alice. Christopher felt deeply wronged and Alice, distressed by their feud, attempted to repair the breach. At Easter 1651, she pleaded with them to make peace and beg one another's pardon. Christian charity was duly restored, the brothers agreed to receive the Easter sacrament, the 'holy feast of love', and Alice blessed God for having made her the 'happy instrument' of their reconciliation. (71–2, 198) But God's providence moved in mysterious ways, for the very next day, Easter Monday, George was drowned while attempting to cross a swollen river. (66–7) Alice was devastated. She had idealized George as a 'dear and loving brother; nay, I may say, a father to us all', and saw his death as a fatal blow to the family. (57–9)

Before the end of the year, Alice and Christopher had both married. On 15 December, Alice reluctantly married William Thornton of East Newton, Yorkshire, the match her uncle had arranged. She made it clear in her autobiography that she had done so only from a sense of duty, submitting to her mother's wishes. She had deep reservations about Thornton's family, which was puritan and parliamentarian in sympathy. Within hours of the ceremony, she fell very ill, with violent head pains and sickness, and was convinced she was dying. Her mother blamed the illness on Alice's rash decision to wash her feet in mid-winter, though acute stress seems a more likely explanation. (75–84) Her brother Christopher, now head of the family, opposed the marriage and did not attend the wedding. Only a few months earlier, he had married the young woman to whom George had previously been betrothed, Eleanor, eldest daughter of Sir John Lowther of Westmorland. (74, 194–5) Such a development, strange to modern eyes, was not exceptional when two families had negotiated a marriage settlement that both considered advantageous. It was destined, however, to bring another catalogue of problems in its wake.

Christopher now joined battle with his two surviving siblings. Money was at the root. Alice had helped George over the annuities payable out of the Kirklington estate by agreeing that £500 of her portion could be switched from that source to his estates in Ireland, though the family had lost control of these after the rebellion. The lifting of sequestration and George's death had reduced the annuity burden, giving Christopher a stronger financial position than his brother had enjoyed. Alice and her mother therefore saw no need to renew her concession, but Christopher was annoyed and sought to retaliate. The annuity arrangements had been laid out in their father's will, filed in Dublin, but the will had been lost in the upheavals of the Irish rebellion. George had possessed a certified copy, which on his death passed to Christopher. Christopher claimed this too was now lost, and then cast doubt on the idea that a will had ever existed. And on that ground, he now flatly refused to pay the annuities and legacies due to his brother John and Alice. (75–6) Alice held firm, refusing to surrender her rights. Several years earlier the siblings—including Christopher—had together made a copy of the copy, and this document was still in

Alice's possession. It had never been authenticated, however, and so had no legal standing. (192–9)

Alice's ageing mother had hoped that marriage would guarantee her daughter's security. Her husband and his parliamentarian family could protect her (and her young brother) in the new republican world, and defend what was rightfully theirs. For the remainder of her life, eight years, she maintained the young couple at Hipswell, along with their servants and soon their young children, at her own expense. Out of her modest jointure, she paid for John's schooling and later his expenses at Cambridge. She sold the lands she had bought, conveying the proceeds to Alice and her children, and settled her personal estate on Alice and her family by deed of gift and in her will. At the same time, she eased the financial pressures on Christopher by agreeing that he could pay Alice's portion in modest annual instalments. Even so, Christopher deeply resented her generosity to Alice, and insisted that his mother's entire estate ought to pass to him. (104–5) When she fell gravely ill, in November 1659, he did not visit her sickbed, and he did not attend her funeral. The house at Hipswell had been hers only for life, and he ordered Alice and her family to leave. And though his mother's will was soon proved in London, Christopher refused to accept it. Before long he was deploying his earlier tactics, claiming that no will would be found, that one had never existed, and that his mother's whole estate should therefore pass to him. Alice was shocked and disgusted by this further attempt to defraud her, and told him so in blunt terms. (106–21)

The hopes that Alice's mother had placed in her daughter's marriage did not bear fruit. William Thornton was an affectionate husband, but indecisive, indolent, and with poor judgement in financial matters. (181–2, 203–4, 214n, 240, 260–2, 269–70, 281–2) Alice bore nine children between 1652 and 1667, with difficult labours that sometimes proved almost fatal, and was seriously ill on several other occasions. Married life became a dreary succession of pregnancies, sicknesses, deaths, and financial crises. Like many women, she worried that if she died in childbed, her husband would remarry and fail to protect their children from his relatives or his new wife. In 1662, pregnant and as yet with only two daughters living, she discovered that he had the right to alter the entail, which meant that if he remarried and had a son, the girls could be left destitute. She persuaded him to enter a bond to make proper provision for them. (281–2) During another pregnancy, several years later, Alice fretted again about her children, two girls and now an infant son, if they were left orphans. Thornton would almost certainly remarry and if he too died, for his health was always poor, they would be extremely vulnerable. This time she made arrangements to safeguard all the documents and deeds that related to her property rights, and three of her kin pledged to raise the children. (145–7) She then devised a long-term solution, through a marriage between her elder daughter and a young clergyman, Thomas Comber, her chaplain and curate of the parish. He was a capable young man, and would make a reliable ally. Her daughter would remain close by, and Comber could oversee the upbringing of Alice's younger daughter and infant son Robert. (154–6) Her husband died while the negotiations were still in train, but the marriage went ahead in secret a few weeks later, in November 1668. (175, 231–2) When it was made public, six months later, it met with considerable suspicion from

Thornton's kin. The bride (yet another Alice) was only 14, the bridegroom was too poor to offer a jointure, and there was malicious gossip of an improper relationship between Alice herself and her chaplain. (224–7, 235–9) She remained unmoved. Ever since moving to her husband's country she had told herself that it was 'my duty to stand my ground in a strange place, and amongst strange people' with very different religious, political, and family loyalties. (215)

William Thornton died heavily in debt, not least through the machinations of Alice's brother. Alice had to struggle on alone to raise the children, sort out the estate, and negotiate with Christopher. There was a further strange twist in this story. The original of their father's will, assumed to have been lost forever, had miraculously resurfaced in Dublin in 1653, which checked Christopher's design to avoid paying anything to his siblings. Predictably, he refused to accept it was genuine, and launched suits against Thornton over the tangled web of obligations and debts surrounding the Wandesford estates in Ireland. These disputes dragged on for a decade, with final settlements concluded only in 1664. Even then, Alice never received a significant proportion of what she had been due. (182–7, 192–204) And after Thornton died, without leaving a will, Christopher took advantage of her vulnerable position to force her to sign a general release of her claims in Ireland before he would pay anything due to her and her administrators. (265–9)

Alice spent her later years in reduced circumstances. Her joys lay in her children. She was proud of her son-in-law Comber, who rose to become Dean of Durham.[2] She was very fond of her daughter Alice ('Naly'), and happy to see her younger daughter Kate also satisfactorily married. And she was devoted to her young son Robert, 'the son of prayers and vows', whom she had dedicated from birth for the Church. She recorded the child's words of piety and wisdom in loving detail. Robert flourished at school and university, but died in 1692, aged only 30. It was another devastating blow. (139–44, 261–5, 308–11)

Alice Thornton wrote her autobiography for her children and descendants. That presented her with a challenge: how could she record her wrongs without blackening her brother's character, thereby tarnishing family honour and laying herself open to the charge of disloyalty? Christopher, after all, was the family's head. He had been created a baronet in 1662, and his own son was elevated to the Irish peerage within Alice's lifetime. Acutely conscious of the problem, Alice adopted the familiar device of shifting the blame to others. She had done this in describing the earlier feud between George and Christopher. Forced to accept that her beloved George had been led astray by 'idle stories', she insisted that at all other times he had been 'a very wise and understanding person', and blamed his youthful lapse on a treacherous servant. (71) It was much harder to explain away Christopher's vindictive behaviour over several decades, but she tried. Her 'poor brother', as she generally called him, was also a victim. Though 'naturally of a good and sweet disposition', he was too easily 'overcome', 'imposed upon', and led astray by bad counsel. She pointed the finger of blame at his avaricious father-in-law, Sir John

---

[2] His life is in *ODNB*.

Lowther, she insisted, had urged him to destroy their father's will and other settlement deeds, so that he and his descendants could enjoy the entire inheritance unencumbered. Lowther and his friends were similarly to blame for Christopher's numerous 'unhandsome' and 'dishonest' dealings over the next twenty years. (75–6, 105, 119–21, 160, 182–3, 195, 198–9) And whenever it was impossible to extenuate her brother's behaviour, Alice chose 'to be silent in these things . . . wishing rather to cover all things of the nature of disputes betwixt such near relations'. (76) Writing to her husband in 1664, she reflected that though Christopher had done nothing to deserve her love, she would try to follow Christ's injunction to love our enemies. (291) Recording his death in 1686, she brought herself to remember him as her 'beloved brother', and 'the father [head] of that family from which he was descended'. (39n)

Whether Christopher would have been able to vindicate his actions seems doubtful but must remain an open question. All we have are a few brief passages in Alice's account that hint at a slightly more balanced picture of their relationship. Christopher had acted as godfather at the christening of her third child, in 1655. (92) Her shock at his malicious behaviour after their mother's death was partly, she tells us, because he had 'formerly pretended so great an affection towards me', a statement that contradicts almost everything else she tells us about him. And she notes that he did eventually accept he had been wrong to claim that their mother had died intestate. (120) His affection may not have been wholly pretended. Christopher had distrusted her husband's kin from the start (as Alice did), and may well have feared they would outmanoeuvre and cheat her. When her daughter married Thomas Comber, Christopher intervened to ensure that the girl's long-term interests were protected. Comber, as a young curate, could offer no jointure, so Christopher made him pledge to settle all his future earnings on his wife and their children. (228–9) After Thornton's death, Christopher intervened again, insisting that the moneys still due as part of Alice's portion should go to her, and not to Thornton's administrators to clear his debts. (265–7) These episodes hardly cancel out the mass of contrary evidence, but they hint at a more complex sibling relationship, and provide another explanation for Alice's longing to extenuate his behaviour.

Alice's account of her youngest brother, John, was also not wholly reliable. She tells us that John had suffered even more from Christopher's unkindness. He never received the annuities or the £6,000 legacy due to him from their father's estates in Ireland. She depicts him as pious and bookish, and suffering chronic ill health. Without the resources or spirit to press his claims, he had sunk into a deep and prolonged melancholy before dying in December 1666. (76, 159–63, 194) The narrative gives no hint that despite his handicaps John had been able to pursue a public career, sitting and playing an active role in the House of Commons from 1662 until his death. That accords with Alice's claim that he possessed many of the qualities of her beloved George, but not with her picture of a man totally destroyed by his brother's malice.[3] (161)

---

[3] Basil Duke Henning, ed., *The House of Commons 1660–1690* (1983), iii.667.

There are several parallels between the narratives of Alice Thornton and Elizabeth Freke, discussed in Chapter 5. Both writers emphasized their sufferings, both indulged heavily in self-pity, and both were burdened with unsatisfactory husbands. Both also possessed a steely resolve that enabled them to weather the storms that raged over many years. Alice was always prepared to stand her ground, defy her enemies, and defend her rights. She might be only a woman, she told Christopher when he attempted to defraud her after her mother's death, but she deserved her fair share of their mother's blessing. She was also two years his senior, she reminded him, and she used her seniority to assert her moral right to a share of their mother's favour. And in this case, she told him sternly, she had the law as well as moral right on her side, for their mother had left a will showering the blessings on her, not him. (114n–15n, 120).

Elizabeth Freke met the challenge of describing her unhappy life without laying herself open to the charge of besmirching family honour by producing a contradictory text that veered between angry outbursts and expressions of love, gratitude, and devotion. Alice Thornton, by contrast, tried to extenuate her brother's bad behaviour, and chose to pass over in silence the most damning details in the interests of family honour and solidarity. The 'bond of nature', she lamented, had done nothing to soften her brother's cruelty towards her and hers, but it always held Alice firmly in its grip. (291)

DOROTHY OSBORNE (1627–95)

Dorothy Osborne remains a familiar figure today through the engaging love letters she wrote to her future husband, William Temple, in the years 1652–4. It was a covert liaison pursued in defiance of her family, and Dorothy burned Temple's replies after reading them. Her own letters reveal a keen intelligence, droll wit, and sharp pen. She poked fun at the foibles of others, and at her own too, for she was highly self-aware and self-critical. What makes her letters particularly valuable for this study is the complex relationship she depicts with her older brother Henry, who had appointed himself, in effect, her guardian and mentor.[4]

Dorothy belonged to a prominent royalist family in Bedfordshire. Her father and brothers had been active in the civil wars; two brothers had been killed, and her father had been forced to compound for his estates, confiscated by parliament. Dorothy shared their political and religious outlook. In the early 1650s, she was living at the family home at Chicksands with her father and brother Henry. Her mother died in 1651, and her father, Sir Peter, was now elderly and frail. Her oldest surviving brother, John, born in 1616, was married and living in Gloucestershire, though he occasionally visited. The other surviving brother, Robert, only a year

⁴ Page numbers in the text refer to *The Letters of Dorothy Osborne to William Temple*, ed. G. C. Moore Smith (Oxford, 1928). There is a more recent edition by Kenneth Parker, *Dorothy Osborne's Letters to Sir William Temple, 1652–1654* (Aldershot, 2002). *N&Q* numbers refer to 'Henry Osborne's Diary', *Notes and Queries*, 12th series, vii (October 1920).

older than her, lived in London and played relatively little part in her life. She was saddened to hear of his drowning in 1653, but reflected prosaically that his death would improve her eldest brother's inheritance. (89, 107) Dorothy had been only 9 when her sister Elizabeth, seventeen years her senior, married Sir Thomas Peyton and moved away to Kent. Elizabeth died six years later, so the sisters were denied any opportunity to build an adult relationship. It would have been hard for the Osborne siblings, differing widely in age and mostly living apart, to develop or maintain much sense of family solidarity. When the three surviving brothers visited Chicksands briefly in July 1653, Dorothy marvelled that the siblings would all be together, 'which I do not think we ever were twice in our lives'. (64)

All these things magnified the importance of the relationship between Henry and Dorothy, the two siblings still living at the family home. Henry, born in 1619 and so eight years her elder, took over the responsibilities that would normally have belonged to his father or eldest brother. He was anxious to see his sister well married, but the brothers did not consider Temple a suitable match. His family was not wealthy, and Henry judged it unsound in both politics and religion. Though Temple's father had once served the king, he had sat in the Long Parliament after the civil war and held legal office in Ireland under the Commonwealth.[5] (139, 142) Henry tried hard to block the correspondence between Dorothy and Temple, and tried equally hard to interest his sister in more suitable matches. He paraded before her a succession of candidates, both at Chicksands and in London. These unwanted encounters, though stressful, provided Dorothy with a rich store of comic material. The suitors ranged widely in age, temperament, and also, surprisingly, politics. Among them were Oliver Cromwell's son Henry, and Sir Thomas Osborne, later to become Earl of Danby and chief minister under Charles II. Both these men she respected, but she had great fun at the expense of another wooer, the widower Sir Justinian Isham. Henry had hoped that a man famed for his learning and gravity would appeal to his serious-minded sister; instead, Dorothy scorned the 'emperor Justinian', as she dubbed him, as a vain, conceited coxcomb, and ridiculed his solitary love letter as a piece of 'sublime nonsense'. She pitied his daughters, living like prisoners under his despotic rule in his 'vile house' at Lamport. If she was forced to marry him, she predicted, she and his daughters would soon rise up together in rebellion against 'the common enemy'. (6–9, 90) A procession of other suitors fared little better. (5–6, 22, 48, 51, 54, 79, 132; *N&Q, passim*)

Dorothy hated her brother's relentless campaign to break her liaison with Temple, and to push her into a marriage with someone she could not love. Sometimes Henry would tease, mock, and laugh at her; at other times, his anger and abuse left her feeling tortured and tormented. (64) When John visited he would tease too, though they had a more low-key relationship and did not quarrel. (68) With Henry, by contrast, Dorothy had several blazing rows, and sometimes

[5] *ODNB*, Sir William Temple and Dorothy Osborne. On their complex personalities and relationship, see Cedric Brown, *Friendship and its Discourses in the Seventeenth Century* (Oxford, 2016), chap. 7. On the siblings, see Carrie Hintz, *An Audience of One. Dorothy Osborne's Letters to Sir William Temple, 1652–1654* (Toronto, 2005), esp. 88–102.

they did not speak for days. She could occasionally find black humour in her predicament. She commented on one occasion that Henry appeared so enraptured by Isham that he must be in love himself. If he wanted to marry her suitor, she joked, she would not stand in his way. (54) At other times, when they were not speaking to each other, they would still bow and curtsey on retiring for the night. Conscious how absurd this empty ritual must appear, she told Temple that 'you would have died with laughing to have seen us'. (56, 139) But she found their quarrels deeply distressing. Once they had been thought 'the kindest brother and sister', and now they were merely 'the most complimental couple in England'. (56)

The siblings' relationship was emotionally complex. Dorothy's wishes were relatively straightforward: she loved Temple, refused to abandon him, and hoped Henry would eventually relent and allow them to marry. Henry's goals and emotions were far less straightforward, as Dorothy recognized. He criticized the very idea of love in marriage. Most people who married for love soon came to regret it, he told her, and challenged her to name any examples to prove the opposite. She found it embarrassingly difficult to do so. Moreover, she recognized that their brother John, who had married more for love than money, was unhappy in his marriage and more melancholy than ever. (44, 47, 93–4,107) Henry believed that money should always be the primary consideration, a view Dorothy steadfastly rejected. She also found his ideas distasteful when he spelled out what sort of person he considered would make her an ideal husband: a wealthy man who was devoted to her, but for whom she cared little. In such a marriage, he explained, she would always be able to manipulate her husband and get her own way in everything. If she married Isham, he argued, she would be easily able to manipulate and control him. Dorothy agreed, but could see no happiness in such a marriage. (47–8, 110)

In all this, Henry was thinking of his own interests too. At present, he enjoyed a commanding position in the household, with his ailing father confined to his chamber and often bedridden. But when their father died, their brother John would inherit the estate. Henry might well have to leave, and even if allowed to remain, would be in a subordinate position at his brother's bidding. His sister might also have to move out, for John's own wife (for whom Dorothy cared little) would naturally want to manage the household. So for his sister to marry a rich, doting husband would provide an ideal solution for them both: Henry could go on living with his sister, and on favourable terms. All this was spelled out very plainly, as Dorothy reported to Temple: her brother was 'resolved to follow me if he can, which he thinks he might better do to a house where I had some power, than where I am but upon courtesy myself'. (47) Yet Henry was not driven by self-interest alone. He cared deeply for his sister's welfare and happiness. In July 1652, his diary records, 'I vowed a vow to God to say a prayer every day for my sister and when she is married to give God thanks that day every day as long as I lived.' (*N&Q*, 305) He sometimes sent Dorothy passionate letters, especially after their rows, reflecting emotions far more intense than was normal between a brother and sister. Indeed, she warned him that a stranger would think they came from a lover. She told Temple ruefully, or teasingly, that his own letters were 'not half so kind' as those from her brother. But then, she added, 'he is always in the extremes'. And 'since our last quarrel he has courted me more than ever', sending her fine presents, including a china chest 'as pretty a thing as I have seen'. (47–8, 148) So there was another reason for Henry to wish on her a husband for whom she did not care: in such an arrangement, he might hope to remain the centre of her affections, if only he could break her attachment to Temple. On one occasion, Dorothy described her brother to Temple as his 'rival'. (140) The situation carries echoes of Webster's Jacobean tragedy *The Duchess of Malfi*, where Duke Ferdinand becomes deeply jealous of the love that has blossomed between his twin sister, the widowed duchess, and her steward. His possessiveness, and its incestuous undercurrent, bring the tragedy to its bloody end. Why Dorothy reported her brother's infatuation to Temple remains less clear. Perhaps she hoped it would galvanize him into action to drive matters forward.

Dorothy's feelings towards her brother, though less intense, were also complex and conflicted, and sometimes left Temple confused. She resented her brother's constant and overbearing interference, his contempt for her values, and his disparaging comments about the man she loved. At the same time, she accepted that he genuinely cared for her and believed he was acting in her best interests. And there was something more, as she tried to explain. She was not afraid of her brother's anger, she told Temple, and when he ranted and raged, she could despise him,

> but when he asks my pardon with tears, pleads to me the long and constant friendship between us and calls heaven to witness that nothing upon earth is dear to him in comparison of me, then I confess I feel a strange unquietness within me.

She could see that Henry was suffering too. (133)

The courtship reached a dramatic turning point in the winter of 1653–4. At the end of November, Henry's relentless pressure finally wore down Dorothy's resistance, and she promised to abandon her dream of marrying Temple. She endured a miserable Christmas at Chicksands, going through the motions of the festive season. Temple was about to leave for Ireland, and he visited Chicksands early in January to say farewell. Henry was away when he arrived, and when he returned on the 13th, Dorothy told him she had informed Temple that their relationship was over. 'God be praised', Henry wrote in his diary, and he was delighted to see Temple looking suitably crestfallen. In reality, this was all a charade, for Dorothy had abruptly reversed her decision and she and Temple had just entered into a binding secret engagement. (129–31; N&Q, 325) She managed to keep the secret from Henry, but their relationship remained tense. Well aware that she still loved Temple, he continued to disparage him, which triggered further angry exchanges. After one of them, Henry came into her chamber and confessed 'in a pitiful tone' that he was dreading another sleepless night, tormented by his thoughts. She had resolved to ignore him, but his confession softened her heart and they drifted into a long discussion of melancholy and then religion. It eased them both into a calmer mood, at peace with each other and the world. They begged one another's pardon, and expressed their mutual 'humble, charitable kindness'. Equally important, Henry promised to speak no more of her feelings for Temple, and to place everything in God's hands. Should they ever marry, he told her, he would leave her, 'not out of want of kindness to me, but because he cannot see the ruin of a person that he loves so passionately and in whose happiness he had laid up all his'. (139–40)

A few weeks later it became clear that their ailing father was dying, a development that brought the affair to its climax. On 9 March, Dorothy told her brother that she would have Temple after all. Sir Peter died on 11 March, and on the 13th, the day of the funeral, she told Henry that she had tied her hands so far that the decision was irrevocable. She could and would marry no other. (280; *N&Q*, 326) It was now Henry's turn to give way, worn down by his sister's stubborn determination. But her father's death left Dorothy now wholly dependent on her brothers, 'kindred that are not friends', a situation she described as 'the most unsupportable to my nature'. With Chicksands now at the disposal of her brother John, she did not know if she would be allowed to remain. (155) In the event she lived henceforth with relations, mainly her brother-in-law, Peyton, or in lodgings in London, and Henry did likewise. Now that her father was dead, Dorothy no longer felt bound to conceal her engagement. In any case, Henry had already broadcast the news, which he presented as an unmitigated disaster. Dorothy was outraged, and saw this as an act of malice and revenge. It was 'so barbarous a cruelty', she wrote in fury, 'that I shall never look upon him as a brother more'. (155–6) It was a dramatic breach of the peace pact they had made only a few weeks earlier. But Henry would have felt, with some justice, that his sister and Temple had blatantly deceived him.

Temple's family were equally unhappy at the news, for they had hoped for a much wealthier bride. Both families slowly and reluctantly came to terms with the situation, and opened negotiations on the terms of a marriage settlement. Temple was highly surprised when Dorothy insisted that Henry must play an active role, despite her bitter complaints over his past conduct. They had all been spoken in anger, she explained, and she trusted him to behave fairly. A powerful bond clearly existed between the siblings that even months of bitter conflict could not destroy. Moreover, she insisted, it would appear highly improper for her closest kin not be involved in such a matter. No one seems to have suggested that her brother John should take on the task. (179–81)

The following months brought several new setbacks. Dorothy was struck down with smallpox, and almost died. Negotiations over the settlement proved fraught, and Henry's diary records that on 22 December 1654 he and his sister 'utterly fell out about it'. Only three days later, on Christmas Day, the couple were privately married. (183) But in marrying while the financial arrangements were still contested, they must have known that further troubles lay ahead. Sir Peter Osborne had made provision several years earlier for Dorothy to have a marriage portion of £4,000, and three days after the wedding she and Temple wrote asking for the documents to be delivered. Henry refused, convinced that the Temples neither would nor could offer an acceptable jointure for his sister. Within a few weeks, the parties were locked in litigation in Chancery, and it was not until late July that they agreed a final settlement. (185–94) Money, we may suspect, was not the only issue at stake. Henry (later Sir Henry) lived until 1675, but he never married.

Sir William Temple, as he became, went on to a distinguished diplomatic career. He and Dorothy played some part in facilitating the marriage between William of Orange and Princess Mary, later William III and Mary II. What relationship Dorothy maintained with her brothers remains largely shrouded in darkness. Henry noted in his diary in May 1656 that his sister had left for Ireland, where the new couple were to remain for several years. But in October 1664, the diary records his visit to Chicksands, and his return to London in the company of Dorothy, Temple, and Temple's sister. That suggests at least some degree of reconciliation. (*N&Q*, 345–6)

This story has one more sibling dimension. Temple's sister, Martha, eleven years his junior, adored him and devoted her entire life to serving his interests. Her name often surfaces in Dorothy's letters. Before Dorothy's wedding, they had never met, so her affectionate and admiring comments reflect what she had heard from Temple, and signalled that she understood and respected their close sibling bond. In 1662, Martha married Sir Thomas Giffard, a marriage that was cut dramatically short by his death only two weeks later. She never remarried, and remained a widow for sixty years. For most of her life, Martha lived happily with Temple and Dorothy, and she composed an admiring biography of her brother during his lifetime.[6] If Dorothy's marriage poisoned relationships between the Osborne siblings, it did no harm to the bond between Temple and his sister. And that must reflect at least in part the good sense and moderation of both Dorothy and Martha.

    [6] G. C. Moore Smith, ed., *The Early Essays and Romances of Sir William Temple, Bt, with The Life and Character of Sir William Temple by his sister Lady Giffard* (Oxford, 1930).

11

James Yonge and John Cannon
Favouritism and Sibling Rivalry

JAMES YONGE (1647–1721)

The journal of James Yonge, a gifted and successful Plymouth surgeon, seethes with resentment. Looking back over fifty years in 1708, he still felt deeply hurt and was angry at his parents' open favouritism towards his older and younger brothers. The journal offers no explanation for their behaviour. Most members of the family appear to have been strong-willed, independent-minded, and plain-speaking, which gives some clue to their acrimonious relationships.

James Yonge's resentment reached back to his childhood. It may have begun in 1658, when he was 11 years old and doing well at the local grammar school. His father, a surgeon, fell seriously ill and, expecting to die, wanted to see his two older sons settled. The elder, John, was accordingly apprenticed to a surgeon at Plymouth Hospital, while James was removed from school and apprenticed for nine years to a surgeon serving in the Cromwellian navy.[1] (27–8) James quickly adapted to life at sea, and found his master a reasonable man. But in 1661, he was sent to serve as assistant in the *Mountagu*, under an old army surgeon who knew nothing of sea affairs and proved a cruel and demanding taskmaster. He supplies no details of the 'misery' he suffered, but commented tersely that he often wished himself dead. He also noted that in over a year he 'heard not one line or received one penny' from his father. (39) Back in England, he visited his family in the autumn of 1662, for the first time in almost two years, and encountered such hostility from his father that he vowed never to return. Hopes that his old master would provide some relief were dashed when his master decided to give up the sea and returned the apprenticeship indentures. (53) James was now forced, by 'severe usage' and threats, to bind himself apprentice to his own father for a further seven years, having already served five under his old master. Miserable at this injustice, he was embittered to see his elder brother John 'maintained like a prince', while he had to make do with old clothes and hobnailed boots, with 'not one penny in my pocket'. In December that year, his brother John, now out of his apprenticeship, married a handsome wife who brought him a portion of £150, and was able to set up his own business.

<hr>

[1] For his life, see *ODNB*. Bracketed numbers refer to *The Journal of James Yonge [1647–1721], Plymouth Surgeon*, ed. F. N. L. Poynter (1963).

James, by contrast, was shipped off as ship's surgeon to the Newfoundland fisheries, with very few clothes or medical supplies. (53–4)

Over the next few years, he made several similar voyages. He performed his surgical duties well, and wrote a valuable description of the fisheries' organization and methods. These were, he wrote later, some of the happiest days of his life. (14, 54–60, 111–38) Returning to Plymouth in September 1669, he discovered several major changes. His brother John had lost his wife, given up his shop, and engaged himself to go on a voyage to the East Indies. This drastic step had been triggered by a fierce quarrel with his mother, and James thought them both to blame. John regretted his 'rash undertaking' even before he sailed, and was to sicken and die in India the following year. (123, 141) The journal offers no words of regret for his death. James had accompanied his brother as far as Exeter on his way to London to join the East Indiaman, but any warm feelings were quickly dispelled when he returned home. With his elder brother gone, he thought he might at last find some parental favour. But he discovered that, before leaving, John had 'buzzed my father in ear' that their mother 'had a design to make me elder and greater than he', presumably by persuading her husband to make James his main heir. This supposed 'design' was probably no more than a spat in her quarrel with John, and the journal provides no evidence of any maternal affection towards James. Whatever the facts, the effect was to poison still further his relations with his father, and he decided to escape by signing up for yet another voyage to Newfoundland. (123)

Arriving back in Plymouth in September 1670, James now finally 'took leave of the sea, having seen in fourteen years a great many parts of it, enough for one' (though his arithmetic was at fault here). (137) He was still only 23. His thoughts were now fixed on marriage, and he had already fallen for a young woman named Jane Crampporn. Confiding his hopes to his mother, he 'desired her to sift my father'. But his father, though approving his plan to settle ashore and marry, wanted him to find a richer bride. It was several months before he would even allow an approach to Jane. He then objected that she would bring a dowry of only £150, and though he was not offering anything towards a marriage settlement, he refused to give his consent. James was in despair. It was Jane who saved the day, by badgering her widowed mother to improve the terms on offer, and James finally persuaded his father to agree. The couple married in March 1671, after he had fitted up his surgeon's shop and furnished their house. (139–41) The couple lived very happily together, his career blossomed, and his family soon grew.

There was to be another and yet more hurtful episode in James Yonge's story of parental bias. At Christmas 1679, his youngest brother Nathaniel married a merchant's daughter from Fowey, in Cornwall. His parents welcomed this match with delight. 'Though the fortune was but £250', James fumed, his father, who 'would never advance or settle a penny on my elder brother John or myself in marriage', gave the couple £100 and the reversion of a house and his shops on the quay after his and his wife's deaths. Even more painful, he also gave them immediate possession of the house in which James was living with his wife, four children, and five servants, and where he ran his business. This extraordinary act 'almost broke my heart', he recalled. It also soon became 'the general wonder of the town' that he and his family 'should be turned out of doors to make way for a younger brother'. Moreover, their father was maintaining Nathaniel and his bride in the parental home, so they had no need to take over James's premises. His father soon discovered that his actions had outraged local public opinion, and he sank into melancholy and deep remorse, turning his anger against his wife and Nathaniel. He fell seriously ill, and died only a few months later. 'In all his sickness', James recalled, 'he hated the sight of my brother and was discontented with my mother as she that had drawn him into this unnatural act, as he always called it.' Before his death he was reconciled with James, 'and died in very good charity with me', though not, the journal makes clear, with either his wife or Nathaniel. (160–1) His widow survived for many more years, dying in 1700 at the age of 82. James notes that she 'enjoyed her memory &c to the last,' but offers no word of affection or sadness. (209) Autobiographies in this period often devote many pages to the writer's ancestry. Yonge, by contrast, does not even supply his parents' names, though he gives those of his children, grandchildren, siblings, and their spouses. His father, he recalled, 'was always a haughty and passionate man'. (161) Yonge never really forgave him, or his mother.

Relations with Nathaniel remained predictably difficult, poisoned by resentment over the favouritism his brother had once enjoyed. Tensions gradually eased sufficiently for Nathaniel to act as godfather to one of James's children in 1686. The brothers also travelled to London together in 1687, when James was summoned to attend James II's great army camp outside the capital. (197–8) But relations then soured again, and permanently. The journal's final reference to Nathaniel is his death from 'scorbutic asthma' in March 1698. James shed no tears, for they had become bitter political foes. While James was a strong Tory, his brother was 'a zealous Whig' who had campaigned with Plymouth's MP, Sir Francis Drake, to change its charter to favour the Whig cause. (207–8) Local politics were riven by fierce party feuds, and when James served as mayor in 1694–5 he endured a turbulent time. Both he and his opponents wanted to restore the town's old charter, surrendered under royal pressure in 1684, and fill the bench with men who shared their own party allegiance. James was thwarted, but his Whig successor enjoyed more success with the support of Sir Francis Drake. In 1696, Drake secured a new charter that brought in a raft of Whig aldermen James despised. He was dropped from the bench, and saw his nomination as a common councillor as an insult. Nathaniel had campaigned on Drake's behalf, and it was Nathaniel, he believed, who 'had put that indignity upon me'. He never forgave him.[2] (188–9, 190, 205–6) Drake too was never forgiven. When Yonge recorded his 'lingering and tormentary death' in 1715, he added tartly: 'I wish he be not punished worse in the other life.' (229)

---

[2] *Calendar of State Papers, Domestic, 1696*, 423–4. On Drake, see B. D. Henning, ed., *The House of Commons 1660–1690*, 3 vols (1983), ii.233–5.

The journal tells us much less about Yonge's third brother, Samuel, who entered Lincoln College, Oxford, in 1667.[3] (109) The Nonconformist views he developed angered his father and must have incurred James's own disapproval, but the brothers appear to have remained on reasonably friendly terms. James mentions casually in 1672 that a new apprentice from Oxford had been recruited partly through Samuel's agency. (123, 142) In 1679 Samuel, now living in Bristol, married the daughter of the famous Nonconformist minister Henry Stubbes, a woman James came to respect as 'discreet, pious [and] virtuous'. (161) We hear nothing more of relations between the two families until a brief note that Samuel had died on 30 April 1707, aged 60, having been 'distracted 14 years'. (227)

James had only slightly better relationships with his two sisters, also independent-minded. When his sister Ann remarried in 1669, only three months after being left a widow, he commented angrily, 'it was done clandestinely, unknown to any of us, and absolutely against the liking of all her relations'. He considered her new husband a 'covetous sneak', despite his good estate. John Walter was a widower with two children by his first wife, and when he died in 1674, he left nothing in his will to Ann or their two small boys. That would have confirmed James's harsh judgement. (83, 112, 147) In 1681, his much younger sister Joanna married George Tollar, of Fowey, the brother of Nathaniel's wife, once more 'contrary to the good liking and against the consent of my mother and self'. Yonge clearly saw himself as the family head, and was offended that his opinion had been ignored. The bridal couple left for Fowey the same day. (165)

Despite these many bitter clashes, family ties did not break down completely. While James had disapproved of Ann's remarriage, in 1672 he accepted a general invitation to visit the couple at their home in Truro. It was a sizeable party, including his mother, wife, and siblings Samuel, Nathaniel, and Joanna. (143) And while he similarly disapproved of Joanna's marriage, he and his wife called on her and her husband during a visit to Cornwall in 1683. (187) We also find him asking his siblings to act as godparents to his children. Ann, Joanna (twice), and both Nathaniel and his wife (before the great rift) all served in that capacity. (141, 148, 150, 165, 197) Surprisingly, his mother also served twice, perhaps in a gesture of reconciliation. (147, 197)

Yonge's journal shows a deep affection for his wife, Jane, and far more affection for her sister and mother too than for his own parents or siblings. He had fallen passionately in love with Jane, and blessed God for their happy marriage. The only slight 'coolness' in their relationship arose from her practice of attending Noncon-formist meetings, despite his efforts to dissuade her. Jane too was strong-willed, and Yonge had to rest content with her agreement to attend the parish church occa-sionally. (146) Her family had strong Nonconformist ties. Yonge's disappointment, as a firm Anglican and churchwarden, was more than offset by his love for her and gratitude to her family, especially her mother, for their help in advancing his career. (139, 142, 143, 149) Yonge's marriage lasted nearly forty years, and Jane's death in

---

[3] Joseph Foster, *Alumni Oxonienses. The Members of the University of Oxford, 1500–1714* (Oxford, 1891–2), iv.1705.

November 1708 brought him 'inexpressible loss and grief'. He could not bring himself to continue his journal thereafter. (228)

Yonge's son John, whom he took on as an apprentice, shared something of the family's characteristically independent spirit. In 1695, Yonge was planning to send him to study at Leyden, but John had other ideas; he had fallen in love, and he seized an opportunity to marry secretly when both his parents were away. It was a fortnight before they discovered what had happened. Abandoning the plan to send him abroad, Yonge set him up with a house and shop in the city. (197, 204, 205) Most of Yonge's wider kin lived far from Plymouth, and they feature only marginally in the journal. It is striking, nonetheless, that he maintained contact with several, and found them ready to help when the need arose. As a youngster, he had lodged with an aunt, his mother's brother's widow, when his ship lay at Deptford. (34) Some years later, when he needed a horse to carry him down from London to Plymouth, his uncle Morrice, his father's brother, took him to Smithfield and helped him choose. (108) And when he visited Barnstaple in 1674, the town where his wife's mother had been born, he received a warm welcome from her kinsfolk there. (144)

James Yonge is remembered today as a respected surgeon, successful in his career and the author of an important treatise on a new procedure in amputations. He was surgeon in charge of the first naval hospital at Plymouth, rose to become mayor of the town, and was elected a Fellow of the College of Physicians. He also became a Fellow of the Royal Society, and a friend of Robert Hooke, its secretary. He enjoyed a long and happy marriage. But he could never forget or forgive his parents for what he saw as their grossly unfair favouritism towards his brothers. And that injustice lay at the root of the sibling rivalries that overshadowed his life.

JOHN CANNON (1684–1743)

John Cannon, the son of a farmer in West Lydford, Somerset, pursued a far more erratic career as a farm servant, excise officer, schoolteacher, and scrivener. His autobiographical *Chronicles* provide the richest depiction we have of the texture of life in rural parishes and small towns in this period, with vivid sketches of their inhabitants. They provide too a detailed and impassioned account of the rivalries between Cannon and his brother and sister, rivalries that began in early childhood and festered throughout their lives. Biased though he was, Cannon acknowledged that all three siblings bore some responsibility for this unhappy situation. But, like James Yonge, he held his parents mainly to blame, and charged them with cruelty and blatant favouritism.

John was the middle of three children, with an older sister and a brother born one year after him. His story began well. As an infant, he tells us, he was plump, merry, and loved by all, including the maidservants and a benevolent grandfather.[4] (19)

---

[4] Bracketed numbers refer to *The Chronicles of John Cannon, Excise Officer and Writing Master, 1684–1743*, ed. John Money (Oxford, 2010). The editor provides an excellent account of Cannon and his world.

This auspicious beginning proved short-lived. His younger brother, Thomas, at the age of 3 fell awkwardly while playing and suffered a serious rupture. It left him with severe and lasting pain, and he always had to wear a truss. His parents sought out the best medical treatments they could find, and even resorted to folk magic when conventional remedies failed. Understandably, they treated Thomas with special indulgence and his mother, in particular, doted on her younger son. That created in John a sense of grievance, exacerbated by her similar partiality for her daughter Elizabeth. They were both her 'darlings', he complained years later. Whenever the children squabbled or misbehaved, it was always John who was blamed and punished. Their father was more even-handed, but his wife seems to have been the dominant personality, and the alliance of mother, daughter, and younger son created a powerful bloc within the household. (20–2)

The children attended school in the village, where John proved an eager and proficient pupil. His siblings, less interested, made only limited progress. But in 1697, his thirteenth year, disaster struck. His schoolmaster moved to Yeovil, and his parents refused to cover the costs of boarding him there. They decided he was now old and strong enough to be more useful on the farm, and set him to keep sheep, drive a plough, and learn other husbandry skills. He was devastated. He felt that he had 'a natural genius' for books and learning and had already made good progress in Latin, and believed that within a few years he would have been ready for university. His pleas to continue at school, though supported by some of his kin, fell on deaf ears. Instead, he mourned, 'I became a mere clod-hopper.' In defiance, he would take small chapbooks and read them furtively under a hedge or in the barn when he should have been working. (27–30) As he grew older, and the farm work became ever more onerous, he felt trapped in a life of 'Egyptian bondage'. He begged in vain to be allowed to study writing and accounts, as utilitarian substitutes for the higher learning he had once dreamt of. (31) Deepening his sense of grievance was that his siblings had been kept on at school in Wincanton for a further three years, Thomas learning writing and accounts, Elizabeth taught millinery, dancing, 'and the like, all at a vast expense'. Neither profited much, and both soon forgot what little they had learned. (31, 33–4) John's bitterness leaps from the page, despite his shaky syntax:

> Thus those two darlings having the ascendant of their parents who winked at all their actions & by their indulgence they easily obtained anything they desired whilst I, poor I, fared daily by far more inferior. And that learning throwed away to no purpose on my brethren should have been bestowed on me.   (31)

Elizabeth contributed little when she eventually returned home to the farm. She became instead her mother's 'chief favourite, cabinet counsel, privy purse and sole advisor; and whatever she craved, instantly had it'. Too corpulent for much work on the farm, she devoted herself instead to the elaborate and expensive flower garden her mother had created. She had fine clothes, while Cannon and Thomas had to make do with cheap clothes far inferior to those worn by other youngsters in the village. They felt mortified. (31, 33–4)

John Cannon's chronicles, compiled many years later, still burn with resentment. We do not, of course, have his parents' or siblings' perspectives, but it is not hard to find a plausible explanation for many of his parents' decisions. His father had been badly injured and incapacitated by a fall in 1692, and both parents almost died the following year from dangerous fevers. (24) It would have been natural for them, looking ahead, to want their healthy elder son to take on more farm work while Thomas, hampered by his rupture, acquired the skills to pursue a less physically demanding career. Elizabeth's ladylike accomplishments, her mother must have hoped, might attract a good husband. These plans, however reasonable, did not materialize. By 1705, when their father left off running the farm, it was plain that Thomas cared only for husbandry while John, though now highly proficient, saw it as little more than slavery. Moreover, the brothers quarrelled repeatedly, which made a partnership unworkable. So their father chose to place his younger son in charge of his farm, while John moved out to live as manager with his maternal uncle Robert Walter, who had bought some land but lacked farming experience. (52) This arrangement worked well for two years, before ending abruptly when John and his uncle came to blows over how best to plough a particular field. John Cannon could be both obstinate and impulsive, traits that remained throughout his life. He now resolved to move away. His first plan was to become a bookkeeper in Bristol, and when this was thwarted by his mother and sister he vowed, in fury, to find some other way to escape from farming, his family, and Lydford. (55–7) By chance, another option soon presented itself: an invitation to take up a new career as an excise officer. Looking back years later, he regretted his impulsive behaviour and his rash vow. But he held his parents mainly to blame for their unkind treatment and their favouritism towards his siblings. In particular, he resented his mother's indulgence of a sister he dismissed as idle and worthless. His chronicle contains frequent and lengthy digressions on the evil consequences of parental injustice. (21, 28)

John's new career took him far away from Lydford. His father paid him a visit in 1709, and father and son were reconciled. (90) After leaving home he saw his mother again only once more, when word came in 1714 that she was gravely ill. She failed to recognize him until he fell to his knees and craved her blessing and pardon. He stayed three weeks. She rallied briefly, but died a few months later. (115–16, 120) John's visit showed him how much had changed since he had left. His brother had married, lost his wife, and was about to marry again. His sister was also about to wed, having accepted a man who already had two marriages behind him (to two sisters) and had children by both. Cannon disapproved of both marriage plans, but neither parents nor siblings appear to have sought his opinion or approval. He thought Elizabeth's intended, William Middleham, an ill-natured, morose man given to heavy drinking and womanizing. She had turned down several better offers, and rejected every attempt to dissuade her. Obstinacy was clearly a trait the siblings all shared. Moreover, his 'overgreedy' sister had persuaded her parents to agree a settlement her brothers thought excessive, depriving them of what they believed should be their own inheritance. (116–17, 149) John feared, indeed, that in his absence both brother and sister had contrived to secure their own interests at his expense. Fearing that worse would follow, he asked the Excise Board for a posting closer to home, where he could better protect his own interests. (119)

In the event, his sister was to pose no further threat. Only three years later, in 1717, John learned that she was dying and hastened to Lydford for one last meeting. She was greatly relieved to see him, though she died within a few hours. Their final meeting was affectionate, and in his chronicle he praised her as a virtuous wife, tender mother, and 'loving sister', a quality hard to square with everything else he says about her. (149) Her death provides us with a rare glimpse of other perspectives on the sibling relationships. She told John that Thomas had stayed away throughout her illness, following a tiff, and that his behaviour was cruel and unnatural. John agreed, and hurried to his brother's house to urge him, in vain, to set these differences aside. He was shocked too that Thomas had called on him at Shepton Mallet, only two days earlier, and had said nothing about their sister's condition, even though John had enquired after all the family. (148–9) If there was no love between the brothers, there was clearly no more between his brother and sister.

The brothers continued to clash. When he visited his mother for the last time, John sensed that his brother had become highly adept at advancing his own interests. That was underlined when their uncle Robert Walter died in 1715 and left Thomas both his house and estate. John felt deeply aggrieved at the small legacy he received, after his earlier service as Walter's farm manager and guide. (lxvi; 132–4) Thomas was now secure for life, and his father also conveyed some of his own lands and goods to him before his death in 1723. John, by contrast, was very far from secure. He had married in 1714 and had a young family, but he was always reckless with money and in 1721 he lost his position with the Excise. (165) This blow and the deaths of his uncle and father transformed the relationship between the brothers. John inherited his father's house and remaining estate, but also liability for his large debts. To pay off these and his own substantial debts he was soon forced to sell off most of the land and the house too. Creditors descended in swarms, and he was several times arrested for debt. Without land, home, or employment, he commented bitterly, quoting an old proverb, 'I had nothing left but the dog to hold, or worse, not so much as a hair of his tail.' He was reduced to renting 'two little bad houses' in Lydford adjoining his brother's property, for £3 a year. It was a humiliating arrangement 'by which he got the ascendant of me', and he reflected bitterly on the biblical story of Esau becoming the servant of his younger brother Jacob. In the midst of disaster, it was the blighted sibling relationship that hurt most. (172–4)

John Cannon was to live another twenty years, and his circumstances gradually improved. He forged a new career as a schoolmaster and scrivener at Mere and then Glastonbury, while his wife and children remained in Lydford, surviving on his irregular contributions and their own earnings. The relationship between the brothers remained tense. Comfortably installed in his uncle's house and land, Thomas now played a significant role in parish affairs, with spells as churchwarden and constable. That led to more friction. As constable he was, in John's view, far 'too busy in his office', deliberately exacerbating local disputes. Typically, he felt it right to tell him so, at some length, and seemed surprised that his lecture was resented. (471–2, 566) With only a toehold left in Lydford, John was not eligible for parish office. Longing for some other mark of status, he campaigned to be appointed one of the sheriff's men at the Taunton assizes, only to be thwarted by Thomas and his wife, who contrived to have their own son appointed instead. He grumbled that they were 'puffed up and swelled with pride' at their triumph. (332–3)

The brothers' fraught relationship never descended to a total breach. John did not want that, and it would have been problematic given the multiple interconnections of their families, friends, and neighbours. He did annual accounts for Thomas, and the two families managed to enjoy occasional social gatherings. On Twelfth Night in 1737, for example, John and his family spent the evening at his brother's house, and were 'merry till late'. (293; cf. 321, 564) When Thomas and his wife visited Glastonbury, he showed them round the abbey ruins, and on another occasion, when they came to hear a celebrated Quaker female preacher, he laid on a dinner at the Bell Inn, 'where we were merry for a while'. (267–8, 314) Tensions always remained, however, and neither showed much inclination to hold them in check. When John called on his brother one Sunday in January 1736, he found his sister-in-law grieving for the death of a child, and their eldest son depressed by his parents' refusal to support his marriage plans. John did nothing to lighten their gloom. He told his brother that in thwarting his son's wishes, he might well be condemning him to an early grave. He reminded his brother and sister-in-law, unkindly, that years earlier similar miserliness had made one of their daughters pine away and die. He held his sister-in-law mainly to blame, and saw her dominance in the household as further evidence of his brother's poor character. (280, 295)

The brothers were always ready to quarrel over any issue, however trivial. On one occasion, they rowed furiously over the weights and measures in use at different markets, a clash that ended with Thomas ordering his brother out of the house. (455–6; cf. 338) But it was a more important issue that created the deepest rift between them, and indeed their families. Their most wealthy and influential relative was their cousin Mrs Elizabeth Pope, and as a widow with no surviving child she became the focus of fierce competition for her favour and the prospect of a substantial legacy. John had skill in keeping accounts and as a scrivener, and was able to do her many services. One of his children was a favoured god-daughter, and he offered to let her live there as a servant. (355–6) For their part, Thomas and his wife could offer Mrs Pope hospitality as well as company, and they placed a son in her household as bailiff. Thomas felt entitled to call her 'Cousin Betty', assuming a familiarity that John detested. (356, 371) Mrs Pope, capable and level-headed, tried to remain on friendly terms with both parties, which was far from easy. The brothers sometimes rowed even in her presence, and accused each other of feeding her damaging gossip to undermine her trust. Their most dramatic clash came at Christmas 1738. On 26 December, John called on Mrs Pope and was invited to play cards in a foursome. Before long, the little party was interrupted by the uninvited arrival of Thomas with his wife and five or six children. It was their practice, John complained, to come in haste whenever they heard he was with Mrs Pope, to make sure nothing could be said or done to further his interest and damage theirs. John believed that Thomas and his wife used such underhand tactics at every opportunity, and went round to their house next day to tell them so, in blunt terms. That triggered another unseemly row, with Mrs Pope present to see them trade insults and accusations. Eventually John was told 'to be gone and get out'. As he left, he thumped the table with his staff and vowed never to cross their threshold for twelve months. It was a vow he honoured. For the next year, the two families 'kept their distances as the remotest strangers'. (371–2, 392)

The brothers' lifelong feud is easy enough to understand. Rooted in childhood resentments, it was exacerbated by new rivalries in adult life, most notably over Mrs Pope's patronage and the likely disposal of her estate. Both men had difficult personalities. John called his brother peevish, crabbed, foolish, haughty, illiterate, proud, conceited, obdurate, sordid, and insulting. His claim that he himself was reasonable, moderate, and mild is rarely supported by his words or behaviour. His modern editor characterizes him as truculent, vindictive, impulsive, and extravagant. (xxxii)

What gives the feud particular fascination is John Cannon's lifelong preoccupation with the rights he felt he deserved as the elder brother, and as Thomas's superior (he believed) in both character and intellect. The reversal of their fortunes had subverted the natural order. He accepted that he bore some of the blame, having defied his parents' wishes, quarrelled with his uncle, and moved away from home. He also admitted his perennial extravagance, but he continued to feel aggrieved. The *Chronicles* repeatedly criticize his parents' 'severity and austerity'. (28, 30, 31) He recorded their deaths without a single word of sadness or affection, and his sister's death prompted yet more criticism of their unwarranted favouritism. (120, 149, 171) A sense of grievance invaded even his sleep. In December 1737 he had a series of troubling dreams about his siblings, and how his father's will, proved fourteen years earlier, showed they had 'juggled' far more than was due to a sister and younger brother. (320) Resentment at being denied proper respect and deference surfaced in other contexts too. In one of their quarrels, he charged his brother with 'discourteously using me with very ill manners, considering not he was the younger brother'. He also believed that 'being the eldest and therefore first of kin', he had a superior claim to Mrs Pope's favour. (199, 371) Similarly, when he went to effect a reconciliation at the end of his year's self-imposed exile, he thought Thomas should have been the one 'to humble first, being the youngest'. (439–40) Equally revealing is Thomas's own absurd claim, in the course of another quarrel, that 'he was as old or older than me'. That outburst was probably triggered by yet another attempt by John to insist on his seniority and status. (471) More often Thomas retaliated by harping on his brother's 'former extravagances and miscarriages', taunts he knew could not be brushed aside. (199, 372)

The Cannons' story throws vivid light on rivalries across a lifetime, and the significant role they played in the lives of each sibling. But it reveals too how they and their families remained bound together, despite the tensions between them. Living in relative proximity, their circles and affairs overlapped and intersected in a multitude of ways. All three also retained at least some sense of the ties of blood. As she lay dying, Elizabeth was desperate to see her brothers one last time. She was relieved when John arrived, mortified that Thomas still stayed away. John often pontificated on the behaviour that should be natural between brethren. Despite their fiery tempers, the brothers generally tried to avoid a total breakdown. When John vowed to stay away from his brother's house for twelve months, he told his wife and children that he was not asking them also to break off neighbourly relations. And though he never shows Thomas or his wife in a gracious light, their recorded actions go some way to compensate. The brothers quarrelled yet again on 3 January 1743, but two days later both families enjoyed Mrs Pope's hospitality 'in good merriment' until two in the morning. The following day Thomas played host to John and Mrs Pope and their families, all 'well entertained'. Next day John set off back to his school in Glastonbury, and there his chronicles abruptly end. (566–7) The sibling bonds proved impossible to shake off, and they provided at least some occasional moments of warmth.

12

Roger North and his Siblings
The Ties that Bind

'I have here showed', wrote Roger North near the close of the *Life* of his brother Francis, Lord Keeper under Charles II,

> how a half-decayed family with a numerous brood and worn-out estate, of the Norths, by the auspicious character of one child of ten was re-edified; and all the rest lifted into the world with wonderful success; and no one of the whole pack miscarried or were not in all respects (the eldest excepted) mutually helpful and assistant to each other; and none of them tainted with any vice or dishonour, nor the least savour of difference or feud found amongst them; but from the first to the last, they maintained that fraternal amity and correspondence inviolable.[1]

North wrote biographies of three of his brothers and an autobiography, all published after his death. Each work emphasized these powerful family ties. It was a large family remarkable for its close sibling bonds, with the one key exception hinted at in Roger's bracketed aside. Roger was the youngest of fourteen children born to Dudley, fourth Lord North, and his wife, Anne. Ten of them reached adulthood, a considerable success in itself. The eldest son succeeded to the title in due course, his five brothers had successful careers, and their four sisters secured good marriages. Such success had been far from assured. Their father did not inherit the title and estate until long after the children had grown. The third Lord North (another Dudley) held the title for over sixty-seven years, until his death in 1668, living in a style that left the estate in poor condition. Roger's parents had to raise their large brood on a very tight budget and amidst the upheavals of civil war. The children were made aware, from an early age, that the eldest son Charles would inherit the whole estate and that, for the others, 'there was no other means of living to be expected, than what came out of our industry'. It was a lesson they never forgot.[2]

---

[1] Mary Chan, ed., *The Life of the Lord Keeper North* (Lewiston, New York, 1995), 194.
[2] *Notes of Me. The Autobiography of Roger North*, ed. Peter Millard (Toronto, 2000), 79–82, 85; Roger North, *The Lives of . . . Francis North, . . . Sir Dudley North, and . . . Dr John North*, ed. Augustus Jessopp, 3 vols (1890), iii.311–13.

THE BAND OF BROTHERS

Francis, the second surviving son, became a barrister. Ambitious, gifted, and ferociously industrious, he rose swiftly to become Attorney-General, Lord Chief Justice, and Lord Keeper, raised to the peerage as Lord Guilford and presiding in the House of Lords in the absence of the Lord Chancellor. Dudley, next in line, became a merchant and amassed huge wealth during twenty years living overseas. After returning to England, he served as Sheriff of London, entered parliament, and held several government positions. John North, a formidable scholar, had become Master of Trinity College, Cambridge, by his early thirties. The two youngest, Montague and Roger, achieved more modest success in trade and the law, rising, Roger acknowledged, in the slipstream of their dynamic siblings. The *Lives* provide information on them all.[3] By contrast, they say little on the eldest brother Charles, who succeeded as fifth Lord North in 1677. This was a tale of sibling ties and triumphs, with the official head of the family written out of the story.

It was Francis who took on the responsibilities normally undertaken by the heir. Roger called him the 'best brother', 'a common father to us', and the other siblings shared his admiration. He and Roger enjoyed a long and close relationship, though with an age difference of sixteen years it was never remotely one of equals. 'I own that all my portion of knowledge and fortunes are owing to him,' he acknowledged. Roger, though highly capable, always stressed the disparity between their gifts. 'I was a plant of slow growth; and when mature but slight wood,' he explained with excessive modesty.[4] Francis smoothed his professional career from the start. When Roger entered the Middle Temple in 1669, aged 16, Francis supplemented the slender allowance which was all their parents could provide. He gave advice, and helped Roger to become something of an authority in the field of conveyancing. When Francis became Chief Justice of Common Pleas, Roger took on work in his courts, and accompanied him on his circuit as an Assize Judge. He had a chamber in the Temple but lodged with Francis and his wife, without charge; and when the Temple was destroyed by fire in 1678, Francis fitted out rooms for him in his temporary quarters in Serjeants' Inn. When Francis became Lord Keeper in 1682, Roger was called to the bar and immediately made King's Counsel, which brought him bigger cases and higher fees. And when Francis, now Lord Guilford, travelled each day to the Guildhall or Westminster Hall, Roger rode in his coach, and accompanied him to dinner and supper engagements. He now lived in some style in Francis's large household, enjoying the command of servants, and a chariot and horses, all for a contribution of £200 a year, 'a trifle as the world went then', as he recalled. With the Lord Keeper's favour obvious to all, lucrative work flowed into the young man's hands. Roger recognized, however, that it would soon cease if

---

[3] Francis, Dudley, John, and Roger have entries in *ODNB*. For Francis see Chan, *Life*, Introduction; for Dudley see Richard Grassby, *The English Gentleman in Trade. The Life and Works of Sir Dudley North 1641–1691* (Oxford, 1994); for John and Roger see Introductions to Peter Millard, ed., *Roger North: General Preface and Life of Dr John North* (Toronto, 1984) and *Notes of Me*.

[4] *Notes of Me*, 171, 200.

anything happened to his brother, and fretted about his long-term security. To set his mind at rest, Francis sold him an annuity of £200 p.a. for £1,600, 'at an easy rate', with the proviso that Roger would sell it back on identical terms if and when his own estate reached £5,000. It was a typical North arrangement, simultaneously generous and hard-headed. During the years his brother served as Lord Keeper, Roger's practice in Chancery brought him an annual profit of £4,000, which set him up for life.[5]

Francis lost his wife in 1678, and decided to remain single to protect the interests of his children. He spent the vacations at the country estate he had acquired through his wife at Wroxton, near Banbury, and in term time lived at his fine house in Chancery Lane. After dinner he would retire with a few companions, 'and the tea-table followed, where his youngest brother [Roger] officiated; and whom his lordship often set at the head of his table, for want of a lady, to carve'.[6] Roger had become his protégé, assistant, intimate, and quasi-wife. When Francis travelled the country as a circuit judge, Roger recalled keeping 'so close to him that I can safely say I saw him abed every night without intermission for divers years together'. And when Francis became Lord Keeper, 'my meals, company, and pleasures, as well as my business, was at my brother's house . . . it was well known, he had scarce a retired minute without me. I never left him but in bed, and commonly he would unbend himself with a song to my thorough bass before he went into his chamber.'[7] Roger was devastated when Francis died in 1685, 'and with him all my life, hope and joys'.[8] After the Revolution in 1688, he gradually wound down his legal career, bought a small estate at Rougham, in Norfolk, married, and set up a household of his own for the very first time.

Roger wrote his brother's life, in six successive versions, to defend his posthumous reputation from Whig attacks after the Glorious Revolution. Francis had been a stalwart Tory, and as attorney-general and judge he had played a prominent role in the major political trials in the wake of the Rye House Plot. Roger provided a staunch defence of his brother's record in another work, a fiercely Tory account of public affairs in the last years of Charles II and the short reign of James II.[9] As a biographer, Roger worried that his portrait might appear too adulatory to be credible, but insisted that it was honest and accurate. It was his brother's exceptional qualities, he urged, that had made him want to preserve his memory for posterity.[10] He did allow a few glimpses of human frailty. Francis had been a life-long valetudinarian, and Roger admitted 'how apt he was to passion, and upon any offence to inflame'.[11] In his autobiography, Roger revealed some of his brother's other personal flaws. Francis had tempered his kindness with 'little contempts' at his expense, 'sometimes in jest, and often in earnest'. In no position to complain, Roger recognized that his brother 'had somewhat of humour that way, of raising his

---

[5] Chan, *Life*, 190–1; *Notes of Me*, 160–1, 218–22.   [6] Chan, *Life*, 211, 220–2.
[7] *Notes of Me*, 161, 219.   [8] *Notes of Me*, 236.
[9] Roger North, *Examen; or, An Enquiry into the Credit and Veracity of a Pretended Complete History* (1740).
[10] Chan, *Life*, 7–10.   [11] Chan, *Life*, 28, 222.

own by depressing others' characters'. For ten years, Roger endured these painful slights from the brother he worshipped, until they eventually triggered an angry outburst. Francis, he recalled, had appeared bemused by his anger and hurt, but thereafter behaved with more restraint.[12]

While the sibling relationship was very unequal, benefits clearly flowed in both directions. Francis could unwind and relax in his brother's company, as nowhere else. They both found pleasure in music-making, instrumental and vocal, enjoyed 'familiar chat' about current news, and engaged in more intellectual conversation. They enjoyed lively arguments on music and natural philosophy, with their brother John sometimes acting as moderator, and loved devising projects to remodel the buildings and gardens at Wroxton.[13] Roger also provided utilitarian services. As the fees poured in from his brother's burgeoning legal practice, Roger was responsible for counting the money and carrying it to the goldsmith who acted as Francis's banker. Francis had total trust in his brother's honesty and integrity.[14] Roger's most valuable service, however, came after his brother's death. As guardians to the three orphaned children, he and his brother Dudley arranged for their care and education, looked after the estate, and enlarged their inheritance by shrewd investments and land purchases.[15]

Dudley North had enjoyed a very different relationship with his elder brother. Only four years separated them, and despite their contrasting characters they were very close. Dudley, born in 1641, was long his mother's favourite. A lively child, he had no aptitude or interest in book-learning and was 'a kind of a dunce at school'. His parents recognized that he was more suited to trade. It was a family jest that as a little boy he had once tried to make a deal with a stock of only three farthings, and at school he had driven 'a subtle trade among the boys by buying and selling'. Sent to London 'to learn good hands and accounts', Dudley ran wild for a time, developing an addiction to cockfighting and gaming.[16] But he soon mended his ways, and when his parents bound him to a merchant in the Levant Company, trading to the Ottoman Empire, he took his duties seriously. In 1661, his master felt sufficiently confident to dispatch him on a daunting first venture to Archangel as 'supercargo', charged with negotiating the sale of the ship's cargo, loading another, and taking it by sea to Spain, Italy, and on to Smyrna, where he would serve as his employer's factor. Dudley was among strangers, suffered chronic seasickness, and faced formid-able language problems, but rose to every challenge. He spent several months in Russia, and wrote a lively account of what Roger was to dub sardonically 'the delights of Archangel' and the customs of its 'polite people'. Setting sail again, his ship called at several Spanish and Italian ports before reaching Smyrna almost nine months later. He penned similarly vivid accounts of Pisa, Florence, and other places the ship visited en route in letters posted back to Francis. Francis had lent his brother £200, all the money he could command at that point, to help him trade in the East. The two maintained a close correspondence for some years.[17]

---

[12] *Notes of Me*, 160–1.   [13] Chan, *Life*, 14, 44, 248–50; *Notes of Me*, 201, 266.
[14] Chan, *Life*, 43–4.   [15] *Lives*, ii.218–20. Francis left £32,000 in money.
[16] Grassby, *English Gentleman*, 219–22, 324; *Lives*, ii.1–6.
[17] *Lives*, ii.7–33; Chan, *Life*, 191.

Dudley remained abroad for almost twenty years. After his one short visit back to England, he returned with another loan from Francis of 'all that money he had got' to increase his trading stock. For much of the period he was the Company's chief agent in Constantinople, and also developed a lucrative private business, supplying money and jewels to the Ottoman court. Over the years, Roger tells us, he 'acquired an exquisite skill in human nature, and knew how to deal with all the various species of politicians and trickers'. He was a good linguist, and had an imposing presence: tall and 'well-whiskered', with a massive moustache and beard.[18] When he finally returned to England in 1680, Dudley used his fortune to purchase stock in the Royal African Company, buy a large house, and marry. But his very first action on disembarking was to hire a cab to visit his 'best brother', Francis. Their old intimacy, rekindled, reached new heights. Hugely experienced in their very different fields, 'each was an Indies to the other'. Dudley was a fund of information and stories about other lands and peoples, about business, trade, finance, and much else too, for he had a wide-ranging intellectual curiosity. And he could impart his fascinating information 'in a style of ordinary conversation', which Francis found hugely appealing.[19] Dudley also developed strong views on banking, the currency, and the poor relief system.[20] On politics, he soon came to share his brother's views. At Constantinople, the English merchants had believed the alarming accounts they received of the rise of popery and the Popish Plot. Francis convinced him they were fabrications, and Dudley soon adopted his brother's staunch Toryism. That made him a potentially valuable recruit to London's beleaguered Tory interest. On the king's initiative he was persuaded to accept office as Sheriff of London, was knighted, and later served as an Alderman. He found employment under the Crown, too, as a Customs and then Treasury Commissioner. And in 1685, when the new king, James II, called a parliament, his brother's influence was sufficient to secure him a seat in the House of Commons. Though a parliamentary novice, he played an active role in managing the king's interests in matters relating to the royal revenues. Dudley resisted royal pressure to support the repeal of the Test Act, which barred Catholics and Dissenters from public life, but he was viewed nonetheless as a 'ringleader of the Tory party'. The Revolution of 1688 accordingly brought an abrupt end to his political and public career.[21] He did not long survive it; he was in poor health and asthmatic, and extreme corpulence had weakened his knees, leaving him unable to walk or stand for long. He died on 30 December 1691.[22]

Dudley had left England when Roger was a small child, and their own close friendship developed only after his return to England. For his account of Dudley's first forty years, he had to rely on letters and anecdotes, and he recognized that Dudley had drawn a veil over some aspects of his life abroad. While he liked and admired Dudley, we do not find the adulation he showered on their 'best brother'. He did not conceal Dudley's teenage escapades, his sexual adventures in Venice, or

---

[18] Grassby, *English Gentleman*, chap. 2; Chan, *Life*, 27; *Lives*, ii.77–8.
[19] Chan, *Life*, 81–2; *Lives*, ii.169.   [20] Grassby, *English Gentleman*, chap. 10.
[21] Grassby, *English Gentleman*, chaps 6, 7, 10; *Lives*, ii.179–82, 209–15, 221–5.
[22] *Lives*, ii.249–52, iii.228–9.

the fact that he had kept a mistress in Constantinople. It was a fault, he insisted, that 'almost all men there are more or less guilty of'. Dudley had at least spurned the drunken and sexual debauchery that was common among the overseas English merchant community.[23] For the years after Dudley's return, by contrast, Roger had first-hand material in abundance. On Thursday evenings, the brothers would gather at Dudley's house, on Sundays at Roger's lodgings in the Middle Temple, 'and at his lordship's almost every day'. Relishing their 'exquisite unanimity and harmony', they had felt aggrieved when friends worked out these arrangements and wanted to join them.[24]

Despite their intimacy, the North brothers were careful to uphold the professional ethics of their age. They viewed political patronage as wholly legitimate if accompanied by merit, of which they were naturally the judges. Francis secured a parliamentary seat for Dudley in 1685, convinced this was in the interests of both king and country, and seats too for Roger, two brothers-in-law, a cousin, and other kin. All were staunchly Anglican Tories.[25] But Dudley scrupulously avoided telling his brother about a Chancery suit he was pursuing, and Francis learned of it only when the case came before him, as judge. He ruled in favour of Dudley's opponent. Both men were adamant that the integrity of the law must be upheld.[26]

It was Dudley's kindness that saved Roger from despair when their 'best brother' died in 1685. He proved, Roger recalled, 'a most incomparable friend and companion. With him I grew into a close alliance and friendship which continued untainted to his death.'[27] Their mother had made Roger executor of her will, and as he was burdened by legal business when she died, Dudley took on the task of clearing her house. They cooperated effectively as guardians of Francis's children, a responsibility they discharged with scrupulous care. Roger also helped to smooth Dudley's matrimonial path, pleading his cause to a cantankerous prospective father-in-law.[28] They took enormous pleasure in each other's company. When Dudley first arrived back in England, full of curiosity, Roger gladly showed him the sights of London. Together they climbed the Monument, inspected progress on the new St Paul's (and discussed it with Christopher Wren, the architect), and clambered happily over other churches under construction. Both had a passion for buildings and for all things scientific and mechanical, and spent many happy hours talking of 'engines, tackle, etc'.[29] Later, when Dudley was married and paying an annual visit to his now widowed mother-in-law in Bristol, Roger would accompany him, to discharge his duties as Recorder of the city. Afterwards they would spend some time at Wroxton, their late brother's estate in Oxfordshire, to ensure all was in order. Indulging their passion for things practical, they constructed a simple workshop there with bench, hearth, and forge, and delighted in both wood- and metalwork.

---

[23] *Lives*, ii.47, 158; Grassby, *English Gentleman*, 210–11.

[24] Chan, *Life*, 217; *Lives*, ii.194–5.

[25] Chan, *Life*, 124–5; Basil Duke Henning, ed., *The House of Commons 1660–1690* (1983), ii.339 (Robert Foley), iii.149–51 (Sir Dudley North), 155 (Sir Henry North), 154–6 (Roger North), 688 (Sir George Wenyeve).

[26] *Lives*, ii.247; cf. 232–3.   [27] *Notes of Me*, 236.

[28] *Lives*, ii.172–3, 184–5; Grassby, *English Gentleman*, 211–13, 222.   [29] *Lives*, ii.236–40.

(Dudley joked that Roger, being a lawyer, was naturally 'the best forger'.) When Dudley's wife summoned them for dinner, they would emerge 'as black as a tinker'. Roger paints an engaging picture of his brother, a rich man of the world, sitting for hours 'turning a piece of wood . . . all the while singing like a cobbler, incomparably better pleased than he had been in all the stages of his life before'. They also enjoyed sailing in Roger's yacht, moored on the Thames. Sailing was one of Roger's favourite hobbies, and Dudley was content to sit down, declare 'I'll be admiral', and simply talk.[30]

In London, the siblings were sometimes joined by their brother Montague, who had followed Dudley into the Levant trade. Francis had given him a loan, as he had earlier helped Dudley, and placed £1,000 in Dudley's hands to be employed on the young man's behalf. Though Roger did not chronicle Montague's life, we can glean its outlines from his other writings and family correspondence. He served as a factor at Aleppo until Dudley found an opportunity to bring him to Constantinople as his junior partner. Dudley was deeply distressed when Montague caught the plague, describing how 'it troubled him to the heart' to think himself responsible for his brother's plight, having brought him to the city. He hired four nurses to provide constant care, and Montague survived. When Dudley finally returned to England, he left Montague as his successor, though he recognized that his 'penetration in business', as Roger tactfully put it, 'was not equal to his own'.[31] In 1686, Montague paid an extended visit home, and three years later he decided to return to Constantinople overland through France. This proved a bad decision, for by loose talk he aroused suspicions of being a spy. He was arrested and incarcerated in the castle of Toulon, and despite desperate efforts by Dudley and Roger to secure his release, remained a captive for three and a half years. The prison conditions, however, sound remarkably benign. Roger notes that the temperate climate and 'allegedly exquisite diet' that his brother enjoyed at Toulon paradoxically restored his health, so that 'from a very crazy [i.e. decrepit] he became a very athletic and sound gentleman'.[32]

Following his release, Montague abandoned his mercantile career and returned to England. As Dudley had died, he now lived mainly with Roger in London or at Rougham. Always easy-going, his last years passed quietly. 'I am a sort of strange fellow,' he wrote to their sister Ann in 1697, 'an honest, plain, rough fellow that am too old to mend, so my friends must take me as I am.' He died in 1709. Long terrified of being buried alive, he directed that his heart was to be removed half an hour before he was interred. According to a fanciful family legend, the heart, very much still alive, had jumped out of the dish the butler was holding.[33]

Roger's *Life* of his scholarly brother, John, was possibly an afterthought. It conveys admiration for his brother's spectacular academic achievements, though with little of the warmth that characterizes the other *Lives*. And Roger did not hide the fact that his life had often been deeply unhappy.

---

[30] *Lives*, ii.242–6.   [31] Chan, *Life*, 191–2; *Lives*, ii.68–9, 142–3, 159.
[32] *Lives*, ii.244–5; Grassby, *English Gentleman*, 59, 222–3.
[33] *Lives*, ii.143, iii.303, 318–19; BL Add. MS 32500, f.170.

Roger described John as 'a martyr to study', and he appears as a tragi-comic caricature of the archetypal academic. Born in 1645, he was a reserved, studious, and hyper-conscientious child, with 'a non-natural gravity which, in youths, is seldom a good sign'. Excelling at school, he proceeded to Cambridge in 1661 and was elected a Fellow five years later. His formidable command of Latin, Greek, and Hebrew led to his appointment as Professor of Greek in 1672. Dissatisfied with the intellectual calibre of his colleagues at Jesus, he migrated to Trinity, where he was elected Master in 1677, at the age of only 32. Roger proudly recorded all these achievements, while not concealing many less flattering details. Roger himself, as a student, had not enjoyed sharing a chamber with John as his tutor. John had resented his presence and ignored his tutorial responsibilities, while Roger had cowered under his 'grave silent authority', never daring to join in student sports and pleasures.[34] He described John as physically weak and resolutely unathletic; 'his flesh was strangely flaccid and soft, his going weak and shuffling . . . his sleep seldom or never easy'. He could perform well on the public stage, at the Cambridge Acts, and was occasionally merry with young nobles and fellow commoners, but more often shunned company. He kept spiders in his room, in large jars, feeding them flies and tiny morsels of bread, and patiently observing their web-spinning techniques. John was always chronically anxious, an incurable valetudinarian, and frightened of the dark. He would hide under the bedclothes if alone, and once convinced himself there was a ghost in his room, which turned out to be moonlight shining on a towel hanging on the wall. He found his duties as Master of Trinity very stressful. Many of the Fellows disliked him, and the students resented him as 'officiously rigid and strict'. On one occasion, a stone came flying through the window of his dining chamber, narrowly missing his guests.[35]

John's few pleasures came from his books and his bond with Francis, the 'sheet anchor . . . of his life'. He liked to stay with his brother in London and at Wroxton, where the whole family often gathered in vacations. Towards the end of his life, seriously ill, he stayed for a month at Francis's 'country-house' in Hammersmith to recuperate. But back in Cambridge, he suffered a serious stroke, which left him partially paralysed and his speech badly affected. His last years were lonely and miserable, and though still Master of Trinity, he was rarely able to attend to college business. When he felt well enough, he would write highly emotional letters to Francis, expatiating on his brother's brilliance and 'his own wretched unworthiness'. He died at Cambridge in April 1683.[36] The books he had planned on ancient and modern philosophy never materialized, and he left strict instructions for all his writings and letters to be burnt. The family recognized that death had come as a happy release. Roger hoped, nonetheless, that his biography would commemorate 'a bright example of orthodox religion, learning, justice, and good will'. It also incidentally demonstrated once more the shining virtues of their 'best brother' Francis.[37]

---

[34] Millard, *John North*, 141 and *passim*; Chan, *Notes of Me*, 91–2.
[35] Millard, *John North*, 102–3, 109–11, 139, 141, 144–7.
[36] Millard, *John North*, 103–4, 139, 141–2, 152–6, 159, 162.   [37] *Lives*, ii.310–15, 340–2.

THE WOMEN OF THE FAMILY

It would never have occurred to Roger to write lives of the four sisters who survived to adulthood. Women could not pursue glittering careers, and the brothers do not appear to have had such intimate ties with their sisters as with each other. That would be unsurprising: the women had no shared professional interests and far less education, and marriage gave them very different responsibilities. It is clear, nonetheless, that they formed an integral and important part of the sibling network. Mary, the eldest, had married in 1660 and died only two years later, soon after giving birth. Roger was then still a child, but he remembered that his brother Francis had been 'as much in love with her, as was lawful for a brother to love a sister'. It is not hard to see why, for Mary had shared many of his natural gifts. Blessed with high intelligence and a prodigious memory, she would divert her sisters and other young women, busy with their needles, with detailed summaries of the romances popular in such circles, even the speeches and letters they contained, for hours together. She had also formed a female 'order' among the 'lady wits' of her acquaintance, fashioning emblems for them to wear with the motto 'Autarches, in Greek characters, which signified self-sufficient.' In another age, Mary would surely have gone far; but when she married, 'the order all at once melted to nothing'.[38]

Christian, the second sister, married Sir George Wenyeve of Brettenham, Suffolk, in 1665. She remains a rather shadowy figure, though the family letters provide a few clues to the couple's low profile. Wenyeve was considered tight-fisted and inhospitable. Roger was furious in 1682 when he heard that Sir George had helped himself to moneys meant for his daughter Nancy, whom her grandmother had raised. It was a foul trick, he raged. He was furious again when Sir George refused to take in their orphaned nephew Charles, and grumbled that the whole family would be shamed if it failed to provide for a sickly child in need.[39] The episode helps explain his gratitude and relief when Ann proved more obliging. But there was no open breach. In 1692, Roger remarked that a journey his brother-in-law was planning would take him past Brettenham, and added sardonically, 'I know Sir George will pour out his one bottle to your health.'[40] Wenyeve had a large family and a modest house, so his parsimony may have been prudent. And in 1686, as we will see, he and his wife did take in her sister Elizabeth at a critical juncture in her life, and looked after her well.[41]

The two youngest sisters, Ann and Elizabeth, are much better documented, and in both cases their brother Francis played a decisive role in their lives. Their father had set aside some outlying estates to be sold to raise portions for them of £1,500 apiece, but there were no suitors in sight. It was Francis who in 1672 found a husband for Elizabeth from among his legal connections. Sir Robert Wiseman, a

---

[38] Chan, *Life*, 27. In 1740, the work's first editor, Roger's son Montagu, chose to dilute the passage hinting at an almost incestuous passion: *Lives,* i.45–6.

[39] BL, Add. MS 32500, fos. 58, 93-v.   [40] *Lives*, iii.230–1.

[41] BL, Add.MS 32500, f.162; Mary Chan, ed., *Life into Story. The Courtship of Elizabeth Wiseman* (Aldershot, 1998), 22–3, 37.

civil lawyer, was already 'an old man, but very rich, and withal a most just and good-natured person'. It was also Francis who advanced the bride's portion. Instead of a jointure, Wiseman would only commit himself to leave her double the portion should she be left a widow, though he hinted there would be more. While hardly an ideal match, the couple lived happily together in Chelsea, and kept in close touch with the rest of the family. When Francis died, Elizabeth and her husband took in his orphaned daughter, and found her a good school. And when Sir Robert died childless in 1684, he more than honoured his promise by leaving Elizabeth a huge fortune of £20,000.[42]

Ann proved more difficult to settle, for she 'had, in that respect, some disadvantage'. She was plain and totally lacking in self-confidence. Already in her thirties, living alone in the country, she had few pleasures or prospects. Francis came to her rescue by persuading their parents to let her live with him and his wife in London. And as she appeared unlikely to marry, he persuaded his father to give her the modest fortune that would have been her portion, expediting the process by offering to buy the estates that had been set aside for this purpose. So Ann moved to London, living with her brother rent-free. Before long, he had also found her a prospective marriage partner: Robert Foley, son and heir of Robert Foley of Stourbridge, ironmonger to the navy. Once immensely rich, the Foley family's affairs had become hopelessly entangled, and the elder Robert thought an influential legal friend, close to the court, could prove a valuable asset. Francis negotiated a good settlement, and took on the tricky task of persuading the young man to accept a plain bride who was fifteen years his senior. He proved predictably reluctant until he grasped that his father's 'negligence, sottishness, and desperate projects' were threatening to ruin his family, whereupon he accepted the proposal with relief. Francis organized a grand wedding in London in 1674, and boarded the couple in his house for several years. He and Dudley advanced the young man's career, and handled the hugely complex administration of the older Foley's estate when he died. The couple, moreover, 'lived many years very well together'; they had numerous children, and in the event, Ann outlived her husband.[43]

The *Lives* are most informative on the relationships between Francis North and his brothers, with much less on the other sibling relationships. Family letters fill in some of the gaps and they also furnish valuable information on the women, especially Ann. Her elder sister Mary wrote to her frequently in 1660, attempting to boost her low self-esteem. She emphasized how much she valued and missed Ann's company, adding on one occasion that she had been invited to a christening, 'but wanting you I would not go'. In another letter, she rallied Ann over her mortification at being unable to attract men. She should rate herself more highly, Mary retorted, and not trouble herself over men, for 'the general part of that sex is so fickle that their friendship (much less their love) is not worth whistling after'.[44] Years later, however, Ann, now married, came to play an important role in the family's affairs. When Francis died, his brothers faced the problem of where to place

[42] Chan, *Life*, 192, 217; Grassby, *English Gentleman*, 63–5.   [43] Chan, *Life*, 192–4.
[44] BL, Add. MS 32500, fos. 1, 4, 5, 8.

his orphaned children, especially his wayward younger son, Charles. They begged Ann to take him in at Stourbridge, mother and educate him, and try to keep him out of trouble. They promised to cover the costs, and couched their appeals in almost obsequious language. When she agreed, their gratitude was fulsome. A few years later, they begged her to take in the orphaned daughter of their eldest brother Charles, Lord North, and were again hugely grateful when she reluctantly agreed.[45] Ann discharged her responsibilities conscientiously. In return, she felt entitled a few years later to call on Roger and Montague to help launch her own son Dudley into a commercial career. They provided advice and information on a range of options, and the young man sailed for Aleppo in 1699 with assistance from both uncles. The two brothers maintained a very friendly correspondence with Ann for the rest of their lives.[46]

Several of the other nephews and nieces turned out less well. Roger's nephew and namesake, the younger son of Sir Dudley the merchant, presented the toughest challenge. A compulsive womanizer, greedy, foul-mouthed, and arrogant, he was judged 'not fit for a civil family in any respect'. Even so, his uncles did all they could to support and guide him. They paid for his cure when he contracted venereal disease, and helped him even after his mother had cast him off for marrying a 'poxed whore' and abandoning his career. 'I never saw such a creature since I was born,' Roger wrote despairingly to Ann in 1707, 'so void of capacity and devious to vice.' Yet the young man was able to continue sponging off his relations. Their patience reflected the powerful affection they still felt for a brother who had died over fifteen years earlier.[47] None of the nephews inherited the ability or drive of the previous generation, or their fraternal spirit.

The half-glimpsed heroine of the *Lives* is the siblings' mother, Lady Anne. The letters confirm her central role in sustaining the bonds between her children. Roger began work on a joint biography of his parents, and his fragmentary text paints her in glowing colours. His father's parental role, he remarked in a Dickensian turn of phrase, had 'consisted chiefly in the gravity and decorum of his comportment'. He had provided his sons with some basic tuition in logic and metaphysics before they entered university, but Roger remembered him as remote and demanding; his 'humour was to be very tyrannical and vindictive'. Lady Anne, by contrast, was a loving and tireless mother, and an efficient manager of the household's strained finances. There 'never was such an example in the world as our mother', he wrote to his sister Ann in 1689. Her parenting had been 'severe but tender'. It was certainly a tough love; she would beat the children to stop them crying and break their stubborn spirit, and then demand to be thanked. But she could also be familiar, taught them to read, tended their cuts and bruises, and told them stories. She had needed a 'heart of brass', he reflected, to raise her huge family, and she had worked

[45] BL, Add. MS 32500, fos. 86, 88, 90, 91, 93, 96, 105, 110, 162–3.

[46] *Lives*, iii.245–6; BL, Add. MS 32500, fos. 175–6, 178, 182, 184; Add. MS 32501, fos. 15, 18, 22 and *passim*. But on Dudley Foley see also Grassby, *English Gentleman*, 116–17.

[47] *Lives*, iii.256–7; BL, Add. MS 32501, fos. 15, 22, 25, 27–8, 39, 46; Grassby, *English Gentleman*, 216–18.

like a lion. At the same time, she had been secretary, accountant, and nurse to a husband who was crippled for years by the stone.[48] Lady Anne had also built up a stock from her own small savings to help her sons launch their careers. It was her money that enabled Francis and Roger to buy their first law books when they entered the Middle Temple, and she found another £60 to help Dudley set up in Smyrna. It was also Lady Anne who had found Francis a wife. And many years later, when she learned that John was desperately ill at Cambridge, she descended on the college and took over his nursing care, being in experience 'more than a match for a college of physicians'.[49] Most important of all, over many years Lady Anne constantly reinforced the bonds between siblings who were living far apart and differed widely in age. She wrote to them weekly, and expected prompt replies. Her surviving letters supply family news on health, grandchildren's progress, clothes, and accounts of local events and people. She loved to have her children and their families to stay at Kirtling and later, in her widowed years, at her home at Tostock, near Bury St Edmunds. She even took in Francis's two small orphaned boys in 1678, though she found them exhausting. And in September 1680, only months before her death, we find her writing to her daughter Ann that John had just left but that she still had four of his brothers under her roof. Her only regret was that Ann and her husband were not there too.[50]

SIBLING RIVALRY: CHARLES VERSUS THE REST

The conspicuously missing figure in the *Lives* is Charles, the eldest son, who inherited the title as Lord North in 1677. Why, in a family so tight-knit, was there such a rift between the head and all other members? Politics provides one part of the answer. Charles attached himself to the Whig party, stoutly defending Titus Oates, fabricator of the Popish Plot, while his brothers were strong Tories.[51] But tensions had developed much earlier, and were primarily personal. At one level, Charles's siblings were typically resentful younger brothers. When Roger described how John, as a student, had been obliged to live on a pittance, he added sourly that 'more he did not expect, knowing that the hereditary honour must devour the fat of the land'. In part, the sibling bond sprang from their shared resentment at Charles's failure to take on his responsibilities. He had repeatedly refused to deliver even a farthing of the modest annuities he was supposed to pay. Roger recalled that Ann 'had a great dread of being left to any dependence on her elder brother', and Dudley thought that Charles would have done very little for any of his sisters, 'had they come to his care'.[52] Charles appears to have been eager to assert his status and rights as heir while shrugging off his obligations. We should remember, of course, that he

---

[48] Chan, *Life*, 11; *Notes of Me*, 79–82; *Lives*, iii.84–6; Millard, *John North*, 101; BL. Add. MS 32500, f.93.

[49] Chan, *Life*, 25, 209–10; *Lives*, ii.37; Millard, *John North*, 153–4; *Notes of Me*, 94.

[50] Chan, *Life*, 217; *Lives*, iii.211–20, 284–6; BL, Add. MS 32500, fos. 17–44 *passim*.

[51] *Lives*, ii.230; *Calendar of State Papers, Domestic, 1682*, 461.

[52] Millard, *John North*, 103; BL, Add. MS 32500, f.110; Add. MS 32501, f.130v.

did not inherit his title and estate until 1677, and had limited resources to help his younger brothers when they were building their careers. Roger addressed the family tensions in his life of Francis, in a section that was omitted when the work was substantially remodelled and published in 1740 by his son. He insisted that Francis had always tried to maintain a civil and respectful relationship with his elder brother, had often lent him money, and had provided legal advice to him and his wife. Charles would have felt mortified at having to borrow from a younger brother, and he and his wife claimed to be dissatisfied with Francis's legal work, making damning comments which they 'blazoned all over the town'. Roger dismissed their complaints, insisting that Francis had simply refused to bend the law in their interest. Roger may have come closest to the heart of the matter by hinting in discreet language at what we would call a clash of outsized egos. He observed that the 'elder brother (as the use is) thought himself so much superior... that he treated him [Francis] superciliously, which the other, having no low conceit of himself... could not well digest'. Roger considered Charles's behaviour 'bizarre' and irrational. The only extenuation he could offer was the malign influence of Charles's wife, an ambitious woman, who did her best to sow discord between the brothers, 'to hold the dominion more entire to herself'. With that reflection, he consigned the family rift to 'eternal oblivion', where his editor hoped to leave it.[53]

Though Charles never set out his own case on paper, the surviving evidence supports the impression of haughty selfishness. When their mother died, in 1681, she left all her movable property at Kirtling to her younger children, naming Roger as sole executor. Charles demanded that everything they wanted must be removed within a week of the funeral, after which he forbade them entry to the house. Roger was detained by professional commitments, so Dudley spent several hectic days 'taking down, sorting, disposing and contriving packs' of goods, including furniture and brewing vessels. Neighbours gazed in wonder at his feverish activity. Even so, Charles arrived before he had finished, which triggered fierce arguments and a comically fraught night, when the pair were forced to share the only bed still remaining in the house.[54] They were to clash again on several later occasions. Dudley viewed his brother with open contempt, and the king shared his opinion, dubbing Charles 'the one fool in the North family'.[55]

The most serious clash between Charles and his siblings is totally absent from the *Lives*. At its centre was their widowed sister Elizabeth, whose immense fortune had predictably soon attracted a throng of fortune hunters. Among them was Robert Spencer, a cousin of the Earl of Sunderland, secretary of state to James II. Charles North set out to promote this match, hoping by it to ingratiate himself at court. He devised ways to bring Elizabeth and Spencer together on several occasions, sometimes by trickery, and eventually contrived to have them locked in a room alone together. Spencer seized the chance to press his suit, and emerged claiming they had agreed to marry. Charles and his wife insisted they had then witnessed a verbal contract. Elizabeth vehemently denied any such agreement, and turned in

53 Chan, *Life*, 161–4.   54 *Lives*, ii.172–3.
55 Grassby, *English Gentleman*, 220; Chan, *Life*, 163–4; *Lives*, ii.233–4.

distress to her other brothers for help.[56] A fierce struggle ensued, lasting from September to December 1686, documented in a stream of letters and memoranda probably intended to support legal proceedings. Elizabeth had a less firm character than her siblings and admitted frankly that her 'brains . . . at best are not good', which left her vulnerable. It is just possible that Charles believed the match would be in her interests, but his main concern was to promote his own and assert his role and rights as head of the family. He repeatedly drew attention to his position as the 'elder brother to whom by God and nature the love and care of the family is in trust'.[57] He denounced his surviving brothers (Dudley, Montague, and Roger) as 'villains' for helping Elizabeth fend off Spencer's advances, and railed at his sister for her 'damned usage' of her suitor. 'Your younger brothers lead you by the nose,' he complained, 'making you forswear what you love. Vengeance will follow such barbarism.'[58] Charles clung to the fiction that Elizabeth really wanted the match to go ahead, and was only held back by her brothers. That was absurd in the light of her repeated expressions of loathing for Spencer and the actions she took to avoid him. If he ever came near her again, she vowed at one point, 'I'll spit in his beastly face.' And Charles found his insistence on his status as family head cast back in his teeth. 'Brother,' she wrote, 'I thought I might have expected protection from you and not ruin.'[59] Charles tried to silence his brothers with a flurry of promises and threats. If they cooperated, Sunderland would secure a viscountcy for Dudley and a title for Roger; if they persisted in their obstructive course, they would face the anger and vengeance of the king. His efforts failed. His brothers viewed him with contempt, and Roger dismissed him as 'Lord 0' (i.e. Nought).[60] But they feared that Elizabeth might be forcibly abducted, so on their advice she retreated from London and found refuge at Brettenham, sheltered by Christian and her husband. In London, her brothers advised, she would be safe only if 'surrounded by women relations as well as men'.[61] The contest ended with a suit in the Court of Arches, where Elizabeth triumphed and Spencer and Charles were forced to withdraw their claims.[62] Charles had failed either to get his way or impose his authority as head of the family. His siblings had stood firm. This is the only episode in which we have Charles's case spelled out in his own words, and they do nothing to enhance his image.

The following year, Elizabeth married William Paston, Earl of Yarmouth, a marriage that was to last over forty years. It sounds a happy outcome, and Elizabeth was delighted when she became pregnant, in her mid-forties. Pleading that she was 'altogether a novice' in such matters, she persuaded her sister Ann to be with her when the time came, as 'one of my greatest comforts'. They enjoyed a warm relationship, and Ann sometimes stayed at her sister's town house in Soho Square even when the couple were away on their estate in Norfolk.[63] But Elizabeth's story was to end less well, for Yarmouth was a gambler and addicted to wildly speculative

---

[56] Chan, *Life into Story*, 23–7.   [57] Ibid., 56, 60.   [58] Ibid., 14, 21–2, 49–50, 56–7.
[59] Ibid., 47–8, 60, 85.   [60] Ibid., 13, 21, 38, 40, 44–5, 76–7.
[61] Ibid., 28, 33–4, 38, 80, 86.   [62] Ibid., 97–100.
[63] BL, Add. MS 32500, fos. 156–7; Add. MS 32501, fos. 89, 96, 98, 100–1, 105.

ventures. He squandered the huge dowry she had brought, and eventually had to sell or mortgage most of his lands. Moreover, Jacobite sympathies landed him in the Tower for a time, and when he died, two years after his wife, he was still deeply in debt.[64]

Relations between Charles and his brothers always remained tense. The Revolution of 1688 brought him closer to those now in power, and left his siblings exposed. Dudley was soon targeted by Whigs looking for revenge against a Tory hated for his role in the Rye House Plot trials. Charles called on Roger one day, unexpectedly, to warn that unless Dudley appeased his enemies he would be 'infallibly ruined'. Roger retorted that his brother had committed no crime and would refute any charges, and Charles left in high dudgeon. It is possible that he had come in good faith, as he claimed, but it is hardly surprising that Roger suspected his motives. In the event, Dudley emerged unscathed from a parliamentary grilling.[65] His widow was later pursued by his former enemies, but Roger and Montague were able 'to vindicate his honour' in court.[66]

Charles died in January 1691, and despite the years of bitter rancour he named Roger and Dudley as guardians of his three young children. The young heir, William, was not quite 12 and the estate was in poor condition. Dudley died a few months later, which left Roger to shoulder the burden alone. He protected the children's interests with scrupulous care. He saved William from being inveigled into a rash marriage while still in his teens, and did his best to retrench the estate finances despite the young man's spendthrift ways. Headstrong, selfish, and arrogant, the youngster proved difficult to handle, and in 1697, Roger thought it best to let him go abroad, to keep him out of more trouble. William went on to a military career under Marlborough, though it ended abruptly on the Hanoverian succession. A committed Jacobite, he died at Madrid in 1734.[67] Roger enjoyed a much warmer relationship with William's sister, Dudleya, who shared his musical and intellectual interests.[68]

Roger North's *Lives* provide a remarkably rich and vivid depiction of sibling relationships. They are, of course, politically partisan and idealized. Roger worshipped his 'best brother', and offered a sanitized account of his political career. He admired Dudley and respected John. Writing long after their deaths, he looked back on their years together with deep nostalgia. They had 'loved and lived', he recalled with yearning, 'in exquisite unanimity and harmony; which was, upon earth, too much of happiness to have long continuance'.[69] In reality, there had of course been shadows, as even the *Lives* concede. Roger acknowledged his hurt at the semi-humorous slights Francis had inflicted on him over many years. He did not conceal Dudley's swearing or temper, and commented tartly that the huge house his brother had bought and furnished near Goldsmiths' Hall, costing over £4,000,

---

[64] *ODNB*, Elizabeth Wiseman and Robert Paston, 2nd Earl of Yarmouth; *Lives*, ii.235–6, iii.224–5.

[65] *Lives*, ii.227–30; Grassby, *English Gentleman*, 141–4.   [66] *Lives*, ii.190–2.

[67] *Lives*, iii.232–44, 277, 295–8; BL, Add MS 32500, f.162.   [68] *Lives*, iii.259–63.

[69] *Lives*, ii.195.

was a manifestation of foolish 'pride and vanity'. He recalled that John had 'loved between jest and earnest, to tell people of their faults', and did not hide his unpopularity at Cambridge. Other tensions between the brothers are mentioned in passing, and Roger once remarked wryly on the 'the Norths' infirmity, passion'.[70] More important, perhaps, is the sense that Roger always felt overshadowed, almost overwhelmed, by the brilliance and self-assurance of his brother Francis. He was devastated by his brother's death, and felt that his own career and life were effectively over. Yet in reality he was a very able lawyer (and was to become a significant commentator on music and architecture), and he soon found, to his surprise, that his legal career still prospered. It was only after his brother's death that he found the will, or confidence, to marry and establish a household of his own. Roger was not one of the 'victims' of primogeniture, like so many of the younger brothers who feature in this book, but he remained psychologically dependent as long as Francis lived. He acknowledged that in his brother's shadow he had always felt less than fully adult, still in effect 'in my minority, having scarce a character of my own'. Any success could be attributed by the world, and by Roger himself, to his brother's support, patronage, and guidance; any failure was his own. Only after Francis died did he achieve full maturity and social independence.[71]

Yet these shadows do not invalidate the overall picture of sibling intimacy, a picture that is confirmed by the voluminous family correspondence. Brothers and sisters maintained a lifelong bond of mutual affection and support, evolving over time in a network that extended with varying degrees of intimacy to their spouses and several of their nephews and nieces. Francis had taken on the role usually played by the heir, supporting his brothers and brothers-in-law, finding husbands for his sisters, and hosting them all at his country house. Such a role demanded a huge investment of time as well as money, and they repaid him with the gratitude, admiration, deference, and companionship he sought. After his death, Roger and Dudley emerged as the leaders of the family, acting as guardians for his children, and looking after the estate. The longest survivors—Roger, Montague, Ann, and Elizabeth—maintained a warm correspondence to the end of their lives, with Roger providing a stream of personal and legal advice and assistance to his numerous nephews and nieces. He was devoted to his extended family, and loved their company best. Finding in October 1691 that none of his close kin were in town, he wailed that 'I am as solitary in London as in a wilderness, like a jackdaw among rooks'. On a later visit he wrote to Ann, in a vivid image, that he had been 'like an earwig upon a hot shovel, perpetually running about' on family business.[72]

Roger saw the family's story as a triumphant record of solidarity and support. Only Charles had remained remote and aloof, despite the fact that, as Roger insisted, they had 'kept fair with him, till he himself made it impossible to converse'.[73] Charles clearly resented the success of his next brother, who had

---

[70] Chan, *Life*, 166; *Lives*, ii.193–4, 220, 248–9; Millard, *John North*, 142; BL, Add. MS 32501, f.18.
[71] *Notes of Me*, 50–1, 240.   [72] *Lives*, iii.227; BL, Add. MS 32501, f.80 and *passim*.
[73] BL, Add. MS 32501, f.18.

outstripped him in wealth, status, and influence. Francis had taken over his role as the family's head, and the other siblings had all made their way in the world without any assistance from the heir. Contemporaries would have found plenty both to admire and deplore in the family's story. The Norths reflected the ideals of brotherly and sisterly affection, but also, and in extreme form, the familiar tensions between an heir and his siblings.

13

Conclusion

Social relationships are naturally shaped by their cultural, social, religious, and economic contexts. Many family relationships transcend time and place but others, once commonplace, now appear strange to us. The family relationships of early modern England offer us both parallels and sharp contrasts, and reveal the complexity and diversity of the age.[1]

Written records can never provide a full picture of family relationships centuries ago. What survives is heavily weighted towards men in the upper levels of society, and even the letters and personal writings of the most literate men and women were moulded by the cultural conventions of their age. The effect is particularly obvious in courtship letters, where suitors were expected to express devotion in absurdly extravagant language, while the women would respond with decorum and reserve.[2] Similarly, an engaging letter in 1651 from the youthful Roger Fleming to an older brother takes on a different meaning when we discover that he had lifted most of it from a printed text.[3] The voices of ordinary men and women, much harder to hear, often reach us only through legal documents, mediated by notaries.

Throughout the early modern period, contemporaries saw the family as the bedrock of political and social order. Its basic shape survived little changed, despite huge demographic, economic, religious, and political upheavals. Male supremacy was never seriously challenged. Yet the upheavals did have an impact on family structures and relationships. One consequence of rapid inflation and falling real wages was to make ordinary families more dependent on the wife's own earnings. This was a reality ignored by the domestic conduct books, which reflected the values and circumstances of the middling sort and above. A parallel inflation of dowries imposed a heavy burden on the gentry and middling sort, allowing fewer daughters to marry, and the wealthy became increasingly reluctant to slice off outlying lands to provide for younger sons. That helps explain why the plight of younger brothers and the broader issue of primogeniture became such heated issues in this period. Sibling rivalries were fuelled by increasingly severe structural tensions.

We have seen that two principles shaped the ideal sibling relationship. The invocation of mutual love, respect, and support was complemented and qualified

[1] Keith Wrightson, 'Mutualities and Obligations: Changing Social Relationships in Early Modern England', *Proceedings of the British Academy*, 139 (2006), 161.
[2] See e.g. *The Diary and Letter Book of the Rev. Thomas Brockbank 1671–1709*, ed. Richard Trappes-Lomax, Chetham Society, New Series, 89 (1930), 184–6; *The Courtship Narrative of Leonard Wheatcroft*, ed. George Parfitt and Ralph Houlbrooke (Reading, 1986).
[3] *Flemings in Oxford*, i.18–19.

by respect for birth order and gender. Male primogeniture was dominant among the elite, and it influenced most families with landed property. The two principles came together in the concept, most evident in the middling and upper levels, of the family as a collective enterprise with every member committed to its success and the preservation of its good name, and bound by reciprocal moral obligations. The Stouts and the Norths (with one notable exception) provide striking examples. With support mostly hierarchical in the higher levels of society, heirs were expected to provide financial support, career assistance, and help in finding a spouse, and expected service, deference, and gratitude in return. Patterns were more fluid in the lower levels of society, with birth order less significant as we descend the social ladder. But as Keith Wrightson has stressed, 'mutualities and obligations' were key to family and many other social relationships in this period.[4]

Most contemporaries viewed brotherly and sisterly love as natural, even if many fell short in their own behaviour, and they were shocked by behaviour that flouted it. While less was owed to half-siblings, respect and the recognition of kinship were still expected. Anthony Wood was disgusted when a niece went ahead with her wedding on the same day that her half-brother died, 'showing herself thereby', he fumed, 'either a grand fool or a grand beast'.[5] Flagrant breaches of the sibling ideal have left us a substantial body of material, both literary and archival. Yet we also have plentiful evidence of close and enduring bonds at all levels of society. Many siblings took in a nephew or niece, to rescue an orphan or relieve pressure on parents in difficulties. At most levels of society it also made sense to value close kin (including brothers- and sisters-in-law) as a potential safety net in the event of sudden death, illness, or financial ruin. And for those able to sustain close ties, in person or by letter, the sibling bond could prove crucial for emotional well-being.

The virtual disappearance of primogeniture makes it harder for us to appreciate now the strength of its hold and its impact on family relationships. The landed classes valued it as the best way to transmit their estates intact to the next generation. Men could disinherit an unsatisfactory eldest son, but few did so, and they often faced disapproval from their friends. Even the beneficiaries might be troubled by their unexpected good fortune. A diarist recorded the remarkable case of a Mr Glanville, who inherited an estate only because his father had cast off a wastrel elder brother. Glanville occupied the estate for some years, always uneasy at this disruption of the natural order. Eventually, convinced that his brother was now fully reformed, he decided to restore it to the 'proper' heir. His brother was invited to dinner, and 'the last dish was the writings, which conveyed the estate to him'.[6] Equally striking was the behaviour of Sir Thomas Wentworth in 1619. Childless after eight years of marriage, Wentworth sought to preserve the family line by negotiating a match for his younger brother William, and offered to settle £2,000 a year on him and the prospective bride. Should he unexpectedly father any children

<hr>

[4] Wrightson, 'Mutualities and Obligations', *passim*.
[5] Wood, *Life and Times*, iii.194.
[6] J. C. Hodgson, ed., 'The Diary of John Thomlinson', *Six North Country Diaries*, Surtees Society, 118 (1910), 110–11.

of his own, at some later date, he trusted that William, as 'an honest man', would return these lands to the heirs of the senior line.[7]

Yet we have seen that primogeniture was also highly contentious. Younger sons faced the prospect of a painful fall in status, and only a minority proved able to claw their way back, through careers in business or the professions. Many others, raised in the comfortable and leisured culture of the gentry, could not stomach the demands and discipline of trade or the professions, and dropped out. That intensified the fraught issue of reciprocity. How far were the obligations of each party conditional on the other honouring his or her own obligations? Many heirs viewed their siblings as lazy and feckless, while their younger brothers viewed them as mean and arrogant. Both parties tended to see themselves as the injured party, and both often had plausible grounds for doing so. Similar tensions are visible among the middling sort. Samuel Pepys felt responsible for the welfare of his siblings and assumed the right to order their affairs. While grateful for his support, they resented their dependence and his overbearing manner. Nevertheless, the fact that Pepys took his responsibilities so seriously, despite feeling little affection for his siblings and resenting his burden, underlines the strength of social and cultural conventions.

The tensions inherent in primogeniture were exacerbated by the social, economic, and demographic changes of the period. Marriage settlements often limited the ability of wealthy landowners to alienate their land even if they wanted to do so. The rapid expansion of the gentry increased competition among younger brothers for the limited supply of acceptable employment opportunities. While the royal court expanded, aristocratic and episcopal households were shrinking. Until the later seventeenth century, a military career had to be pursued overseas, and naval careers became acceptable only towards the end of the period. Many viewed trade and the professions as beneath them. All this fuelled public debate over primogeniture, a debate intensified by the upheavals of the civil wars. In 1648, the radical chaplain Hugh Peter could justify Pride's Purge, the military coup, by explaining that the younger brother (the army) had forced open the door kept locked by the oppressive older brother (parliament) to free their imprisoned mother (the nation).[8] It is striking too that younger brothers, such as the Leveller John Lilburne, played a significant role in the radical movements of the era. Resentful at their reduced status and with the self-assurance that reflected their birth and upbringing, they made articulate and forceful leaders. In the mid-1650s, one critic urged Cromwell's Parliament to provide relief for younger brothers. He complained that many were reduced to beggary, and that those who turned to crime and died on the gallows brought shame on their families as well as themselves. Annuities, even if paid, were never sufficient for them to marry. Moreover, sex-starved younger brothers must either practise celibacy or campaign for 'the public toleration of stews'—a suggestion that Oliver Cromwell was unlikely to welcome. The author denounced primogeniture as a hateful 'grand monopoly', and called on Parliament to sweep

---

[7] J. P. Cooper, ed., *Wentworth Papers 1597–1628*, Camden Society, 4th series (1973), 120–1.
[8] *A Declaration, Collected out of the Journalls of Both Houses of Parliament*, 3 (13–20 December 1648), 20.

it away or establish plantations overseas where younger brothers could 'establish decrees and constitutions of our own'. But Francis Osborn, another disgruntled younger brother, observed sourly that any change was unlikely as long as parliaments consisted mainly of elder sons.[9] This was a debate, moreover, that extended far beyond the landed classes. The Fifth Monarchists, a radical movement in the 1650s, were mostly small tradesmen and craftsmen, and the desperate rising they staged shortly after the Restoration was led by a cooper. Yet in their manifesto the rebels identified primogeniture as 'one grand branch of tyranny'. Elder brothers, they declared, were like kings within the family, and 'younger brethren are slaves and subjects'. Gerrard Winstanley, the Digger, returned repeatedly to the image of the privileged and oppressive elder brother, and advocated communal ownership of property as a solution to inequality.[10] A generation later the merchant Thomas Tryon, the son of a tiler and plasterer, thought that children should inherit equal shares, regardless of birth order and gender. His suggestion was predictably ignored, along with his teetotal and vegetarian ideas.[11]

A demographic slowdown in the later seventeenth century, coupled with expanding opportunities in the army, navy, commerce, and colonial administration, may have taken some heat out of the issue in the eighteenth century. Moreover, new forms of strict settlement, through the creation of a trust, became dominant from around 1700 and for the first time guaranteed some fixed provision for the daughters and younger sons the couple might produce.[12] But the fundamentals remained unchanged. Or did they? Some recent scholars, both historians and anthropologists, have taken a different view. In a study focusing on the gentry of Georgian England, Amy Harris has argued that 'siblinghood's friendship was meant be an alliance of equals'.[13] Contemporaries certainly idealized sibling love and emotional intimacy, but the distribution of property and power remained far from equal, and this inevitably shaped affective relationships too, as Jane Austen's novels remind us.[14] Amy Harris's thesis parallels a broader European history of kinship sketched out by Christopher Johnson, David Sabean, and their colleagues. They identify two major transformations, one late mediaeval, the other situated between the mid-eighteenth and mid-nineteenth centuries. The first, they suggest, witnessed a shift from a loose mediaeval 'lineage' pattern to one where land and power more often passed down through a single line, most commonly that of the eldest son. Heirs and their siblings now led very different lives, both emotionally and physically distant. By contrast, personal affection lay at the heart of the second

---

[9] Champianus Northtonus, *The Younger Brothers Advocate: or a line or two for Younger Brothers, with their Petition to the Parliament* (1655), 3, 5–7, 15–16 and *passim*. The bookseller George Thomason dated his copy 4 November 1654. *The Works of Francis Osborn, Esquire* (1682), Part II, 142.

[10] *A Door of Hope* (1661), 10; on Winstanley, see Chapter 1.

[11] Thomas Tryon, *Some Memoirs of the Life of Mr Tho. Tryon, late of London, Merchant* (1705), 7, 89–90.

[12] Lloyd Bonfield, *Marriage Settlements 1601–1740. The Adoption of the Strict Settlement.* (Cambridge, 1983), esp. 108–20.

[13] Amy Harris, *Siblinghood and Social Relations in Georgian England* (Manchester, 2012), 57.

[14] See, for example, the behaviour of John Dashwood and his wife towards his half-sisters in *Sense and Sensibility*.

'new kinship regime', dominant by 1800 and reflected in warm sibling ties and frequent intermarriage between cousins and other close kin. The material surveyed in this book (and others), however, is impossible to square with 'emotional indifference' as a central characteristic of the earlier period. Most of the mediaeval and early modern essays in the Johnson–Sabean collections focus on princely and aristocratic families, and on structures of inheritance and power.[15] This book has adopted a far wider social focus, from the landed gentry to the poor. It has also explored other important dimensions of sibling relationships, including the central issue of moral rights and responsibilities. And throughout the early modern period, long before the 'new kinship regime', we have repeatedly found strong emotional relationships between siblings, from love and care to rivalry and hatred. Landed, professional, and mercantile families saw no contradiction between the ideals of equality in love and inequality in wealth and status. Thomas Fuller observed succinctly on the eve of the civil war that a good father 'observeth gavelkind in dividing his affections, though not his estate. He loves them (though leaves them not) all alike'. Sir Henry Slingsby, addressing his two sons in 1658, explained that the elder would naturally inherit most of the estate, as 'the inordinate hope of my house', but assured Harry, his younger son, that he had 'ever been dear and near my heart since infancy'.[16]

As we have seen, primogeniture had diminishing sway as we descend the social ladder. Amy Erickson suggests a consensus in ordinary families that 'eldest sons ought to be privileged—but not too much'.[17] While land commonly passed to the eldest son, manorial customs often provided some protection for other children, and will-makers were guided by equity as well as birth order and gender. Other siblings could expect to inherit money, movables, or livestock, and heirs were often required to pay significant annuities or lump sums out of their inheritance. Across society, moreover, it is clear that parental affection by no means always focused on the first-born son. Some parents loved the youngest child; some longed for a daughter; and others favoured the child whose temperament most resembled their own. Fathers and mothers sometimes favoured different children, and preferences might alter over time. Daughters were brought up to accept their subordinate status, which severely limited their freedom, education, and life opportunities. Nonetheless, as we have seen, many proved able to play active and important sibling roles, supporting both brothers and sisters. One major contrast with the present day is the demographic context: the likelihood of one parent dying while the children were still young, and the near-certainty that parents would lose at least some of their children. That raised the fraught

---

[15] Christopher H. Johnson and David Warren Sabean, eds, *Sibling Relations and the Transformation of European Kinship 1300–1900* (New York, 2011), Introduction and *passim*. Sophie Ruppel's essay in this collection, however, presents findings for seventeenth-century Germany much closer to my own. The Johnson–Sabean schema resembles in part Lawrence Stone's picture of the development of the family in *The Family, Sex and Marriage 1500–1800* (1977). See also Sabean, Simon Teuscher, and John Mathieu, eds, *Kinship in Europe: Approaches to Long-Term Development (1300–1900)* (New York, 2007).
[16] Thomas Fuller, *The Holy State* (1642), 12; Sir Henry Slingsby, *A Father's Legacy* (1658), 45, 52.
[17] Amy Louise Erickson, *Women and Property in Early Modern England* (1993), 77.

issue of remarriage and relations between step-parents and children, and between half- and step-siblings. Though far fewer parents now die young, these issues have obvious modern parallels through the high incidence of divorce. High mortality rates raised another issue, which, thankfully, has now almost vanished. When two or more children fell sick at the same time, which should receive most care? And when it seemed likely that not all would survive, which did parents most long to see live? Though much inevitably remains hidden, it is astonishing to find parents sometimes recording their feelings on such intensely personal matters. That they did so suggests their anguish at having to confront these issues, and a sense of guilt in owning their secret wishes.

As already noted, the demographic and economic changes of the early modern period impacted on both society and the family. The combination of rising population, inflation, falling real wages, and higher unemployment placed greater demands on the better-off. We have seen that kin settled in London often helped younger family members migrating to the capital. In the provinces, the destitute might tramp many miles to seek out a brother or sister, confident of receiving help. The creation of a nationwide system of poor relief tells us that the voluntary support of close kin and neighbours proved inadequate to cope with the scale of the problem. Yet the time it took for the new system to be fully implemented across the nation suggests that voluntary help remained important, even if it rarely entered the written record. It would be wrong, moreover, to focus only on financial issues. Support from close kin took a multitude of other forms, from physical protection to assistance at key points in the life cycle, from childbirth to courtship, marriage, sickness, and old age. Only rarely did such informal help enter the written record. The Lancashire apprentice Roger Lowe, for example, mentions helping his elder brother drive his livestock across country to a new farm, a task that would have involved no financial outlay but demanded considerable time and effort.[18] A multitude of similar examples must have gone unrecorded. We generally catch only fleeting glimpses of the sibling dynamics in ordinary families, and the sense of mutual responsibility that existed alongside personal affection, or even without it. In many families, sibling bonds proved of huge value at critical moments. Despite rivalries and tensions, the sibling relationship was recognized as important and rooted in nature. Contemporaries agreed on that, even if they often disagreed over their responsibilities and fell short in living up to them. It was left to every individual and family, and to preachers, playwrights, and later novelists, to address the issues and explore the emotions raised by the sibling tie.

---

[18] *The Diary of Roger Lowe of Ashton-in-Makerfield, Lancashire 1663–74*, ed. William L. Sachse (1938), 14, 83.

Select Bibliography

MANUSCRIPT SOURCES

Birmingham & Midland Society for Genealogy and Heraldry, Birmingham
Census of Lichfield carried out for Gregory King in 1695, transcript

Bodleian Library, Oxford
Rawlinson MS B382

Borthwick Institute, York
Diocese of York, Cause Papers, H 363, 1499, 4267, 4299, 4315, 4587

British Library
Add. MS 27440, Letterbook of Charles Allestree
Add. MS 28003–5 Oxinden papers
Add. MS 32500–1 North papers
Add. MS 44846 Letterbook of Sir Thomas Peyton
Add. MS 70231 Harley papers
Egerton MS 2715, 2717 Gawdy papers
Harley MS 1026 Diary and letterbook of Justinian Pagitt

Cambridge University Library
K6/33, Ely Diocesan papers

Guildhall Library, London
MS 9064–5 Commissary court act books and papers (now transferred to the London
   Metropolitan Archive)

Leicestershire and Rutland Record Office
ID 41/4, archdeaconry papers

The National Archives, Kew
SP12 and 16, State Papers, Domestic, Elizabeth, and Charles I

Oxfordshire Archives Office
Oxf. c12, archdeaconry papers

West Sussex Record Office
Ep.1/11/1, archdeaconry papers

PRIMARY PRINTED SOURCES

An Account of Many Remarkable Passages in the Life of Oliver Sansom (1710).
Adams, Thomas, *The Devills Banket* (1614).
Adventures by Sea of Edward Coxere, ed. E. H. W. Meyerstein (Oxford, 1945).

Agnew, Jean, ed., *The Whirlpool of Misadventures. Letters of Robert Paston, First Earl of Yarmouth 1663–1679*, Norfolk Record Society, 76 (2013).

Allen, Gemma, ed., *The Letters of Lady Anne Bacon*, Camden Society, 5th series, 44 (2014).

Allison, K. J., ed., 'An Elizabethan Village "Census"', *Bulletin of the Institute of Historical Research*, 36 (1963).

Anderson, R. C., ed., *The Book of Examinations and Depositions 1622–1644*, 4 vols, Southampton Record Society (1929–36).

Ap Robert, I., *The Younger Brother His Apology* ([St. Omer,] 1618).

The Autobiography and Correspondence of Sir Simonds D'Ewes, ed. J. O. Halliwell (1845).

The Autobiography of Alice Thornton, ed. Charles Jackson, Surtees Society, 62 (1873).

The Autobiography of Henry Newcome, ed. R. Parkinson, Chetham Society (1852), pp. 26–7.

The Autobiography of Leonard Wheatcroft of Ashover 1627–1706, ed. Dorothy Riden, Derbyshire Record Society, 20 (1993).

The Autobiography of Sir John Bramston, ed. Lord Braybrooke, Camden Society, OS, 32 (1845).

Autobiography of Thomas Raymond, ed. G. Davies, Camden Society, 3rd series, 28 (1917).

The Autobiography of William Stout of Lancaster 1665–1752, ed. J. D. Marshall (Manchester, 1967).

Axon, Ernest, ed., *Life of John Angier of Denton*, Chetham Society, NS, 97 (1937).

Bacon, Francis, *The Essays*, ed. John Pitcher (1985).

Bagley, J. J., ed., *The Great Diurnall of Nicholas Blundell of Little Crosby, Lancashire, 1702–1728*, 3 vols, Record Society of Lancashire and Cheshire (1968–72).

Bamford, Francis, ed., *A Royalist's Notebook. The Commonplace Book of Sir John Oglander Kt. of Nunwell* (1936).

Barclay, John, ed., *Some Account of the Life of Joseph Pike* (1837).

Bates Harbin, E. H., ed., *Quarter Sessions Records for the County of Somerset*, Somerset Record Society, 23–4, 28, 34 (1908–19).

Behn, Aphra, *The Works of Aphra Behn*, ed. Janet Todd (1992–6).

Bennett, J. E. H. and Dewhurst, J. C., eds, *Quarter Sessions Records for the County Palatine of Chester 1559–1760*, Record Society of Lancashire and Cheshire, 94 (1940).

Bennett, Kate, ed., *John Aubrey: Brief Lives* (Oxford, 2016).

Besse, Joseph, *The Sufferings of the Quakers*, 2 vols (1753).

Bettey, J. H., ed., *Calendar of the Correspondence of the Smyth Family of Ashton Court 1548–1642*, Bristol Record Society, 35 (1982).

Bewley, George, *A Narrative of the Christian Experiences of George Bewley* (Dublin, 1750).

The Bloody Murtherer, or the Unnatural Son his Just Condemnation (1672).

Blundell, Margaret, ed., *Cavalier. Letters between William Blundell and his Friends 1620–1698* (1933).

Blundell, Margaret, ed., *Blundell's Diary and Letter Book 1702–1728* (Liverpool, 1952).

Bruce, John, ed., *Liber Famelicus of Sir James Whitelocke*, Camden Society, OS, 70 (1858).

Burns, S. A. H., ed., *The Staffordshire Quarter Sessions Rolls, 1581–1606*, 5 vols, William Salt Archaeological Society (1931–40).

Bury, Samuel, *An Account of the Life and Death of Mrs Elizabeth Bury* (1720).

Chan, Mary, ed., *The Life of the Lord Keeper North* (Lewiston, New York, 1995).

Chan, Mary, ed., *Life into Story. The Courtship of Elizabeth Wiseman* (Aldershot, 1998).

Chandos, Cassandra, Duchess of, *The Continuation of the History of the Willoughby Family*, ed. A. C. Wood (Eton, Windsor, 1958).

The Christian Progress of that Ancient Servant . . . George Whitehead (1725).

The Chronicles of John Cannon, Excise Officer and Writing Master, 1684–1743, ed. John Money (Oxford, 2010).

Clarke, Samuel, *The Lives of Two and Twenty English Divines* (1660).

Clarkson, Laurence, *The Lost Sheep Found* (1660).

Cockburn, J. S., ed., *Calendar of Assize Records: Essex Indictments, Elizabeth I* (1978).

Cockburn, J. S., ed., *Calendar of Assize Records: Kent Indictments, Elizabeth I* (1979).

Cooper, J. P., ed., *Wentworth Papers 1597–1628*, Camden Society, 4th series, 12 (1973).

The Courtship Narrative of Leonard Wheatcroft, Derbyshire Yeoman, ed. George Parfitt and Ralph Houlbrooke (Reading, 1986).

Cross, Claire, ed., *The Letters of Sir Francis Hastings, 1574–1609*, Sussex Record Society, 69 (1969).

Cunnington, B. Howard, ed., *Records of the County of Wilts.* (Devizes, 1932).

Davies, G., ed., *Autobiography of Thomas Raymond and Memoirs of the Family of Guise of Elmore, Gloucestershire*, Camden Society, 3rd series, 28 (1917).

Davies, Richard, *An Account of the Convincement, Exercises, Services, and Travels of Richard Davies* (1794).

Dekker, Thomas, *The Witch of Edmonton*, ed. Etta Soiref Onat (New York, 1980).

The Diary and Autobiography of Edmund Bohun, Esq., ed. S. Wilton Rix (Beccles, 1853).

The Diary and Letter Book of the Rev. Thomas Brockbank 1671–1709, ed. Richard Trappes-Lomax, Chetham Society, NS, 89 (1930).

The Diary of a West Country Physician AD 1684–1726, ed. Edmund Hobhouse (Rochester, 1934).

The Diary of Bulstrode Whitelocke 1605–1675, ed. Ruth Spalding (Oxford, 1990).

The Diary of Edmund Harrold, Wigmaker of Manchester 1712–15, ed. Craig Horner (Aldershot, 2008).

'The Diary of Isaac Archer 1641–1700', in Matthew Storey, ed., *Two East Anglian Diaries, 1641–1729*, Suffolk Records Society, 36 (1994): 1–200.

Diary of John Rous, 1625–1642, ed. M. A. E. Green, Camden Society, OS, 66 (1856).

The Diary of Ralph Josselin, 1606–1683, ed. Alan Macfarlane (1976).

The Diary of Ralph Thoresby FRS, ed. Joseph Hunter, 2 vols (1830).

The Diary of Roger Lowe, of Ashton-in-Makerfield, Lancashire 1663–74, ed. William L. Sachse (1938).

The Diary of Samuel Pepys, ed. R. C. Latham and W. Matthews (1971–83).

The Diary of Sir Simonds D'Ewes (1622–1624), ed. Elisabeth Bourcier (Paris, 1974).

'The Diary of the Rev. John Thomlinson', ed. J. C. Hodgson, *Six North Country Diaries*, Surtees Society, 118 (1910): 64–167.

The Diary of Thomas Isham of Lamport, ed. Sir Gyles Isham (Farnborough, 1971).

'The Diary of William Coe 1693–1729', in Matthew Storey, ed., *Two East Anglian Diaries, 1641–1729*, Suffolk Records Society, 36 (1994): 201–80.

The Diary of William Lawrence, ed. G. E. Aylmer (Beaminster, 1961).

Dod, John, and Cleaver, Robert, *A Godly Forme of Household Government* (1612).

Doe, Charles, *A Collection of Experience of the Work of Grace* (1700).

A Door of Hope (1661).

Dugdale, Gilbert, *A True Relation of the Practices of Elizabeth Dugdale* (1604).

Dyke, Daniel, *The Mystery of Selfe-Deceiving* (1617).

'A Dyurnall, or Catalogue . . . by Adam Eyre', ed. H. J. Morehouse, *Yorkshire Diaries of the Seventeenth and Eighteenth Centuries*, Surtees Society, 65 (1875).

Earle, John, *Micro-cosmographie* (1628).

Edwards, Thomas, *Gangraena* (1646: facsimile edition, Exeter, 1977).

Emmison, F. G., ed., *Wills of the County of Essex (England). Volume 1, 1558–1565* (Washington, D.C., 1982).

Evans, Arise, *An Eccho to the Voice from Heaven* (1653).

Evans, Nesta, ed., *Wills of the Archdeaconry of Sudbury 1630–1635*, Suffolk Records Society, 29 (1987).

Fair Warning from Tyburn (1680).

'Family History begun by James Fretwell', ed. Charles Jackson, *Yorkshire Diaries of the Seventeenth and Eighteenth Centuries*, Surtees Society, 65 (1875): 162–243.

The Flemings in Oxford, ed. J. R. Magrath, Oxford Historical Society, 44, 62, 79 (1904–24).

Fletcher, John, *The Womans Prize: or the Tamer Tamed*, in Fredson Bowers, ed., *The Dramatic Works in the Beaumont and Fletcher Canon*, iv (Cambridge, 1979).

Fletcher, John, *The Elder Brother*, in Fredson Bowers, ed., *The Dramatic Works in the Beaumont and Fletcher Canon*, ix (Cambridge, 1994).

Fuller, Thomas, *The Holy State* (1642).

Gardiner, Samuel Rawson, ed., *Reports of Cases in the Courts of Star Chamber and High Commission*, Camden Society, NS, 39 (1886).

Gatley, D. A. et al., eds, 'The Stoke-upon-Trent Parish Listing, 1701', *Collections for a History of Staffordshire*, Staffordshire Record Society, 4th series, 16 (1994): 171–225.

Geninges, John, *The Life and Death of Mr Edmund Geninges* (St. Omers, 1614; facsimile reprint Menston, 1971).

Gilkes, R. K., ed., *The 'Bawdy Court' of Banbury. The Act Book of the Peculiar Court of Banbury 1625–1638*, Banbury Historical Society, 26 (1997).

Good Newes from all Quarters (1643).

Gouge, William, *Of Domesticall Duties* (1622).

Gough, Richard, *The History of Myddle*, ed. David Hey (Harmondsworth, 1981).

Guy, Nicholas, *Pieties Pillar* (1626).

Gwin, Thomas, *A Memorial of Anne Gwin* (1715).

Hardy, W. J. and Le Hardy, W., eds, *Hertfordshire County Records* (Hertford, 1905–57).

Hassell Smith. A. et al., eds, *The Papers of Nathaniel Bacon of Stiffkey*, 5 vols, Norfolk Record Society (1979–2010).

Heath, Helen Truesdell, ed., *The Letters of Samuel Pepys and his Family Circle* (Oxford, 1955).

Heywood, Oliver, *Autobiography, Diaries, Anecdote and Event Books*, ed. J. H. Turner (Brighouse and Bingley, 1881–5).

Heywood, Thomas, *The Phoenix of these late Times. Or the Life of Henry Welby* (1637).

Hinde, William, *A Faithfull Remonstrance of the Holy Life and Happy Death of Iohn Bruen* (1641).

Historical Manuscripts Commission. Series:
  9 *Salisbury*
  11 *Gawdy*
  13 *Capt. Stewart*
  23 *Cowper*
  24 *Rutland*
  32 *Fitzherbert*
  35 *Kenyon*
  39 *Eliot Hodgkin*
  52 *Frankland-Russell-Astley*
  53 *Montagu of Beaulieu*

The History of the Life of Thomas Ellwood, ed. C. G. Crump (1900).

Hobson, Joseph, ed., *Memoirs of the Life and Convincement of Benjamin Bangs* (1757).

Howell James, D. E., ed., *Norfolk Quarter Sessions Order Book 1650–1657*, Norfolk Record Society, 26 (1955).

Hughey, Ruth, ed., *The Correspondence of Lady Katherine Paston 1603–1627*, Norfolk Record Society, 14 (1941).

Hunnisett, R. F., ed., *Sussex Coroners' Inquests 1558–1603* (Kew, 1996).

Hunter, Michael and Gregory, Annabel, eds, *An Astrological Diary of the Seventeenth Century. Samuel Jeake of Rye 1652–1699* (Oxford, 1988).

Hutchinson, Lucy, *Memoirs of the Life of Colonel John Hutchinson*, ed. John Sutherland (Oxford, 1973).

Janeway, James, *Invisibles, Realities, Demonstrated in the Holy Life and Triumphant Death of Mr John Janeway* (1673).

Janeway, James, *A Token for Children: Being an Exact Account of the Conversion, Holy and Exemplary Lives, and Joyful Deaths, of several young Children* (1673).

Jarman, E. K. M., ed., *Justice and Conciliation in a Tudor Church Court: Depositions from . . . the Consistory Court of Chester, September 1558-March 1559*, Record Society of Lancashire and Cheshire, 146 (2012).

Johnstone, Hilda, ed., *Churchwardens' Presentments (17th century). Archdeaconry of Chichester*, Sussex Record Society, 49 (1950).

The Journal of Giles Moore 1656–1679, ed. Ruth Bird, Sussex Record Society (1971).

The Journal of James Yonge [1647–1721], Plymouth Surgeon, ed. F. N. L. Poynter (1963).

'The Journal of Mr John Hobson', ed. Charles Jackson, in *Yorkshire Diaries and Autobiographies of the Seventeenth and Eighteenth Centuries*, Surtees Society, 65 (1877).

A Journal of the Life of William Edmundson (1837).

The Journal of Richard Norwood, Surveyor of Bermuda, ed. Wesley Craven and Walter Haywood (New York, 1945).

Kemp, Thomas, ed., *The Book of John Fisher, Town Clerk and Deputy-Recorder of Warwick 1580–1588* (Warwick [, 1945]).

Kenny, Anthony, ed., *The Responsa Scholarum of the English College, Rome, 1598–1685*, Catholic Record Society, 54–5 (1962–3).

Kettle, Anne J., ed., 'Mathew Cradock's Book of Remembrance, 1614–15', *Collections for a History of Staffordshire*, Staffordshire Record Society, 4th series, 16 (1994): 67–169.

The Knyvett Letters (1620–1644), ed. Bertram Schofield, Norfolk Record Society, 20 (1949).

Lee, Sidney, ed., *The Autobiography of Edward, Lord Herbert of Cherbury* (n.d., *c.* 1906).

Le Hardy, William, ed., *County of Middlesex. Calendar to the Sessions Rolls, 1612–16*, 3 vols (1935–7).

The Letters of Dorothy Osborne to William Temple, ed. G. C. Moore Smith (Oxford, 1928).

The Letters of John Chamberlain, ed. N. E. McClure (Philadelphia, 1939).

Letters of John Holles 1587–1637, ed. P. R. Seddon, Thoroton Society, 31, 35 (1975, 1983).

Letters of John Pinney 1679–1699, ed. Geoffrey F. Nuttall (1939).

Letters of Philip Gawdy of West Harling, Norfolk, ed. Isaac Herbert Jeayes (1906).

The Life and Times of Anthony Wood, ed. Andrew Clark, Oxford Historical Society, 19, 21, 26, 30, 40 (1891–1900).

The Life of Adam Martindale, ed. Richard Parkinson, Chetham Society, 4 (1845).

The Life of John Rastrick 1650–1727, ed. Andrew Cambers, Camden Society, 5th series, 36 (2010).

'The Life of Master John Shaw', ed. Charles Jackson, in *Yorkshire Diaries and Autobiographies of the Seventeenth and Eighteenth Centuries*, Surtees Society, 65 (1877): 119–62.

Lister, John, ed., *West Riding Session Records, ii, 1611–1642*, Yorkshire Archaeological Society, 54 (1915).

Lubbock, Basil, ed., *Barlow's Journal of his Life at Sea* (1936).

Maclean, John, ed., *Letters from George Lord Carew to Sir Thomas Roe*, Camden Society, 76 (1860).

Markham, Sir Clement, ed., *Markham Memorials*, 2 vols (1913).

Mayor, J. E. B., ed., *Nicholas Ferrar. Two Lives, by his Brother John and by Doctor Jebb* (Cambridge, 1855).

The Memoirs of Anne, Lady Halkett and Ann, Lady Fanshawe, ed. John Loftis (Oxford, 1979).

Memoirs of Benjamin Lay (New York, 1842).

Memoirs of Sir John Reresby, ed. Andrew Browning (2nd edition, ed. Mary Geiter and W. A. Speck, 1991).

The Memoirs of the Verney Family, ed. Frances Parthenope Verney and Margaret M. Verney, 4 vols (1892, repr. 1970).

Millard, Peter, ed., *Roger North: General Preface and Life of Dr John North* (Toronto, 1984).

Newnham, John, *Newnams Nightcrowe. A Bird that Breedeth Braules in many Families and Housholdes* (1590).

Nicholson, Joseph and Burn, Richard, *The History and Antiquities of the Counties of Westmorland and Cumberland* (1777).

North, Roger, *The Lives of . . . Francis North, . . . Sir Dudley North, and . . . Dr. John North*, ed. Augustus Jessopp, 3 vols (1890).

Northtonus, Champianus, *The Younger Brothers Advocate* (1655).

The Notebook of Robert Doughty 1662–1665, ed. J. M. Rosenheim, Norfolk Record Society, 54 (1989).

The Notebooks of Nehemiah Wallington, 1618–1654, ed. David Booy (Aldershot, 2007).

Notes of Me. The Autobiography of Roger North, ed. Peter Millard (Toronto, 2000).

Nott, H. E., ed., *The Deposition Books of Bristol 1643–1647*, Bristol Record Society, 6 (1935).

Nott, H. E. and Ralph, Elizabeth, eds, *The Deposition Books of Bristol 1650–1654*, Bristol Record Society, 13 (1948).

The Office of Christian Parents (Cambridge, 1616).

Oliver, John, *A Present to be Given to Teeming Women* (1688).

Osborn, Elias, *A Brief Narrative of the Life, Labours and Sufferings of Elias Osborn* (1723).

Osborn, Francis, *The Works of Francis Osborn, Esquire* (8th edn, 1682).

The Oxinden Letters 1607–1642, ed. Dorothy Gardner (1933).

The Oxinden Letters 1642–1670, ed. Dorothy Gardner (1937).

Pask, Brenda M. with Harvey, Margaret, eds, *The Letters of George Davenport 1651–1677*, Surtees Society, 215 (2011).

Penney, Norman, ed., *The First Publishers of Truth* (1907).

Penney, Norman, ed., *Record of the Sufferings of the Quakers in Cornwall 1655–1686* (1928).

Perrin, W. G., ed., *The Autobiography of Phineas Pett*, Navy Records Society, 51 (1918).

Pope, Walter, *The Life of Seth [Ward], Lord Bishop of Salisbury* (1697).

Porter, Stephen, Roberts, Stephen K., and Roy, Ian, eds, *The Diary and Papers of Henry Townshend, 1640–1663*, Worcestershire Historical Society, NS, 25 (2014).

Pound, J. F., ed., *The Norwich Census of the Poor, 1570*, Norfolk Record Society, 40 (1971).

Poynter, F. N. L. and Bishop, W. J., eds, *A Seventeenth Century Doctor and his Patients. John Symcotts 1592?–1662*, Bedfordshire Historical Record Society, 31 (1951).

The Private Correspondence of Jane Lady Cornwallis, 1613–1644 (1842).

Raine, James, ed., *Depositions and other Ecclesiastical Proceedings from the Courts of Durham*, Surtees Society, 21 (1845).

Raine, James, ed., *The Acts of the High Commission Court within the Diocese of Durham*, Surtees Society, 34 (1858).

Ratcliff, S. C. and Johnson, H. C., eds, *Warwickshire County Records*, 9 vols (Warwick, 1935–64).

Rede, Sarah, *A Token for Youth: or, Instruction to Children* (1760).

The Remembrances of Elizabeth Freke, 1671–1714, ed. Raymond A. Anselment, Camden Society, 5th series, 18 (2001).

The Repenting Sinner Pardoned: Being a brief Relation of the wicked Life and penitent pious Death of James Wilson of Wolverhampton (1669).

Rider, W. *The Twins. A Tragi-Comedy* (1655).

Rogers, John, *Ohel or Beth-shemesh. A Tabernacle for the Sun* (1653).

Rosen, Barbara, ed., *Witchcraft in England 1558–1618* (Amherst, Mass., 1991).

Sachse, W. L., ed., *Minutes of the Norwich Court of Mayoralty 1630–1631*, Norfolk Record Society, 15 (1942).

Sachse, W. L., ed., *Minutes of the Norwich Court of Mayoralty 1632–1635*, Norfolk Record Society, 36 (1967).

Salt, D. H. G., ed., *Staffordshire Quarter Sessions Rolls, Easter 1608-Trinity 1609*, Staffordshire Record Society, 70 (1950).

Savile, Alan, ed., *Secret Comment. The Diaries of Gertrude Savile 1721–1757*, Thoroton Society, 41 (1997).

Searle, Arthur, ed., *Barrington Family Letters 1628–1632*, Camden Society, 4th series, 28 (1983).

Shepard, Thomas, 'Thomas Shepard's Memoir of his Own Life', in Alexander Young, ed., *Chronicles of the First Planters of the Colony of Massachusetts Bay* (Boston, 1846), pp. 499–558.

Sir George Sondes his plaine Narrative to the World (1655).

Slingsby, Sir Henry, *A Father's Legacy* (1658).

Slocombe, Ivor, ed., *Wiltshire Quarter Sessions Order Book 1642–1654*, Wiltshire Record Society, 67 (2014).

Smyth, John, *The Berkeley Manuscripts, The Lives of the Berkeleys*, 3 vols (Glasgow, 1883–5).

Snell, F. J., ed., 'A Devonshire Yeoman's Diary: William Honeywell of Ashton 1596–1614', in G. L. Apperson, ed., *Gleanings after Time* (1907), pp. 160–75.

Some Account of the Life of Joseph Pike, ed. John Barclay (1837).

Some Remarkable Passages in the Holy Life and Death of Gervase Disney, Esq. (1692).

Spicksley, Judith M., ed., *The Business and Household Accounts of Joyce Jeffreys, spinster of Hereford, 1638–1648* (Oxford, 2012).

Strange and Wonderful News from Lincolnshire [*sic*] (1679).

Taylor, John, *An Humble Desired Union betweene Prerogative and Priviledge* (1642).

Thomson, Sheila D., ed., *The Book of Examinations and Depositions before the Mayor and Justices of Southampton 1648–1663*, Southampton Record Society, 37 (1994).

Tixall Letters; or the Correspondence of the Aston Family and their Friends during the Seventeenth Century, ed. Arthur Clifford (1815).

Tryon, Thomas, *Some Memoirs of the Life of Mr Tho. Tryon, late of London, Merchant* (1705).

Underhill, Edward Bean, ed., *The Records of the Church of Christ meeting at Broadmead, Bristol, 1640–1687* (1847).

(Vario, Charles,) *The Modern Farmers Guide* (Glasgow, 1768).

Walker, Anthony, *The Vertuous Wife, or the Holy Life of Mrs Elizabeth Walker* (1694).

(Walker, Henry,) *Spirituall Experiences of Sundry Beleevers* (1653).

Wall, Alison D., ed., *Two Elizabethan Women: Correspondence of Joan and Maria Thynne 1575–1611*, Wiltshire Record Society, 38 (1983).

Whitehead, George, et al., *Piety Promoted by Faithfulness* (1686).

Whiting, John, *Early Piety Exemplified* (1711).

Williams, J. B., ed., *Memoirs of the Life and Character of Mrs Sarah Savage*, 4th edition (1829).

Willis Bund, J. W., ed., *Worcestershire County Records: Calendar of the Quarter Sessions Records, 1591–1643* (Worcester, 1900).

Wilson, Thomas, *The State of England Anno Dom. 1600*, ed. F. J. Fisher, in *Camden Miscellany*, 16 (Camden Society, 3rd series, 52, 1936): 1–47.

Winstanley, Gerrard, *The Law of Freedom in a Platform* (1652).

Woodforde, Dorothy Heighes, ed., *Woodforde Papers and Diaries* (1932).

The Works of Anne Bradstreet, ed. Jeannine Hensley (1967).

SECONDARY SOURCES

Adair, Richard, *Courtship, Illegitimacy and Marriage in Early Modern England* (Manchester, 1996).

Anstruther, Godfrey, *The Seminary Priests. A Dictionary of the Secular Clergy of England and Wales 1558–1850*, 4 vols (Great Wakering, Essex, 1969–77).

Avery, Gillian, 'The Puritans and their Heirs', in *eadem* and Julia Briggs, eds, *Children and their Books* (Oxford, 1989), pp. 95–118.

Bailey, Joanne, *Unquiet Lives. Marriage and Marriage Breakdown in England 1660–1800* (Cambridge, 2003).

Beier, A. L., *Masterless Men. The Vagrancy Problem in England, 1560–1640* (1985).

Ben-Amos, Ilana Krausman, *Adolescence and Youth in Early Modern England* (New Haven 1994).

Ben-Amos, Ilana Krausman, *The Culture of Giving: Informal Support and Gift-Exchange in Early Modern England* (Cambridge, 2008).

Bonfield, Lloyd, *Marriage Settlements 1601–1740. The Adoption of the Strict Settlement.* (Cambridge, 1983).

Brodsky Elliott, Vivien, 'Single Women and the London Marriage Market: Age, Status and Mobility, 1598–1619', in R. B. Outhwaite, ed., *Marriage and Society* (New York, 1982), pp. 81–100.

Capp, Bernard, *When Gossips Meet. Women, Family and Neighbourhood in Early Modern England* (Oxford, 2003).

Capp, Bernard, *England's Culture Wars* (Oxford, 2012).

Capp, Bernard, 'The Travails of Agnes Beaumont', in Bronach Kane and Fiona Williamson, eds, *Women's Agency and the Law, 1300–1700* (2013), pp. 113–124.

Caraman, Philip, *William Weston. The Autobiography of an Elizabethan* (1955).

Charlton, Kenneth, *Women, Religion and Education in Early Modern England* (1999).

Chaytor, Miranda, 'Household and Kinship: Ryton in the late 16th and early 17th Centuries', *History Workshop*, 10 (1980): 25–60.

Collins, Stephen, 'British Stepfamily Relationships, 1500–1800', *Journal of Family History*, 16 (1991): 331–44.

Coster, Will, *Baptism and Spiritual Kinship in Early Modern England* (Aldershot, 2002).

Crawford, Patricia, *Blood, Bodies and Families in Early Modern England* (Harlow, 2004).

Crawford, Patricia, *Parents of Poor Children in England, 1580–1800* (Oxford, 2010).

Cressy, David, *Literacy and the Social Order. Reading and Writing in Tudor and Stuart England* (Cambridge, 1980).

Cressy, David, *Birth, Marriage and Death* (Oxford, 1997).

Davidoff, Leonore, *Thicker than Water. Siblings and their Relations 1780–1920* (Oxford, 2012).

Daybell, James, *Women Letter-Writers in Tudor England* (Oxford, 2006).

Dubrow, Heather, 'The Message from Marcade: Parental Death in Tudor and Stuart England', in Betty S. Travitsky and Adele F. Seeff, eds, *Attending to Women in Early Modern England* (Newark, Delaware, 1994), pp. 147–67.

Earle, Peter, *A City Full of People. Men and Women of London 1650–1750* (1994).

Erickson, Amy Louise, *Women and Property in Early Modern England* (1993).

Fletcher, Anthony, *Gender, Sex and Subordination in England 1500–1800* (1985).

Fletcher, Anthony, *Growing Up in England: the Experience of Childhood 1600–1914* (New Haven, 2008).

Foyster, Elizabeth, 'Marrying the Experienced Widow in Early Modern England: the Male Perspective', in Sandra Cavallo and Lyndan Warner, eds, *Widowhood in Medieval and Early Modern Europe* (Harlow, 1999), pp. 108–24.

Froide, Amy, *Never Married. Singlewomen in Early Modern England* (Oxford, 2005).

George, Margaret, *Women in the First Capitalist Society* (Brighton, 1988).

Goody, Jack, Thirsk, Joan, and Thompson, E. P., eds, *Family and Inheritance. Rural Society in Western Europe 1200–1800* (Cambridge, 1976).

Gowing, Laura, *Domestic Dangers. Women, Words, and Sex in Seventeenth-Century London* (Oxford, 1996).

Gowing, Laura, 'Secret Births and Infanticide in Seventeenth-Century England', *Past and Present*, 156 (1997): 87–115.

Gowing, Laura, 'The Politics of Women's Friendship in Early Modern England', in *Love, Friendship and Faith in Early Modern Europe, 1300–1800*, ed. Laura Gowing, Michael Hunter, and Miri Rubin (Basingstoke, 2005), pp. 131–49.

Grassby, Richard, *The English Gentleman in Trade. The Life and Works of Sir Dudley North 1641–1691* (Oxford, 1994).

Grassby, Richard, *Kinship and Capitalism. Marriage, Family, and Business in the English-Speaking World, 1580–1740* (Cambridge, 2001).

Griffiths, Paul, *Youth and Authority. Formative Experiences in England 1560–1640* (Oxford, 1996).

Hanawalt, Barbara A. 'Childrearing among the Lower Classes of Late Medieval England', *Journal of Interdisciplinary History*, 8 (1977): 37–56.

Harris, Amy, *Siblinghood and Social Relations in Georgian England* (Manchester, 2012).

Hartman, Mary S., *The Household and the Making of History* (Cambridge, 2004).

Heal, Felicity and Holmes, Clive, *The Gentry in England and Wales, 1500–1700* (Oxford, 1994).

Healey, Jonathan, *The First Century of Welfare. Poverty and Poor Relief in Lancashire 1620–1730* (Woodbridge, 2014).

Hemphill, C. Dallett, *Siblings. Brothers and Sisters in American History* (Oxford, 2011).

Herbert, Amanda E., *Female Alliances. Gender, Identity, and Friendship in Early Modern Britain* (New Haven, Conn., 2014).

Hindle, Steve, *On the Parish? The Micro-Politics of Poor Relief in Rural England c.1550–1750* (Oxford, 2004).

Hodgkin, Katharine, 'Elizabeth Isham's Everlasting Library: Memory and Self in Early Modern Autobiography', in Sally Alexander and Barbara Taylor, eds, *History and Psyche: Culture, Psychoanalysis, and the Past* (Basingstoke, 2012), pp. 241–64.

Houlbrooke, Ralph A., *The English Family* (1984).

Houlbrooke, Ralph A. 'Death in childhood: the practice of the "good death" in James Jameway's *A Token for Children*', in Anthony Fletcher and Stephen Hussey, eds, *Childhood in Question. Children, Parents and the State* (Manchester, 1999), pp. 37–56.

Hubbard, Eleanor, *City Women. Money, Sex and the Social Order in Early Modern London* (Oxford, 2012).

Ingram, Martin, *Church Courts, Sex and Marriage in England, 1570–1640* (Cambridge, 1987).

Johnson, Christopher and Sabean, David Warren, eds, *Sibling Relations and the Transformations of European Kinship 1300–1900* (New York, 2011).

Lake, Peter and Stephens, Isaac, *Scandal and Religious Identity in Early Stuart England* (Woodbridge, 2015).

Laslett, Peter, *Family Life and Illicit Love in Earlier Generations* (Cambridge, 1977).

Laslett, Peter, *The World We Have Lost Further Explored* (1983).

Laslett, Peter and Harrison, John, 'Clayworth and Cogenhoe', in H. E. Bell and R. L. Ollard, eds, *Historical Essays 1600–1750* (1963), pp. 157–81.

Levy Peck, Linda, *Court Patronage and Corruption in Early Stuart England* (London, 1993).

McCall, Fiona, *Baal's Priests. The Loyalist Clergy and the English Revolution* (Farnham, 2013).

Macfarlane, Alan, *The Family Life of Ralph Josselin. A Seventeenth-Century Clergyman* (Cambridge, 1970).

Macfarlane, Alan, *The Origins of English Individualism* (Oxford, 1978).

Manuel, Frank E., *A Portrait of Isaac Newton* (Cambridge, Mass., 1968).

Mears, Natalie, *Queenship and Political Discourse in the Elizabethan Realm* (Cambridge, 2005).

Mendelson, Sara, 'Anne Dormer and her Children', in Naomi J. Miller and Naomi Yavneh, eds, *Gender and Early Modern Constructions of Childhood* (Farnham, 2011), pp. 117–26.

Mendelson, Sara and Crawford, Patricia, *Women in Early Modern England* (Oxford, 1998).

Mendelson, Sara and O'Connor, Mary, ' "Thy Passionately Loving Sister and Faithfull Friend": Anne Dormer's Letters to her Sister, Lady Trumbull', in Naomi J. Miller and Naomi Yavneh, eds, *Sibling Relations and Gender in the Early Modern World* (Aldershot, 2006), pp. 206–15.

Miller, Naomi J. and Yavneh, Naomi, eds, *Sibling Relations and Gender in the Early Modern World* (Aldershot, 2006).

Montrose, Louis, ' "The Place of a Brother" in *As You Like It*: Social Process and Comic Form', *Shakespeare Quarterly*, 32 (1981): 28–54.

Muldrew, Craig, *The Economy of Obligation: the Culture of Credit and Social Relations in Early Modern England* (Basingstoke, 1998).

O'Day, Rosemary. *The Family and Family Relationships, 1500–1900* (Basingstoke, 1994).

O'Hara, Diana, *Courtship and Constraint: Rethinking the Making of Marriage in Tudor England* (Manchester, 2000).

Osborn, Louise Brown, *The Life, Letters, and Writings of John Hoskyns 1566–1638* (New Haven, 1937).

Pollock, Linda, *A Lasting Relationship. Parents and Children over Three Centuries* (Hanover, New Hampshire, and London, 1987).

Pollock, Linda, 'Younger Sons in Tudor and Stuart England', *History Today*, 39 (June 1989): 23–9.

Postles, Dave, 'Surviving Lone Motherhood in Early-Modern England', *The Seventeenth Century*, 21 (2017): 160–83.

Prior, Mary, 'Women and the urban economy: Oxford 1500–1800', in Mary Prior, ed., *Women in Early Modern Society 1500–1800* (1985), pp. 97–117.

Quaife, G. R., *Wanton Wenches and Wayward Wives* (1979).

Questier, Michael, *Conversion, Politics and Religion in England 1580–1625* (Cambridge, 1996).

Reinke-Williams, Tim, *Women, Work and Sociability in Early Modern London* (Basingstoke, 2014).

Rowse, A. L. *The Case Books of Simon Forman* (1976).

Seaver, Paul, *Wallington's World. A Puritan Artisan in Seventeenth-Century London* (1985).

Sharpe, J. A., *Crime in Seventeenth-Century England. A County Study* (Cambridge, 1983).

Sharpe, J. A. and Dickinson, J. R, 'Revisiting the "Violence We Have Lost": Homicide in Seventeenth-Century Cheshire', *English Historical Review*, 131 (2016): 293–323.

Sharpe, Pamela, *Population and Society in an East Devon Parish. Reproducing Colyton 1540–1840* (Exeter, 2002).

Slack, Paul, 'Vagrants and Vagrancy in England, 1598–1664', in Peter Clark and David Souden, eds, *Migration and Society in Early Modern England* (1987), pp. 49–76.

Slater, Miriam, *Family Life in the Seventeenth Century. The Verneys of Claydon House* (1984).

Smith, Richard, ed., *Land, Kinship and Life-Cycle* (Cambridge, 1984).

Spufford, Margaret, 'First steps in Literacy: the Reading and Writing Experiences of the humblest seventeenth-century Spiritual Autobiographers', *Social History*, 4 (1979): 407–35.

Stone, Lawrence, *Uncertain Unions. Marriage in England 1660–1753* (Oxford, 1992).

Swain, John T., *Industry before the Industrial Revolution. North-East Lancashire c.1500–1640*, Chetham Society, 3rd series, 32 (1986).

Tadmor, Naomi, *Family and Friends in Eighteenth-Century England* (Cambridge, 2001).

Thirsk, Joan, 'Younger Sons in the Seventeenth Century', *History*, 54 (1961): 358–77.

Thomas, Keith, 'Children in Early Modern England', in Gillian Avery and Julia Briggs, eds, *Children and their Books* (Oxford, 1989), pp. 45–77.

Todd, Barbara J., 'The Remarrying Widow: a Stereotype Reconsidered', in Mary Prior, ed., *Women in English Society 1500–1800* (1985), pp. 54–92.

Tomalin, Claire, *Samuel Pepys: the Unequalled Self* (Harmondsworth, 2003).

Underwood, Lucy, *Childhood, Youth and Religious Dissent in Post-Reformation England* (Basingstoke, 2014).

Walker, Claire, 'Recusants, Daughters and Sisters in Christ: English Nuns and their Communities in the Seventeenth Century', in Stephanie Tarbin and Susan Broomhall, eds, *Women, Identities and Communities in Early Modern Europe* (Aldershot, 2008), pp. 62–76.

Walker, Garthine, 'Keeping it in the Family: Crime and the early modern Household', in Helen Berry and Elizabeth Foyster, eds, *The Family in Early Modern England* (Cambridge, 2007), pp. 67–95.

Walsham, Alexandra, *Church Papists. Catholicism, Conformity and Confessional Polemic in Early Modern England* (1993).

Walsham, Alexandra, '"Out of the Mouths of Babes and Sucklings": Prophecy, Puritanism and Childhood in Elizabethan Suffolk', in Diana Wood, ed., *The Church and Childhood (Studies in Church History, 31)* (1994), pp. 285–99.

Walsham, Alexandra, 'The Reformation of the Generations. Youth, Age and Religious Change in England, c.1500–1700', *Transactions of the Royal Historical Society*, 6th series, 21 (2011): 93–121.

Westfall, Richard S., *The Life of Isaac Newton* (Cambridge, 1993).

Whyman, Susan E., *Sociability and Power in Late-Stuart England. The Cultural Worlds of the Verneys 1660–1720* (Oxford 1999).

Whyman, Susan E., *The Pen and the People. English Letter Writers 1660–1800* (Oxford, 2009).

Willen, Diane, ' "Communion of the Saints": Spiritual Reciprocity and the Godly Community in Early Modern England', *Albion*, 27 (1995): 19–41.

Wilson, Adrian, *Ritual and Conflict. The Social Relations of Childbirth in Early Modern England* (Farnham, 2013).

Winchester, Barbara, *Tudor Family Portrait* (1955).

Wrightson, Keith, *English Society 1580–1680* (1982).

Wrightson, Keith, 'Mutualities and Obligations: Changing Social Relationships in Early Modern England', *Proceedings of the British Academy*, 139 (2006): 157– 94.

Wrigley, E. A. and Schofield, R. S., *The Population History of England 1541–1871. A Reconstruction* (1981).

ONLINE RESOURCES

'The Diary of Elizabeth Isham' (http://www.warwick.ac.uk/fac/arts/ren/projects/isham/).

Elizabeth Isham, 'Book of Rememberance' (http://www.warwick.ac.uk/fac/arts/ren/projects/isham/).

Old Bailey, Ordinary's Accounts (http://www.oldbaileyonline.org/).

Old Bailey Sessions Papers (http://www.oldbaileyonline.org/).

The Oxford Dictionary of National Biography (Oxford, 2004; http://www.oxforddnb.com/).

Index